Stefanie Kisgen
The Future of Business Leadership Education
in Tertiary Education for Graduates

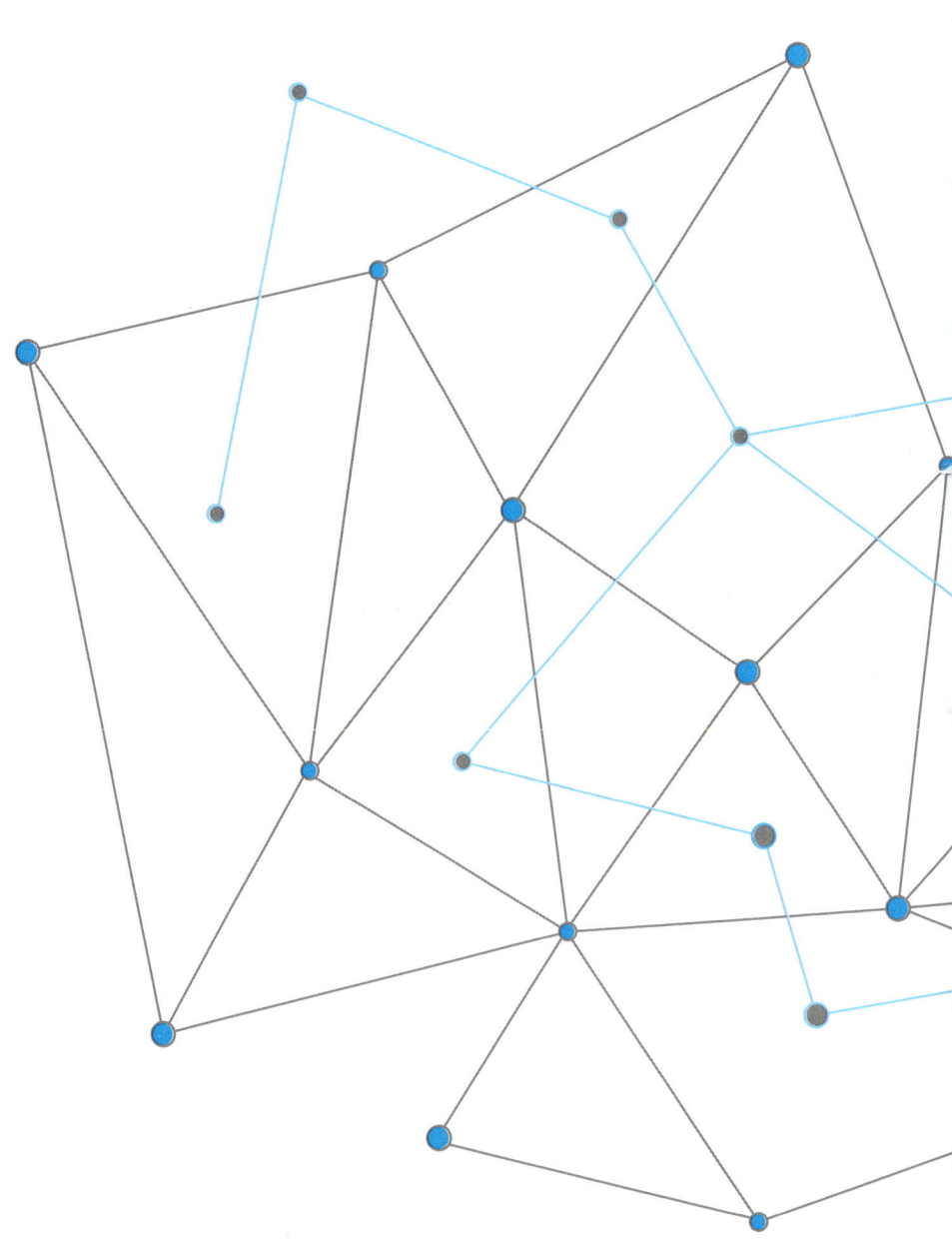

Stefanie Kisgen

The Future of Business Leadership Education in Tertiary Education for Graduates

LMU
LUDWIG-MAXIMILIANS-UNIVERSITÄT MÜNCHEN

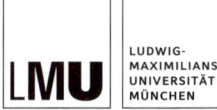

SCHOOL OF INTERNATIONAL BUSINESS AND ENTREPRENEURSHIP
STEINBEIS UNIVERSITY BERLIN

Stefanie Kisgen
The Future of Business Leadership Education in Tertiary Education for Graduates
Zugl. Inaugural-Dissertation zur Erlangung des Doktorgrades der Philosophie an der
Ludwig-Maximilians-Universität München
Referent: Prof. Dr. Rudolf Tippelt, Lehrstuhl für Allgemeine
   Pädagogik und Bildungsforschung
Korreferent: Prof. Dr. Hartmut Ditton, Lehrstuhl für Allgemeine
   Pädagogik, Erziehungs- und Sozialisationsforschung
Tag der mündlichen Prüfung: 31.01.2017

Imprint

© 2017 Steinbeis-Edition

All rights reserved. No part of this book may be reprinted, reproduced, or utilised in any form by any electronic, mechanical, or other means now known or hereafter invented, including photocopying, microfilming, and recording or in any information storage or retrieval system without written permission from the publisher.

Stefanie Kisgen
The Future of Business Leadership Education in Tertiary Education for Graduates

1st edition, 2017 | Steinbeis-Edition, Stuttgart
ISBN 978-3-95663-130-6

Published in the scientific series of SIBE
Likewise Ludwig-Maximilians-Universität Munich, dissertation 2017

Layout: Meike Haverkamp
Cover picture: ©mypokcik/Shutterstock.com, edited by Steinbeis-Edition
Production: Kraft Premium GmbH, Ettlingen

Steinbeis is an international service provider in entrepreneurial knowledge and technology transfer. The Steinbeis Transfer Network is made up of about 1,000 enterprises. Specialized in chosen areas, Steinbeis Enterprises' portfolio of services covers research and development; consulting and expert reports as well as training and employee development for every sector of technology and management. Steinbeis Enterprises are frequently based at research institutions, especially universities, which are constituting the Network's primary sources of expertise. The Steinbeis Network comprises around 6,000 experts committed to practical transfer between academia and industry. Founded in 1971, the Steinbeis-Stiftung is the umbrella organization of the Steinbeis Transfer Network. It is headquartered in Stuttgart, Germany. Steinbeis-Edition publishes selected works mirroring the scope of the Steinbeis Network expertise.

193005-2017-05 | www.steinbeis-edition.de

Preface

We are facing great challenges; both on a societal as well as a commercial level; globally, nationally and individually. The continued, uninhibited growth of the population, the excessive consumption of resources, climate warming, the extinction of species and the dissimilar spread of wealth are only a few, yet significant problems of our earth.

When today, the day at which you read these lines, comes to a close tonight, there will be approx. 250,000 less trees, and approx. 70,000 more fellow human beings net.

Since the United Nations conference on Environment and Sustainability in Rio de Janeiro in 1992, the term sustainability has constantly gained international recognition and - one may discuss this critically - commitment.

In the so-called Rio Declaration, sustainable development is simultaneously geared toward

> Providing all people and nations, particularly the developing countries, with the necessary commercial and cultural opportunities;
> Granting all people a fair share in all resources of this our earth in social justice;
> In the interest of future generations, limiting the utilization of all natural resources, raw materials, plants and animals to an extent that the world is able to regenerate itself under its own steam, ensuring that future generations still find humane living conditions.

Sustainability in the corporate world consequently means carrying the responsibility for creation, the society as well as customers and employees.

The economy - and thus the corporations - is facing great challenges today. (In part entirely) new business and value-creation models have to be developed and realized in light of the scientific and technological developments, the global competition and the emphasis on sustainability. At the same time, the level of innovation quality to be realized has to be immensely greater than in the past in order to maintain and expand competitiveness in the product as well as the service sector. This also includes more disruptive or even radical innovations.

Next to those mentioned above, catch words for the challenge include: digitization, the usage of artificial intelligence, automation, new organizational structures, the service sector and value creation at the location of the revenue and profit realization, etc.

In order to have these challenges become a value-adding reality for one's own company requires, first and foremost, people with leadership and value-adding powers. In the corporate world, the issues of the past were generally quite solvable by managers with the respective methodical expertise. Today's challenges and those of the future are fundamentally of a corporate nature and require a high degree of entrepreneurship to arrive at a solution. Entrepreneurship with future-oriented and sustainable leadership and executive power. A self-learning algorithm is quickly installed, a 3D printer quickly positioned and a new production site at a new location is realized relatively quickly. However, there is a great deficit in executive leaders who are a credit to their name.

Creative personalities with leadership power are, among other, the result of development processes and thus also development processes in the tertiary educational sector.

With her work, Stefanie Kisgen takes up the discussion about the future-oriented design of business leadership education and provides a consolidated, structured foundation of the discussion status.

With an evaluation of selected Master's programs in leadership education, she shows in a critical and science-based manner the level of things based on clearly defined criteria and thus illustrates that also education is facing major challenges in this sector.

With a Delphi-based scenario study, incorporating more than 100 experts worldwide and consisting of corporate personalities, representatives of business associations, executives from the tertiary education sector, students and politicians, she develops scenarios for the post-graduate business leadership education in the tertiary education sector for the year 2030.

With this thesis, Stefanie Kisgen managed to positively structure the current, understandably controversially conducted discussion about the future-oriented design of leadership education by reducing it to clearly verbalized scenario options. She therefore makes an extremely valuable contribution to the definition of education objectives and the dissipation and realization of respective education strategies. The tertiary education sector is thus enabled to make an essential contribution to the lucrative solution of the aforementioned challenges.

Future needs origin - so the German philosopher Odo Marquard; the future of leadership education has to reflect again on its principles once expressed by Plato, and realize the formation of creative personalities as a sustainable and thus uppermost objective. For the economy, this is the objective of creating educational processes which allow the development of creative personalities who are capable and willing to think, to act and to lead on an entrepreneurial and sustainable level. Stefanie Kisgen's thesis provides much more than just a readable contribution.

I wish a lot of profit with this read.

Herrenberg, March 2017
Werner G. Faix

Acknowledgements

First, I would like to thank my supervisor, Professor Dr. Rudolf Tippelt, for his guidance and advice throughout the process of my doctoral research. I am also thankful to the second reader, Professor Dr. Hartmut Ditton and the third reader Professor Dr. Jörg Jantzen for their interest in my research topic, their time, and willingness to be my examiners.

This doctoral research is part of a joint research project of the Department of Educational Science at Ludwig-Maximilians-University (LMU) Munich, Germany and Steinbeis School of International Business and Entrepreneurship (SIBE), Germany. Therefore, I greatly appreciate the valuable support and contributions made by SIBE. My sincere thanks also go to my business partner and mentor at SIBE, Professor Dr. Dr. h. c. Werner G. Faix for his support, inspiring discussions and thoughtful comments.

I also thank the participants of the cross-country real-time Delphi survey for donating their time to share their valuable insights and suggestions as well as IEL (Brazil) and Post University (USA) for their support and network. In addition, I would like to thank all pretest panelists and workshop participants for sharing their valuable time and contributions.

I would like to thank the following people for their support and advice, especially Dr. Heiko von der Gracht, Dr. Shalaka Sharad Shah, Prachi Nawathe, Friederike Niederberger, and Meike Haverkamp.

Lastly, I would like to thank my parents and my sister for their continuous support throughout my entire life and the process of the dissertation. Last but not least, I would like to extend my heartfelt thanks to my partner Thomas for his unconditional support, patience and encouragement without which the successful completion of this dissertation would have been impossible.

Herrenberg, November 2016
Stefanie Kisgen

Abstract

Purpose

Contributing to further improve and continuously develop business leadership education in tertiary education for graduates to become state of the art, by:

> Introducing the principles of business leadership education in tertiary education based on sound theory

> Uncovering how business leadership education is practiced in contemporary exemplary Master's programs

> Defining objectives and creating different alternatives (scenarios) for business leadership education in tertiary education for the long-term future (2030) that comprise potential systematic pedagogical approaches through which objectives can be achieved

Methodology

Theoretical foundations; qualitative research; Delphi-based scenario study comprising mixed methods analysis of Delphi survey, along with a set of multiple methods of futures studies for scenario development, such as portfolio analysis, cross impact analysis, and scenario axes analysis

Findings

1) Holistic model and definition of business leadership; 2) contemporary holistic human-centered concept of education that allows individuals to develop their personalities; 3) seven principles for curriculum design of business leadership education; 4) four future scenarios, two wildcards for the long-term future (2030) of business leadership education in tertiary education based on Delphi results

Practical implications

Main stakeholder groups (higher education institutions, students, organizations, and politics) obtain an in-depth understanding of the meaning of business leadership and business leadership education in tertiary education, were prepared to cope with different potential future settings that may arise from different alternative scenarios, wildcards and a checklist for transfer into practice. A roadmap was compiled for higher education institutions in order to launch (redefined) Master's programs.

Keywords

business leadership education; tertiary education; curriculum design; personality; competency development; innovation; real-world setting; Delphi-based scenario study

Executive Summary

Business leadership is largely concerned with leadership in the business context, particularly with regard to leadership in business corporations, companies, enterprises, organizations etc. Business schools and business leadership education in tertiary education are faced with multiple challenges. At least since the (global) financial crisis of 2007-2009, critical and controversial debates ensued on the quality of business leadership education, particularly with regard to ethical dimensions. Against this background, and along with the current development of the political, economic, social, and technological environment, business leadership education in tertiary education for graduates has to be scrutinized and – where appropriate – redesigned. In order to equip tomorrow's business leaders with the necessary competencies to cope with the challenges of a complex and uncertain world in the 21st century that is driven by globalization and accelerated technological advancements, a pedagogical infrastructure is required that nurtures the development of a students' (creative) personality.

As traditional leadership definitions and approaches are not adequate, a holistic model and definition of business leadership was elaborated. Furthermore, a contemporary holistic human-centered concept of education was developed. This concept is deeply rooted in humanistic tradition, enriched by contemporary pedagogical perspectives. It aimed at the personal-potential of the individual, to convert it into actions, render it apparent in actions and allows individuals to develop their personalities. Based on the holistic understanding of business leadership and human-centered concept of education, seven principles for curriculum design of business leadership education in tertiary education for graduates were designed as a modus of orientation and guidelines. They laid the foundation for subsequent qualitative research of contemporary exemplary Master's programs in business leadership education. Synthesizing the essential results of the evaluation procedure yielded that the educational approach is diametrically opposed to the earlier findings of this research.

To define the objectives for the long-term future (2030) of business leadership education in tertiary education, the Delphi-based scenario study was proposed. A rigorous systematic research approach was applied to enhance quality and validity of different scenarios. 16 projections concerning four strategic perspectives of stakeholders on business leadership education in tertiary education were formulated and surveyed regarding the probability of occurrence, desirability and impact in case of occurrence. 105 experts (13.78%) from 13 countries and 16 industries participated in this real-time Delphi survey. Quantitative and qualitative data were interpreted separately as well as together. Based on the results of the Delphi survey, a set of multiple methods of futures studies such as portfolio analysis, cross impact analysis and scenario axes analysis were applied, resulting in four different scenarios comprising potential systematic pedagogical approaches through which the respective objectives can be achieved. Two additional wild cards, i.e. extreme situations with low-probability and serious impact in case of occurrence, were developed. The final scenario transfer prepares decision makers to apply theoretical results at their individual practice, based on a checklist for the main stakeholder groups and a roadmap for higher education institutions. Thus, main stakeholder groups were prepared to cope with different potential future settings that may arise. Moreover, this research contributes to further improve and continuously develop business leadership education in tertiary education to become state of the art.

Contents

Abbreviations XII
List of figures XIV
List of tables XVI
Glossary XIX

Part 1: Introduction XXII
    1. Research Background 1
    2. Aim of research and research questions 3
    3. Field of research 4
    4. Research design and process 6

Part 2: Business leadership education in tertiary
           education for graduates 12
    1. Aim of research 13
    2. Formulation of research questions 13
    3. Business leadership education in tertiary education
       for graduates – theoretical foundations 14
       3.1 Conceptualizing business leadership 15
           3.1.1 Definitions 15
           3.1.2 Theoretical approaches 17
               3.1.2.1 Traditional approaches to leadership 18
               3.1.2.2 Excursus: Business leader selection process –
                        Assessment center 23
               3.1.2.3 Interdisciplinary considerations on leadership 26
           3.1.3 Preliminary conclusions 28
           3.1.4 Business leadership – A holistic model 30
               3.1.4.1 Shaping the future – Goal identification
                        and goal setting 30
               3.1.4.2 Creating sustainable value – Realization of innovations ... 33
               3.1.4.3 Leading into the future – Creative personality 37
               3.1.4.4 Fostering self-organized actions –
                        Business leadership competencies 42
               3.1.4.5 Business leadership – At a glance 50
           3.1.5 Conclusions 53
       3.2 Conceptualizing business leadership education
           in tertiary education 55
           3.2.1 Preliminary notes on education 55
           3.2.2 Focusing on the segment of tertiary education 66
               3.2.2.1 General trends and challenges in tertiary education 71

   3.2.2.2 Trends and challenges in business leadership education in tertiary education in particular 80
  3.2.3 Preliminary conclusions 91
  3.2.4 Curriculum in tertiary education 93
  3.2.5 Principles for curriculum design of business leadership education in tertiary education 96
   3.2.5.1 Principle 1 – Educational goals 97
   3.2.5.2 Principle 2 – Personality as educational ideal 99
   3.2.5.3 Principle 3 – Educational contents 103
   3.2.5.4 Principle 4 – Educational methodologies 107
   3.2.5.5 Principle 5 – Educational settings 119
   3.2.5.6 Principle 6 – Evaluation 122
   3.2.5.7 Principle 7 – Financing 125
  3.2.6 Conclusions 126
4. Business leadership education in tertiary education for graduates – Evaluation of exemplary Master's programs 129
 4.1 Methodology 130
  4.1.1 Development of evaluation criteria 130
  4.1.2 Selection of exemplary Master's programs 132
  4.1.3 Data collection 135
  4.1.4 Data analysis 135
   4.1.4.1 Document analysis 136
   4.1.4.2 Content analysis 137
  4.1.5 Interpretation and discussion 140
   4.1.5.1 Educational goals 144
   4.1.5.2 Educational ideal 152
   4.1.5.3 Educational contents 152
   4.1.5.4 Educational methodologies 159
   4.1.5.5 Educational settings 164
   4.1.5.6 Evaluation 170
   4.1.5.7 Financing 173
  4.1.6 Limitations and future research 175
 4.2 Conclusions 176
5. Conclusions Part 2 178

Part 3: Delphi-based scenario study: Business leadership education in tertiary education for graduates in the year 2030 182

1. Aim of research 183
2. Formulation of research questions 185
3. Methodology: Framing of Delphi-based scenario study 185
 3.1 Principles of scenario planning 185

3.2	Study design and procedures	189
4.	Delphi method	191
4.1	Principles of the Delphi method	191
4.2	Real-time Delphi approach	194
4.3	Delphi procedures	196
4.3.1	Development of projections	196
4.3.2	Selection of experts	200
4.3.3	Data collection	202
4.3.4	Data analyses	208
4.3.4.1	Quantitative data analysis	208
4.3.4.2	Qualitative content analysis	209
4.3.5	Results and discussion	212
4.3.5.1	Overview	212
4.3.5.2	Stakeholder dimension providers (universities/business schools)	219
4.3.5.2.1	Projection 1 – Personality & leadership competencies	220
4.3.5.2.2	Projection 2 – Educational setting & development of competencies	225
4.3.5.2.3	Projection 3 – E-learning	229
4.3.5.2.4	Projection 4 – Individualization	235
4.3.5.2.5	Projection 5 – Allocation to schools	239
4.3.5.2.6	Conclusions for stakeholder dimension providers	245
4.3.5.3	Stakeholder dimension participants/ learners (students)	246
4.3.5.3.1	Projection 6 – Requirements for leadership positions	247
4.3.5.3.2	Projection 7 – Entre- & intrapreneurship as a basis for innovations	252
4.3.5.3.3	Projection 8 – International internships & development of competencies	257
4.3.5.3.4	Projection 9 – Transfer of knowledge by "real-world projects"	262
4.3.5.3.5	Conclusions for stakeholder dimension participants	267
4.3.5.4	Stakeholder dimension purchasers (employers/companies)	268
4.3.5.4.1	Projection 10 – Return on education (ROE)	268
4.3.5.4.2	Projection 11 – Transformation of working environment & working conditions	273

- 4.3.5.4.3 Projection 12 – International and intercultural experiences 277
- 4.3.5.4.4 Projection 13 – Corporate universities 282
- 4.3.5.4.5 Conclusions for stakeholder dimension purchasers 287
- 4.3.5.5 Stakeholder dimension politics 288
  - 4.3.5.5.1 Projection 14 – International student mobility & recognition of degrees 288
  - 4.3.5.5.2 Projection 15 – Funding of tertiary education 293
  - 4.3.5.5.3 Projection 16 – Duration of Master's programs 298
  - 4.3.5.5.4 Conclusions for stakeholder dimension politics 303
5. Scenario development 304
   - 5.1 Prioritization 305
     - 5.1.1 Portfolio analysis 305
     - 5.1.2 Cross impact analysis (CIA) 309
   - 5.2 Scenario axes analysis 315
   - 5.3 Scenario stories 319
     - 5.3.1 Scenario 1 – 2030: Management education 10.0 319
     - 5.3.2 Scenario 2 – 2030: Leadership trailblazer – grasping the 24/7 e-learning landscape & experiencing real-world settings 322
     - 5.3.3 Scenario 3 – 2030: Management education in the armchair 325
     - 5.3.4 Scenario 4 – 2030: Leadership explorer – coping with the blended learning environment online and off & exploring real-world settings 328
   - 5.4 Discontinuities and the surprising future 331
     - 5.4.1 Wildcard 1 – Eradication of Master's degree programs 332
     - 5.4.2 Wildcard 2 – Structural discontinuity 333
   - 5.5 Expert check 334
6. Transfer 334
7. Limitations and future research 340
8. Conclusions Part 3 342

Part 4: Conclusions 346
1. Conclusions and remarkable results 347
2. Contributions of research 352
3. Limitations and future research 355
4. Practical implications 357

References 360

Appendix 420

Abbreviations

AACSB	Association to Advance Collegiate Schools of Business
AC	Assessment Center
ADF	Aalto University Design Factory
B.C.	Before Christ
BMWi	Bundesministerium für Wirtschaft und Energie
CBE	Competency-Based Education
CEMS	Community of European Management Schools and International Companies
CEO	Chief Executive Officer
CERI	Centre for Educational Research and Innovation
CFSB	Constitution of the Free State of Bavaria
CHRO	Chief Human Resource Officer
CIA	Cross Impact Analysis
C-level	C stands for Chief; this adjective describes high-ranking executive titles within an organization
Con	Convergence of opinion (variation of standard deviation)
D	Desirability
DBA	Doctor of Business Administration
EBC	Experience-Based Curriculum
ECTS	European Credit Transfer and Accumulation System
ed-tech	education technology
EP	Estimated probability of occurrence
EHEA	European Higher Education Area
EU	European Union
GDP	Gross Domestic Product
GMAT	Graduate Management Admission Test
HHL	Handelshochschule Leipzig (Leipzig Graduate School of Management / Germany)
I	Impact
IBM	International Business Machine Corporation
ICT	Information and communications technology
InQ	InnovationQuality
IQR	Interquartile range
ISCED	International Standard Classification of Education
IT	Information Technology

KMK	Kultusministerkonferenz
KPI	Key Performance Indicator
LMX	Leader-Member Exchange
LPC	Least Preferred Coworker
MBA	Master of Business Administration
MOOC	Massive open online course
NGO	Non-Governmental Organization
OECD	Organisation for Economic Co-operation and Development
PKS	Projekt-Kompetenz-Studium
ROE	Return on education
RT	real-time
SD	Standard deviation
SIBE	Steinbeis School of International Business and Entrepreneurship (SIBE) GmbH
STEEPL	Social, Technological, Economic, Environmental, Political and Legal framework
TGC	Talent Growth Curriculum
TOEFL	Test of English as Foreign Language
UDHR	Universal Declaration of Human Rights
UN	United Nations
UNESCO	United Nations Educational, Scientific and Cultural Organization
USA	United States of America
VDL	vertical dyad linkage
VUCA	Volatility, Uncertainty, Complexity, Ambiguity
WEF	World Economic Forum
WFS	World Future Society
WHU	WHU Otto Beisheim School of Management/Germany

List of figures

Figure 1.	The strategic triangle of business development	7
Figure 2.	Research design and process	9
Figure 3.	Business objectives based on company's needs pyramid	30
Figure 4.	The concept of having / being a personality	40
Figure 5.	Knowledge, qualifications and competencies	44
Figure 6.	A general set of leadership competencies	47
Figure 7.	Business leadership – A holistic model	51
Figure 8.	Definition of business leadership	54
Figure 9.	Text field "Personhood"	63
Figure 10.	Conceptualizing education: The educational cycle	65
Figure 11.	Developments of high importance to European higher education institutions over the past three years	75
Figure 12.	Population aged 30-34 with tertiary educational attainment (ISCED 5-8), by country, 2015 (%)	77
Figure 13.	Population aged 30-34 with tertiary educational attainment (ISCED 5-8), by sex, EU-28, 2005-2015 (%)	78
Figure 14.	Expected level of complexity	84
Figure 15.	The complexity gap	84
Figure 16.	Top factor: CEOs say technology is the chief external influence on their enterprises	85
Figure 17.	Prime sources of sustained economic value	86
Figure 18.	Engaging employees	87
Figure 19.	Organizational attributes to engage employees	88
Figure 20.	Role of online education versus classroom education	90
Figure 21.	Academic plans in sociocultural context	95
Figure 22.	Knowledge, qualifications and competencies in the curriculum	101
Figure 23.	Model for business leadership education	102
Figure 24.	Educational contents of business leadership education	107
Figure 25.	Learning cycle in the format of a research process	110
Figure 26.	Learning model – School of Accounting and Finance/ University of Waterloo	115
Figure 27.	Ideal course of Experience-Based Curriculum	119
Figure 28.	Model on evaluation and quality assurance in the field of education	122
Figure 29.	Evaluation procedures for exemplary Master's programs	130
Figure 30.	The balance of predictability and uncertainty in the business environment	184
Figure 31.	Process of Delphi-based scenario study	190
Figure 32.	Delphi panel composition according to countries	206
Figure 33.	Portfolio analysis – estimated probability vs. impact	306
Figure 34.	Portfolio analysis – estimated probability vs. desirability	307

Figure 35.	Cross impact matrix	311
Figure 36.	Intensity of influences (total active / total passive)	312
Figure 37.	Intensity of activity and interconnectedness	313
Figure 38.	Index of leverage (degree of activity and interconnectedness)	314
Figure 39.	Business leadership education in tertiary education in Master's programs in the year 2030. Four scenarios in a nutshell	318
Figure 40.	Scenario 1 – Management education 10.0. Scenario pathway	321
Figure 41.	Scenario 2 – Leadership trailblazer. Scenario pathway	325
Figure 42.	Scenario 3 – Management education in the armchair. Scenario pathway	327
Figure 43.	Scenario 4 – Leadership explorer. Scenario pathway	331
Figure 44.	Roadmap for sponsor of research	339

List of tables

Table 1.	General trends and challenges in tertiary education	92
Table 2.	Trends and challenges for business leadership education in tertiary education	93
Table 3.	Selected programs of Financial Times Masters in management ranking 2013	134
Table 4.	Selected programs of U.S. News ranking Best Business Schools 2013	134
Table 5.	Example of the process of coding according to the coding system	138
Table 6.	Overview of main codes and sub-codes and the number of statements	139
Table 7.	Educational goals defined by selected Master's programs	148
Table 8.	Elements of proposed goals in selected Master's programs goal definition	150
Table 9.	Educational contents of selected Master's programs based on minimal criteria for theory	155
Table 10.	Educational contents of selected Master's programs based on minimal criteria for reality and reflection	158
Table 11.	Educational methodologies of selected Master's programs	162
Table 12.	Evaluation methods of selected Master's programs on the macro and meso level	173
Table 13.	Study fees for selected Master's programs	175
Table 14.	Key factors and literature for development of final set of projections	200
Table 15.	Panel invitations and participants according to stakeholder groups	205
Table 16.	Delphi panel composition according to age groups	207
Table 17.	Delphi panel composition according to position within organization	207
Table 18.	Panel information – general overview	212
Table 19.	Quantification of projections (n=105)	217
Table 20.	Statistical data for projection 1 (n=105)	222
Table 21.	Details of comments for projection 1	222
Table 22.	Selected pro and contra comments of the experts for projection 1	224
Table 23.	Statistical data for projection 2 (n=105)	226
Table 24.	Details of comments for projection 2	226
Table 25.	Selected pro and contra comments of the experts for projection 2	227
Table 26.	Statistical data for projection 3 (n=105)	231
Table 27.	Details of comments for projection 3	231

Table 28.	Selected pro and contra comments of the experts for projection 3	233
Table 29.	Statistical data for projection 4 (n=105)	236
Table 30.	Details of comments for projection 4	236
Table 31.	Selected pro and contra comments of the experts for projection 4	238
Table 32.	Statistical data for projection 5 (n=105)	242
Table 33.	Details of comments for projection 5	242
Table 34.	Selected pro and contra comments of the experts for projection 5	244
Table 35.	Statistical data for projection 6 (n=105)	248
Table 36.	Details of comments for projection 6	248
Table 37.	Selected pro and contra comments of the experts for projection 6	250
Table 38.	Statistical data for projection 7 (n=105)	253
Table 39.	Details of comments for projection 7	253
Table 40.	Selected pro and contra comments of the experts for projection 7	254
Table 41.	Statistical data for projection 8 (n=105)	258
Table 42.	Details of comments for projection 8	258
Table 43.	Selected pro and contra comments of the experts for projection 8	260
Table 44.	Statistical data for projection 9 (n=105)	263
Table 45.	Details of comments for projection 9	263
Table 46.	Selected pro and contra comments of the experts for projection 9	264
Table 47.	Statistical data for projection 10 (n=105)	270
Table 48.	Details of comments for projection 10	270
Table 49.	Selected pro and contra comments of the experts for projection 10	271
Table 50.	Statistical data for projection 11 (n=105)	274
Table 51.	Details of comments for projection 11	274
Table 52.	Selected pro and contra comments of the experts for projection 11	275
Table 53.	Statistical data for projection 12 (n=105)	278
Table 54.	Details of comments for projection 12	279
Table 55.	Selected pro and contra comments of the experts for projection 12	281
Table 56.	Statistical data for projection 13 (n=105)	283
Table 57.	Details of comments for projection 13	283
Table 58.	Selected pro and contra comments of the experts for projection 13	285
Table 59.	Statistical data for projection 14 (n=105)	290
Table 60.	Details of comments for projection 14	290

Table 61.	Selected pro and contra comments of the experts for projection 14	292
Table 62.	Statistical data for projection 15 (n=105)	294
Table 63.	Details of comments for projection 15	295
Table 64.	Selected pro and contra comments of the experts for projection 15	297
Table 65.	Statistical data for projection 16 (n=105)	299
Table 66.	Details of comments for projection 16	300
Table 67.	Selected pro and contra comments of the experts for projection 16	301
Table 68.	Checklist: Are stakeholders prepared for Master's programs in 2030?	337

Glossary

The attentive reader of this research may ask about concrete disambiguation of similar but different terms. Therefore, please consider the following notes to the pivotal concepts of this research.

1. Business leadership

Although a very similar core notion of leadership that may be generalized for different domains, military, political, educational, or business leadership, may differ in a particular way due to the specific missions of the domain (Palmer, 2009). The term *leadership* in this research is largely concerned with leadership in the business context, particularly with regard to leadership in business corporations, companies, enterprises, organizations etc. For reasons of unambiguousness, leadership in this research is specified as business leadership (Gordon, 1961; Harvey, 2001; Palmer, 2009). A holistic model and definition (see Part 2, chapter 3.1.4.5 / 3.1.5) for business leadership are elaborated in a deductive process.

2. Business leadership, management, entrepreneurship and intrapreneurship

There are several discussions regarding the terms *leadership* and *management* (see Part 2, chapter 3.1.1). If there is a differentiation between management and leadership, it is not to be conceived based on traits or behavioral aspects rather than the basis of the time horizon, a leader or manager focusses on. Based on the pyramid of needs for companies (see Figure 3), one may conclude that management primarily focusses on company's need to survive, while leadership focusses on the company's need to grow and shape the future. However, it must be stated clearly that there is no unambiguous differentiation between management and leadership, as overlaps are possible.

Additionally, reference is made in this research to the terms *entrepreneurship* and *intrapreneurship*. Generally, the term entrepreneurship refers to the creation of new companies and intrapreneurship refers to leaders within a company, which act like an entrepreneur but do not take the entrepreneurial risk and autonomy. Considering Schumpeter's oeuvre, the terms entrepreneurship and intrapreneurship are closely connected with the term *business leadership* due to the immense importance of innovations as one of the main tasks required from business leaders. Based on Schumpeter, who described the entrepreneur (intrapreneur) as not merely an innovator but also as leader, the construct of *entrepreneurial leadership* emerged only recently. By combing, integrating, and exploring both entrepreneurship and leadership, the entrepreneurial leader is expected to cope with a rapidly changing business environment (see Part 2, chapter 3.1.2.3).

3. Business leader

The English term *leader* or *business leader* in this research corresponds to the German term *Führungskraft*, which is based on the principal direction of this research and the principal understanding of leadership and management in this research.

4. Education

In this research, the English term *education* corresponds to the German term *Bildung* "as a kind of umbrella term" (Autio, 2014, p. 18). It has to be noted that the term *Bildung*, which is a central concept in educational sciences, has a long tradition. However, it appears exclusively in the German language and has no equivalent in any other (Raithel, Dollinger & Hörmann, 2009). In this research, the English term *education* is used in a broad sense, comprising such concepts as nurture and socialization among others, which is in line with Faix and Mergenthaler (2015).

5. Personality

The English term *personality* (vs. *character*) in this research corresponds to the German term *Persönlichkeit*. In line with Faix and Mergenthaler (2015), character is subsumed under personality, namely that "'[p]ersonality means something more than 'Character'" (Faix & Mergenthaler, 2015, p. 14).

6. Competence and competency

After reviewing literature on competencies, it can be stated that various terms are used in the context of competencies, which are closely connected, yet not exactly the same according to different fields of research, different concepts and different languages. First, the terms skills, abilities, qualifications, key qualifications, and potentials are very often used synonymously for competencies both scientifically and in the every-day language (Weinert, 1999). Second, the English language uses both spellings of "competency" and "competence". Strebler, Robinson and Heron (1997) provided a plausible reasoning. Thus, "competency" has been used to refer to the behaviors individuals need to express (behavioral approach); whereas "competence" has been used to refer to minimum standards of competent performance (standard approach). In this research, the English spelling and term *competency* (vs. *competence* or *skill*) corresponds to the German term *Kompetenz*, based on Strebler, Robinson and Heron (1997). The interpretation of competencies in this research is based on the work of Erpenbeck (2012a / b); for details please see Part 2 (chapter 3.1.4.4).

7. Curriculum

In line with Lattuca and Stark (2009), the terms *curriculum* or *program of studies* are used synonymously and in a broad conception as an "academic plan", which is embedded in a complex sociocultural context with its various influence factors. In this broad sense, a curriculum comprises at least the educational purpose and goals, educational contents and sequence, resources, teaching and learning processes as well as assessment and evaluation. Furthermore, a curriculum is conceived being dynamic in process that has to be continuously adjusted.

8. Tertiary education and higher education

Tertiary education - provided by universities or other higher education institutions that are approved by the competent state authorities - is the level of education following secondary schooling. According to the International Standard Classification of Education (ISCED) provided by UNESCO, the term tertiary education was chosen as the official term in this research. The terms *tertiary education* and *higher education* are used synonymously.

Notes to linguistic usage

Wherever possible and advisable, quotations and references in this research are based on reliable translations of the original works, e.g. Plato's (1969) *Poilteia* (*Rebublic*), Humboldt's (1793 or 1794 / 2000) *Theorie der Bildung des Menschen* (*Theory of Bildung*).

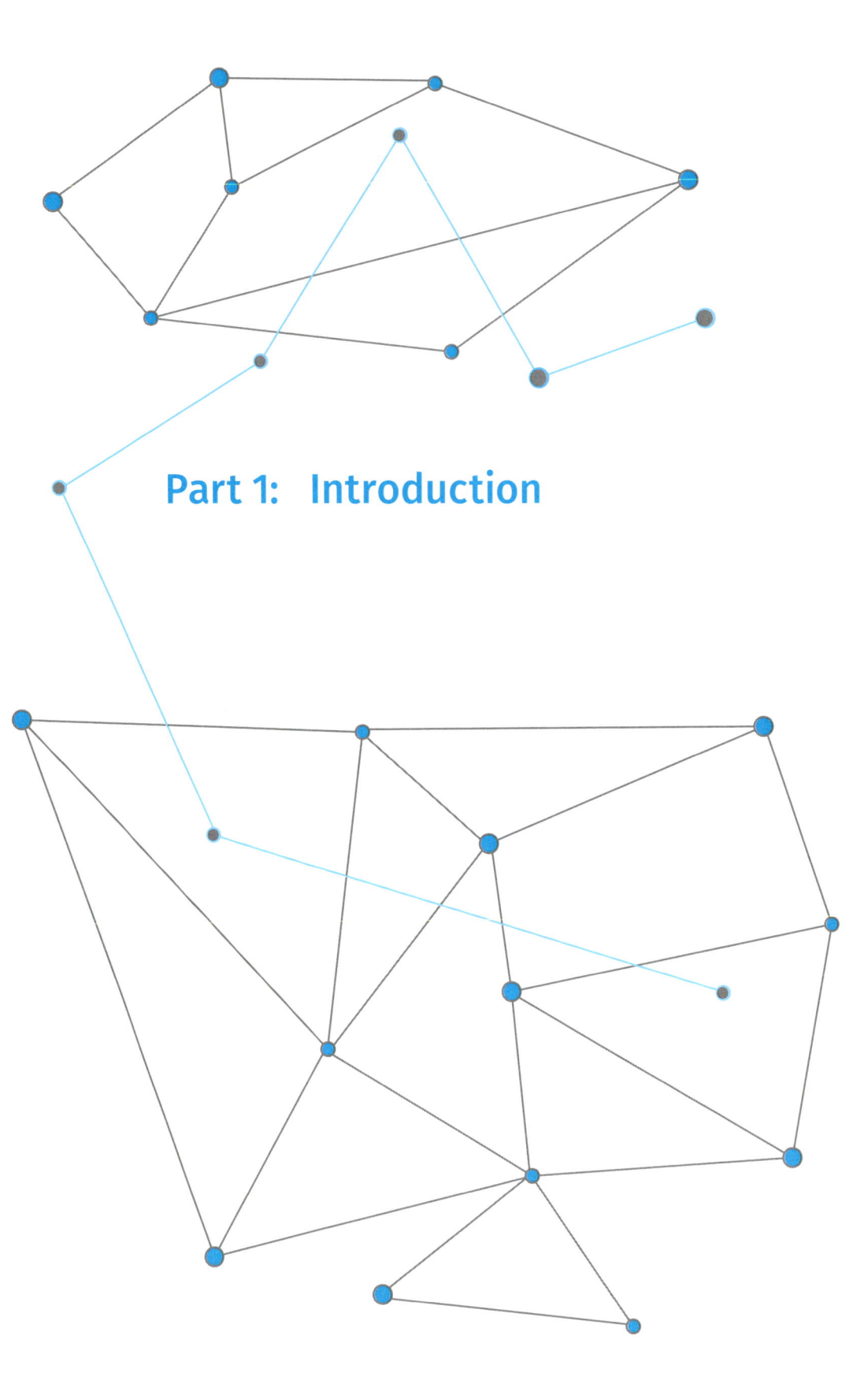

Part 1: Introduction

Leadership is not a new phenomenon. On the contrary, leadership as a subject is of great interest since ancient times. However, scientific research on leadership is barely one hundred years old (Yukl, 2013). This, in turn, coincides with the emergence of business leadership. Business leadership, as the term implies, is largely concerned with leadership in the business context, particularly with regard to leadership in business corporations, companies, enterprises, organizations etc. (Gordon, 1961; Harvey, 2001; Palmer, 2009). The origins of business leadership are located in the USA and can be considered a consequence of industrialization, mass manufacturing and the need for management (Canals, 2011a; Thomas et al., 2014). Consequently, business schools and business programs evolved as academic institutions and domains, where the principles of management and leadership could be systematically learned, developed, and researched. Nevertheless, business schools and business programs today are faced with multiple challenges. At least since the (global) financial crisis of 2007-2009, critical and controversial debates ensued on the quality of business leadership education, particularly with regard to its ethical dimensions. Against this background, and along with the current development of the political, economic, social, and technological environment, business leadership education in tertiary education for graduates has to be scrutinized and – where appropriate – redesigned in order to cope with the challenges of the 21st century.

In order to lay the foundation of this research, this introduction explains the research background of the studied topic, defines the aim of research and research questions, explicates the field of research and, ultimately, introduces the research design and structure of this thesis.

1. Research Background

Globalization, technological advancements, and digitization are the main drivers of the global acceleration of transformation, uncertainty, and complexity (DDI, 2015; IBM 2010a). Increased acceleration, in turn, represents an immense challenge for business leadership due to the half-life period of knowledge and shorter product life cycles common in industry and service economy. (Future) competiveness of business corporations, companies, enterprises, organizations etc. largely depends on their capacity for innovation (Faix et al., 2015; IBM, 2012b; IBM 2016). Setting goals as prime task of leadership (Thom, 2015; Welge & Al-Laham, 2003) means identification and setting innovation goals (Drucker, 2010; Faix et al., 2015). Setting innovation goals of tomorrow today, in times of accelerated transformation, uncertainty, and complexity, is challenging leaders of any discipline on any level and business leaders in particular. Not to put too fine a point on it, the company's future and competiveness is determined by the quality of their business leaders. Moreover, companies / organizations are faced with a shortage of specialists, talents and leaders due to demographic change (Manpower Group, 2014).

Considering contemporary business leadership education in tertiary education for graduates, it is assumed that it neither meet the requirements of the present nor, for that matter, the future. On the contrary, it is rather traditional. Traditional in the context of business leadership education in tertiary education for graduates means that the majority of students – aspiring business leaders – were selected due to previous Bachelor's degrees, GMAT scores, TOEFL scores, and other test results. The curricula impart knowledge and qualifications / skills, but do not (adequately) promote competency development in future leaders. Furthermore, the future job performance of a graduate as a leader cannot be predicted based on the successful completion of contemporary business leadership education in tertiary education. To summarize the aforementioned assumptions, business leadership education in tertiary education predominantly focus on imparting knowledge and qualifications / skills, but do not promote the holistic development of the business leader's personality.

Based on current debates, a brand new definition seems to be indispensable in order to design contemporary and future-oriented business leadership education in tertiary education, namely from a pedagogical perspective, which is the topic of this research.

Business leadership education in tertiary education for graduates has to facilitate a pedagogical infrastructure that holistically caters to the need of developing (creative) personalities who will contribute to the world.

2. Aim of research and research questions

Against the research background outlined previously, an overall aim of research will contribute to further improve and continuously develop business leadership education in tertiary education to become state of the art, which is concretized on two levels.

Firstly, it is aimed at introducing the principles of business leadership education in tertiary education for graduates based on thorough literature review. Therefore, it is indispensable to obtain an overview of the meaning of business leadership. Furthermore, the research attempts to uncover how business leadership education in tertiary education is practiced in exemplary Master's programs for graduates.

Secondly, based on theoretical foundations and analysis of contemporary practice, it is aimed at defining objectives and creating different alternatives (scenarios) for business leadership education in tertiary education for graduates for the long-term future (2030). The intention is to illustrate possible systematic pedagogical strategies to achieve the respective goal.

In order to deal with the defined aim of research, it is imperative to formulate the relevant and concrete research questions, which are developed based on the research background and theory. Thus, the following principal research questions guide the design and implementation of this research:

1. What is the goal of business leadership education in tertiary education for graduates and how should business leadership education in tertiary education for graduates be designed?
2. How is business leadership education in contemporary tertiary education practiced in exemplary Master's programs for graduates in the light of the theoretical framework?
3. How do experts assess future projections for business leadership education in Master in Management programs in tertiary education for the year 2030 according to their estimated probability of occurrence (EP) (scale 0-100 %), desirability (D) (5-point Likert scale) and impact (I) (5-point Likert scale), and how do they support their quantitative evaluations for the three dimensions?

4. Which different future alternatives (scenarios and wildcards) can be developed for business leadership education in Master in Management programs in tertiary education for the year 2030, based on quantitative and qualitative data of the (real-time) Delphi study?

3. Field of research

Certainly, as Grint (1997) stated, "It would be strange if leadership was the only human skill that could not be enhanced through understanding and practice" (p. 2). Considering Grint's statement along with the background and aim of the research outlined earlier, the focus here is the pedagogical perspective on business leadership education in tertiary education for graduates.

Thus, within the academic discipline of pedagogy, this research is allocated to the field of general education and empirical educational sciences. Nevertheless, some explanatory notes are needed in this context. Firstly, empirical educational sciences is a multifaceted field of research referring to various other disciplines, such as sociology, psychology, economics, history, philosophy etc., including a broad field of quantitative and qualitative research methodologies. It is a matter of concern in a regional as well as international and intercultural context across one's entire lifespan (Tippelt & Schmidt, 2010). Secondly, considering the field of research in higher education (Hochschulforschung) as a part of empirical educational sciences (Ditton & Reinders, 2011; Teichler, 2010), it cannot be attributed solely to the academic discipline of pedagogy. Research in higher education is a rather inter- or transdisciplinary research topic as it is affected by other disciplines such as economics or sociology (Wolter, 2011). Thirdly, in order to elucidate the theoretical foundations of business leadership education in tertiary education for graduates it is indispensable to understand the meaning of business leadership. The phenomenon of leadership covers a broad spectrum and cannot be attributed solely to one academic discipline (Rosenstiel & Comelli, 2003). Leadership is a rather complex (interdisciplinary) research topic, which is part of various academic disciplines: business studies, economics, history, pedagogics, philosophy, political sciences, psychology, sociology, social sciences etc.

The inter- and transdisciplinary influences have to be considered in this research. In the process, the primary topics within the field of general education and empirical educational sciences are elaborated substantially in order to approach the overall aim of research, which is to contribute to the further improvement and continuously development of business leadership education in tertiary education to become state of the art.

The societal and economic relevance of the topic is demonstrated by a vast amount of research literature, such as monographs (e.g. Bijedić, 2013; Faix & Mergenthaler, 2015), anthologies (e.g. Snook, Nohria & Khurana, 2012) and research articles (e.g. Brungardt, 1996; White & Guthrie, 2016) in different journals such as Journal of Leadership Education, Journal of Leadership Studies, Leadership Quarterly etc. Furthermore, various other disciplines are referred to, including the respective research literature such as competency development (e.g. Erpenbeck 2012b, Gervais, 2016; Weinert, 2001), e-learning (e.g. Halarnkar & Kulkarni, 2013; OECD, 2005), innovations (e.g. Faix et al., 2015; Schumpeter, 1911 / 2008), leadership theories (e.g. Northouse, 2013; Yukl, 2013) etc. A careful selection of this volume of literature was made in order to integrate the existing literature and state of the art in research on leadership education / management education and its associated topics in this work as far as possible and necessary.

Furthermore, different methodology approaches are integrated in this research. Firstly, qualitative analysis is conducted in order to find out, how business leadership education in contemporary tertiary education is practiced in exemplary Master's programs for graduates in the light of the theoretical framework. To define the objectives for business leadership education in tertiary education, the Delphi-based scenario study is proposed. The development and description of alternative scenarios and wildcards are based on quantitative and qualitative Delphi results that are interpreted and integrated in a mixed-methods approach followed by a set of multiple methods of futures studies, such as portfolio-analysis, cross impact analysis and scenario axes analysis. This specific combination of different methods is best suited to answer the questions of this research and thereby to achieve the aim. However, various examples were found in research in educational sciences that integrate at least one of the aforementioned methods.

Thus, the Delphi research was published e.g. for the impact of knowledge society on educational processes and structures (BMBF, 1998), tertiary education in general (Gregersen, 2011), competency in higher education didactics (Paetz et al., 2011) etc. Furthermore, scenario analysis and methodological research were published e.g. for tertiary education in general (CERI, 2008) and the specific field of management education in tertiary education (Thomas et al., 2014). However, the latter provide a general overview on the future of management education. A combination of a (real-time) Delphi-based scenario study along with portfolio-analysis and scenario axes analysis was found for professional training (Becker & Gracht, 2014). Consequently, it can be stated that the different methodological approaches are recognized in the field of general education and empirical educational sciences. Nevertheless, a profound theoretical and empirical analysis to conceptualize a holistic educational concept of business leadership education in tertiary education for graduates was not found. Thus, the research gap in the field of business leadership education in tertiary education should be closed.

4. Research design and process

In order to answer the research questions, and thereby achieve its aim, this thesis follows a rigorous research design and process, which shall be presented in this section.

According to the German philosopher Odo Marquard, humankind can only endure times of accelerated transformation by relying on the past. Considering the past means to foster the necessary know-how and confidence face the future (Schmitter & Schreiber, 2003). Odo Marquard stated, "The future needs a solid past." (as cited in Faix & Mergenthaler, 2015, p. 108; see also Marquard & Zimmerli, 1995). Although Marquard's statements were also reviewed and found to be conservative (e.g. Schmitter & Schreiber, 2003), this statement has to be interpreted for this research. In this context, it seems to be indispensable to analyze the current situation and its history in order to understand what is happening, to be prepared and anticipate aspects of the future, an approach also suggested by Heijden (2005). Assuming a dynamic development process of the (business) environment with multiple interpretations and therefore multiple possible futures, alternative scenarios should be developed to cope with different potential future settings that may arise. Vice versa, using different scenarios for the future also help to better understand the meaning of a current situation and "to come to a reasonable judgement on the degree of robustness of a specific decision across the range of uncertainty" (Heijden, 2005, 94). Thus, "a systematic approach based on the strategic triangle of business development developed by SIBE" (Nagel et al., 2013, preamble) originally introduced as "Strategic triangle of the transformation process" by Faix, Buchwald and Wetzler (1994) according to Figure 1 should be applied to systematically scrutinize the field of business leadership education in tertiary education for graduates.

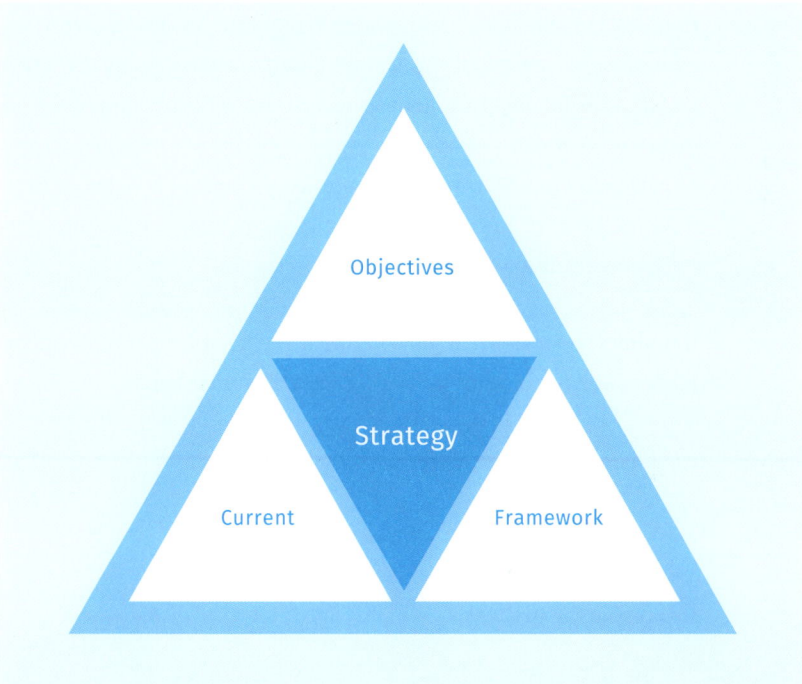

Figure 1.   The strategic triangle of business development. Adapted from Nagel et al., 2013, p. 27.

Adapting the process of the strategic triangle within an overall research design and process (Figure 2), according to Nagel et al. (2013), eight steps have to be taken (p. 31). The basic structure of this thesis follows these eight steps:

Step 1:   Deciding to use the transformation process by research based on a defined research gap.

Step 2: Analyzing the current situation based on literature review and a theoretical approach on one hand and based on a qualitative analysis of exemplary Master's in Management programs on the other. In order to consider the framework conditions that might have an impact on the studied topic, trends and challenges in tertiary education, and in the discipline of business leadership education were examined based on thorough literature review.

Step 3: Defining and evaluating of current potentials and risks for business leadership education based on the results of previous steps.

Step 4: Defining the objectives for business leadership education in tertiary education by means of the Delphi-based scenario study. Creation and description of alternative scenarios and wildcards are based on quantitative and qualitative Delphi results that are interpreted and integrated in a mixed-methods approach, followed by a set of multiple methods of futures studies, such as portfolio-analysis, cross impact analysis and scenario axes analysis.

Step 5: Defining the strategy by developing a checklist for relevant stakeholders and a roadmap for the sponsor of this research.

Step 6: Implementation of strategy

Step 7: Monitoring achievement of objectives.

Step 8: Reentering the process.

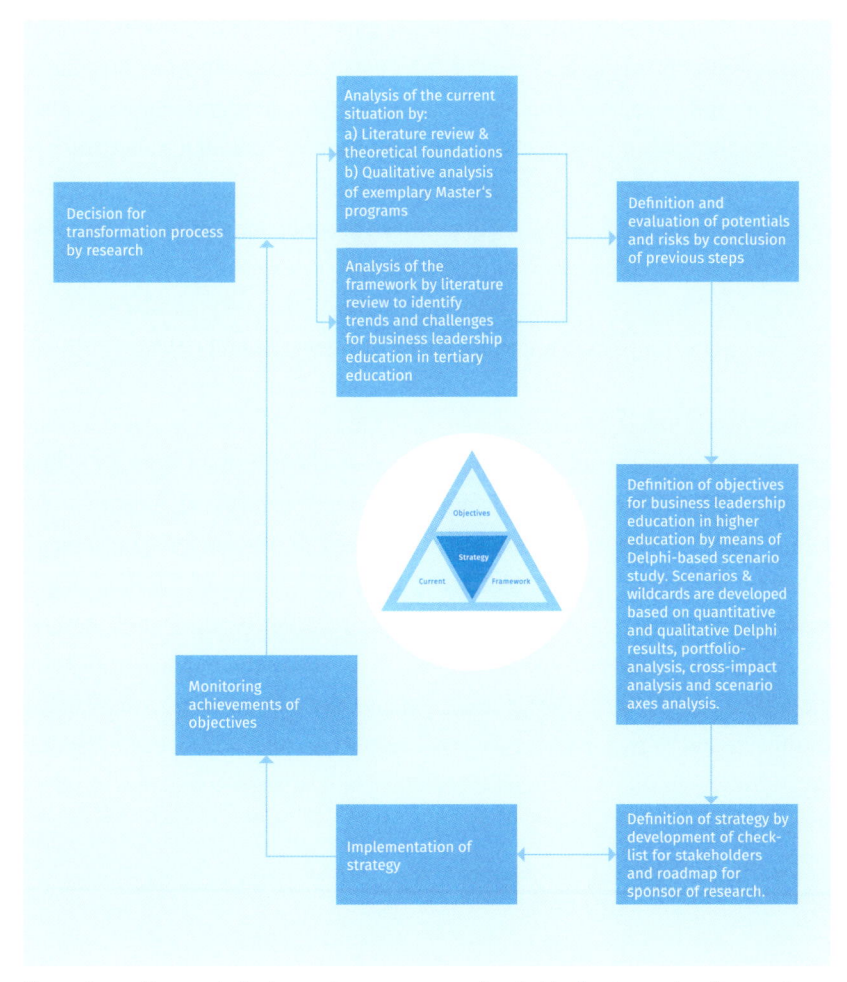

Figure 2. Research design and process according to the business development process of Faix, in: Nagel et al., 2013, p. 31.

Thereby, the overall research design and structure of this research also comprise the foresight process that consists of three main phases, namely scanning (the actual environment on uncertainties), foresight (look in the future) and transfer (of findings in implementation) (Horton, 1999; Voros, 2003). The overall research design was chosen due to its distinctive action orientation and holistic approach.

To systematically follow the eight steps of the overall research design, a rigorous methodological structure should be applied within each step. Focus of this thesis are steps 1-5 in Part 2 and Part 3 of this work, while steps 6-8 were outlined in Part 4 and should be part of a subsequent implementation.

The remaining work is structured in three parts. To elucidate the theoretical foundations of business leadership education in tertiary education for graduates in the following Part 2 of this work, it is indispensable to understand what business leadership means. Hence, the essentials of business leadership are crystallized in a first step before light is shed on the pedagogical perspective of business leadership education in tertiary education for graduates. Based on these theoretical considerations, contemporary practice of a sample in business leadership education in tertiary education is analyzed following a rigorous systematic evaluation approach based on qualitative research.

In a next step, objectives for the long-term future of business leadership education in tertiary education for graduates have to be identified in Part 3 of this work. In order to enhance the quality and validity of different scenarios, the Delphi-based scenario development is proposed. Methodology is introduced in detail. A suitable overall process to conduct the Delphi-based scenario study in this research is developed and applied. Therefore, the Delphi method is carried out as basis for the subsequent scenario method, which is also the main structure of Part 3 of this work. Finally, Part 4 of this work summarizes this thesis and its remarkable results, contributions of research, its limitations and recommendations for future research. It concludes with practical implications of this research project.

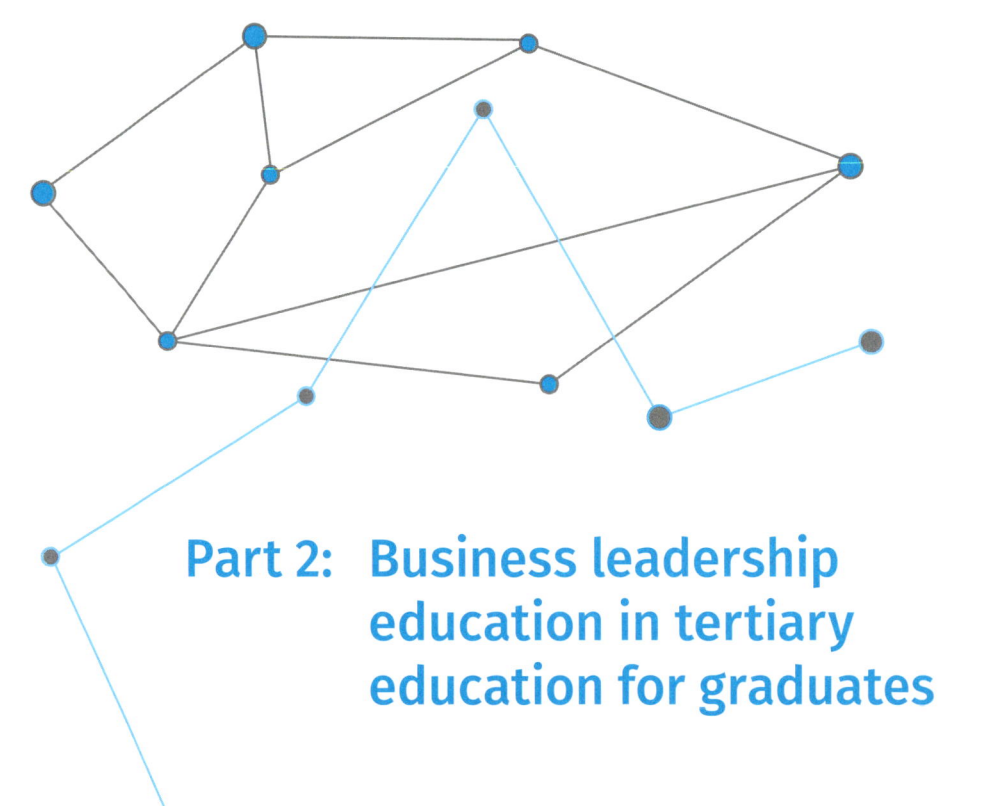

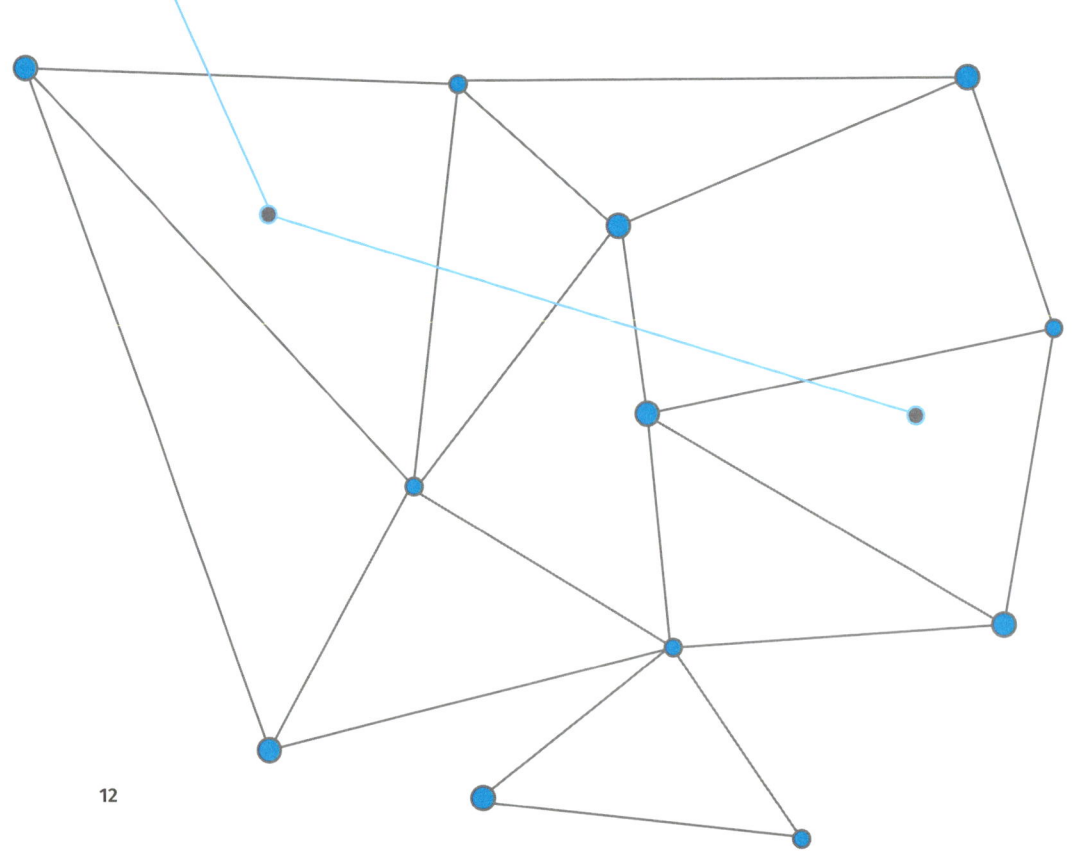

Part 2: Business leadership education in tertiary education for graduates

1. Aim of research

The interest in the field of leadership and in learning leadership has rapidly increased within the last decades (Kellerman, 2012a). Due to today's (and future) demographic and economic development in a technological, global, interconnected and dynamic environment, a critical reflection on theoretical and practical approaches to business leadership education in tertiary education for graduates is required.

Principal purpose of this chapter is to introduce the principles of business leadership education in tertiary education for graduates based on thorough literature review. Therefore, it is indispensable to obtain an overview of the meaning of business leadership. Furthermore, the research attempts to uncover how business leadership education in tertiary education is practiced in exemplary Master's programs for graduates.

2. Formulation of research questions

In order to deal with the defined aim of research regarding business leadership education in tertiary education for graduates from a theoretical and practical perspective, it is imperative to formulate the relevant and concrete research questions. Therefore, the following principal research questions guide the design and implementation of this chapter:

1. What is the goal of business leadership education in tertiary education for graduates and how should business leadership education in tertiary education for graduates be designed?
2. How is business leadership education in contemporary tertiary education practiced in exemplary Master's programs for graduates in the light of the theoretical framework?

In order to answer the research questions, the following chapter is structured in two parts. Theoretical foundations of business leadership education in tertiary education for graduates are scrutinized in a first step based on thorough literature review, before exemplary contemporary Master's programs were evaluated in light of the theoretical framework.

3. Business leadership education in tertiary education for graduates – theoretical foundations

Leadership as a subject is of great interest since ancient times, "but scientific research on leadership did not begin until the twentieth century" (Yukl, 2013, p. 18). In fact, the phenomenon of leadership covers a broad spectrum and cannot be attributed solely to one academic discipline (Rosenstiel & Comelli, 2003). Leadership is a rather complex (interdisciplinary) research topic, which is part of various academic disciplines: business studies, economics, history, pedagogics, philosophy, political sciences, psychology, sociology, social sciences etc. With its different research interests, the various academic disciplines focus on a variety of leadership aspects. Moreover, the particular (e.g. organizational or social) context of leadership may influence the specific type of leadership in practical application. Although a very similar core notion of leadership that may be generalized for different domains, military, political, educational, or business leadership may differ in a particular way due to specific missions of the domain (Palmer, 2009). The term leadership in this research is largely concerned with leadership in the business context, particularly with regard to leadership in business corporations, companies, enterprises, organizations etc. For reasons of unambiguousness, leadership in this research is specified as business leadership (Gordon, 1961; Harvey, 2001; Palmer, 2009).

Addressing the relevant question whether leaders are born or made, a balanced approach says that leaders are both born and made. Studies of twins based on quantitative behavioral genetics methods reveal that the genetic influence on leadership role occupancy is 30 %. The remaining 70 % are not based on genetic effects and influences shared by twins in a common family environment, only on all possible personal and exogenous incidents across one's lifespan that may affect leadership development (Arvey et al., 2006; Arvey et al., 2007). Thus, many individuals are born with attributes and qualities that help them in becoming a leader. On the other hand, early childhood development, appropriate education, and work related experiences promote and foster leadership abilities (Bass, 1990; Conger, 1992; Brungardt, 1996; Murphy & Johnson, 2011; Schmidt-Huber & Tippelt, 2014). Certainly, as Grint (1997) stated, "It would be strange if leadership was the only human skill that could not be enhanced through understanding and practice" (p. 2). Therefore, the focus of this research is the pedagogical perspective on business leadership education in tertiary education for graduates. In order to elucidate the theoretical foundations of business leadership education in tertiary education for graduates, it is indispensable to understand what business leadership means. Hence, the essentials of business leadership are elaborated in a first step before light is shed on the pedagogical perspective of business leadership education in tertiary education for graduates.

3.1 Conceptualizing business leadership

In general, it seems to be widespread knowledge what the term (business) leadership means, without being able to define it precisely. Therefore, in a first step, definitions available in literature are presented along with traditional approaches on leadership, which are mainly derived from the discipline of psychology. Since several aspects of the aforementioned theoretical approaches on leadership play a role in (future) business leaders' assessment and selection, we shall shed light on the selection procedure of (potential) business leaders. In a third step, findings of different disciplines, mainly from human ethology and organizational sciences, are compiled due to their high impact on leadership, and to obtain a comprehensive overview on the studied topic. Nevertheless, business leadership is undergoing a drastic change due to economic, demographic and societal reasons in a dynamic technological and global world. Therefore, a holistic model of business leadership is deduced from theoretical considerations that are proposed to meet contemporary demands and lay the foundation for a contemporary humanistic approach on business leadership education in tertiary education.

3.1.1 Definitions

Reviewing the vast amount of research literature on leadership, one can conclude that many different definitions have been developed in order to explain the term leadership (Northouse, 2013; Rost, 1991; Yukl, 2013). Bass (2007) stated, "There are almost as many different definitions of leadership as there are persons who have attempted to define the concept". He concluded, "The meaning of leadership may depend on the kind of institution in which it is found" (p. 16). The following definitions represent examples from literature. Hemphill & Coons (1957) define leadership as "the behavior of an individual…directing the activities of a group towards a shared goal" (p. 7). According to House et al. (1999), leadership is "the ability of an individual to influence, motivate, and enable others to contribute toward the effectiveness and success of the organization" (p. 184). Yukl (2013) broadly defines leadership as a "process of influencing others to understand and agree about what needs to be done and how to do it, and the process of facilitating individual and collective efforts to accomplish shared objectives" (p. 23). Some essentials of leadership can be extracted by comparing different definitions. Hence, leadership includes an influential process between leaders and followers to act in order to achieve common goals (Northouse, 2013; Steyrer, 2009; Yukl, 2013).

Another school of thought defines leadership in contrast to management, which is typically represented by the authors Warren Bennis and John P. Kotter. Bennis' and Nanus' (1985) frequently cited statement is that "managers are people who do things right, and leaders are people who do the right thing" (p. 21). According to Kotter (1990), "leadership and management are two distinctive and complementary systems of action. Each has its own function and characteristic activities. Both are essential components for success in an increasingly complex and volatile business environment" (p. 3). He elaborated that managers have to cope with complexity, produce predictability and order when overseeing the (day-to-day) operations, while leaders have to cope with change, to envision and set (future) directions. As Kotter (1990) proposes, management is important as organizations become increasingly larger and more complex, while leadership is imperative in a more competitive and volatile business world due to many factors, such as technological change, global competition, and changing demographics.

Moreover, controversy not only surrounds the terms leadership and management, reference is also made to a third term, which is entrepreneurship. Czarniawska-Joerges and Wolff (1991) concisely defined the three terms leadership, management, and entrepreneurship as follows:

> "Leadership is seen as symbolic performance, expressing the hope of control over destiny; management as the activity of introducing order by coordinating flows of things and people towards collective action, and entrepreneurship as the making of entire new worlds." (p. 529)

In order to explore the term entrepreneurship, the comprehensive work of Joseph A. Schumpeter, an Austrian economist, has to be mentioned. At the beginning of the 20th century, he scrutinized the characteristics of the corporation and the function of an entrepreneur. He pointed out that it is an entrepreneur's main task to create rather than manage an existing company by carrying out innovations. Realizing innovations is not merely assigned to entrepreneurs, but also to intrapreneurs that are working in business corporations (Schumpeter, 1911 / 2008). Moreover, in Schumpeter's perception, the entrepreneur was not only described as innovator, but also as leader (Grebel, 2004). Huynh (2007) concluded that Schumpeter's definition of an entrepreneur was equivalent to that of a leader.

Nevertheless, due to a globalized and digitized dynamic world and the increased pressures on companies' competitiveness, the construct entrepreneurial leadership emerged recently (Huynh, 2007; McGrath & MacMillan, 2000). By combing, integrating, and exploring both entrepreneurship and leadership, the entrepreneurial leader is expected to cope with the fast changing business environment "to exploit opportunities to reap advantage for the organisation before and faster than others" (Karmarkar, Chabra & Deshpande, 2014, p. 160).

Controversial debates about the ideal leadership definition are ongoing. Yukl (2013) noted that this question should be answered based on empirical research rather than on subjective judgements.

3.1.2   Theoretical approaches

Furthermore, not only the definitions of leadership, but also the theoretical approaches on leadership are manifold. In order to provide a comprehensive overview, different models shall be examined. In a first step, traditional leadership approaches prevalent in (research) literature on leadership shall be elucidated. Leadership approaches that dominate (research) literature are rooted in psychological research (Parry, 1998) which, in turn, is the scientific domain of the assessment center, a widespread and well accepted instrument used for the selection of (potential) business leaders. Due to its relevance in business leadership, the assessment center is outlined as an excursus. Finally, research findings of different disciplines with a high impact on leadership shall be presented.

3.1.2.1 Traditional approaches to leadership

Due to the extraordinarily high number and variety of definitions and theoretical approaches – approx. 1500 definitions and approx. 40 theories of leadership[1] according to Rhode and Packel (2011) – a choice had to be made in order to present the most common theories and the current state of discussion in research literature on leadership. Leadership approaches that are predominantly presented in (research) literature mainly derive from the discipline of psychology (Parry, 1998).

Brodbeck, Maier and Frey (2002) structured the different approaches in four main categories:

1. Personalist approach, wherein stable personal traits explain leaders' success (e.g. trait approach)
2. Behavioral approach that focuses on stable behavioral patterns (e.g. leadership styles) and skills that can be learned
3. Contingency theory that additionally comprises situational variables (e.g. employee's or organization's situation) and
4. Power and influence concepts, which describe leadership as a reciprocal social influence process between leaders and followers.

The main approaches are exemplary and roughly outlined in the following section in order to present the current state of discussion in standard literature on leadership.

The trait approach (Brodbeck, Maier & Frey, 2002; Frey & Spielmann, 1997; Northouse, 2013; Steyrer, 2009; Yukl, 2013) is seen to be one of the earliest attempts to scrutinize leadership at the beginning of 20th century. The theories – also known as "great man" theories – attempt to identify specific traits, which great leaders in social, political, and military fields characterize and possess, based on the assumption that people were born with these traits and that these traits are personality dispositions, which are relatively stable over time and situations. Findings of this research are revealed e.g. in Stogdill

---

[1] Rhode and Packel (2011, p. 6) refer to two sound references a) Bass and Stogdills's Handbook of Leadership from the year 1990 and b) Gareth Edwards: In search for the Holy Grail: Leadership in Management from the year 2000. Thus, it may be assumed that – instead of remaining constant or decreasing – the numbers have increased to the present day.

(1948), Ghiselli (1966), Korman (1968) and Gibb (1969). The aim of this approach is to understand and identify an ideal profile for leaders, comprising all relevant traits for successful leadership. Several strengths as well as shortcomings of this approach were elucidated e.g. by Northouse (2013). On the positive side, intuitively appealing, outstanding longevity, breadth and depth of research along with a focus on the leader component as well as definition of a benchmark for an ideal leader e.g. in assessment procedures were elaborated. Along with the strengths, several shortcomings were depicted. Thus, the trait approach is criticized due to conflicting, ambiguous, and sometimes uncertain results in research, an endless list of traits, an isolated view failing to take situations into account, subjective determinations, and subjective interpretation of the important traits and, finally, failing to evaluate the leaders' performance. Brodbeck, Maier and Frey (2002) emphasize that predictability for the leaders' future performance is overestimated due to methodological reasons of research. However, findings in research are ambiguous, uncertain, and controversially debated throughout a time, when this approach is still – or once again – popular in research and practical application e.g. in order to determine individual's leader potential, to identify, select and develop leaders.

While the focus of leadership research in the trait approach (Brodbeck, Maier & Frey, 2002; Northouse, 2013; Steyrer, 2009) was on leaders' personal characteristics, the style approach exclusively accentuates the behavior of the leader, particularly leaders' actions towards followers in different contexts. In this approach, which is based on the assumption of stable behavioral patterns, two main types of behaviors were elaborated, namely task behaviors and relationship behaviors. The style approach emphasized how leaders apply one, or combine task and relationship behaviors in order to influence followers to achieve goals. Comprehensive research was done in this field, wherein Iowa studies (in the late 1930s), Ohio State studies (in the late 1940s), Michigan studies (in the 1950s) along with research done by Blake and Mouton (in the early 1960s) build the basis. In addition, several strengths and weaknesses were compiled for this approach, e.g. by Northouse (2013).

The style approach is valuable since it broadened the scope of research on leadership by including leaders' behaviors rather than exclusively focusing on personality traits. Further positive sides of the style approach are the extensive research in this field, highlighting two important main types of leadership behavior (task and relationship behavior) and its heuristic value. On the opposite side, a universal style that could be adapted in almost every situation in order to ensure effective leadership could not be identified. This weakness can be compared to the trait approach, which failed to identify the ultimate personal traits. Neither task nor relationship behavior can be associated with performance. Finally, the style implied to be most effective – meaning high task in combination with high relationship orientation –, was not supported. According to Brodbeck, Maier and Frey (2002), findings are also applied in practice, e.g. in selection or evaluation procedures of (potential) leaders by measuring external assessments on various dimensions of leaders' behaviors.

According to Frey and Spielmann (1997), both personalist and behavioral approaches of leadership research do not comprise a theoretical model in the strict sense; only the two concepts of trait and style approach comprise a wide variety of empirical studies. However, the contingency theory reflects another shift in leadership research. Several contingency theories were developed in the 1970s and 1980s, e.g. path-goal theory, situational leadership theory (Yukl, 2013), wherein Fiedler's contingency theory (Fiedler, 1964; Fiedler, 1967; Fiedler & Chemers, 1974) was "the most widely recognized" (Northouse, 2013, p. 123), in fact "the only explicitly developed leadership theory in social psychology" (Frey & Spielmann, 1997, p. 167). Instead of focusing on only the leader, Fiedler's contingency theory accentuated the conjunction of the leader and the appropriate situation in which the leader works.

The term *contingency* means that a leader's performance depends on the leader's behaviors in specific situations or contexts (Northouse, 2013; Steyrer, 2009). Therefore, both leadership style and situations were measured. In order to measure the leadership style, the Least-Preferred-Coworker (LPC) scale, which is seen to be a personality-like measure, was used. This scale distinguishes highly task-motivated people (low LPCs) from socio-independent (middle LPCs) and relationship-motivated people (high LPCs). In order to measure situations, three situational variables – leader-member relations, task structure and position power – are assessed. By dichotomizing the three dimensions of situations in combination with three variables, eight different types of situations result (2x2x2=8) that consider the degree of leader's situational control. Based on empirical research, certain styles were shown to be effective in certain situations, e.g. those people who are task-motivated (which means a low LPS score) will be effective in very favorable as well as unfavorable situations (Northouse, 2013; Steyrer, 2009). Fiedler's theory is based on the assumption of a stable leader's personality, behavior, and leadership style, which does not change (in the short or even medium term), and that leaders are incapable of adapting their behavior to different situations in a flexible manner (Fiedler, 1967).

Consequently, Fiedler's model implies that the situation has to be matched to leader's behavioral disposition or, when the situation cannot be changed, to install the most adequate of the leaders. Brodbeck, Maier and Frey (2002) emphasize that Fiedler's model still has a high degree of plausibility for practitioners. They conclude that the leadership style has to be adapted to the situation in a flexible way; although this seems to be reasonable, it does not correspond to Fiedler's assumption of an invariable leadership style. For the contingency theory, several strengths and weaknesses were compiled e.g. by Northouse (2013) and Steyrer (2009). On the positive side, a vast amount of research supports at least the core concepts of Fiedler's model. Moreover, it emphasizes the impact of situations on leaders; it provides useful information about different types of leadership and the type, which is most likely to be effective in certain situations. Therefore, Fiedler's contingency theory has some predictive character. Last, Fiedler's model does not require leaders to perform in all situations. In contrast, several shortcomings were discussed. First, although the theory is supported by many studies, it has been criticized that it does not adequately explain the link between certain leadership styles and situations. Mainly, the situational variables do not describe situations thoroughly, e.g. followers' personal characteristics were not included; dichotomization of the situational variables in favorable or unfavorable strongly simplifies reality etc. Second, validity of the LPC scale has been questioned, and third, the theory is not user-friendly in real-world situations.

Despite their great contributions in leadership research, all the three aforementioned approaches were criticized due to theoretical and methodological reasons. Causal relations between leader's traits, behaviors, situations and outcomes could not be demonstrated due the interaction of a multitude of factors (Brodbeck, Maier & Frey, 2002).

Considering the substantial contribution by the aforementioned approaches it has to be noted, that they focused on leadership from the perspective of the leader (e.g. trait approach and style approach) or the situation and / or context (e.g. contingency theory). A further shift in leadership theory was made by emphasizing leadership as a (reciprocal social influence) process. Since influence is seen to be "the essence of leadership" (Yukl, 2013, p. 188), power and influence concepts were elucidated. These concepts try to explain various constructs of power and influence, sources and types as well as their implications for effectiveness and outcomes (e.g. Brodbeck, Maier & Frey, 2002; Yukl, 2013). The leader-member exchange (LMX) theory by Graen and his colleagues scrutinizes leadership as a process of interactions between leaders and followers. While the early studies, called vertical dyad linkage (VDL) theory, emphasized the vertical linkages leaders build with each of their followers, resulting in two general types of relationships. Dansereau, Graen and Haha (1975) distinguished between relationships that were built upon expanded and negotiated role responsibilities and those that were built upon a formal employment contract. These two different groups of employees were called in-group and out-group, resulting in the description how well leaders and followers cooperate and the nature of differences between the in- and out-group. Consequently, the style approach that is based on the assumption of stable leader's behavior was disproved (Frey & Spielmann, 1997). In the later studies, the effect of the leader-member exchanges on organizational performance was elaborated, particularly the relation of the leader-member exchanges on positive effects for leaders, followers, groups and the organization (Graen & Uhl-Bien, 1995). Further research in this field focused e.g. on employees' perceptions of leader-member exchange (Atwater & Carmeli, 2009), relationship of LMX theory to empowerment (Harris, Wheeler & Kacmar, 2009) and on how these exchanges between leaders and followers can be used for leadership-making (Graen & Uhl-Bien, 1991). Leadership making in this context is based on the assumption that a leader should create high-quality exchanges and effective dyads with all followers and establish networks within the organization in order to achieve the organization's goals and the leader's career progress. Graen and Uhl-Bien (1991) describe the process of leadership making. The authors suggest a three-phase-process from 1) stranger phase, 2) acquaintance phase to 3) partnership phase, which develops gradually over the time.

Consequently, individuals and organizations should benefit from the good working relationships. Northouse (2013) pointed out several strengths and weaknesses for this approach. On the positive side, the LMX theory is seen to be a descriptive approach that elucidates the different types of relationships leaders develop with followers of in-groups versus out-groups in order to achieve organizational goals. In contrast to other approaches the LMX theory strongly accentuates the specific relationship between the leader and each follower. Effective leadership depends on high-quality leader-member exchanges and consequently on effective communication. Moreover, the LMX theory reproves leaders to be fair even in the leader's relationships with each follower. Finally, the LMX theory is grounded in a variety of research that link the practice of LMX to positive organizational outcomes. In contrast, early VDL studies undermine the general principle of fairness because it divides the work unit into different groups, which were treated differently. Consequently, perceived inequalities may result in negative impact for individuals and organizations. In addition, the LMX theory does not describe how high-quality exchanges and relationships can be created. Furthermore, contextual factors that may have an impact on LMX relationships were not adequately described. Last, measurement procedures used in the LMX theory were questioned. Despite controversial discussions, the concept represents a further contribution and progress in leadership research.

Following the structure and categorization of leadership theories according to Brodbeck, Maier and Frey (2002), the aforementioned approaches roughly delineate scientific research on leadership provided in psychological research on leadership within the last century. Along with these main approaches in psychology, further paradigms emerged (e.g. transformational leadership, servant leadership, authentic leadership), which are presented in educational books, standard literature and research.

As several aspects of the aforementioned theoretical approaches on leadership play a role in (future) business leaders' assessment and selection, the selection procedure of (potential) business leaders shall be presented.

3.1.2.2 Excursus: Business leader selection process – Assessment center

A widespread and well accepted instrument used for business leaders' selection is the assessment center (AC) that determines a leader's future job performance. AC have been employed in many companies in USA since the late 1950s, were subsequently introduced in the UK and ultimately in Germany at the end of the 1960s. Today, the AC is extensively used in organizations throughout the world (Sarges, 2001). According to Nerdinger, Blickle and Schaper (2008), the AC is a mixture of diverse behavior-oriented simulation exercises (e.g. presentation, role-plays, group discussion), wherein the qualified assessors observe and rate participants simultaneously based on predefined dimensions. Usually, a group of candidates were assessed over a period of two to three days (Sarges, 2001).

In spite of its widespread use, (academic) discussions due to methodological and ideological issues of AC are ongoing (Sarges, 2001). Therefore, the quality criteria for ACs must be taken into account. The evaluation of ACs is best done through predictive validity. Predictive validity is the ability to predict future job performance, job-related learning (in training as well as development programs), and other criteria (Schmidt & Hunter, 1998). Furthermore, the predictive validity coefficient is directly proportional to the practical economic value or utility of the assessment method (Brogden, 1949; Schmidt et al., 1979). Research evaluating the ability of personnel assessment methods predicting future job performance and future oriented learning especially training programs has been performed since the first decade of the 20th century. In early 1920s, it has been reported that the findings from various studies conducted on the same assessment procedure had no consensus with respect to their results (Schmidt & Hunter, 1998). Gaugler et al. (1987), in their meta-analysis of 50 assessment center studies comprising 107 validity coefficients, yielded an average predictive validity coefficient of .37, suggesting a weak correlation between results of ACs and prediction of future job performance. Another meta-analysis by Hermelin, Lievens and Robertson (2007), based on 26 studies and 27 validity coefficients, reported an even weaker relationship ($r = .28$) between the overall AC ratings and workplace outcomes. However, variations in predictive validity are evident in different studies (Schoelmerich, Nachtwei & Schermuly, in press) and cultural differences (Becker et al., 2011). This implies that not all ACs are able to predict the future job performance of leaders. Relying on mere ACs to select future leaders therefore seems to be insufficient and in many instances misleading.

The comprehensive methods used by ACs have another issue with construct validity. Construct validity is the degree to which a test measures what it claims, or purports, to be measuring (Cronbach & Meehl, 1955). Regardless whether the AC provides a correct prognosis, the type of psychological constructs are not yet clear (Sarges, 2001). Overall, the quality criteria for ACs are still debatable. There is a need for a standardized and more thorough instrument to review the quality of ACs. It has been recommended that AC quality should be weighed against scientific standards as well as a norm of organizations for the purpose of enhancing predictive validity of ACs (Schoelmerich, Nachtwei & Schermuly, in press). Another criticism mentioned by Schuler (2007) is that ACs are not conducted by psychologists in most cases. Therefore, the scores from psychometric tests, which are also a part of ACs, are either ignored or incorrectly interpreted.

Due to many discussions on the quality of AC and ideological debates on cost-benefit-ratio, many attempts were made to improve predictive and construct validity of the AC method. ACs traditionally used comprehensive testing methods, a collection of relevant measurements. This complex examination was a type of "character check". In the end, an up to date selection procedure emerged, which included a palette of investigation methods for a period of three days, carried out on a group of candidates under the close observation of the selection panel (assessors). The following analyses were conducted for candidates: Resume or life career analysis, expression analysis, mind analysis, action analysis, leader's test, and group discussion. As well as tests and explorative interviews, individual and group exercises were included as simulations of important leadership situations. According to Sarges (2001), the following aptitudes are assessed in the AC (p. 8). These are 1) cognitive aptitude comprising e.g. knowledge range, logical-analytical thinking, planning ability, 2) motivational-emotional aptitude comprising e.g. energy and general ambition, courage to take risk and initiative, self-confidence, and 3) social-interactive aptitude e.g. extraversion, communication, cooperativeness and the ability to work in a team. Furthermore, also the potential to learn should be assessed.

In spite of the low quality of assessment experienced in ACs, organizations are opting for this due to the fact that most of the companies still use this as a reliable measure. However, it has to be pointed out, that the main purpose of ACs may lie in a culture-directed selection of (potential) business leaders. This is given, when assessors are (higher) leaders and select (potential) business leaders best suited to the company's organizational culture. Currently, the assessment center is one of the most popular diagnostic procedures. It is not only utilized for the selection of external applicants as well as a potential diagnosis for internal employees in companies; it also serves as a deciding factor for career paths and measures of personnel development (Schuler, 2007).

3.1.2.3 Interdisciplinary considerations on leadership

Along with traditional leadership approaches that are rooted in the discipline of psychology, various other disciplines focus on different aspects that are of high relevance for the research on leadership. For the purpose of this exercise, it was important to compile findings of different disciplines mainly from human ethology and organizational sciences in order to receive a comprehensive overview on the topic.

Nevertheless, considering the field of human ethology in the context of leadership approaches, it is more than plausible but woefully neglected. Consequently, studying leadership does not automatically provide valuable insight in this research area. However, the contemporary Austrian researcher Irenäus Eibl-Eibesfeldt performed remarkable work in this field, above all with his works of *Grundriß der vergleichenden Verhaltensforschung* (1967) and *Die Biologie des menschlichen Verhaltens: Grundriß der Humanethologie* (1984). Eibl-Eibesfeldt explored the fundamentals of biological and cultural human behavior. He thereby constituted the field of human ethology. Characteristics, which play a major role for humans' leadership behavior were thereby determined as universalities of human behavior. These characteristics encompass reputation, authority, aggression, status, communication, solicitude, identification with a group etc. Furthermore, Felix von Cube, a contemporary German educationalist, introduced findings of human ethology in pedagogics. He thereby influenced educational processes and contents for leaders. Three of his major works *Fordern statt verwöhnen: Die Erkenntnisse der Verhaltensbiologie in der Erziehung (1986)*, *Lust an Leistung: Die Naturgesetze der Führung (1998)* and *Führen durch Fordern: Die BioLogik des Erfolgs* (2003) elucidate his major findings.

Moreover, another field of high importance for leadership research is the research on entrepreneurship, which is "a relatively distinctive field within the organizational sciences" (Vecchio, 2003, p. 304) with its foundations in both psychology and economics. As outlined earlier, the Austrian economist Joseph A. Schumpeter is referred to as "forefather of entrepreneurship" (Karmarkar, Chabra & Deshpande, 2014, p. 164). In his oeuvre *Theory of Economic Development (Die Theorie der wirtschaftlichen Entwicklung*, 1911 / 2008), he not only emphasizes innovations as a necessary requirement for entrepreneurship (and intrapreneurship) and sustainable competitiveness of a company, but also refers to the entrepreneur (intrapreneur) who is in charge of innovations. Browsing research literature on this topic reveals that Schumpeter's entrepreneur (intrapreneur) was also perceived as a leader (Grebel, 2004; Huynh, 2007), which is also concisely pointed out by Czarniawska-Joerges and Wolff (1991):

> "The core of entrepreneurial motivation is similar to that of leaders, but entrepreneurship mainly fits contexts which are new and cannot be dealt with by means of experience or routine. Entrepreneurship is leadership in exceptional situations and, we might add, is most likely to entail the creation of such situations. Schumpeter stressed repeatedly that entrepreneurship is never a matter of individuals only. It is a phenomenon which has to be analyzed and identified within a complex conglomerate of factors" (p. 533).

Considering Schumpeter's justifications of entrepreneurship (intrapreneurship) also means considering the entrepreneurial personality, which is of major interest in the research on entrepreneurship (Bijedić, 2013; Braukmann, Bijedic & Schneider, 2008; Creuznacher, 2008) and for entrepreneurship education (Bijedić, 2013; Creuznacher, 2008; Walterscheid, 1998).

However, research on both entrepreneurship and leadership are treated as separate areas. After having consciously scrutinized this phenomenon, Vecchio (2003) suggests "to view entrepreneurship as simply a type of leadership that occurs in a specific setting and, ... a type of leadership that is not beyond the reach or understanding of available theory in the areas of leadership and interpersonal influence" (p. 322). Nevertheless, as mentioned earlier, a construct that recently emerged is entrepreneurial leadership (Huynh, 2007; McGrath & MacMillan, 2000). Due to a globalized and digitized dynamic world and the increased pressures on companies' competitiveness, a combination, integration and exploration of both entrepreneurship and leadership, the entrepreneurial leader is expected to cope with the fast changing business environment.

Furthermore, several other approaches emerged in contemporary debates on leadership. These approaches are not theories in the strict sense and cannot be allocated to a specific discipline. They rather try to provide answers to current (socioeconomic) questions and trends within the broad field of leadership. These topics encompass e.g. cross-cultural leadership (Hanges et al., 2016; Northouse, 2013), diversity in leadership (Eagly & Chin, 2010; Yukl, 2013), women and leadership (Cook & Glass, 2014; Northouse, 2013), ethical leadership (Fischer, Frey & Niedernhuber, 2013; Frey et al., 2010; Palmer, 2009; Schmidt-Huber & Tippelt, 2014; Yukl, 2013) etc.

3.1.3 Preliminary conclusions

Following the structure of this chapter, it has to be pointed out that many different definitions of leadership coexist depending on the institution where they were developed and their purpose. Along with different definitions, several theoretical approaches on leadership exist. Leadership approaches that are predominantly presented in (research) literature, mainly derive from the discipline of psychology, and were presented according to four categories, namely personalist approach, behavioral approach, contingency theory, and power and influence concepts. Thus, it has to be pointed out that they offer valuable contributions to research on leadership.

Considering the approaches from psychology, various strengths as well as (methodological) shortcomings were outlined. Steyrer (2009) concluded: "The 'optimum', all-encompassing leadership model does not exist. Each leadership theory has its strengths, its explanatory value and practical usefulness, but also its weaknesses, blind spots and often simplified fundamental assumptions" (p. 88).

Furthermore, it has to be pointed out that the approaches on leadership deriving from the discipline of psychology reflect a mere fragmentary instead of a holistic perspective on leadership, failing to provide an acceptable measure of the leader's performance. Frey and Spielmann (1997) noted: „Despite, or particularly because of the quite intense research in this field over the past two decades, a general theory of leadership, which could integrate the multitude of doubtlessly existing partial knowledge is still not apparent" (p. 172).

In a second step, the AC as a widespread instrument used for the selection of (potential) business leaders was outlined due to its importance for business leadership. Considering ACs from a positive point of view, the main purpose of ACs may lie in a culture-directed selection of (potential) business leaders when assessors are (higher) leaders. In spite of various improvements, not all ACs are able to predict leaders' future job performance. The exclusive reliance on ACs to select future leaders therefore seems to be insufficient and in many instances misleading.

In a third step, findings of different disciplines (mainly from human ethology and organizational sciences) were compiled due to their high impact on leadership and to obtain a comprehensive overview of the examined topic. Characteristics, which play a major role for humans' leadership behavior and which were determined as universalities of human behavior shall be considered in further research on leadership and impact on educational processes and contents for leaders. Finally, entrepreneurship rooted in organizational sciences plays a major role for the research on leadership. It has to be summarized that Schumpeter's entrepreneur (intrapreneur) who is in charge of innovations was also perceived as a leader. Considering Schumpeter's justifications of entrepreneurship (and intrapreneurship) also means emphasizing the entrepreneurial personality. A recently emerging construct is entrepreneurial leadership combining both entrepreneurship and leadership. Due to a globalized and digitized dynamic world and the increased pressures on companies' competitiveness, the entrepreneurial leader is expected to cope with the fast changing (business) environment.

An observation by Burns (1978, p. 1 f.) – as true today as when he made it nearly forty years ago – can summarize the sections before: "If we all know too much about our leaders, we know far too little about *leadership*. We fail to grasp the essence of leadership that is relevant to the modern age". He then concluded: "Leadership is one of the most observed and least understood phenomena".

Based on these preliminary conclusions, due to various external (political, economic, socio-cultural, technological and legal) influencing factors on (business) environment and for the purpose of this research, theoretical foundations have to meet the following demands:

1. Since business leadership undergoes a drastic change, theoretical foundations of this research shall imply a contemporary and holistic understanding of business leadership in a dynamic environment.
2. This contemporary and holistic understanding of business leadership in a dynamic environment shall lay the foundation for a contemporary humanistic approach on business leadership education in tertiary education that can cater to the changing needs of business leaders.

3.1.4 Business leadership – A holistic model

In order to achieve a holistic perspective on business leadership, both the organizations' (functional) needs and the leader's' perspective have to be elucidated and integrated in an outcomes based approach, following stringent deductive reasoning.

3.1.4.1 Shaping the future – Goal identification and goal setting

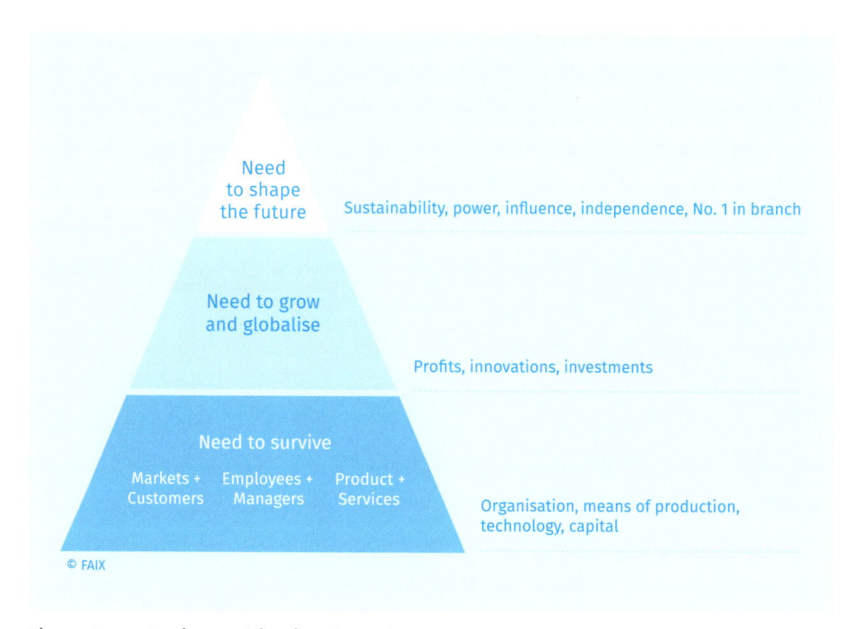

Figure 3. Business objectives based on company's needs pyramid according to Faix. Adopted from: Nagel et al., 2013, p. 47.

The pyramid of needs for companies shall be starting point of the following considerations. The pyramid of needs for companies presented in Figure 3 was elaborated by Faix similar to Maslow's pyramid of human needs, comprising three levels (Rasner, Füser & Faix, 1999; Nagel et al., 2013). In the first level, the company's need to survive is shown as basic principle, followed by level two, which is the need to grow (e.g. by globalization) and, last, level three is the need to sustainably shape the company's future.

According to Nagel et al. (2013), reaching a next level can be considered a vivid process; only a fraction of companies reach the second level and only a few companies succeed by reaching the highest level. Although there are different demands to be met at each level, two basic principles have to be pointed out for this research. First, all companies – irrespective of their individual level and irrespective of the time horizon – have to set (corporate) goals[2]. Second, all companies should aim to reach level three in order to sustainably shape the (company's and society's) future and consequently contribute to economic growth and wealth.

With regard to the macro economic environment of both corporate business world and society – and consequently of individuals – the acronym "VUCA" describes a volatile, uncertain, complex and ambiguous world (Horney, Pasmore & O'Shea, 2010). The term VUCA-world was first used by the U.S. army in the 1990s and later introduced in civil life and corporate management (DDI, 2015). According to an international survey, which was conducted by an international top talent management consultancy among 13,124 leaders and 2,031 organizations in 48 countries, 25 % of organizations reported that their leaders are not VUCA-capable, while only approx. 18 % recognized their leaders as being "very capable" (DDI, 2015). Moreover, those organizations, which specified their leaders to be VUCA-capable, "are three times more likely to have financial performance commensurate with the top 20 percent" (DDI, 2015, p. 11). Another survey, conducted by IBM (2010a) among 1,541 CEOs, general managers and senior public sector leaders in 60 countries and 33 industries, depicts that organizations perceive significant changes in the new economic environment regarding volatility, uncertainty, complexity and structural changes. Notably, 60 % of the respondents are "experiencing a high / very high level of complexity" (IBM, 2010a, p.18). 79 % expect the level of complexity to increase over the next five years, while only 49 % consider themselves prepared for the expected complexity.

By returning to the micro economic level, a more complex or even "VUCA" world implies not only that leaders are required to foster change (Rosenstiel & Comelli, 2003), but also that setting goals is not as easy as it was in the past (Faix & Mergenthaler, 2015; Gausemeier, Fink & Schlake, 1996). It has to be noted that setting goals as prime task of leadership means to create the future of tomorrow today. Thom (2015) highlights the leaders' responsibility

---

2   The term *goal* is used as long-term horizontal aims in this research while objectives are specific, directional, measurable ends that relate directly to goals, which is in line with Wachs & Schofer (1969) and Skutsch & Schofer (1973).

to identify and set corporate goals for the purpose of locomotion. He defines goals as "targeted future states" (p. 37). In goal setting theory, the term goal is defined as "object or aim of an action" (Locke & Latham, 2013, p. 4). Locke and Latham (2013) based their goal setting theory, which was developed in 1990, on nearly 400 empirical studies. They concluded firstly that specific and high goals lead to higher performance than no or abstract goals, irrespective whether they are self-set or set in a participative process with an individual or group. Secondly, a linear relationship between the level of goal difficulty and performance was supported. According to Locke (1967, as cited in Locke & Latham, 2013, p. 5), "the performance of participants with the highest goals was over 250 % higher than those with the earliest goals". Ability, feedback, commitment, complexity of task, and situational constraints are moderating variables that either increase or weaken the effects, while choice / direction, effort, persistence, and strategy enhance a positive effect on performance. Moreover, not only the validity of goal setting and its usefulness in the workplace were concluded, but also to work motivation.

Corporate goals are integrated a part of common leadership definitions, as earlier presented. They are recognized as one of the basic and primary functions of management and leadership in order to shape a company's development and future (Welge & Al-Laham, 2003), and the goal setting theory supports a positive impact on performance and motivation. A profound description of the goal setting procedure can be found in Eisenbeis (2008). The author points out that the goal setting procedure is a continuously ongoing process. Since the process is influenced by pluralistic interests of different stakeholders, e.g. investors, corporate management / leadership, employees, customers, suppliers, society or government, the goal setting procedure is considered to be a multi-personal and interactive approach, in which a reciprocal process of bottom-up and top-down is considered to be successful. Research on goals is considered to be of high importance (Eisenbeis, 2008). Nevertheless, it is reported to be one of the major difficulties with regard to methodology and contents (Macharzina & Wolf, 2005). Furthermore, it was observed that goal identification procedure is woefully neglected in leadership literature, in leadership education, training, and development. The goal identification procedure – premise of the overall procedure – has to answer the question, which goals have to be pursued. Anyway, Kotter (1990) explained the setting of directions as an inductive rather than a mystical process of leaders based on a wide range of data, identification of patterns, linkages and relationships in order to understand phenomena. A systematic overall development process for organizations that can be easily applied to projects or even individuals can be found in Nagel et al. (2013).

Gausemeier, Fink and Schlake (1996) not only emphasize the need of concrete goals, but also specify that the focus of corporate goals has shifted in recent years. While key performance indicators for liquidity and profits seemed to be reasonable principles for corporate management in the 1970s, companies today also have to focus on the future and future potentials in order to succeed. Consequently, a multidimensional system of (corporate) goals comprising social, political, economic, and ecological elements have to replace – or at least supplement – the goal of profit maximization. Drucker (2010) noted that the concept of profit maximization is not only meaningless, but also dangerous. He pointed out that the source of confusion was the fact that classical economists consider profit maximization a basic theorem in order to describe a reality that could not be explained by their theory of economic equilibrium. Considering profit and profitability as basic requirements, the only one valid purpose of companies, which are institutions of society, is to generate a customer. Drucker then arrived at two basic functions companies have to fulfill. Those two functions are marketing and innovation. Innovation goals are crucial points within a company's development process. Considering a company's development process to be an innovation development process, the identification and setting of innovation goals is not only imperative but also its fundamental point (Faix et al., 2015). Therefore, the following section shall emphasize the importance of innovations for business leadership and present essential perspectives on innovations for the purpose of this research.

3.1.4.2 Creating sustainable value – Realization of innovations

Drucker (1993) conceived that "innovation is the specific instrument of entrepreneurship. It is the act that endows resources with a new capacity to create wealth. Innovation, indeed, creates a resource" (p. 30). Based on a content analysis of 60 definitions of innovation, Baregheh, Rowley and Sambrook (2009) proposed the more comprehensive definition of "innovation [being] the multi-stage process whereby organizations transform ideas into new /

improved products, service or processes, in order to advance, compete and differentiate themselves successfully in their marketplace" (p. 1334).

Nevertheless, as Schumpeter's reputation as "prophet of innovation" (McCraw, 2007) has been established, the roots of his thoughts should be synthesized. In his work *Theorie der wirtschaftlichen Entwicklung (Theory of Economic Development)*, first published in 1911, Schumpeter (2008) clarified the term *development*. Thus, "by development…we shall understand only such changes in economic life as are not forced upon it from without but arise by its own initiative, from within" (p. 63). He furthermore stated:

> "Development in our sense is a distinct phenomenon, entirely foreign to what may be observed in the circular flow or in the tendency towards equilibrium. It is spontaneous and discontinuous change in the channels of the flow, disturbance of equilibrium, which forever alters and displaces the equilibrium state previously existing" (p. 64).

The specific role to initiate and realize economic development is attributed to the entrepreneur and entrepreneurial actions. Development comprises five cases, which are specified by Schumpeter (1911 / 2008):

> "This concept covers the following five cases: (1) The introduction of a new good – that is one with which consumers are not yet familiar – or a new quality of a good. (2) The introduction of a new method of production, that is one not yet tested by experience in the branch of manufacture concerned, which need by no means be founded upon a discovery scientifically new, and can also exist in a new way of handling a commodity commercially. (3) The opening of a new market, that is a market into which the particular branch of manufacture of the country in question has not previously entered, whether or not this market has existed before. (4) The conquest of a new source of supply or raw materials or half - manufactured goods, again irrespective of whether this source already exists or whether it has first to be created. (5) The carrying out of the new organization of any industry, like the creation of a monopoly position (for example through trustification) or the breaking up of a monopoly position." (p. 66)

In order to realize economic development, stagnation has to be excluded. Rather, the premise of economic development is innovation. The term *innovation* was popularized after the publication of Schumpeter's two volumes of *Business Cycles*, first published in 1939. Innovation is briefly defined as "the doing of new things or the doing of things that are already being done in a new way" (Schumpeter, 1947, p. 151). Innovations consequently imply "creative destruction" (Schumpeter 1942 / 2003). According to Faix and Mergenthaler (2015), "Innovation thus describes the sometimes radical metamorphosis of what already exists – that active power that creates the new by destroying the old" (p. 12).

Zillner and Krusche (2012) distinguish innovations according to three different levels, which are incremental, radical and disruptive innovations. Thus, incremental innovations are explained as renovations or improvements. Based on existing know-how and detailed knowledge, the focus of incremental innovations is the existing product portfolio. In contrast, radical innovations focus on new developments for existing problems. Moreover, disruptive innovations imply new developments for new problems. Faix and Mergenthaler (2015) concretized Schumpeter's five cases of economic development described earlier by differentiating between radical (p. 31) and incremental (p. 34) innovations. The authors also adapted the wording according to company's contemporary perspective. Consequently, the following paths lead to innovations:

> Development and introduction of a new product or new product feature and development and deployment of a new service or new service feature

> Development and introduction of new production methods or optimization of existing production methods and development and introduction of new business processes or optimization of existing business processes

> Development of new markets or penetration / reactivation / expansion of existing (international) markets

> Development of new purchasing markets or improvement / reactivation / expansion of existing (international) purchasing markets

> Development and introduction of new organizational structures or improvement / reorganization / expansion of existing organizational structures

Research on innovation portrays that innovation goes beyond the technical dimension; its relevance is not only in the business or financial world, but it stretches to the society as well. Innovation is not specifically a "thing" (Drucker, 1993, p. 31). Drucker (1993) gave an appropriate example to highlight the aspect of social innovation. He said

> "Management, that is, the 'useful knowledge' that enables man for the first time to render productive people of different skills and knowledge working together in an 'organization', is an innovation of this century. It has converted modern society into something brand new, something, by the way, for which we have neither political nor social theory: a society of organizations." (p. 31 f.)

Faix and Mergenthaler (2015) describe types of innovations that are most relevant to contemporary economy based on and complementary to Schumpeter's idea. They are as follows:

> *Social innovation*: It involves introduction and development of novel structures for activities and procedures.

> *Financial innovation*: It involves introduction and development of novel investment and financing instruments along with behaviors of market participants.

> *Infrastructural innovation*: It involves introduction and development of novel instruments and procedures that primarily aid the mobility of people, goods and information and secondarily facilitate the access to or logistics of goods and information.

> *Business model innovation*: It involves introduction and development of business models (value proposition / value creation architecture / income models).

With regard to the overall economic and sustainable perspective, it has to be stressed the action-driven part of Schumpeter's approach to innovation, since he described the transformation of ideas into reality and action as decisive necessity (Swedberg, 2002). Since innovations ultimately have to contribute to sustainable competitive advantage and to create value for organizations (Baregheh, Rowley & Sambrook, 2009), novel knowledge or ideas have to be transformed in value-creating reality as a basic premise (Faix & Mergenthaler, 2015). Furthermore, Faix et al. (2015) introduced the term *Innovation Quality (InQ)*. By combining the two terms *innovation* and *quality*, the authors defined a model and formula in order to quantify the value of innovations. Based on this model and the result, the question whether innovations contribute in a new or (only) incremental way to organizations' value.

Building a bridge from theory to (corporate) practice Drucker (2010) noted that the basic definitions of company's business and purpose have to be transformed into goals in order to achieve results. He also specified that goals have to be set for each of the company's key areas. In the context of this research, it has to be concretized that setting innovation goals is the need of the hour (Faix & Mergenthaler, 2015; Faix et al., 2015). Innovation goals are indispensable in order to successfully and sustainably shape a company's future.

Thus, it can be concluded that 1) setting (corporate) goals is one of the primary management / leadership tasks in order to shape a company's future; 2) the goal setting procedure is a multi-personal and interactive approach; 3) the goal identification procedure is rarely neglected in standard leadership literature; 4) goals have to focus on the future and future potentials. Defining the profit maximization as a (corporate) goal is seen to be obsolete in a (business) environment that is characterized by volatility, uncertainty, complexity, and ambiguity. In order to succeed and sustainably shape company's future innovation goals have to be set for each of the company's key areas.

3.1.4.3   Leading into the future – Creative personality

As Faix and Mergenthaler (2015) stated, "Innovations are not bolts from the blue and they do not come from nowhere; they are the result of human activity" (p.13). Considering the skepticism and resistances innovators are faced with in identifying and – above all – realizing innovations, it has to be noted that this is not a problem of recent times, but rather an implicit part of the development history. Despite the controversial opinions and interpretation of Machiavellis's oeuvre, his observation in *The Prince* (1515 / 2012) is as true as when he made it more than five hundred years ago:

> "And it ought to be remembered that there is nothing more difficult to take in hand, more perilous to conduct, or more uncertain in its success, than to take the lead in the introduction of a new order of things, because the innovator has for enemies all those who have done well under the old conditions, and lukewarm defenders in those who may do well under the new. This coolness

arises partly from fear of the opponents, who have the laws on their side, and partly from the incredulity of men, who do not readily believe in new things until they have had a long experience of them."

It is no coincidence that the importance of leadership for (the effectiveness of) organizations has been highlighted by practitioners and scientists, resulting in a vast amount of publications. Focusing on research literature, Zillner and Krusche (2012) stated that "innovation requires leadership" (p. 18).

In ancient Greece, Plato already emphasized the nature of an ideal political leader. In book 6 of Plato's (1969) oeuvre *Politeia (Republic)*[3], the combination of both qualities "to know the ideal reality of things" and "experience" (484c) belong to one and the same person are pointed out. Along with the combination of intellectual and practical abilities belonging to one and the same person, their spirit – enamored with the eternal and constant essence – was proved to be "akin to truth, justice, bravery and sobriety" (487a). Those persons, who "are perfected by education and maturity of age" (487a) then have to be assigned to political leaders (see also Erler, 2007).

Considering the explanation given so far, organizations must have competent business leaders. Leaders in this context not only have to know and be able to explain theoretically how a good idea may function. According to Faix and Mergenthaler (2015), the requirement for innovations is – as mentioned earlier – "human activity" (p.13), so that leaders were also capable of actively realizing innovations. Realization of innovations in real-world settings means that leaders have to handle and deal with uncertainty, complexity, resistances and irritations of the external (market) as well as the internal (organizational) environment, while simultaneously being aware of rules, values and norms that influence (and determine) market and environment. The question about leaders' nature arises not merely because of the challenging task, but also due to its importance for organizations. The main buzzword in answering this question is 'simply' personality. Frey clarified that filling a leadership position does not mean the appointment of "the best specialist", but "the most suitable personality", which he described in a positive and a negative sense: "…people who possess both technical and social competencies and are guided by val-

---

3 Both the date of the dialog and the era of Plato's Politeia are a contentious issue. According to Erler (2007), it seems to be plausible, that the final version of Politeia was completed in the late 370s (B.C.).

ues. Thus, leaders, who do not assume their responsibility and rather focus on their own power-hungry self-fulfillment, have to be removed from their leadership position". (Frey in EAM, 2011, p. 32)

Many researchers on leadership refer on the term personality (e.g. Faix, Rütter & Wollstadt, 1995; Furtner & Baldegger, 2013). As mentioned before, Schumpeter (1911 / 2008) attributed the role of initiating and realizing economic development (by innovations) to the entrepreneur and entrepreneurial actions. Moreover, in his *Theory of economic development* (1911 / 2008), he characterized the entrepreneur's person (Schäfer, 2008; Swedberg, 2002). Based on these fundamentals and on latest research, Bijedić (2013) considers "the entrepreneurial personality to be the main objective of entrepreneurship education" (p. 115). According to her understanding, entrepreneurial thinking and acting is based on entrepreneurial personality. In order to explain the concept of entrepreneurial personality in her research, she referred to the trait approach (see also Braukmann, Bijedic & Schneider, 2008).

In awareness of the complexity of human personality and various theories (Friedman & Schustack, 2012), personality in this context should not be based on a (long) list of personality traits or qualities in order to predict a person's future behavior or action. In pursuing a holistic approach on (business) leadership education, this research refers on a more comprehensive concept of personality. Faix and Mergenthaler (2015) defined a humanistic model of personality, which is not only based on sound historical, philosophical and anthropological knowledge but also on the basic premise of the unique individuality of each person (see also Blumenthal et al., 2012a). According to Erpenbeck[4] (2012a), such understanding of personality is deeply rooted in history and philosophy. However, "it stands in direct conflict of all descriptive attempts to find clear indicators for the measurement of personality in terms of a psychophysical object. It resists psychometric claims" (Erpenbeck, 2012a, p. 61).

Based on Rütter's (2008) triad of "being a person", "person potential" and "personality" (p. 111) and the inherent principle that each person has a certain person potential, Faix and Mergenthaler (2015) conclude "that every person has the singular potential to realize his personality in a unique manner

---

[4] Erpenbeck (2012a) has pointed out the different perspectives on personality between explanatory and descriptive psychology.

by taking action that shapes his personality" (p. 102).[5] The authors have elaborated the concept of personality on two levels. One is *'having a personality'* and the other *'being a personality'*. These two-fold approaches of personality lead to the so called *"Schöpferische Persönlichkeit"* simply translated from German as "creative personality". An overview of elements of a creative personality is presented in Figure 4. A creative personality is the result of the spiritual combination of *'having a personality'* and *'being a personality'* through actions.

HAVING A PERSONALITY
Individual constellations of »spiritual elements«

ACTIONS
Synergetic interaction of »spiritual elements«

Knowledge

BEING A PERSONALITY
Individual degree of appreciation that a person and their actions receive from society as well as the degree of influence the person has on society, based on these actions.

Competencies

Respect

Temperament and character

Charisma

Identity

Authority

Values and virtues

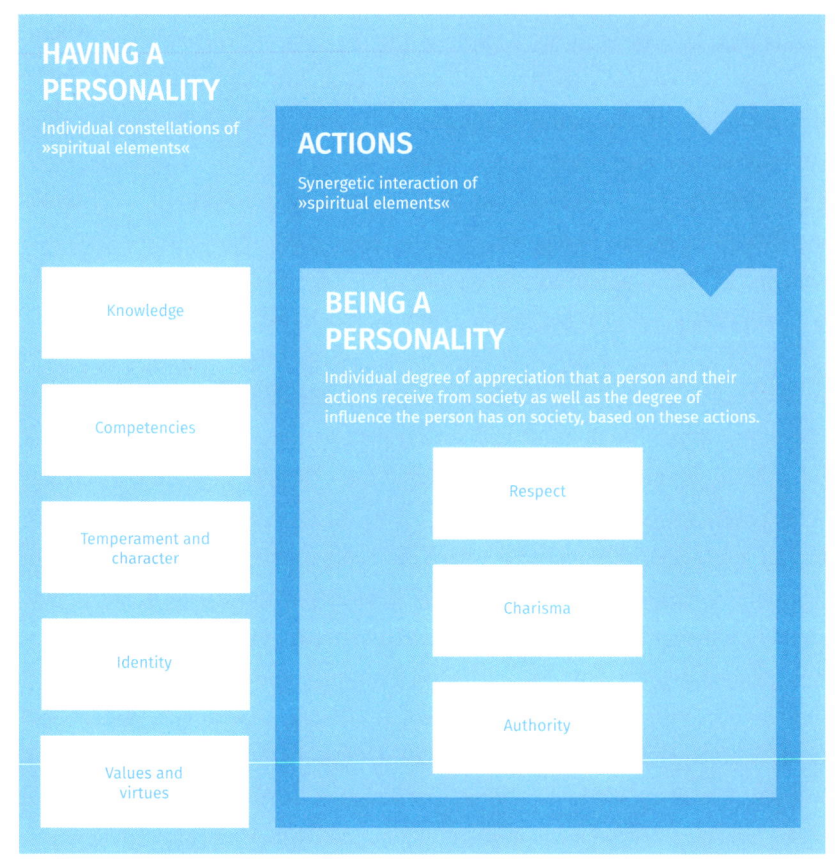

Figure 4. The concept of having / being a personality. Adapted from Faix & Mergenthaler, 2015, p. 131.

The aspects of having a personality depicted in Figure 4 show that having a personality is a culmination of five elements such as knowledge, competencies, temperament & character, identity, values & virtues. *Having a personality* sig-

---

5   The following part and description is partially literally and partially analogously published in Faix, W. G., Kisgen, S., Shah, S., & Faix, A.-V. (2017). Fostering creative personalities through real-world experiences – SIBE as a representative example! The Journal of Competency-Based Education, to be published.

nifies an individual, who executes concrete actions. Each of the five elements depict a specific function, namely the ability to act based on knowledge and competencies, the willingness to act (having a temperament) along with displaying behavior that reflects intention, character, identity, values and virtues. As pointed out before, a creative personality is a combination of having and being a personality. Along with the aspects of having a personality presented earlier, the aspects of being a personality play an equally important role in fostering a creative personality. The term *being a personality* is principally social in nature. Faix and Mergenthaler (2015) assert that being a personality is characterized by charisma, respect, and authority. For detailed definitions of each element of having and being a personality, see Faix and Mergenthaler (2015). Actions are the linking or even the synergy of having and being a personality. The person and the results of a person's actions were evaluated and acknowledged by a community (society, organization etc.), which, in turn, determines the degree of influence a person has on the community (society, organization etc.) due to these actions. Thus, the authors describe the synergistic interaction of the aforementioned elements as a social process. Consequently, a community honors the individual and his actions (respect), leading to charisma and influence over this community (authority). The authors declare '*having a creative personality*' and '*being a creative personality*' to be the educational ideal (*Bildungsideal*). They furthermore conclude that assuming a leadership position in a community, which is an urgent requirement due to the particular importance of innovations, seems to be closely connected to the development of a creative personality, which is in turn closely linked – among other things – to education.

Personality as described in the construct of creative personality – based on latest research[6] – can be developed. In fact, Faix and Mergenthaler (2015) take a step forward when they explain the terms education and personality development to be synonymous and the acquisition of knowledge, competencies etc. to be subsumed under the term of education. Hence, competencies are to be seen as part of the personality that enables people to actively participate in and contribute to a community, society or even the world.

Given the immense relevance of competencies, conceived as dispositions for self-organized action, innovations, business leadership and consequently

---

6   Latest findings in epigenetics by Blech (as referred to in Faix & Mergenthaler, 2015, p. 124) show that humans' genes can be influenced by humans' behavior and external stimuli.

business leadership education, the following section sheds light on the field of competencies.

3.1.4.4 Fostering self-organized actions – Business leadership competencies

Development of leadership personality is conceived as a reciprocal influencing process between an individual and the environment. Thus, an important contribution in developing a creative personality is developing competencies an individual possesses. Considering the modern research on competency[7], the term cannot be solely assigned to one particular discipline, but it is used by various disciplines: management theory, human resources management, pedagogy, and politics (Hoffmann, 1999). Approaching the term *competency*, two aspects require mentioning. Firstly, the terms skills, abilities, qualifications, and effectiveness are often used synonymously for competencies both scientifically and in every-day language (Weinert, 1999 and 2001). Secondly, literature reveals that there is no one and only definition of competency, but that numerous definitions of competency are used (De Vos, De Hauw & Willemse, 2015; Strebler, Robinson & Heron, 1997; Weinert, 1999). Consequently, different meanings emerged, resulting in different approaches and concepts of competencies. Klink and Boon (2003) consider competencies to be a blurry concept. Moreover, Jubb and Robotham (1997) state that "the concept of competencies…continues to remain one of the most diffuse terms in in the management development sector, and the organizational and occupational literature" (p. 171).

Two[8] distinct meanings of competency have been posited by Strebler, Robinson and Heron (1997): competency can be conceived as 'behaviors that one must exhibit', and 'as minimum standards of performance'. A deeper review of competency literature (Hoffmann, 1999, p. 276) defines competencies on three levels, namely observable performance (Boam & Sparrow, 1992; Bowden & Masters, 1993), standard, or quality of the outcome of the person's perfor-

---

7   The history of the term competency and research on competency is described e.g. in Erpenbeck (2012b).
8   The following part and description is partially literally and partially analogously published in Faix, W. G., Kisgen, S., Shah, S., & Faix, A.-V. (2017). Fostering creative personalities through real-world experiences – SIBE as a representative example! The Journal of Competency-Based Education, to be published.

mance (Rutherford, 1995; Hager, Athanasou & Gonczi, 1994), and the underlying attributes of a person (Boyatzis, 1982; Sternberg & Kolligian, 1990).

The following extracts of literature show different definitions of competency. One of the earliest definitions is provided by Faix and Laier (1989 / 1991), who refer to social competency as an "interrelation of self-confidence, responsibility and maturity" (p. 62) to take and realize actions. Spencer and Spencer (1993) define competencies as "an underlying characteristic of an individual that is causally related to criterion-referenced effective and / or superior performance in a job or a situation" (p. 9). Westera (2001) defines competence as "the ability to produce successful behaviors in non-standardized situations" (p. 82). Competence is "an individual's ability to execute his tasks and meet external demands in a practical and designed fashion in relation to the current situation" (Docherty & Marking, 1997, p. 23.) According to Weinert (2001), competencies are dispositions to act that are embedded in complex action systems and cannot be characterized by basic cognitive abilities or simple skills. Remarkable work and research on competency is carried out by Erpenbeck and Rosenstiel (2007), who define competencies as "dispositions to self-organized action" (p. XXIII). The interpretation of competencies in this research is based on the work of Erpenbeck due to the aforementioned understanding. According to Erpenbeck (2012b), competencies are action-oriented attempts to capture and improve options for future action. They are self-organization dispositions of mental and physical action (Erpenbeck & Heyse, 2007). Disposition describes complete development of the inner pre-conditions up to a certain point, which psychologically regulates the activity (Kossakowski, 1981). Thus, dispositions comprise individual traits along with results of development (Erpenbeck & Sauter, 2014). In his presentations, Erpenbeck often defines competencies as "capabilities of self-organized action. The mental and physical acting becomes self-organized in open critical and decisive situations in complex and often chaotic systems" (e.g. Erpenbeck, 2009, p. 25). According to Erpenbeck and Rosenstiel (2007), competencies are not mere abilities one possesses, but refer to particular aptitudes and qualifications that facilitate creative action in uncertain and complex situations. It involves reflexive and creative problem-solving actions with regard to complex and meaningful situations, which emerged from development processes. Thus, as presented in Figure 5, the authors clearly distinguish knowledge and qualifications from competencies. Vice versa, competencies comprise knowledge and qualifications. Moreover, competencies imply more e.g. norms, rules, and values, which are "constitutively interiorized" (Erpenbeck, 2012b, p. 14) and regulate self-organized actions as the premise to the capability of acting in open, uncertain and complex situations.

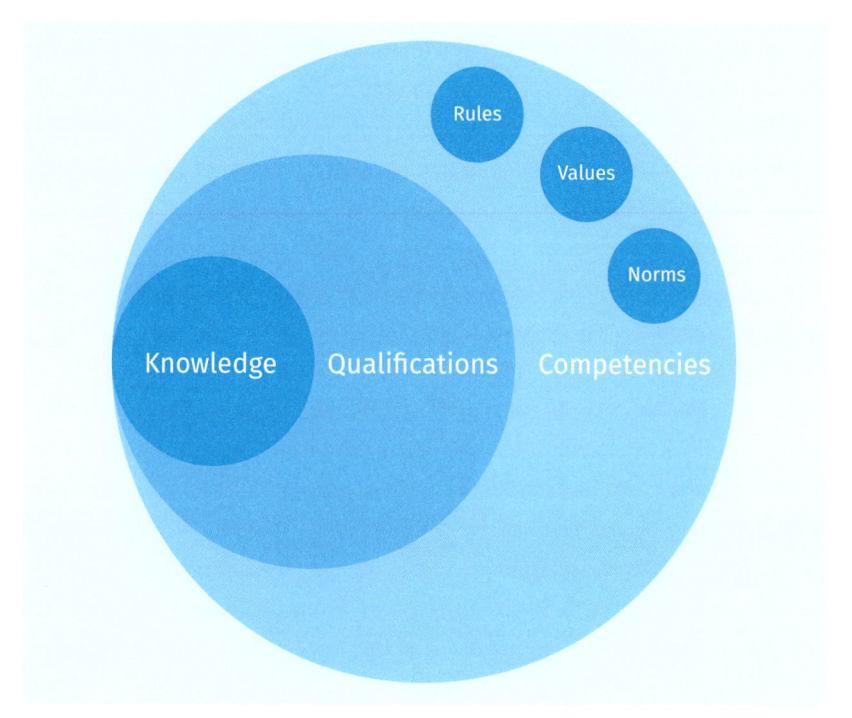

Figure 5. Knowledge, qualifications and competencies. Adapted from Erpenbeck & Rosenstiel (2007), p. XII.[9]

In comprehensive correspondence, Arnold & Erpenbeck (2014) elaborated that "knowledge is not competency". Erpenbeck (2012b) pointed out the relevant relation of qualification and competency. He affirms that an individual's competency development requires the individual to have high qualifications. "Highly competent individuals are necessarily highly qualified" (Erpenbeck, 2012b, p. 17).

In order to clearly distinguish between knowledge, qualifications, and competencies, the terms knowledge and qualifications have to be explained. In contrast to meaning (mean) and belief (believe), knowledge focus on the truth, which is the result of handling the world cognitively (Tenorth & Tippelt, 2012). In order to acquire knowledge, a process of understanding is a basic

---

9   In order to distinguish the terms clearly, the first circle in this research focus on knowledge. In the original version in Erpenbeck and Rosenstiel (2007) the first circle comprises knowledge (in a strict sense) and skills.

premise in which information (e.g. alphabets, numbers, symbols) is classified in a context that is based on the individual's experiences, in a context of meanings and problems (Klein, 2001). Moreover, knowledge can be implicit and explicit and serves as a base for many derivatives, such as opinions, judgements regarding oneself, others and the world, as well as competencies (Faix & Mergenthaler, 2015).

As there is no general definition for the term qualification (Heid, 2012), qualifications in this context are described as clearly defined aggregates of knowledge and skills a person has to possess in order to fulfill job-related tasks and the set standards. Qualifications are action-oriented and easy to verify (Erpenbeck, 2012b). Thus, certificates, diploma etc. verify "that a person has demonstrated certain knowledge or skills in an arranged and thus artificial situation" (Faix & Mergenthaler, 2015, p. 136). In pedagogics, the term qualification, which is mostly used with judgmental connotations (Heid, 2012), is distinguished from education. Rather, according to Faix & Mergenthaler (2015), considered "no longer adequate" in an open, uncertain and complex environment where individuals have to "face and react to the new" (p. 137). Consequently, this understanding underlines the importance of competencies for innovations and business leadership.

Moreover, it is also worth noting the categorization of basic competencies provided by Erpenbeck & Rosenstiel (2007). Basic competencies can be categorized as personal, action-oriented, technical and methodological, and social-communicative competencies. This taxonomy was used in a comparable manner by (almost all) researchers on competency (Erpenbeck, 2012b). The definitions of each basic competency according to Erpenbeck and Rosenstiel (2007, p. XXIV) are described as follows:

1. Personal competencies: The dispositions of a person to act reflexively and self-organized, i.e. to assess one's own abilities, to develop productive attitudes, values, motives and self-perception, to unfold one's own talents, motivation, intention to perform and creatively develop and learn in and outside of the working environment.

2. Competencies to take and realize action: The dispositions of a person to take active and comprehensive action in a self-organized manner and to direct this action to realize these aims, intentions and plans – either for oneself, for and with others, in a team, company or organization. These dispositions comprise the

capacity to integrate one's own emotions, motivations, skills and experiences and all other competencies – personal, technical and methodological, and social-communicative – into one's own determination and to successfully realize these actions.

3. Technical and methodological competencies: The dispositions of a person to act in a mentally and physically self-organized manner when solving problems, i.e. creatively solving problems, classifying and evaluating knowledge; it comprises dispositions to arrange tasks, problems and solutions methodologically in a self-organized manner and to creatively develop the methods further.

4. Social-communicative competencies: The dispositions of a person to organize himself so that he can communicate and cooperate with others, i.e. creatively discuss, integrate himself in a group and in a relationship to others and to develop new plans, tasks and goals.

For the purpose of this research, it is important to consider the aforementioned explanations for several reasons. Firstly, competencies as defined by Erpenbeck and Rosenstiel (2007) based on self-organization theory[10] clearly mean the disposition to self-organized action, which is indispensable to act in open, uncertain, and complex situations. Thus, there is a close connection to the identification and realization of innovations carried out in an uncertain, complex, and fast changing environment. Secondly, competencies comprise more than knowledge and qualifications; they rather include interiorized rules, values, and norms that regulate self-organized actions and are a basic premise for the capability to act in open, uncertain, and complex situations. Competencies are the result of development processes. Thus, competencies can be developed systematically, which directly leads to the following and last point. Finally, based on the categorization of basic competencies and the need for a business leadership position, a specified competency profile comprising specific sub-competencies, which are required to fulfill a business leadership position, can be developed. Based on the comprehensive research on development and measurement of competencies (Erpenbeck & Rosenstiel, 2007; Erpenbeck & Heyse, 2007; Erpenbeck & Sauter, 2014; Keim, Erpenbeck & Faix, 2012) individual's competencies can be assessed, measured, analyzed, and developed to suit specific goals (Keim, to be published).

---

10 For details on the principle of self-organization, see Haken (1990), the founder of synergetics.

The School of International Business and Entrepreneurship (SIBE), which is part of Steinbeis University Berlin – a private business school located in Germany –, created such a general competency profile systematically based on interviews, analytics, evaluation of studies, expert panels and surveys. By doing so, SIBE was able to reduce various required managerial competencies to a common denominator – irrespective of a special industry, organization, or level of hierarchy. Even if this general set comprising 16 sub-competencies does not entirely match a specific job profile on a certain level of a specific organization in a specific industry, it should at least fit to a large degree (Sax in Blumenthal et al., 2012b). It comprises the following 16 sub-competencies presented in Figure 6:

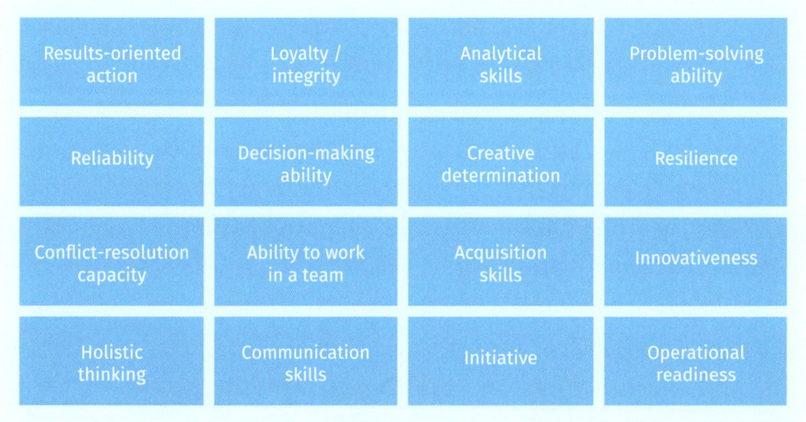

Results-oriented action	Loyalty / integrity	Analytical skills	Problem-solving ability
Reliability	Decision-making ability	Creative determination	Resilience
Conflict-resolution capacity	Ability to work in a team	Acquisition skills	Innovativeness
Holistic thinking	Communication skills	Initiative	Operational readiness

Figure 6.   A general set of leadership competencies. Adapted from Faix and Mergenthaler, 2015, p. 202.

For detailed definitions of each sub-competency, see Faix and Mergenthaler (2015).

This general set of managerial competencies has been successfully applied within the competency development seminars of the SIBE Master's programs since the year 2007. SIBE Master's programs in Management studies consequently follow the principle of an Experienced-Based Curriculum (EBC)[11] (Faix, Schulten & Auer, 2009; Faix & Mergenthaler, 2015; Faix et al., 2017a). Within this curriculum, every Master's student at SIBE had and has to pass a seminar cycle on competency development in order to assess, measure,

---

11   The German original term was Projekt-Kompetenz-Studium (PKS), which was originally translated into English as Talent Growth Curriculum (TGC). Due to latest discussions in research on competency-based learning in higher education, the term was generally rephrased in Experienced-Based Curriculum (EBC).

analyze, and develop the individual's managerial competencies with respect to specific targets in a very individual manner. More than 1,100 Master's students have already passed this cycle; approx. 600 Master's students are currently enrolled. During the 24 months of their Master's program in Management studies, students have to pursue the competency development cycle comprising self-studies, seminars, reflection, transfer, documentation in papers[12] and evaluation in order to explore and foster personal development based on a systematic process. Part of this systematic process is an assessment procedure based on the comprehensive research of Erpenbeck (Erpenbeck & Heyse, 2007; Erpenbeck & Rosenstiel, 2007; Keim, Erpenbeck & Faix, 2012), which is carried out three times in the duration of the Master's program.[13] Each assessment procedure includes a self-assessment and assessments by eight peers based on the Poffenberger's research[14], which are randomly selected (Keim, Erpenbeck & Faix, 2012), as well as an assessment by – usually – the student's supervisor and mentor in the job. SIBE has defined key performance indicators (KPI) in order to evaluate student's success at the end of the program. First, the student is situated in the target lane (SOLL-Korridor) with regard to the 16 sub-competencies, which were defined as a general set of managerial competencies. Second, student's self-assessment is correlated with the assessment by others. Finally, the student will have achieved the self-set personal development goals (Faix, Schulten & Auer, 2009; Faix & Mergenthaler, 2015; Keim & Wittmann, 2012; Kisgen, 2010 & 2013).

Based on latest findings, which are the result of quantitative longitudinal research based on approx.1,100 Master's students as well as qualitative research based on nine papers written by Master's students, positive competency development can be supported. The strongest competency development was reported for the three sub-competencies operational readiness, innovativeness and resilience (Keim, to be published). Thus, the general set of 16 managerial

---

12   Papers are written assignments based on scientific standards that focus on reflection of the real-world business project students carry out within a company during the duration of the Master's program (for completed projects please see Faix et al., 2013). Thereby, based on the principle of SIBE's EBC students realize transfer between theory and practice. One paper focuses on the students' own and individual personal development. This is because students have to pursue their own and individual personal development for the duration of the Master's program along with the real-world business project, which the students carry out within a company.
13   Erpenbeck stated that SIBE has set a benchmark among German universities in the field of competency development by consequently realizing the PKS/EBC (Erpenbeck, 2012).
14   According to Poffenberger's research and based on eight anonymous raters the mean value varies negligibly – based on the premise that there are no modifications in the mode of survey – when the number of raters increases (Poffenberger as reffered to in Keim, Erpenbeck & Faix, 2012). For detailed information, see Keim, Erpenbeck and Faix (2012).

competencies is not merely based on sound analysis, but also consolidated by longitudinal research.

A survey on competency management in German companies (Bauer & Karapidis, 2013) yielded that about 60 % (n=518) of the companies practice competency management systematically. In turn, these companies achieve considerable higher effects compared to companies, which practice competency management unsystematically. Thereby, competency management comprises several components, which are establishing a competency model, designing a target competency profile and measuring existing competencies, among others. Due to the survey results, competency management contributes to increase a company's performance capability, master change, and transformation, increase the capacity for innovation as well as the employee's performance, among others. Furthermore, 80 % of the companies, which already practice competency management systematically, assume that the importance of competency management will grow within the next two years.

Furthermore, not only the competency management of individuals within organizations is of high importance, but also the competency management of organizations as "core element of learning organizations" (Tippelt, Mandl & Straka, 2003, p. 353).

Debates and research on competencies continuously increase (Erpenbeck, 2012b). Along with different perspectives in research, which were referred to previously, some basic viewpoints in debates on competences should be addressed. European debates on competences (as a consequence of the Bologna Declaration[15]) primarily focus on the attempt to develop "European instruments in order to promote mobility and transparency" (Grootings, 1994, p. 5). Thus, qualifications should be used transnationally for a European labor market. In this context, a key question emerges with regard to the comparability of vocational and university degrees as well as achievements in training and development. On the other hand, the German debate on competences emphasizes "to remove or compensate existing dysfunctionalities by developing competences and responding to changed requirements in an economic environment" (Werner, 2005, p. 168). While higher education in USA has long been

---

15   Bologna Declaration was adopted 1999 in Bologna/Italy by European Ministers of Education in order to develop a European Higher Education Area. Thus, within this area students' and graduates' mobility should be promoted based on comparability of degrees; for details see Bologna Declaration (1999) and/or European Commission/EACEA/Eurydice (2015).

considered one of the best in the world, debates about innovation in higher education are raised due to concerns about cost and quality. Rising tuition fees along with rising student depts and challenging value proposition have stimulated discussions about competency-based education (CBE) as an alternative to traditional higher education programs (Franklin & Lytle, 2015; Kelchen, 2015; Lacey & Murray, 2015; McClary & Gaertner, 2015).

Moreover, debates on competencies are not only focused on tertiary education, but on the high importance of education throughout one's entire life, and to thrive in the 21st century (WEF, 2015; WEF, 2016). According to the World Economic Forum (WEF, 2015, p. 2):

> "To thrive in today's innovation-driven economy, workers need a different mix of skills than in the past. In addition to foundational skills like literacy and numeracy, they need competencies like collaboration, creativity and problem-solving, and character qualities like persistence, curiosity and initiative.
>
> Changes in the labour market have heightened the need for all individuals, and not just a few, to have these skills. In countries around the world, economies run on creativity, innovation and collaboration. Skilled jobs are more and more centred on solving unstructured problems and effectively analyzing information."

Having highlighted the importance of business leadership competencies and having introduced in the individual but essential aspects of business leadership, the individual aspects were integrated in a holistic model.

3.1.4.5 Business leadership – At a glance

Based on the aforementioned, several but essential aspects of business leadership a broad understanding of business leadership were developed, which shall be consolidated in a holistic model of business leadership. Figure 7 presents this holistic model of business leadership comprising several but essential aspects. Thus, creative personalities contribute to a sustainable corporate development by realizing innovations. This implies that creative personalities are not only able to identify, set and achieve innovation (and personal) goals, but also possess business leadership competencies. Creative personalities are able to realize innovation quality and consequently shape the (corporate) future. Moreover, business leadership is not a matter of the individual business leader. In fact, the business leader is embedded and acts in a complex socio-cultural context with its manifold reciprocal influencing factors comprising employees, corporate leadership / management, organizational culture, customers, suppliers, government, society, nature etc. Consequently, it is indispensable that the business leader is able create effective exchanges and dyads with employees and other stakeholders and to create strong networks within and outside the organization.

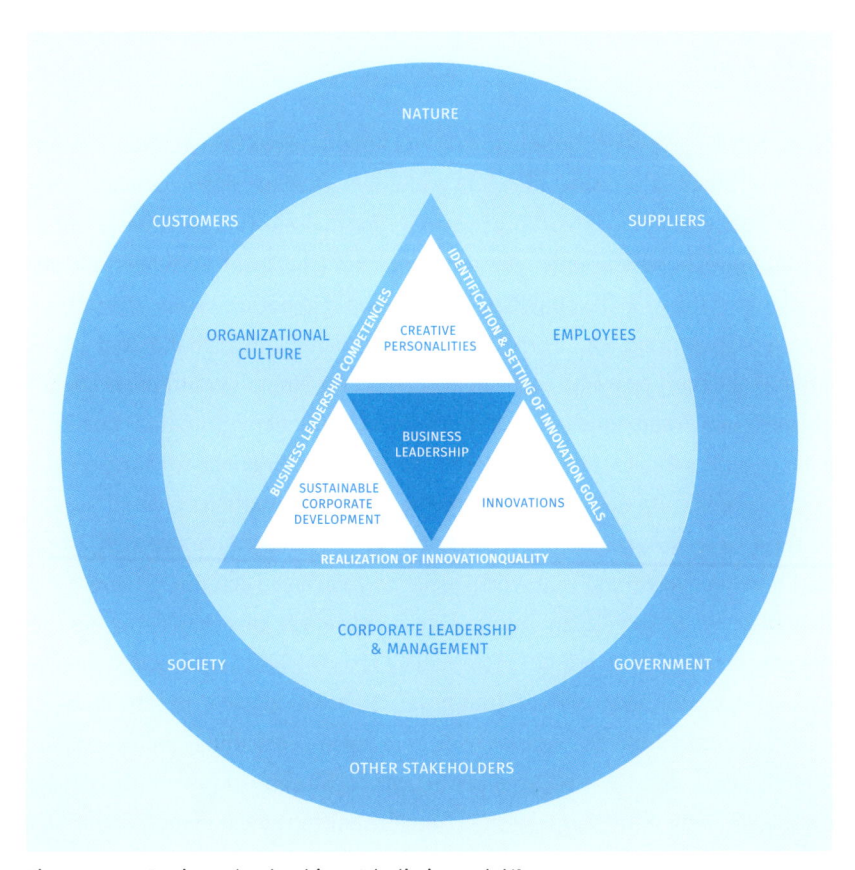

Figure 7.   Business leadership – A holistic model.[16]

Despite a broad understanding of business leadership, concrete and specific KPIs can be defined in order to evaluate the performance of (potential) business leaders:

---

16   The holistic model of business leadership is based on sound theory. Impetus and the very idea was the model of the creative personality in the innovation process. The latter was developed by Faix and Mergenthaler (2015). The authors incorporated the management definition provided by Adolf Stepan from Technische Universität Wien in a workshop discussion. According to this defintion, management means that actors contribute to corporate goals by their actions (strategies).

> Contribution through innovation(s): What does the (potential) business leader contribute to the organization through innovation(s)?

> Goal identification, goal setting, and achievement: Is the business leader able of identifying and setting both professional (innovation) and personal goals and of achieving those goals?

> Business leadership competencies: What are the (current) status and development of business leadership competencies according to the target lane with regard to the general set of 16 business leadership competencies? Does self-assessment correspond with the assessments by others?

Those KPIs are relevant for individuals and organizations in order to select and develop (potential) business leaders and / or to evaluate business leaders. By directing the company's working processes for the selection and development of (potential) business leaders to the holistic model of business leadership education and the KPIs developed above, one could hypothesize that the performance of (potential) leaders can be better predicted, rather than based on existing (selection) procedures. Evaluating KPIs developed within the model of business leadership for the selection and development of (potential) business leaders means to base ones decision on results from previous working results that emerged from real-world settings vs. artificial situations created in ACs. In order to obtain meaningful results, it might be advisable to expose (potential) business leaders to real-world projects, which are unique and limited in time in order to solve corporate business challenges that may contribute to the organization's value and (sustainable) future. Thus, real-world business projects are indicators for the (potential) business leaders' performance in uncertain and complex situations were self-organized action is indispensable. Thereby, goal identification, goal setting, and achievement procedure may be evaluated along with the project's contribution to the company's value and future as well as the business leader's competencies. The verification of the previous assumption could be a project for future research.

Since the perspectives of different disciplines may vary, the prioritization and ranking of the different KPIs may also vary. While the business perspective may prioritize the (monetary) contribution to organizations through innovations, individuals may favor personal development through competency development or the goal aspect. Regardless of the different perspectives, the individual elements cannot be considered separately; rather – although the elements may be complementary or interdependent – all elements are equal as one entity. This entity is indispensable fill the term business leadership with live.

3.1.5 Conclusions

Between the vast amount and variety of definitions and theoretical approaches to leadership, an exemplary selection was made in this research in order to present the current state of discussion in (research) literature. Without doubt, they offer immense and valuable contributions in leadership research. Nevertheless, various strengths and (methodological) shortcomings were outlined. Furthermore, it has to be pointed out that the (traditional) definitions and approaches merely reflect a fragmentary instead of a holistic perspective on leadership, failing to acceptably measure a leader's performance.

In a second step, the assessment center that belongs to the most popular diagnostic procedures was roughly outlined. Considering ACs from a positive point of view, the main purpose may lie in a culture-directed selection of (potential) business leaders when assessors are (higher) leaders. In spite of various improvements, (not all) ACs are able to predict leaders' future job performance. Reliance on just ACs to select future leaders therefore seems to be insufficient and in many instances misleading.

Moreover, findings of different disciplines mainly from human ethology and organizational sciences were compiled due to their high impact on leadership, and in order to obtain a comprehensive overview of the studied topic. Thus, a person's leadership behavior not only plays a vital role in business leadership, but also in entrepreneurial leadership. The latter, a relatively new construct, combines both entrepreneurship and leadership and emphasizes the leader's personality. Due to a globalized and digitized dynamic world and the increased pressures on companies' competitiveness, the entrepreneurial leader is expected to cope with the fast changing (business) environment.

Based on these preliminary conclusions, due to various external (political, economic, socio-cultural, technological, and legal) influencing factors on the (business) environment and with respect to the research topic within the field educational sciences, a contemporary and holistic model of business leadership was developed. This holistic model comprises both the business perspective, i.e. goals and innovations and the perspective on the leader's individual personality, i.e. creative personality, business leadership competencies and networks. Thus, the understanding and definition of business leadership presented in Figure 8 was developed and shall be applied in this research.

> *Creative personalities* contribute to a sustainable corporate development by realizing innovations. This implies that creative personalities are not only able to identify, set and achieve innovation (and personal) goals, but also possess business leadership competencies. Creative personalities are able to realize innovation quality and consequently shape the (corporate) future. Moreover, business leadership is not a matter of the individual business leader. In fact, the business leader is embedded and acts in a complex sociocultural context with its manifold reciprocal influencing factors comprising employees, corporate leadership/management, organizational culture, customers, suppliers, government, society, nature etc. Consequently, it is indispensable that the business leader is able to create effective exchanges and dyads with employees and other stakeholders and create strong networks within and outside the organization.

Figure 8. Definition of business leadership.

Based on this holistic understanding of business leadership, concrete and specific KPIs were defined in order to evaluate the success of (potential) business leaders. Those KPIs are relevant for individuals and organizations in order to select, develop, and evaluate (potential) business leaders. It was assumed (hypothesized) that the performance of (potential) leaders can be better predicted based on these KPIs than on existing (selection) procedures. This assumption (hypothesis) has to be a subject of future research.

However, although the term *leadership* in this research is largely concerned with leadership in the business context, particularly with regard to leadership in business corporations, companies, enterprises, organizations etc., the several aspects and the holistic model of business leadership presented above can easily be adapted to other domains by considering the domain's specific mission and characteristics.

This contemporary and holistic understanding of business leadership in a dynamic environment shall lay the foundation for a contemporary humanistic approach on business leadership education in tertiary education that can cater to the changing needs of business leaders, which will be elucidated in the following chapter.

3.2 Conceptualizing business leadership education in tertiary education

"Leadership does not simply happen. It can be taught, learned, developed" (Giuliani, 2002, p. xii). Considering this attitude and transferring it to the field of education, the following chapter follows the holistic understanding and model of business leadership outlined previously. Before concretizing business leadership education in tertiary education, it is imperative to consider, what *education* implies in general. Therefore, in a first step, the term education shall be concretized, culminating in a contemporary understanding of education. In a next step, the focus will be on the segment of tertiary education along with its trends and challenges of tertiary education in general that are discussed across the globe. Furthermore, contemporary trends and challenges of business leadership education in tertiary education in particular, which were also part of transnational debates, shall be elucidated. Based on current debates, a brand new definition seems to be indispensable in order to design contemporary business leadership education in tertiary education from a pedagogical perspective. The pedagogical infrastructure for business leadership education in tertiary education is determined in the *curriculum*.

Barnett and Coate (2005) accurately stated that "the idea of curriculum goes to the heart of what we take higher education to be, of what it might be and should be in the twenty-first century" (p. 16). Nevertheless, in order to answer the research question – how business leadership education in Master's programs for graduates in tertiary education shall be designed –, it is not intended to define an ideal curriculum on a detailed level. Rather, the general principles of academic freedom and unity of research and teaching and each higher education institution's individual culture and (research) focus shall be respected in order to promote diversity. Therefore, seven main principles for a curriculum of business leadership education in Master's programs in tertiary education shall be proposed.

3.2.1 Preliminary notes on education

Concretizing the term *education* is important, as it will deepen the understanding of business leadership education in tertiary education. In this research, the term education corresponds to the German term *Bildung* and is used "as a kind of umbrella term" (Autio, 2014, p. 18) in a broad sense, comprising such concepts as nurture and socialization among others, which is in line with Faix and Mergenthaler (2015). It has to be pointed out that education along with pedagogy is not only embedded in culture, structures and policies (Alexander, 2000). Rather, the term *Bildung*, which is a central concept in educational sciences, has a long tradition[17] and appears exclusively in the German language and has no equivalent in any other (Raithel, Dollinger & Hörmann, 2009). Due to the breadth and variety of issues, the comprehensive, yet conflicting claims *Bildung* has been critically discussed for a long time (Rütter, 2008; Tenorth, 2012). Consequently, there is no generally accepted definition; in fact, a distinct definition of the term contradicts the core of the education concept (Dörpinghaus & Uphoff, 2011). In distinctive and catchy wording, Tenorth states that "*Bildung* is what remains if we forget everything that we ever learned in school" (as cited in Jung & Pinar, 2016, p. 39), which is complemented by Jung and Pinar (2016) with the words "specifically the individual's capacity for freedom accomplished in part through individuation" (p. 39).

Understanding the roots an early education concept can be found in ancient Greece, captured in the allegory of the cave at the beginning of book 7 (514a ff.) in Plato's (1969) oeuvre *Politeia (Republic)*. This allegory metaphorically illustrates education to be an about-turn of soul toward the realm of true being; which is a painful process since familiar attitudes and environment have to be relinquished.[18] The allegory of the cave not only implies valuable approaches, but is also (epistemological) basis for the contemporary concept of education. Another crucial impact on the concept of education was the Age of Enlightenment. The ideas of Jean-Jacques Rousseau – notably with his educational novel *Émile ou De l'Éducation (*1762 / 2010), which was revolutionary at that time –, and Immanuel Kant, notably with his works *Beantwortung der Frage: Was ist Aufklärung? (1784)* and *Über Pädagogik (1803)* among others, were important contributions along with Wilhelm von Humboldt's oeuvre. Humboldt's education theory is central point of the neo-humanistic movement and a response to the utilitarian approach found in the late Enlightenment pedagogy. Education during this period is considered a purposeful process, which

---

17 For details, please see Rütter (2008). For introduction and comparison of two curriculum theories (Anglo-American curriculum and European-Scandinavian Bildung-Didaktik) and their intellectual affiliation, please see Autio (2014).
18 For sound considerations of Plato's allegory of the cave from perspective of educational theory, please see Benner and Stępkowski (2011). For more details on pedagogical theory and educational program in Plato's oeuvre, please see Szaif (2003) and Gill (2003). For critical considerations on Plato's Politeia from a contemporary perspective, please see Wiersing (2001).

aims to systematically shape people to make them useful for economy, nation, and society – but, simultaneously, it was ensured that they remain in their socio-economic class. In contrast, education from Humboldtian perspective can be conceptualized as education of humans, which does not cater to a specific function humans have to carry out; rather, to foster humans' inherent power and capabilities (Dörpinghaus, Poenitsch & Wigger, 2012). The contrast between utilitarian and Humboldtian perspective is expressed even more blatantly by Menze (1975). Thus, Humboldt intended "to repel education that pretends to breed humans but rather promote education as a human right, as the pursuit of humanity and freedom" (Menze, 1975, p. 17).

In his work *Ideen zu einem Versuch, die Gränzen der Wirksamkeit des Staates zu bestimmen (The Sphere and Duties of Government; 1792 / 1854)*, Humboldt stated: "The true end of Man, or that which is prescribed by the eternal and immutable dictates of reason, and not suggested by vague and transient desires, is the highest and most harmonious development of his powers to a complete and consistent whole." Humboldt's humanistic perception of education as a response to transition of that time, when the lore of traditions was challenged, was to rethink and redesign education by his work *Theorie der Bildung der Menschen (Theory of Human Education or Theory of Bildung, 1793 or 1794 / 2000)*[19]. In the fragment under this name, the general principles of a theory on education were outlined only roughly, since "the theoretical strength of the concept can only unfold entirely in the analysis of human's faculty of speech" (Giel & Flitner, 2010, p. 316).

With regard to this research nucleus of Humboldt's (1793 or 1794 / 2000) *Theory of Bildung* is the following:

> "At the convergence point of all particular kinds of activity is man, who, in the absence of a purpose with a particular direction, wishes only to strengthen and heighten the powers of his nature and secure value and permanence for his being. However, because sheer power needs an object on which it may be exercised and pure form or idea needs a material in which, expressing itself, it can last, so too does man need a world outside himself. From this springs his endeavor to expand the sphere of his knowledge and his activity, and without himself being clearly aware of it, he

---

19 It is not ultimately determined, when the fragment given this name was written. Information vary between end of 1793 and 1794 or 1795 (Giel & Flitner, 2010).

is not really concerned with what he obtains from the former or what he achieves outside him by means of the latter, but only with his inner unrest that consumes him. In pure, ultimate terms, thought is never more than an attempt of the mind to be comprehensible to itself, whereas action is an attempt of the will to become free an independent in itself. Man's entire external activity is nothing but the striving against futility. Simply because both his thought and his action are not possible except by means of a third element, the representation and cultivation of something that is actually characterized by being non-man, that is, world, he seeks to grasp as much world as possible and bind it as tightly as he can to himself.

It is the ultimate task of our existence to achieve as much substance as possible for the concept of humanity in our person, both during the span of our life and beyond it, through the traces we leave by means of our vital activity. This can be fulfilled only by linking of the self to the world to achieve the most general, most animated, and most unrestrained interplay." (p. 58)

To engage in Humboldt's *Theory of Bildung*, the five most important principles for this research should be outlined. Firstly, Humboldt emphasized humans to be in the center "of all particular kinds of activity". Secondly, Humboldt points out humans' drive ("*inner unrest*")[20] to develop and enhance their powers and ensure value and consistency. Peoples' drive is evident in both their thoughts and actions (Lüth, 2000). Thirdly, the basic premise for the development of power, the securing of value and consistency is the world. According to Menze (1975), Humboldt conceived world as a concept comprising society, other people, history, cultural products etc. Thereby, humans' relation to the world is outlined as an interdependency ("interplay"), wherein both human and world change. By way of human actions, which are based on their individual capabilities, they change the world, which in turn – as new is the object of capabilities' – also affects humans. This "interplay" is pivotal for human's educational process (Dörpinghaus, Poenitsch & Wigger, 2012; Menze, 1975). With regard to the interplay expressed by Humboldt Menze (1975) notes:

"Capabilities are not complete; rather, they are developed and 'shaped' when man deals with the world for which they are needed.

---

20 According to Lüth (2000) – who intelligibly analyzed Humboldt's Theory of Bildung in a series of closed readings – Theory of Bildung is linked with anthropology, since Humboldt emphasized humans' striving. For further considerations with regard to the nature of man and anthropology in Humboldt's work, see Lüth (2000).

> Such an education can be fostered systematically insofar as man's relations to the world, which challenge certain capabilities and leave others to remain idle, are favored." (p. 29)

The fourth important principle is "the concept of humanity in our person" that Humboldt emphasizes as "ultimate task of our existence." In this context, Menze (1975) notes loosely that the "human individuality shall be educated and represent itself in its humanity" (p. 46). He then outlined that man is not one of many but "he / she [the individual human] portrays the endlessly humanity as – necessarily – confined individuality" (p. 47); he then refers to education, which is a process of formative development and a result of reflection. Such a process in Humboldt's wording not only lasts for the "span of our life", but "beyond"; in Menze's (1975) interpretation "life is not a possession, it is rather a task, a permanent exercise that caters to self-fulfillment and self-determination, thus a never-ending struggle. Hence, a 'completed' life or a 'concluded' education does not exist" (p. 49).

Carrying this train of thought to extremes, human's life is supposed to be self-determined, shaped by highest consciousness and personal responsibility, Menze (1975) notes:

> "Accomplishments achieved by people who are reduced to certain functions, can be provided in an almost identical manner by others. However, the individual character of one's own life, one's own 'education', cannot be delegated to others... Each person has to live and design his own life. He has to grow to become his own man." (p. 51).

Concluding the principle of man's individuality based on Humboldt's original and Menze's interpretation, one may conclude the more education (in Humboldtian sense) the more individuality, and the more humanity. Education is the constitutive and decisive challenge of man's life. Moreover, man's life simply is education – comprising both, the process of education and the product itself.

The fifth and final principle of Humboldt's *Theory of Bildung*, which shall be elucidated in this research, is freedom. In this fragment, Humboldt points out that man's challenge is "the will to become free and independent in itself" through action. Following Lüth's (2000) explanations, not only due to humans' power, but also due to their "results obtained through the agency of these powers" (p. 66), humans aim to ensure value and persistence, to find fulfillment. Thus, education and freedom are connected inseparably; moreover, education challenges individuals to use their freedom and to reject any heteronomy (Menze, 1975).

Thus, Humboldt's *Theory of Human Education* – a response to the radical change of that time –, which was and is not only a great demand, but also idealistic and even keen in its nature (Tippelt, 2013). However, comparing contemporary debates on education, one may conclude that Humboldt's thoughts are as true today as when they were conceived more than two hundred years ago.

Not only Humboldt was convinced by the impact of education on improving humankind's existence (Menze, 1975). Also the Dalai Lama, himself "driven by the simple desire to contribute to the greater good of humankind and all living creatures" (Dalai Lama & Alt, 2016, p. 21), emphasizes in the later part of his explanations that creating a better world, bringing about change in thinking can primarily be realized through education.

A new perspective on education based on traditional roots was elaborated by Autio, a contemporary Finnish researcher with special research focus on the comparison between German and European-Scandinavian *Bildung-Didaktik* and American curriculum studies. According to Autio (2014), hermeneutics is crucial in conceiving *Bildung-Didaktik* traditions. He delineates that "*Bildung* can be referred to as a theory of education with a two-layer sense and in with a broader meaning than the English 'education'" (p. 18). Autio (2014) furthermore points out that *Bildung* means:

> "to become, first, socialized to one's culture through school and other official curricula, and then, second, individuated by one's own studies, activities, and hobbies and 'transcending' (the Hegelian *Aufhebung*) the official education and curriculum. The final, ideal aim of *Bildung* … is the individual's competence to be able to lead a public life; to participate in a knowledgeable way in cultural activities, public affairs, and politics; and to critique – ideally to reconstruct – society by transforming one's self through continuous study and different, idiosyncratic activities" (p. 18).

According to the researcher, *Bildung* in a broader conception comprises four constitute elements that create the basic framework of any curriculum. These are 1) *moral*, 2) *cognitive*, 3) *aesthetic,* and 4) *practical* elements. While the last three elements can be categorized within the sphere of instrumental rationality (*Verstand*), the first element, *moral*, can be rationally categorized within the non-instrumental sphere and rationality (*Vernunft*)[21]; consequently, it is the moral that makes education educative.

> "Ideally, the educational and educative aim of the moral in *Didaktik* traditions is to encourage thinking, to make subjective yet knowledgeable judgments and decisions, to think against the subject matter, to think against oneself, to transcend and to transform." (Autio, 2014, p. 18)

Nida-Rümelin, a contemporary German philosopher, refers to the Humboldtian idea in several of his works and states the basic impulse that emanates from humanism to be an issue now more than ever; not only since the overall discourse on human rights is based on humanism (Nida-Rümelin, 2011). In his work *Philosophie einer humanen Bildung* he points out: "A humanistic concept of education is based on the *ideal of autonomy*. The ability to lead a life by one's own rules, freely and responsibly, is a primary goal of humanistic education" (Nida-Rümelin, 2013, p. 60). He furthermore delineates:

> "Human education should consider the entire person...Human practice requires coherence...The primary goal of human education is to help develop this coherence and thus enable a coherent life, to help ensure that people are at peace with themselves in different stages of their lives" (Nida-Rümelin, 2013, pp. 230 f.).

In developing a holistic concept of education Tippelt (2013), a contemporary German educational researcher, creates a link to Kant's and Humboldt's ideas. Thus, using one's own rationality critically is the basis for the ability to make decisions, solve problems, resolve conflicts and for creative determination of every human being and that these were ambitious but essential objectives of a holistic concept of education. Such holistic concept of education has to be based on personality and the universal idea of human dignity that contribute to shape the life of mankind humanely and effectively. He furthermore points out that education comprises inclusion, development and subsump-

---

21 According to Cicero's De re publica (2013, III, 33) that originates from 54-51 B.C., man's rationality (Vernunft) is consistent with nature. According to Kreutz's (2008) interpretation of Cicero „Man's nature is the foundation of nature; nature and rationality (Vernunft) are directly interrelated. Rationality (Vernunft) ... is everlasting, irreversible, coherent, consistent, and stringent" (p. 67 f.).

tion of knowledge and experiences in all phases of life, from early childhood, throughout adolescence and up to old age. General aspects for all spans of life were qualification, competency development, social integration, political participation, finding cultural identity and ethical orientation. Nevertheless, he concluded:

> "The formative power of education can only be fruitful if the individual manages to repeatedly stabilize his identity while going through a biographical series of ever more complex and often new demands. 'Humans in the modern age' are described here as particularly reflected, differentiated, open and individuated. The core of the modern educational mandate is therefore to find the cultural identity of each individual." (Tippelt, 2013, p. 251)

Another view on education was thoroughly elaborated by Rütter, a contemporary German educational researcher. Based on a sound reflection on education and its roots in Plato's *Politeia* (*Republic*), Rütter (2008) developed a concept of human's education in his work *Bildungsarbeit,* emphasizing man's personhood (*Personalität*). As presented in Figure 9, starting point of this consideration is the term *person*, from which the later term *personhood* originates. Personhood is conceived in a comprehensive way as individuality, which is not used in the common sense of uniqueness but due to its origin in late Latin as indivisibleness comprising six aspects of a person that are generativity, sociality, uniqueness, naturalness, culture and spirituality, which interact in synergy. For detailed definitions of each aspect of personhood and their synergistic interaction, see Rütter (2008). As Figure 9 shows, personhood in turn implies three meanings, namely *being a person*, *person potential* and *personality*. These three meanings are thoroughly distinguished. Thus, *being a person* constitutionally means that "each human being is a person – at least from conception to death" (p. 178). The second meaning, *person potential,* means the entirety of a person's inherent potentials. Finally, by taking action and realizing the entire person's potential the personality is shaped, which is considered to be a lifelong process.

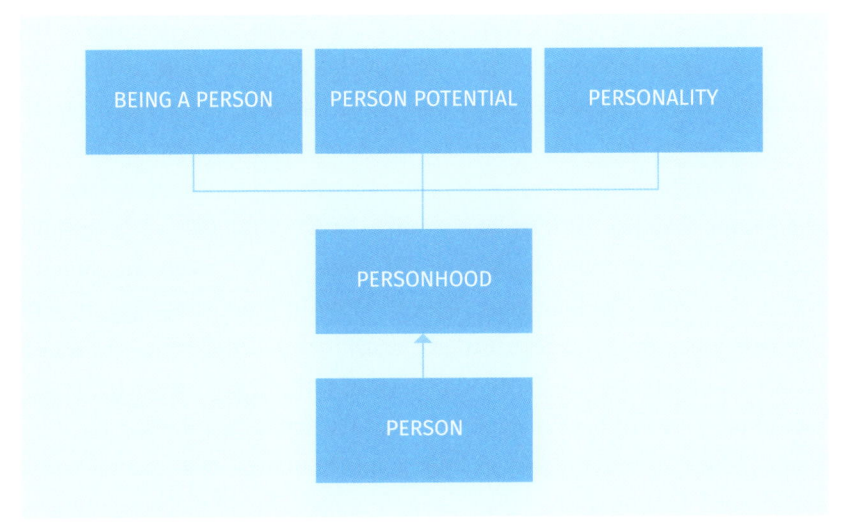

Figure 9. Text field "Personhood". Adapted from Rütter, 2008, p. 111.

Rütter (2008) finally concludes:

> "What is general of education? ...'Education' stands for the process by which a person actualizes one's own person potential and thus gradually forms one's own personality. A person takes this path throughout one's live, step-by-step through the various phases of one's live, through social situations and thus through communication, interaction and collaboration, through conflict and collision with other persons and through crises in one's struggle for life....In brief, 'education' stands for 'personality'. Because, what a person develops from his personal (internal and external) potential – creatively from intellectual act to intellectual act, throughout one's entire life and one's struggle for life – that is one's personality" (p. 303)

Based on the several aspects of humanistic approach throughout history on education as previously outlined, Faix and Kisgen developed a contemporary holistic human-centered concept of education (Faix et al., 2017a). Figure 10 elucidates the holistic concept of education that in turn allows individuals to develop their personalities. Thus, the prime purpose of education is conceived as an end in itself. By facing the world, which is defined as nature, other humans, society, organizations etc., the individual's personal development is initiated. Facing the world means that one has to strive for as much experiences as possible, with, in and through the world and transform the world as much as possible into one's own person in order to achieve the educational goal, which is personality that in turn is a result of actions. Basic premise of the holistic concept of education is the model of creative personality as described in chapter 3.1.4.3. A creative personality is the result of the spiritual combination of *having a personality* and *being a personality* through actions. *Having a personality* comprises five elements such as knowledge, competencies, temperament and character, identity, values and virtues. *Being a personality* is characterized by charisma, respect, and authority. Actions are the connecting, or, even more, the synergetic elements of having and being a personality. Competencies, which are described as dispositions to act, are inherent to personality. Competencies can be developed systematically and play an important role in the personal development process. Consequently, following this concept of education and the personal development process by facing the world and thereby developing their competencies, personalities and contributing to the world by their actions and individual creativity is essential for one's own development, the development of society, sciences and arts, economy etc. This kind of contribution is also elaborated by Joachim Gauck, the Federal President of Germany within the context of society. He notes, "Only when we believe in the potentials hidden within us, if we use and apply them, we shall be satisfied with ourselves and can be a blessing for others" (Gauck, 2012, pp. 61 f.).

Thus, the contemporary holistic concept of education as outlined above is based on the premise and understanding of general education in terms of Plato in order to educate all elements of a person, which is in line with Faix and Mergenthaler (2015). A contemporary view on general education (*Allgemeinbildung*) was elaborated by Klafki (2000). In an up-to date concept of general education, he concluded:

> "Allgemeinbildung as Bildung *for all* to develop the capacity for self-determination, participation, and solidarity.
> An outline and the critical discussion *of the general as that which concerns us all* in our epoch, and
> Bildung *of all* the dimensions of *humane capacities* that we can recognize today.
> Allgemeinbildung must even now also be understood as *political Bildung*, as a capability for active participation in a process of on going democratization." (p. 103.)

It can be concluded that Faix's and Kisgen's concept of education is deeply rooted in humanistic tradition, enriched by Rütter's distinctive thoughts on the triad of personhood comprising the elements *being a person*, *person-potential* and *personality*. Thus, this approach of education is aimed at the personal-potential of the individual, to convert it into actions and render it apparent in actions.

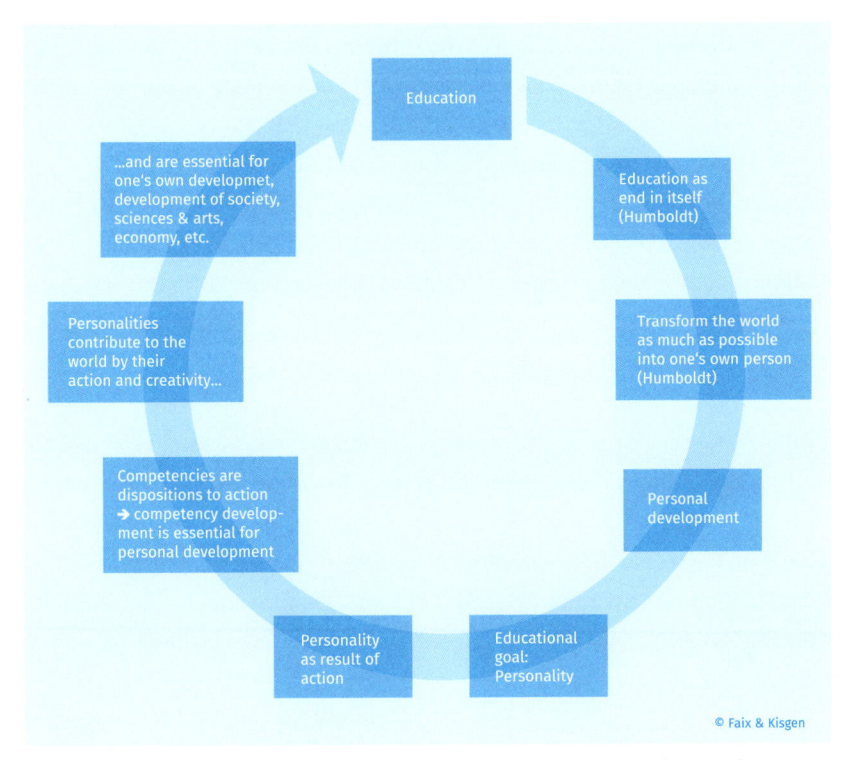

Figure 10. Conceptualizing education: The educational cycle by Faix and Kisgen. Adapted from Faix et al., 2017a.

Taking both the concept of business leadership and the concept of education outlined in this research seriously, it can be concluded that "to thrive in the 21st century, students need more than traditional academic education" (WEF, 2016, p. 4). Rather, education has to facilitate a pedagogical infrastructure that holistically caters to the need of developing (creative) personalities that will contribute to the world.

Before focusing the pedagogical infrastructure, which is defined in a *curriculum*, and elaborating and proposing seven main principles for contemporary business leadership education in tertiary education, the segment of tertiary education shall be elucidated in the following section.

3.2.2 Focusing on the segment of tertiary education

Starting point of the journey to tertiary education shall be the universal principles of Human Rights codified in the *Universal Declaration of Human Rights* (UDHR) adopted by the United Nations General Assembly in the year 1948. *Article 26, paragraph 1* of the UDHR (1948) states that "Everyone has the right to education" and that "higher education shall be equally accessible to all on the basis of merit". *Article 4* of the subsequent *Convention against Discrimination in Education* (1960), adopted by the General Conference of the United Nations Educational, Scientific and Cultural Organization (UNESCO), demands from the States Parties to "make higher education equally accessible to all on the basis of individual capacity".

Within a state's education system, tertiary education is the level of formal education that follows completion of a school providing secondary education. In general, upon completion of a course or program, certificates, diplomas, or academic degrees will be awarded. According to the International Standard Classification of Education (ISCED) 2011 scheme provided by the UNESCO, the only United Nations (UN) agency with a mandate in higher education:

> "Tertiary education builds on secondary education, providing learning activities in specialised fields of education. It aims at learning at a high level of complexity and specialisation. Tertiary education includes what is commonly understood as academic education but also includes advanced vocational or professional education. It comprises ... short-cycle tertiary education, Bachelor's or equivalent level, Master's or equivalent level, and doctoral or equivalent level, respectively. The content of programmes at the tertiary level is more complex and advanced than in lower ... levels." (UNESCO, 2012a, p. 46)

For the purpose of this research, which is focused on the Master's (or equivalent) level (ISCED level 7), core characteristics[22] for Master's level programs described by UNESCO (2012a) are presented as follows:

1. "Programmes … are often designed to provide participants with advanced academic and / or professional knowledge, skills and competencies, leading to a second degree or equivalent qualification. Programmes at this level may have a substantial research component but do not yet lead to the award of a doctoral qualification. Typically, programmes at this level are theoretically-based but may include practical components and are informed by state of the art research and / or best professional practice. They are traditionally offered by universities and other tertiary educational institutions. …

2. Entry into [Master's or equivalent level] programmes preparing for a second or further degree normally requires the successful completion of a [Bachelor's or equivalent level or Master's or equivalent] programme. …Additionally, it may be required to take and succeed in entry examinations. [Master's or equivalent level] programmes have a significantly more complex content than programmes at [Bachelor's or equivalent level] and are usually more specialised. Upon completion, individuals may continue their education at … doctoral-level education … although not all [Master's or equivalent level] programmes give direct access to [doctoral or equivalent level]." (UNESCO, 2012a, p. 55)

Following the characteristics provided by UNESCO for the design of Master's programs, it is important to define theoretically-based and / or professionally-based content in order to maintain knowledge, skills and competencies. Master's programs may comprise a considerable research part. Moreover, it is important to define entry requirements in order to maintain a certain standard and to prepare for a potential following (doctoral) level. Therefore, more complex and specialized content compared to lower levels is required.

Within the European Union (EU) introduction of Bologna process was of high importance. The Bologna Declaration was adopted 1999 in Bologna / Italy by

---

22 For the purpose of this research, principal characteristics 241 and 243 were selected; the remaining principal characteristics, classification criteria, and complementary dimensions are thoroughly read and registered but are not focus of this research. For a complete list, please see UNESCO (2012a). ISCED 2011 provides 8 different levels; ISCED 2011 level 7 corresponds to ISCED 1997 level 5. For details, please see UNESCO (2012a).

29 countries, represented by their European Ministers of Education in order to develop a European Higher Education Area (EHEA). It was intended to make European higher education more comparable, compatible, competitive, and attractive for students and thereby also to enhance students' and graduates' mobility (Bologna Declaration,1999; European Commission / EACEA / Eurydice, 2015; Eurostat, 2016b). One year later, in 2000, European heads of state and government adopted the Lisbon Strategy that aims the EU *"to become the most competitive and dynamic knowledge-based economy in the world, capable of sustainable economic growth with more and better jobs and greater social cohesion"* (European Council, 2000) by 2010. Education was then defined to be one of the main disciplines in reaching this goal. Thus, the Bologna Process and the Lisbon Strategy were considered the main frameworks and driving force directing the European way and the response to globalization in tertiary education (Marginson & Wende, 2007).

The term *tertiary education* and the several levels comprised in the context of the Bologna Process are in line with ISCED provided by UNESCO.[23] Eurostat – a Directorate-General of the European Commission – introduces the tertiary education statistics with the following overall definition and purpose of tertiary education:

> "Tertiary education – provided by universities and other higher education institutions – is the level of education following secondary schooling. It is seen to play an essential role in society, by fostering innovation, increasing economic development and growth, and improving more generally the wellbeing of citizens." (Eurostat, 2016b)

This definition clearly emphasizes the high importance of tertiary education not only for individuals but also for society, innovation, and economic growth.

In order to supplement national explanations, a general description for Germany is provided by the Standing Conference of the Ministers of Education

---

[23] Organisation for Economic Co-operation and Development (OECD) also refers to the term tertiary education and classification defined in ISCED provided by UNESCO. Please see Glossary of Statistical Terms on website OECD (https://stats.oecd.org/glossary/index.htm).

and Cultural Affairs (*Kultusministerkonferenz; KMK*)[24]. According to KMK (2015), general objectives of tertiary education are:

> "Teaching and study are to prepare students for a profession in a certain sphere of activity, imparting to them the particular knowledge, skills and methods required in a way appropriate to each course so as to enable them to perform scientific or artistic work and to act responsibly in a free, democratic and social state governed by the rule of law. These purposes of study are common to all types of higher education institution.
>
> Thus, the mandate bestowed by the legislator, in line with the traditional principle of the unity of teaching and research, is to provide professional training to students in a way that directly involves scientific and academic research and artistic development." (p. 147)

Thus, KMK underlines the purpose of tertiary education, namely to enhance students' employability, enable them to fulfill scientific or artistic work and to act responsibly in a free democratic and social state governed by law. Moreover, the principle of the unity of teaching and research is an essential element of higher education. However, it has to be noted that KMK emphasizes particular knowledge, skills and methods that have to be imparted by tertiary education, but does not – at least not explicitly – mention competencies. In contrast, UNESCO (2012a) refers to knowledge, skills, and competencies. In this context, the perspective of the German Council of Science and Humanities (*Wissenschaftsrat*)[25] shall be elucidated, as it provides the German Federal Government and the State (*Länder*) Governments with advice on the structure and development of higher education and research. According to the "Recommendations for the relationship of higher education to the labor market" ("*Empfehlungen zum Verhältnis von Hochschulbildung und Arbeitsmarkt*") (Wissenschaftsrat, 2015), three dimensions were elaborated for educational goals of higher education, which are technical sciences, personality development and employability. Although the three dimensions are of high importance, their

---

24 The KMK is a consortium of ministers in charge of education, schooling, and higher education institutions, research and cultural affairs. They define the joint interests and the objectives of all 16 federal states in the Federal Republic of Germany. While the Federation is responsible for the fields of admission to higher education institutions and degrees from higher education institutions, main responsibility in supervision, definition of objectives and organizational structures etc. of institutes of higher education is primarily organized within the individual federal states. For details, please see KMK (2015) or the individual federal states respectively.
25 For details and the history of the Wissenschaftsrat, please see Bartz (2007).

accentuation may vary due to the course of study, discipline or type of higher education institution. The three dimensions are explained as follows.

The purpose of technical science is to „enable students to select, apply and adapt specific theories and methods according to the situation, and independently and critically handle scientific findings" (Wissenschaftsrat, 2015, p. 40). Ultimately, the preparation for the labor market concerns the qualification of the students, which is designed directly and specifically for professional life including all its multifaceted and dynamic challenges after graduation. The dimension of personality development "is designed to promote socialization into science, identification with a subject and its scientific community and development of a scientific and professional ethos" (Wissenschaftsrat, 2015, p. 40). Personal development in the context of tertiary education furthermore includes the development of personal and social competencies, such as self-organization, team, communication and conflict skills and the future role of graduates in society, politics and culture.

Moreover, the *Wissenschaftsrat* emphasizes the social relevance and function of higher education:

> „University education fulfills a variety of functions for society as a whole as well as each individual student. From a systematic perspective, the qualifications of the university sector are primarily designed to help ensure the innovative ability and adaptability of society and economy. From the individual perspective, a university degree is designed to most of all open professional and personal development options." (Wissenschaftsrat, 2015, pp. 48 f.)

Due to the original aim that is providing advice to the German Federal Government and the State (*Länder*) Governments on the structure and development of higher education and research, the *Wissenschaftsrat* developed recommendations based on sound analysis. In the introduction to their recommendations, referring to the objectives and functions of higher education it is stated:

> "In order to meet its inherent responsibility for innovative and development capability of society and economy, universities have to regularly and thoroughly reflect on their respective qualification objectives and make them transparent for prospective students as well as employers. Based on these objectives, the curricula have to be adapted - focus should hereby be the ability students and grad-

uates to learn, judge, and solve problems as well as the multiple options available to them after graduation. Ultimately, the study proposals of universities should be designed in such a manner that the needs of the labor market can be considered and student success rate can be increased." (Wissenschaftsrat, 2015, p. 94)

While the ISCED provided by UNESCO clearly categorize tertiary education and the respective levels, the more comprehensive notes on tertiary education by Eurostat and KMK underline the purpose and high importance of tertiary education for (the individual's) contribution to society. Moreover, the *Wissenschaftsrat* not only emphasizes the social relevance and function of higher education for society as a whole and the individual students; also, three dimensions of educational goals for higher education were elaborated and a holistic perspective on higher education was presented. In their recommendations referring to objectives and functions of higher education, institutions' responsibility is highlighted. They are not only responsible to scrutinize but also to refine their qualification objectives on a regular basis. The offered courses have to consider the needs of the labor market and increase the student success rate.

Within this framework of challenging demands and a quite complex structure – comprising supranational defined (basic) standards, intragovernmental regulations and nationally specified laws, rules and regulations and the individual higher education institution's orientation, culture and research focus – study programs have to be integrated, developed, implemented (incl. quality assurance systems), improved and refined. As tertiary education is a highly debatable issue across the globe, contemporary trends and challenges are elucidated in the following section.

3.2.2.1 General trends and challenges in tertiary education

Recalling the manifold perspectives of the supranational and national level as previously outlined shows the extraordinary importance of tertiary education for both the individual learner and society as a whole, innovation and economic development (see also Gogolin & Tippelt, 2003). The causal effects were also confirmed by scientific studies. Recent studies not only show the positive benefits of higher education on individual's and society by elucidating financial and nonpecuniary (e.g. civic participation and health-related behaviors) aspects

(Anger, Plünnecke & Schmidt, 2010; Baum, Ma & Payea, 2013); rather, Valero and Reenen (2016) explored the impact of universities on economic growth. The researchers used the World Higher Education Database provided by the International Association of Universities in collaboration with UNESCO. Based on a dataset of nearly 15,000 universities in approx. 1,500 regions across 78 countries, the researchers scrutinized the changes in the number of universities in regions and their effects on subsequent growth between 1950 and 2010. Their findings show a positive correlation between increases in the number of universities and future growth of GDP per capita, i.e. doubling the number of universities per capita implies a growth of 4 % in future GDP per capita. Positive spillover effects from universities to neighboring regions were found. Although small in magnitude, part of the positive relationship between growth and universities can be explained by increase of human capital and greater innovation. Finally, a highly significant correlation between the presence of a university in a region and recognition of a democratic system was shown.

Nevertheless, along with the crucial role of tertiary education from a strategic global perspective for the long-term development and well-being of individuals and society, it is faced with considerable complexity, changes, and great challenges. Major challenges for tertiary education along with new opportunities were (already) discussed on the UNESCO World Conference on Higher Education in 1998 resulting in *World Declaration on Higher Education for the Twenty-First Century: Vision and Action* and *Framework for Priority Action for Change and Development of Higher Education*. Many new challenges for higher education were specified in the *Preamble* of the *World Declaration on Higher Education for the Twenty-First Century: Vision and Action* (1998). The increase in student enrolments worldwide (also discussed as massification), equality of conditions for access to and during the course of studies, skills-based training, employability of graduates, quality in teaching, research and services, staff development, establishment of co-operation agreements and equitable access to the benefits of international co-operation and finally challenges related to finances were the main challenges. In contrast to the multifaceted challenges new opportunities were outlined, such as sharing knowledge, international co-operation and exchange and technologies in order to better produce, transmit, manage, access and control knowledge.²⁶ Furthermore, it is concluded in the *Preamble* that:

> "Higher education itself is confronted therefore with formidable challenges and must proceed to the most radical change and renewal it has ever been required to undertake, so that our society, which is currently undergoing a profound crises of values, can transcend mere economic considerations and incorporate deeper dimensions of morality and spirituality. It is with the aim of providing solutions to these challenges and of setting a process of in-depth reform in higher education worldwide that UNESCO has convened a World Conference on Higher Education in the Twenty-First Century". (UNESCO, 1998)

In order to master substantial change, UNESCO (1998) urges to strongly involve all stakeholders that are governments, higher education institutions, students and their families, teachers, the public and private sectors of economy, business and industry etc. in the change process.

The urgency of change for tertiary education was also clearly stated by Richmond (2009):

> "Although universities have resisted significant change for centuries, change is coming. A variety of forces are likely to influence the future of the academy, and most of these influences are coming from outside the traditional university structure. The forces that are changing universities are the demographic shift of students from predominantly male to predominantly female; the rapid increase in technologies, especially information technologies; an ongoing reduction in the proportion of public funding devoted to higher education; changes in the roles of faculty; and the advent and strength of for-profit institutions." (p. 31)

Based on current debates, definition seems inevitable in order to design and build a framework for tertiary education that caters to contemporary (societal) needs. Various approaches to solve those (global) problems were elaborated. The following two works shall be exemplary and are presented due to their high impact.

---

26   For further details and debates on trends and challenges in tertiary education please see e.g. Altbach, 2016; Altbach, Reisberg & Rumbley, 2009; Glass, 2014; Gül et al., 2010; Lin and Pleskovic, 2008; Marginson and Wende, 2007; OECD, 2007; Salmi and Hauptman, 2006; Tremblay, Lalancette & Roseveare, 2012; UNESCO, 2015.

Based on many challenges and opportunities with which higher education is confronted, the OECD Secretariat developed four scenarios as part of its ongoing project on the future of higher education (CERI, 2008). The scenarios focus on higher education up to 2030 with regard to quality access in times of globalization. Title of the first scenario is "Open Networking" (p. 2) that describes higher education in 2030 to be highly internationalized based on broad networks comprising higher education institutions, students, scholars, and actors such as industry. Second scenario with the title "Serving local communities" (p. 4) delineates higher education institutions focused or refocused on national or local level. In the third scenario called "New Public Responsibility" (p. 6), tertiary education is mainly publicly funded. Financial incentives as well as market forces are considered. The final scenario, "Higher Education Inc." (p. 8), describes that tertiary education institutions compete worldwide in order to provide commercial and economic research and education services. The four scenarios show different potential futures for higher education in general. Each of the four scenarios provides a short scenario story along with key drivers and related developments that may affect future development. Finally, questions are raised that enable the reflection on possible consequences of the respective scenario.

A further ongoing debate refers to an international agreement on the recognition of higher education qualifications. First efforts to develop "a global normative instrument on the recognition of qualifications in higher education" (UNESCO, 2015) were made by UNESCO in 1992. Afterwards, UNESCO and OECD jointly elaborated the "Guidelines for Quality Provision in Cross-border Higher Education", which were adopted in 2005 by the UNESCO General Conference. These guidelines aim to protect both students and other stakeholders from discredited providers and inferior quality and are still relevant to elaborate a global convention on the recognition of higher education qualifications. The project status was reported and presented in 2015, debates are still ongoing and are part of future work of international experts, committees and consultations both on theme-specific and regional level. The progress report with a preliminary draft of the convention is expected in 2017 (UNESCO, 2015).

In terms of the European level, results of a survey by Sursock and Smidt (2010) show the considerable and very important impact of Bologna-driven changes on higher education institutions. The survey was addressed to higher education institutions. 821 individual institutions replied, representing 15 %

of European higher education institutions. More than 70 % of the sample pertains to universities offering doctoral education. The sample represents 43 % of the students enrolled in European higher education institutions. Thus, the top five most important changes for institutions over the last ten years were enhanced internal quality processes (60 %), enhanced cooperation with other higher education institutions (53 %), more autonomy (43 %), enhanced cooperation with industry (42 %) and more diversified funding (41 %) (p. 18), indicating the importance of international attractiveness and competiveness of higher education institutions. Figure 11 shows the developments that were of high importance for the institutional strategy over the past three years. Along with Bologna-driven changes that affect higher education institutions, e.g. the Bologna process itself (78 %), quality assurance reforms (63 %) and internationalization (61 %) exogenous forces are likely to influence higher education institutions, e.g. demographic changes (26 %).

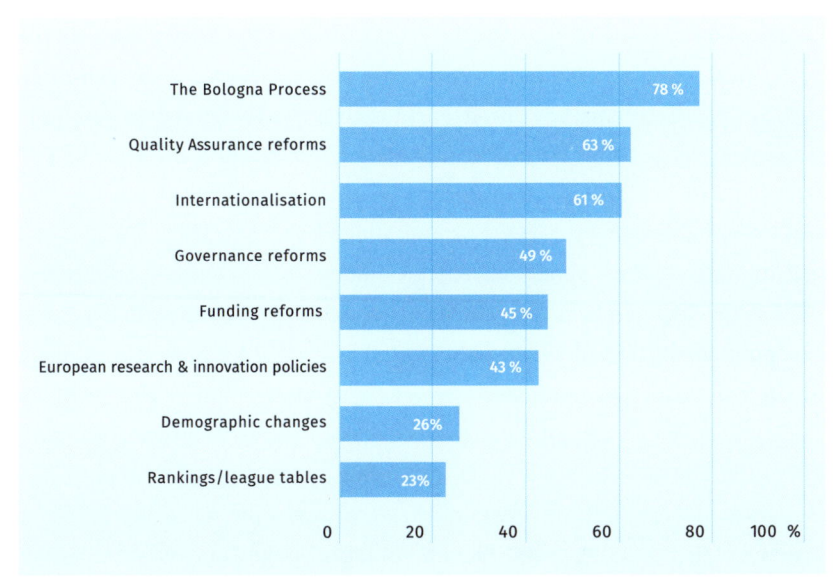

Development	%
The Bologna Process	78 %
Quality Assurance reforms	63 %
Internationalisation	61 %
Governance reforms	49 %
Funding reforms	45 %
European research & innovation policies	43 %
Demographic changes	26%
Rankings/league tables	23%

Figure 11.   Developments of high importance to European higher education institutions over the past three years. Adapted from Sursock and Smidt, 2010, p. 26.

Considering the survey results, one may conclude that the Bologna process – without assessing the individual issues and their impact – has triggered a certain dynamic in higher education institutions. Developments resulting directly from the Bologna process are important for institutions' competiveness but also exogenous forces have to be considered.

Even if a positive dynamic between higher education institutions can be detected, it is stated that EHEA is not yet completely implemented. The implementation report of the Bologna process states:

> „Graduates too often discover that they do not have the skills and competences they need for their future careers. Higher education is still not easily accessible for young people from disadvantaged backgrounds. Student-centred learning, based on carefully planned goals, remains underdeveloped. And the potential of digital technologies to transform learning and teaching has not yet been grasped everywhere." (European Commission / EACEA / Eurydice, 2015, p. 3)

Nevertheless, higher education institutions are decisive partners within the EU's 2020 strategy of striving for growth. The objective is that at least 40 % of population in the age of 30-34 in the EU should attain tertiary education qualification by 2020. Also part of the 2020 strategy is the improvement of the performance of education and training systems at all levels and the increased participation in tertiary education. Furthermore, the EU Council adopted the strategic framework for European cooperation in education and training (ET 2020) in the year 2009. Four objectives were set. First, lifelong learning and mobility shall become a reality. Second, quality and efficiency of education and training shall be improved. Third, equality, social cohesion, and active citizenship shall be promoted. Finally, creativity and innovation (comprising entrepreneurship) shall be enhanced on all levels of education and training. Along with the above-mentioned aim of at least 40 % of population between 30-34 years that should attain tertiary education qualification another headline target was set to be achieved by 2020. Thus, at least 20 % of higher education graduates (in EU average) should have realized a period of their study or training (comprising work-placements) of higher education abroad; thereby, at least 15 European Credit Transfer and Accumulation System (ECTS) credits or duration of at least three months should be established (Eurostat, 2016b).

As Figure 12, based on educational attainment statistics provided by Eurostat, shows, 38.7 % of the population in the age of 30-34 in the EU-28 had completed tertiary education in 2015. Figure 12 reveals a differentiated situation in the EU Member States. 17 Member States had already achieved or exceeded the proportion, which was also the case in Switzerland, Norway, and Iceland. On the other hand, the lowest proportion of population having completed tertiary education were reported in Italy, Romania, Malta, and Slovakia as well as in former Yugoslav Republic of Macedonia, where the share of people having completed tertiary education was below 29 %. Member states have set individual goals they want to achieve, e.g. Luxemburg has set a goal of 66 %, Italy 26 %. In 2015, 12 EU Member States had already attained their goal. The share of people having completed tertiary education in Germany – which is categorized in the bottom third of EU Member States – was 32.3 % in 2015. Germany's national target for the proportion of 30-34 year-olds with tertiary educational attainment should be at least 42 % by 2020. Considering the national German perspective on the actual situation, a proportion of 45.7 % (2014) in the age group of 30-34 years having completed tertiary education was reported. In EU statistics, a share of 31.4 % (2014) was reported, based on different ISCED levels that are comprised in EU and in German national statistics. Germany explicitly refers to the Presidency conclusions on education targets in the Europe 2020 Strategy specified at the 3013th education, youth and culture Council meeting in 2010 and therefore does not agree with the EU data (Bundesministerium für Wirtschaft und Energie (BMWi), 2016).[27]

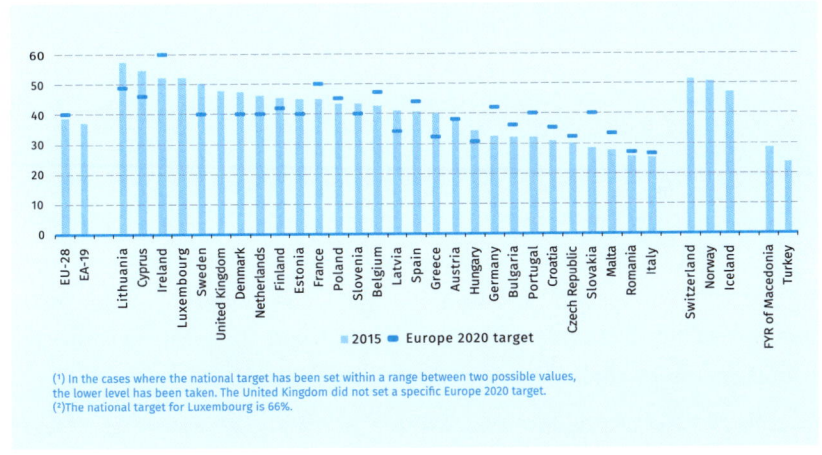

Figure 12. Population aged 30-34 with tertiary educational attainment (ISCED 5-8), by country, 2015 (%); t2020_41. Adapted from Eurostat (2016a).

Specifying data by sex for EU-28 as a whole reveals that women in the age of 30-34 have already achieved the EU 2020 target in the year 2012, when the proportion of women with tertiary educational attainment in EU-28 was

---

27   According to the Presidency conclusions on education targets in the Europe 2020 Strategy provided on 3013th education, youth and culture Council meeting in 2010 "Member States may in justified cases include national qualifications currently classified at ISCED level 4 into the definition of their national target for tertiary or equivalent education" (Council of the European Union, 2010).

40.2 % (vs. males with 31.8%). In 2015, the proportion of women having completed tertiary education was 43.4 %, while men in this age group achieved 34.0 % (see Figure 13). As Figure 13 shows, the share of women that have completed tertiary education has increased more rapidly than men in the period of 2005-2015. Hence, the gender gap has widened.

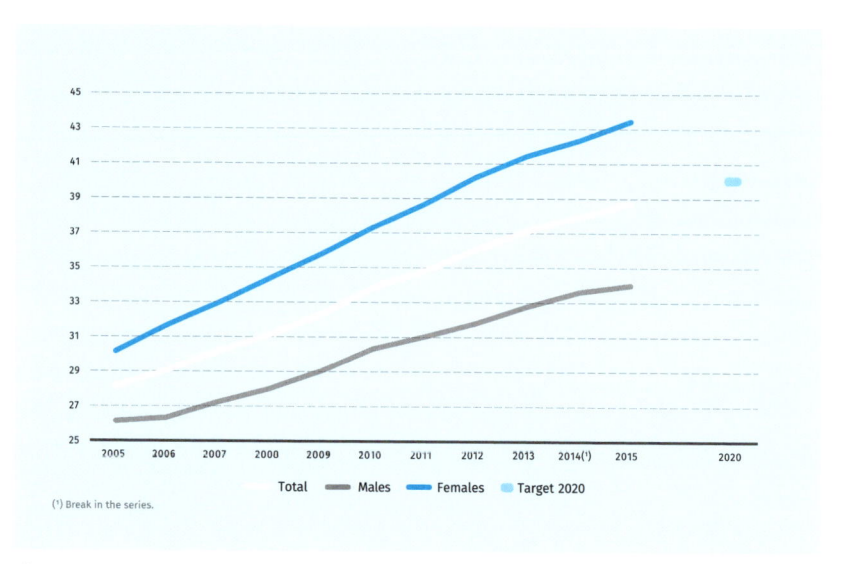

Figure 13. Population aged 30-34 with tertiary educational attainment (ISCED 5-8), by sex, EU-28, 2005-2015 (%); t2020_41. Adapted from Eurostat (2016a).

The prominent role of higher education within the EU 2020 strategy and the inclusion of tertiary education in the big EU picture may be highly appreciated. However, critical debates are ongoing on the issue of increasing the share of people who have completed tertiary education (Nida-Rümelin, 2014). Therefore, at least for the German educational system with its system of vocational education, this benchmark has to be critically examined.

On the national level, the *Wissenschaftsrat* has elaborated the "Theses for the Future Development of the System of Higher Education and research in Germany". The *Wissenschaftsrat* (2000) stated that the German system of tertiary education and research had a dynamic development on the one hand, however, with regard to the institutional level

> "it is too inflexible and its contribution to the solution of problems in industry, society and politics is inadequate. Energetic reforms and financial support of a far higher order than is currently available are necessary in order to exploit the potential of the

higher education and research system to the full in the present and at the same time to lay the foundation for further development." (Wissenschaftsrat, 2000, p. 6)

Therefore, the *Wissenschaftsrat* (2000) has recommended the accomplishment of three decisive actions. In the first action, research and teaching is to be more application orientated, which is interpreted as better utilization, not as a degradation of pure research. Consequently teaching should have a greater association with the actual practice. Therefore, cross-institutional funding by Federal government and states was recommended, which has to comply with certain principles, e.g. transparent processes. As a shift is assumed in the demand of personnel from higher educational qualifications to "academically sound, practice-oriented training and qualification profiles" (p. 7), a principal shift of resources was concluded in favor of the *Fachhochschulen* (universities of applied sciences). The second action refers to the advancement of internationalization of the German system of higher education and research as a whole. It is not enough to merely strengthen exchange and co-operation; also internationalization of research and teaching content require additional attention. Moreover, focus is also directed toward transnational institutional structures (on a European level), in order to encourage pure research. Third action postulated intensified use of information and communication technologies, as higher education institutions and in particular universities were expected to hold a leading position. It is explicitly formulated that electronic media shall be of greater use in teaching. Furthermore, "virtual institutions" (p. 7) in combination with associated institutions abroad were suggested, attempting to raise international profile. The accomplishment of this basic but indispensable actions was required for further reforms that are necessary in different sectors, e.g. increasing mobility, fostering competition and co-operation, enhancing autonomy, multiplying resources and renewing the unity of research and teaching.

The challenges and opportunities outlined above are still (necessary) debatable issues on supranational, intergovernmental, national, and organizational level as well as within the transnational research community. Moreover, they are of great relevance due to tertiary education's key role in creating wealthier and more open societies (Beall, 2013).

Based on the trends and challenges in the sector of tertiary education in general, trends and challenges in the discipline of business leadership education in particular shall be elucidated in the next step.

3.2.2.2 Trends and challenges in business leadership education in tertiary education in particular

Following the elaboration of trends and challenges in the segment of tertiary education in general, the next step focuses on trends and challenges in business leadership education in tertiary education in particular. The spheres of influence in the discipline of business leadership education in tertiary education can be determined as coming from inside and outside of the traditional university structure. A selection of internal factors of business schools and business programs is described in Canals (2011a), referring to mission, relevance, governance, faculty development, financial deficit and humanistic approach.[28] External trends and challenges are emerging from (critical) debates on (conventional) practices of business schools, from demands of the corporate world and the dynamic (market) environment in which corporations operate. External trends and challenges resulting from these forces and their meaning and (assumed) consequences for business leadership education in tertiary education shall be presented in the following section.

Starting point shall be a perspective on management and leadership on the basis of economic history that rose with the emergence of the modern corporation in the early 20th century and the shaping of (mass) manufacturing, the subsequent sales of manufactured products (e.g. automobiles, electricity) and their distribution. Thus, as pointed out by Canals (2011a), professionalization of managers and business leaders, which gradually succeed the entrepreneurs or investors who initiated the business, became very important in 20th century. Consequently, business schools[29] and business programs evolved as academic institutions and domains, where the principles of management and leadership could be systematically learned, developed, and researched. Thus,

---

28 For details please see Canals (2011a); more challenges are presented in Lorange (2008) and Thomas (2007).

29 The world's first business school is reputed to be ESCP in France that was established in 1819 (Parker, 2015), while Wharton within the University of Pennsylvania is reputed to be the first business school founded in USA in 1881 (Canals, 2011a). For the history of business schools in USA, please see Canals (2011a); for history, current conditions and future perspectives of business schools please see Thomas, Lorange & Sheth (2013) and Thomas et al. (2014).

business leadership and business leadership education still have a young history prospering in the second half of the 20th century due to economic growth. Nevertheless, as Canals (2011b) delineates, the (global) financial crisis of 2007-2009[30] shed light not only on notable weaknesses of market capitalism and implications within a global economy, but also corporate leadership and quality were challenged. Questions referred to e.g. what could companies generally have done differently in assessing risks and evaluating investment decisions, whether goals were set realistically, but also what kind of leaders were selected by companies and, in turn, educated and developed by business schools or universities. Thus, questions were not only directed to the corporate world, but also to business schools.[31] Critical and controversial debates were initiated on quality of business leadership education, particularly with regard to its ethical dimensions (Moules, 2015; Palin, 2013; Podolny, 2009). Consequently, the focus was not only on ethics in curricula (Palin, 2013), but also on newly emerging approaches, e.g. critical leadership studies (Collinson & Tourish, 2015; Parker, 2015). Debates are still ongoing and are fueled by emerging scandals in the corporate world, e.g. Volkswagen emissions scandal in 2015 (Weibel, 2015). Thus, it seems to be appropriate when Parker (2015) notes: "Given everyday business scandals – whether concerning corruption, pollution or eye-watering salaries – the business schools often come across like drug dealers who blame the addicts while profiting from the sales" (p. 42).

Another storyline pertains to ongoing debates – predominantly held in USA, the mother of management and leadership education – on outcomes of management and business leadership education in order to justify an adequate cost-benefit ratio. In this context, appropriate and contemporary pedagogy and methodology is also a relevant (debatable) issue. As explained above (chapter 3.1.4.4), rising tuition fees along with rising student debts[32] and challenging value proposition have stimulated discussions about competency-based education (CBE) as an alternative path to traditional higher education programs. Thus, the Association to Advance Collegiate Schools of Business (AASCB), the main accreditation body for business schools that urges "programs to spend less time on research and pedagogy and focus on helping businesses solve current problems" (Gellman, 2016), proposes a shift towards a more practice-oriented education. Gellman (2016) furthermore points out

---

30 For details, please see The Economist (2013).
31 For more details, please see Canals (2011a and 2011b). For studies that have addressed leadership behaviors, please see Kerr and Robinson (2011); Tourish and Hargie (2012).
32 According to Burke and Butler (2012), total student debt in the USA exceeded 1 trillion USD (p. 4).

that requirements for accreditation[33] were revised by AASCB based on input from corporate leaders, encouraging schools to intensify relationships, cooperation with companies, and increase the proportion of practitioners, lecturers, and / or adjunct professors among their teaching staff. Michael Arena, chief talent and development officer for General Motors Co. and member of AACSB board of directors, expects business graduates to master the "practice of theory in a less-than-ideal context" (as cited in Gellman, 2016). Also in corporate leadership development, a number of companies increasingly focus on experiments, as described by Ashkenas and Hausman (2016). Focal point of this approach is "a real business challenge that leaders need to solve, instead of a hypothetical case study or simulation. In order to succeed, they have to act, step outside of their comfort zone, and adapt their approach". Moreover, 80 % of the 75 participants accomplished their projects and "produced tangible results and business insight". Even though leadership development and leadership education in tertiary education may be a different kettle of fish, corporate perspective is indispensable, as it reflects corporate requirements on (future) business leaders. In turn, corporate needs have to be considered for the program design in tertiary education.

A huge number of surveys, usually conducted by (consulting) firms, provide insight into the corporate (real-world) perspective. A set of studies conducted by the International Business Machine Corporation (IBM) – one of the worldwide leading IT and consulting companies – received special attention due to the immense empirical sample. The studies provided by IBM are generally based on a sample of more than 1,000 C-level subjects. Based on the aforementioned immense empirical sample and four additional criteria, being quality, international relevance, actuality along with representation of various perspectives on business leadership by actual business leaders – namely Chief Executive Officers (CEOs) and Chief Human Resource Officers (CHROs) – and future business leaders (students) several studies by IBM were considered to provide sound findings. The selected studies and their respective sample were as follows:

1. IBM (2010a). *Capitalizing on Complexity. Insights from the Global Chief Executive Officer Study*. Somers / NY: IBM Global Business Services. The research is based on face-to-face interviews with 1,541 CEOs, general managers and senior public sector leaders worldwide in 60 countries and 33 industries to "better understand the challenges and goals of today's CEOs." (p. 6).

---

[33] For critical considerations on accreditation, please see Burke & Butler, 2012.

2. IBM (2012a). *Connected generation. Perspectives from tomorrow's leaders in a digital world. Insights from the 2012 IBM Global Student Study.* Somers / NY: IBM Global Business Services. The research is based on a survey of more than 3,400 college and university students worldwide "to better understand the opinions, perceptions and aspirations of our future employees, customers, leaders and citizens." (p. 1). The results of the student survey were compared to those of Global CEO Study 2012.

3. IBM (2012b). *Leading Through Connections. Insights from the Global Chief Executive Officer Study.* Somers / NY: IBM Global Business Services. The research is based on face-to-face interviews with 1,709 CEOs and senior public sector leaders worldwide in 64 countries and 18 industries "to better understand their future plans and challenges in an increasingly connected economy." (p. 58).

4. IBM (2016). *Redefining competition. Insights from the Global C-suite Study – The CEO perspective.* Somers / NY: IBM Global Business Services. The research is generally based on input from 5,247 C-suite executives "to find out what they think the future will bring and how they're positioning their organizations to prosper in the 'age of disruption'" (p. 1); this distinctive edition focuses on the perspectives of 818 interviewed CEOs worldwide.

5. IBM (2010b). *Working beyond Borders. Insights from the Global Chief Human Resource Officer Study.* Somers / NY: IBM Global Business Services. The research is based on a worldwide survey in 61 countries of 707 executives; almost 600 have been surveyed face to face to "understand the challenges, opportunities and goals of today's Chief Human Resource Officers." (p. 60). The results were compared with 2010 IBM Global CEO Study.

Considering opinions of both chief officers and students provides a complete picture about the need to carefully develop updated business leadership (training and) education. Key findings of these five surveys that are of high relevance for this research can be grouped in the following conceptual context:

1. Complexity, uncertainty and unpredictability
2. Technology, innovation and collaboration
3. Purpose, goals[34] and mission and ethics and values,

which shall be elaborated on in the following section.

---

34   IBM surveys asked for purpose and mission; the term goal was added in this research for reasons of unambiguousness.

Following on from the finding in the VUCA-world and IBM's CEO study (IBM, 2010a) outlined in chapter 3.1.4.1, it has to be pointed out that six out of ten CEOs expressed that the significantly complex economic environment saturates leaders' thinking. Moreover, 79 % expect an upward trend in the level of complexity over the next five years. Figure 14 shows the rising level of complexity and the respective CEOs opinions about it.

Expected level of complexity
CEOs agree complexity will only continue to rise.

Currently experiencing high/very high level of complexity
60%

Expect high/very high level of complexity over five years
79%

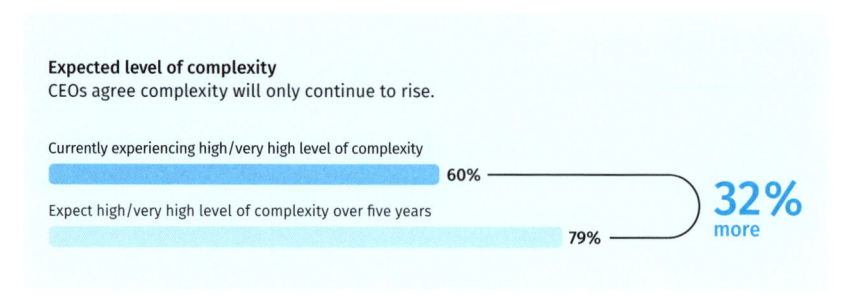

32% more

Figure 14.   Expected level of complexity. Adapted from IBM, 2010a, p. 18.

The major challenge for CEOs is a "complexity gap" (see Figure 15), which is reported to be a greater challenge than was measured throughout the past eight years of IBM's CEO research. Thus, eight out of ten CEOs expressed that the complex environment is growing faster, and fewer than half of them are ready to handle this challenge (IBM, 2010a).

The complexity gap
While eight out of ten CEOs anticipate significant complexity ahead, less than half feel prepared to handle it.

Expect high/very high level of complexity over five years
79%

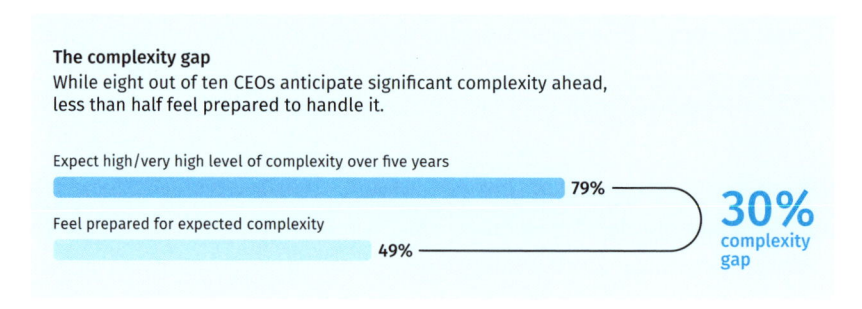

Feel prepared for expected complexity
49%

30% complexity gap

Figure 15.   The complexity gap. Adapted from IBM, 2010a, p. 19.

The perspective of future leaders reveals that 70 % of the students believe the high impact of complexity on organizations to be the result of interrelation of economic, social and physical systems, compared to 60 % CEOs. Students are highly aware of the complexity, which they will encounter throughout their career (IBM, 2010a).

Along with complexity, uncertainty, unpredictability and economic volatility have impact on organizations. As it is stated by one CEO, "*We are entering an era of ten to twenty years of new significant investment. There is opportunity and uncertainty that we have not seen before*" (Tom King, President, National Grid U.S. as cited in IBM, 2010a, p. 20). Moreover, a U.S. government agency leader asserted "There isn't a single day I come into work when I know what will happen" (as cited in IBM, 2012b, p. 12).

In the 2012 IBM CEO study, most important of all exogenous forces that have impact on organizations over the next three to five years is technology, which is also consistently ranked first in 2016 CEO perspectives (see Figure 16). This perspective is supported by other members of C-suite level.

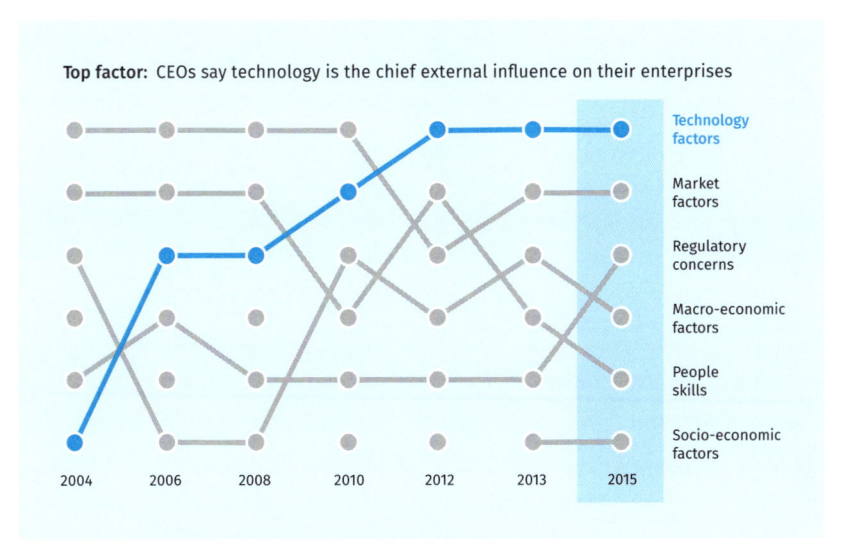

Figure 16. Top factor: CEOs say technology is the chief external influence on their enterprises. Adapted from IBM, 2016, p. 2.

Based on the findings of IBM (2012b), technology is not only a risk for organizations, which has to be anticipated in time in order to compete and survive. CEOs expect technology also to be "an enabler of collaboration and relationships – those essential connections that fuel creativity and innovation" (IBM, 2012b, p. 14). In the IBM study four years later, the results are supported and specified. Joshua Oigara, CEO of Kenya Commercial Bank states: "Technology is the epicenter of change. It enables businesses to leapfrog their competitors in meeting customers' needs" (as cited in IBM, 2016, p. 2). Thus, technology is not only a driver of change, but specified as four particular components that are relevant in the short-term; mobile solutions ranked first, followed by cognitive computing, internet of things and cloud computing.

As Figure 17 shows, technology fundamentally affects human capital (71 %), customer relationships (66 %), and innovation (52 %), which are key sources of sustained economic value.

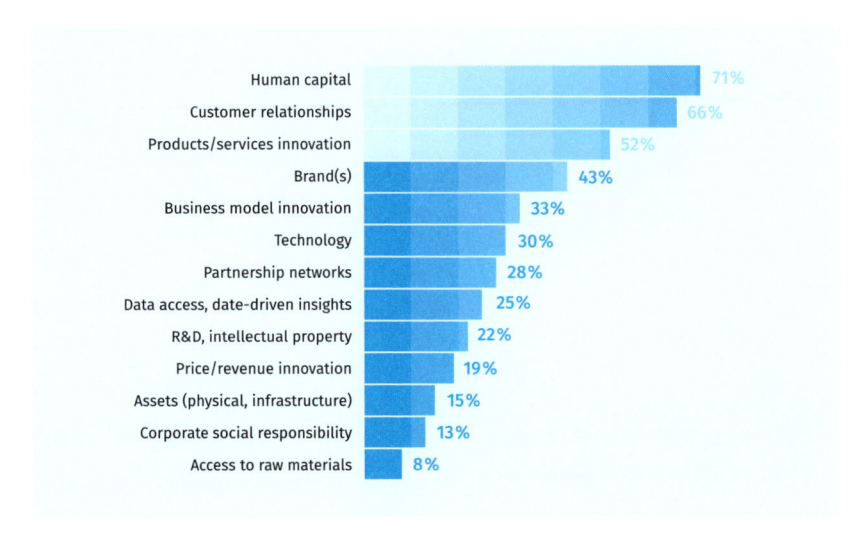

Source	Percentage
Human capital	71%
Customer relationships	66%
Products/services innovation	52%
Brand(s)	43%
Business model innovation	33%
Technology	30%
Partnership networks	28%
Data access, date-driven insights	25%
R&D, intellectual property	22%
Price/revenue innovation	19%
Assets (physical, infrastructure)	15%
Corporate social responsibility	13%
Access to raw materials	8%

Figure 17. Prime sources of sustained economic value. Adapted from IBM, 2012b, p. 15.

In contrast to CEOs, students are more concerned with the impact of market and macroeconomic factors on organizations before technology factors. The differing results between CEOs and students may be explained with the fact that students grew up with mobile and social technology so that they "have already integrated technology into their world view" (IBM, 2012a, p. 2). Nevertheless, looking ahead in the medium-term future of three to five years, CEOs expectations for the use of social media and internet were as high as those of students.

In order to compete and survive, according to the findings of IBM (2012b), CEOs strive for the empowerment of employees through values on one hand, and amplification of innovation with partnerships on the other. As one CEO stated, "It is important for employees to see the company's values as a reflection of their own. Values are at the core of the social contract between company and employee" (Wichian Mektrakarn, CEO, AIS as cited in IBM, 2012b, p. 20). Therefore, it is important for organizations to compose their core values. It is not easy to induce thinking and behavior in employees that synchronizes with organizations values. It is necessary that employees truly believe in the purpose, goals and mission and the ethics and values put forth by organizations as shown in Figure 18.

Attribute	%
Ethics and values	65%
Collaborative environment	63%
Purpose and mission	58%
Ability to innovate	51%
Industry leadership	40%
Stability of the organization	37%
Work-life balance	35%
Personal autonomy	31%
Financial rewards	31%
Work flexibility	24%
Cultural diversity	21%
Customizable compensation	18%
Comprehensive mentoring	18%

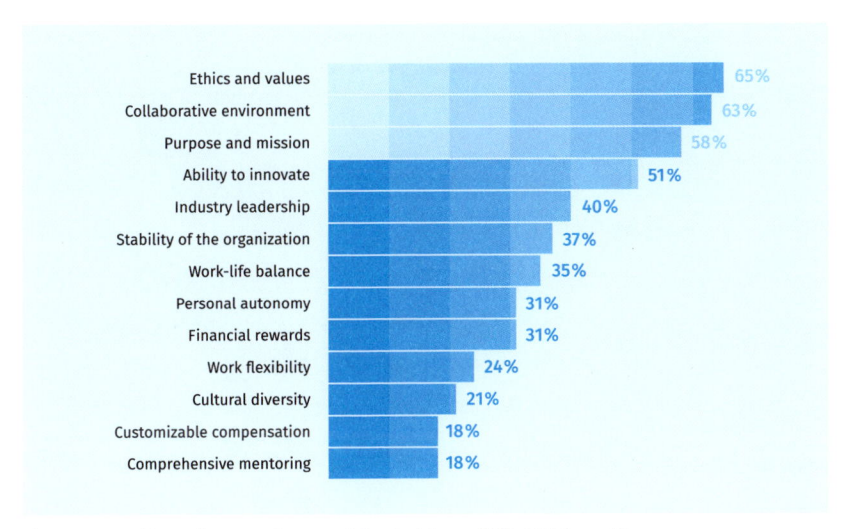

Figure 18.   Engaging employees. Adapted from IBM, 2012b, p. 20.

Aligning company values with personal values is also a key difference in attracting and retaining employees – at least in mature markets – among other aspects such as compensation and benefits, creating career growth opportunities, balancing work and life demands etc. (IBM, 2010b).

Comparisons between the CEO study (IBM, 2012b) and the student study (IBM, 2012a) reveals that a collaborative environment is important for both, CEOs and students (IBM, 2012a). While students ranked it as the most important organizational aspect to engage employees, CEOs ranked it the second most important (see Figure 19). However, referring to the other employee engagement aspects reveals many differences. Thus, it has to be noted that students place a high priority on autonomy and flexibility, which are necessary for innovations and work-life balance. In addition, major differences have to be pointed out with regard to the attributes ethics and values, and purpose and mission. As previously outlined, a culture of ethics and values was ranked first by CEOs, while students ranked it fourth. Likewise, purpose and mission were ranked third by CEOs, while students ranked it fifth. As ethics, values, and missions are assumed critical by the millennial generation, these different results were interpreted as a contradiction to widely held assumptions according to IBM (2012a). Nevertheless, students are more likely to recognize the importance of ethics in organizations once they are engaged in full-time employment.

Organizational attributes to engage employees

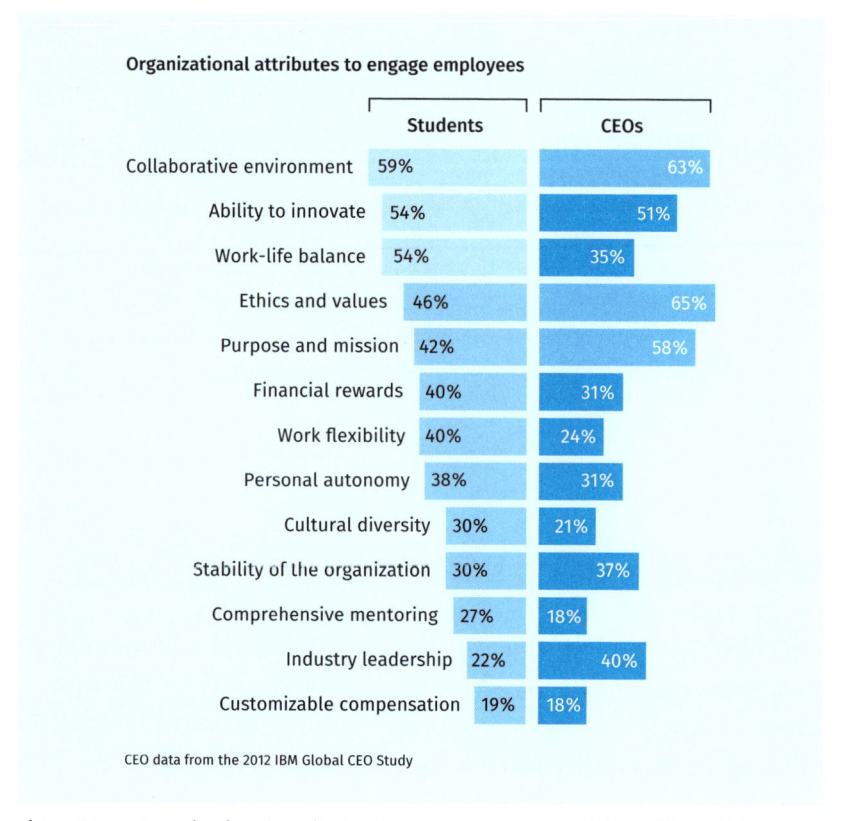

Attribute	Students	CEOs
Collaborative environment	59%	63%
Ability to innovate	54%	51%
Work-life balance	54%	35%
Ethics and values	46%	65%
Purpose and mission	42%	58%
Financial rewards	40%	31%
Work flexibility	40%	24%
Personal autonomy	38%	31%
Cultural diversity	30%	21%
Stability of the organization	30%	37%
Comprehensive mentoring	27%	18%
Industry leadership	22%	40%
Customizable compensation	19%	18%

CEO data from the 2012 IBM Global CEO Study

Figure 19. Organizational attributes to engage employees. Adapted from IBM, 2012a, p. 11.

Anyway, "CEOs are looking for hard outcomes. Through diversity of thought and the free flow of ideas, they expect innovation" (IBM, 2012b, p. 19). In context of innovations, IBM's CEO study 2012 revealed that financially successful organizations are more inclined to foster innovations with external partners. Consequently, organizations not only have to endeavor to be more open with employees, but also with customers and external partners. Collaboration is even more underlined in IBM's recent study (IBM, 2016). Not only emerging technologies allow enterprises to rethink the ways in which they involved their partners and customers. Digital engagement is expected to increase over the next three to five years, as it is presumed to gain in competitiveness and business intelligence. Therefore, working within an "open web of interdependent entities" seems to be more valuable than "a solo entity" (p. 4).

CEOs try to find ways in anticipating or creating disruptive innovation, as described in 2012 CEO study (IBM, 2012b) and supported by the recent CEO study (IBM, 2016). Chris Hilger, President and CEO of Securian Financial Group in USA, states: "*We need to institutionalize innovation. Innovation exists within our organization; we simply need to give it the time and the tools*" (as cited in IBM, 2016, p. 12). Moreover, CEOs of most successful enterprises emphasize experimentation and agility, as they are assumed preconditions for disruptive innovation. As previously outlined (see chapter 3.1.4.2), innovations do not grow on trees; rather they are the result of activity.

Innovation and planning for growth is also seen by CHROs, since

> "Innovation is the lifeblood of any enterprise, driving efficiency and facilitating new product and service development. But innovation is more than the creative application of acquired skills; it is the sum of an enterprise's capabilities, experiences and institutional knowledge. And maintaining the innovative edge requires capitalizing on this collective intelligence." (IBM, 2010b, p. 44)

The relation between innovation and collective intelligence is clearly underlined. Collective intelligence in this context, as outlined in IBM's CHROs study (IBM, 2010b), not only means organizations to become efficient by sharing and applying decisive knowledge and practices across the organization, but also to discover new ways of improvement through communication with costumers or other external partners, e.g. by evaluating feedback.

Finally, findings provided by IBM's student study (IBM, 2012a) with regard to (tertiary) education are relevant for this research. The first relevant aspect refers to online education. While digital channels are of high importance for students in creating customer relationships, they still prefer the face-to-face classroom settings for their own education. Only 26 % of students found online education to be of higher value than classroom education (see Figure 20). A differentiated analysis yielded different results between students in mature markets versus emerging markets. The latter found higher value in online education (38 %) compared to students in mature markets (20 %). Thus, online education may create value and contributes to accessing education. An 18 years-old U.S. student stated: "*Increased access to (college) education is the value of online education programs, not necessarily their competitiveness with physically attending class*" (as cited in IBM, 2012a, p. 7). In a global perspective, online education was less valuable than traditional face-to-face classroom education for 50 % of students.

Role of online versus classroom education

- 26% More valuable
- 50% Less valuable
- 24% Neither more nor less valuable

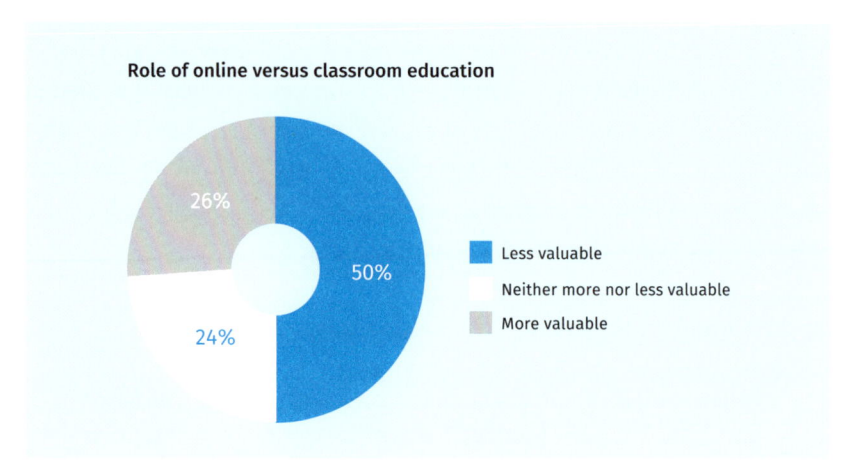

Figure 20. Role of online education versus classroom education. Adapted from IBM, 2012a, p. 7.

However, asking students how they assess "the extent to which their formal education prepares them for working life across multiple dimensions" (IBM, 2012a, p. 13). Findings show that formal education prepares well for collaboration with others and the use of technology. Although formal education has improved compared to the previous survey conducted two years earlier, some improvements are yet to be realized. Thus, emerging and growth markets as well as social and environmental sustainability require attention. Moreover, in order to prepare future leaders, the students' original quotes seem to be valuable and have to be considered. A 21-years-old student from New Zealand states: *"Businesses need to have a greater influence on what and how tertiary (college) education is provided – with more tangible skills and work-place experience given greater focus"* (as cited in IBM, 2012a, p. 13). The following statement by a 21-years-old student from the United Kingdom coincides: *"We need to step away from the traditional 'trait approach' leadership and manager characteristics and look to people who enable change"* (as cited in IBM, 2012a, p. 16).

Despite some minor discrepancies, the five studies selected by IBM comprising opinions of chief officers and students revealed a general agreement on different topics. Complexity and uncertainty / unpredictability, technology, innovation and collaboration, purpose, goals[35], mission, ethics, and values are aspects

---
35   Please see footnote 2.

that chief officers and students consider crucial. In turn, those aspects have a high impact on contemporary business leadership (training) and education. Moreover, students provided valuable perspectives on (tertiary) education.

As previously outlined, several drivers for business leadership education in particular were elucidated. These drivers emerge from critical debates on the discipline in general due to business scandals on one hand, and debates on outcomes and justification of cost-benefit ratio of education on the other. Moreover, debates on innovative pedagogy are ongoing, proposing a shift towards more practice-oriented education, e.g. fortifying ties with companies, including practitioners in teaching, and real-world challenges in education. Finally, findings of several studies emphasize corporate needs for (future) business leadership that have to be considered in the curricula design.

3.2.3   Preliminary conclusions

In order to systematically scrutinize and deductively develop business leadership education in tertiary education based on the holistic model of business leadership conceptualized in chapter 3.1 a contemporary human-centered perspective of education was concretized. The holistic educational cycle described in chapter 3.2.1 is deeply rooted in humanistic philosophy; it allows individuals to develop their personalities, becoming apparent in actions. As education is conceived as a loop, it is similarly conceived as a life-long process.

However, the focus of this research is business leadership education in tertiary education. Therefore, the topics of tertiary education in general and the discipline of business leadership education in particular were characterized. Tertiary education means focusing on the level of formal education that follows the completion of a secondary education school. (Tertiary) education is not only anchored in the universal principles of Human Rights, but also deeply embedded in the respective culture and society of a nation. Moreover, tertiary education has a political, economic, and societal mandate. It is seen to play an important role not only for the individual student's personality and competency development, but also in society by fostering innovation, economic development, and growth.

Due to its high importance, tertiary education is influenced by supranational, intergovernmental and national laws, rules and regulations and the individual higher education institution's distinctive orientation, culture and research focus. The various spheres of influence underline the complex structure and challenging demands, which are facing tertiary education. As tertiary education is a highly debatable issue across the globe, contemporary trends and challenges were highlighted in general and for the discipline of business leadership education in particular. Many challenges for higher education were previously touched on or specified in detail. Table 1 provides an overview comprising the most important trends and challenges along with opportunities for tertiary education in general.

General trends and challenges in tertiary education
- Access and completion
- Competency- and skill-based education
- Demographic changes
- Employability of graduates
- Funding
- Globalization and internationalization
- Increase in students enrolments (massification)
- Quality in teaching
- Staff development
- Research and services

Opportunities:
Shared knowledge + International co-operation & exchange + Technology

Table 1.   General trends and challenges in tertiary education.

Along with the general trends, challenges and opportunities that were elaborated with respect to tertiary education, further spheres of influence were delineated for business leadership education in particular. These forces can be determined coming from inside and outside the traditional university structure. A selection of internal factors of business schools and business programs was briefly presented in chapter 3.2.2.2. However, external trends and challenges were discussed and summarized in Table 2.

Trends and challenges for business leadership education in tertiary education
> Critical debates on the discipline in general due to business scandals
> Debates on outcomes and justification of cost-benefit ratio of education
> Debates on innovative pedagogy comprising proposal of a shift towards more practice-oriented education (e.g. strengthening ties with companies, including practitioners in teaching, including real-world challenges in education)
> Findings of several studies emphasize the corporate need for (future) business leadership and have to be considered in curricula design
Opportunities: Clear positioning of the discipline business leadership education + Implementation of innovative pedagogy

Table 2. Trends and challenges for business leadership education in tertiary education.

With regard to current leadership education, Kellerman (2012b) critically highlights:

> "[...] that leaders of every sort are in disrepute; that the tireless teaching of leadership has brought us no closer to leadership nirvana than we were previously; that we don't have much better an idea of how to grow good leaders, or of how to stop or at least slow bad leaders, than we did a hundred or even a thousand years ago." (p. xiv)

Based on current debates a brand new definition seems to be indispensable to design contemporary business leadership education in tertiary education from a pedagogical perspective.

3.2.4 Curriculum in tertiary education

Pedagogical infrastructure for business leadership education in tertiary education is determined in *curriculum* or program of studies. The terms *curriculum* or program of studies are used synonymously in this research, which is in line with Totté, Huyghe and Verhagen (2013). Concretizing the term and concept *curriculum* is necessary, as it will clarify the understanding of pedagogical infrastructure for business leadership education in tertiary education.

The term *curriculum* used within the context of tertiary education is not clearly defined; rather, it is characterized by fuzzy use (Barnett & Coate, 2005; Fraser & Bosanquet, 2006). Barnett and Coate (2005) state, "The very idea of 'curriculum' is unstable, its boundaries uncertain" (p. 5). Furthermore, a void of treatment of curriculum in tertiary education in policy domain, research literature and by practitioners is uncovered[36] (Barnett & Coate, 2005; Tight, 2012). Barnett and Coate (2005), researchers from United Kingdom, noted that valuable texts on curriculum in tertiary education could be found either in school education or in the USA. Nevertheless, in recent years, attention for *curricula* rose as a consequence of the Bologna process. Thus, the main focus was on curriculum development and learning outcomes (Jenert, 2016; Totté, Huyghe & Verhagen, 2013). However, according to Salden, Fischer and Barnat (2016), research on didactics in tertiary education was (re-)established once again at a later stage, resulting in remarkable scientific publications (e.g. Brinker & Tremp, 2010; Gerholz & Sloane, 2013).

Basically, two conceptions can be found in research literature (Totté, Huyghe & Verhagen, 2013). In a strict sense, curriculum is conceived to focus on structure and (a list of) content in one single course. In contrast, broader conceptions go beyond this, not only include each and every course within one program (Biggs & Tang, 2007), but also consider the big picture of a curriculum. Salden, Fischer and Barnat (2016) describe "curriculum development as a complex process, wherein structural requirements have to be met, various stakeholders involved and reasonable didactical solutions found in order to achieve the aimed learning outcomes" (p. 133). Totté, Huyghe and Verhagen (2013), who have developed a conceptual framework for curriculum development to be used by various involved stakeholders, conceive curriculum as

> "a dynamic environment that cannot be grasped within one snapshot. It develops continuously due to environmental demands and contextual changes. Therefore to make the conceptual scheme useful in different contexts ... and for different stakeholders ... the curriculum is approached from different points of view" (p. 2).

Remarkable work was also done by Lattuca and Stark (2009). They define curriculum as an "academic plan" in order to "remedy the lack of a comprehensive definition of curriculum" (p. 4). In their conception, various aspects have to be considered in developing an "academic plan", being at least purposes, content, sequence, learners, instructional processes and resources, evaluation and adjustment. Moreover, they developed a model that illustrates the various spheres of influence on curriculum development. As Figure 21 shows, curric-

---

[36] Reasons for the absence are explained in Barnett and Coate (2005).

ulum as an "academic plan" is embedded in the respective sociocultural context with its educational environment, which is influenced by three factors including external influences (e.g. government, market forces etc.) and internal influences. The latter are divided in two parts institutional (e.g. governance, resources etc.) and unit level influences (e.g. discipline, faculty or students).[37]

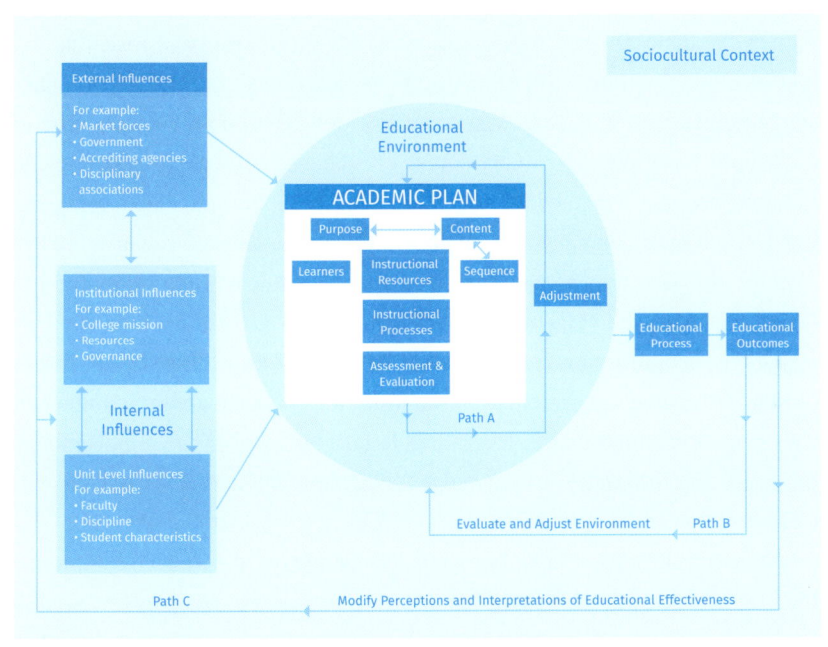

Figure 21. Academic plans in sociocultural context. Adapted from Lattuca & Stark, 2009, p. 5.

Against this background, it may be not surprising that curriculum in general is also perceived as a mechanism to stimulate change in the future, not only of education but also in society and culture (McCulloch, 2016). A curriculum, then, is not so much a static instrument as dynamic in process (Barnett & Coate, 2005). It is embedded in its sociocultural context with its multitude of influencing factors. Thus, it is the duty of higher education institutions to continuously evolve and improve the curriculum.

Basic principles, which allow a curriculum of business leadership education in tertiary education to strive for contemporary and future (societal) demands, shall be elaborated in the following section.

---

[37] For sound work and description of influencing factors on conception of study programs in German speaking literature, please see Pfäffli, 2015, i.e. pp. 110 ff.

3.2.5 Principles for curriculum design of business leadership education in tertiary education

In order to answer the research question – namely, how business leadership education in Master's programs for graduates in tertiary education shall be designed – it is not intended to define an ideal curriculum on a detailed level. Rather, the general principles of academic freedom[38], unity of research and teaching, and the individual culture and (research) orientation of each higher education institution shall be respected in order to maintain diversity. Therefore, main principles for a curriculum of business leadership education in Master's programs in tertiary education shall be proposed, considering the importance of consistency and coherence (Totté, Huyghe & Verhagen, 2013). Thereby, the basic idea of proposing principles is in line with Bourdieu (1990). Bourdieu developed *Principles for reflecting on the curriculum,* published after he led a commission for the French Minister of Education, Lionel Jospin during Mitterrand's presidency. The commission was instructed "to reflect on the curriculum and to plan a revision of it, bearing in mind the importance of the coherence and unity of knowledge" (Bourdieu, 1990, p. 307), but was not directly involved in curriculum design. Bourdieu's principles were not only based on intellectual inquiry, but were also of a general nature. For example, the first principle proposes that *"Course content must be regularly reviewed so that new knowledge demanded by scientific progress and changes in society ... can be introduced"* (p. 308). According to Albright (2016), Bourdieu's principles were "pragmatic recommendations about pedagogical reform" (p. 537). The author furthermore concluded that Bourdieu's contributions to curriculum studies are as topical today as when he made them in the 1980s.

General principles in this research focus on business leadership education in tertiary education from a pedagogical point of view. Therefore, five main questions and aspects that are based on Klafki's (2012) didactic approach shall be elucidated to design business leadership education in Master's programs for graduates in tertiary education. Klafki is renowned as "one of the most distinguished contemporary scholars in Didaktik[39] tradition" (Westbury, 2000, p. 16).

---

38 For Germany, the principle of freedom of research and teaching is determined in the Basic Law for the Federal Republic of Germany (2012) (Art. 5).
39 For introduction and comparison of two curriculum theories (Anglo-American curriculum and European-Scandinavian *Bildung-Didaktik*) and their intellectual affiliation, please see Autio (2014). Furthermore, Klafki (1995), Künzli (2000) and Westbury (2000) provide valuable information and comparisons.

Thus, the following five questions provide direction for the answer to the research question of this chapter:

1. What are educational goals of business leadership education in tertiary education?
2. Which educational contents *(Bildungsinhalte)* have to be chosen for business leadership education in tertiary education based on educational goals?
3. Which methodologies and organizational forms are best suited in business leadership education in tertiary education based on defined educational goals and contents of education?
4. Which educational settings[40] are best suited for business leadership education in tertiary education?
5. How to control and evaluate business leadership education in tertiary education?

In addition to Klafki's structure two further questions have to be answered due to relevant explanations on the educational ideal *(Bildungsideal)* of (creative) personality and funding that are of high importance for business leadership education in higher education. Therefore sixth and seventh questions are:

6. How to facilitate educational framework for business leadership education in tertiary education that enables students to develop the educational ideal *(Bildungsideal)* that is (creative) personality?
7. How can business leadership education in tertiary education be funded?

Consequently, seven main principles for a curriculum of business leadership education in Master's programs in tertiary education shall be proposed that will provide answers to the questions above.

3.2.5.1 Principle 1 – Educational goals

First and pivotal question in curriculum design refers to educational goals (Klafki, 2012; Schaper, Schlömer & Paechter, 2012). According to Tenorth and Tippelt (2012), educational goals denote skills, qualifications, capabilities, and

---
[40] Klafki uses the term „media", which is conceived in this research in a broader sense as "educational settings".

competencies learners should achieve upon completion of a specific course or program. Educational goals are (more) general in nature compared to learning objectives and learning outcomes[41] that have to be defined for each and every module and course within one program resulting in a consistent and coherent (curriculum) entity (Schaper, Schlömer & Paechter, 2012).

Crossing to the field of this research, which is business leadership education in tertiary education, educational goals were developed in a deductive process. Therefore, as a kind of umbrella provided generally in tertiary education, students' "enculturation" (Gilbert & Reiner, 2000, p. 265) into scientific education and environment shall be prioritized as a general principle and purpose. Even though not all students will pursue their careers as scientists, it is important that Master's programs enable students to familiarize themselves "with the practices of knowledge-building as exercised by the general community of scientists" (Gilbert & Reiner, 2000, p. 265). In doing so, the greatest possible number of students shall be able to participate in scientific debates and / or to grasp the utility of scientific knowledge.

Based on the holistic model of business leadership, which was thoroughly developed in chapter 3.1 and the conceptions of (tertiary) education previously outlined, the (creative) personality, which is in line with Faix and Mergenthaler (2015), undoubtedly has to be the superior educational ideal. Thus, educational goals of business leadership education in Master's programs for graduates in tertiary education are proposed as follows[42]:

1. Master's programs in business leadership education for graduates aim to enable learners to develop their (creative) personalities systematically.

2. Master's programs in business leadership education for graduates aim to develop learners' various (business leadership) competencies throughout the Master's program; (business leadership) competencies are inherent to the model of (creative) personality and can be developed systematically. They play a pivotal role in the learner's development of personality and the success in (business) leadership.

---

[41] For more details and relevance of learning outcomes that gained in importance as a consequence of the Bologna process, please see Schermutzki (2012). For legitimation of educational goals, please see Tippelt (1979).
[42] The following part and description is partially literally and partially analogously published in: Faix, W. G., Kisgen, S., Shah, S., & Faix, A.-V. (2017). Fostering creative personalities through real world experiences – SIBE as a representative example. The Journal of Competency-Based Education, to be published.

3. Master's programs in business leadership education for graduates aim to empower learners to contribute to organizations in a valuable way through exposure to and completion of (a) real-world project / s, which is / are limited in time and unique in order to solve (a) corporate / entrepreneurial business challenge / s. Conducting (a) real-world project / s is a mandatory part of the curriculum.

4. Master's programs in business leadership education for graduates aim to enable learners to identify and set both personal and professional goals and empower them to achieve these goals.

5. Master's programs in business leadership education for graduates aim to enable learners to create and utilize valuable networks, which play a vital role in succeeding in (business) leadership.

Due to the high importance of (creative) personality that is defined as superior educational ideal for business leadership education in tertiary education, second principle was developed and elucidated in the following section.

3.2.5.2 Principle 2 – Personality as educational ideal

The term *ideal* denotes the embodiment of the perfection, "a standard or principle to be aimed at" (Oxford Dictionaries). Referring to the field of education, an educational ideal has to be aimed at in the course of an educational process. The definition of educational ideals has its origin in ancient world, when Cicero conceptualized his ideal of a great orator with his all-embracing knowledge in his oeuvre *De Oratore* (55 B.C.). Thus, the ideally educated orator was important to serve in the courts and in public life (May, 2010). In the course of the history, new educational ideals emerged and the old were discarded, supplemented or adapted. Referring to Germany in the 19th century until the mid of the 20th century, the German "cultural nation" (*Kulturnation*) defined itself by education (*Bildung*) and thereby distinguished itself from other nations – e.g. England or France" (Tenorth, 2013). As previously outlined (see chapter 3.2.1), Humboldtian educational ideal was and still is of very high importance (Herbold, 2013; Nida-Rümelin, 2014; Tenorth, 2013). Shortly after that period, Max Weber (1864-1920), a well-known German sociologist famous for his work *Protestant Ethic and the Spirit of Capitalism* (1904 / 1905 / 1930), reflected on the passing values of the German educational ideal. He defined an educational ideal in contrast to a specific profession (*Beruf*) in order "to re-attain the value and status of educated, free-thinking experts in a modern setting" (Myers, 2004, p. 284).

As the aforementioned examples show, educational ideals are embedded in the respective political, social, cultural, economic, educational and scientific context of a society. Consequently, an educational ideal is determined based on a society's appreciation of education. Two contemporary perspectives shall be pointed out. Firstly, on a supranational level, according to the universal principles of Human Rights (see also Part 2, chapter 3.2.2), "[e]ducation shall be directed to the full development of the human personality" (Article 26, paragraph 2, UDHR, 1948). Secondly, on a regional level within Germany, according to the Constitution of the Free State of Bavaria (CFSB), "[s]chools shall not only impart knowledge and skills, but also develop the nobleness of the heart and character" (Article 131, paragraph 1, CFSB, 1998 / 2014). Notwithstanding, an ideal requires a clear separation from educational objectives, which have been previously prepared (chapter 3.2.5.1). While the latter should be achievable and measurable during a defined period, an educational ideal should be pursued throughout one's entire life. Even if, by nature, it is never achieved, one should attempt to come close. If an educational ideal was not formulated, it would also – presumably – not be systematically pursued.

Contemporary conception of education in this research is deeply rooted in humanistic philosophy. It has to be adapted for business leadership education in tertiary education. Considering both parts, business leadership and (tertiary) education as previously outlined, the educational ideal almost suggests itself, i.e. creative personality, which is in line with Faix and Mergenthaler (2015). Therefore, the question as to how an educational framework in business leadership education in tertiary education can be facilitated, which enables students to develop the educational ideal that is (creative) personality, has to be answered.

The answer to this question requires a logical train of thought. Starting point is the contemporary conception of education (see chapter 3.2.1 and Figure 10), wherein personality was set as an educational goal. Personality is defined as result of action. In turn, competencies, which are described as dispositions to act, are inherent to personality. Competencies can be developed systematically and play an important role in the personal development process. Consequently,

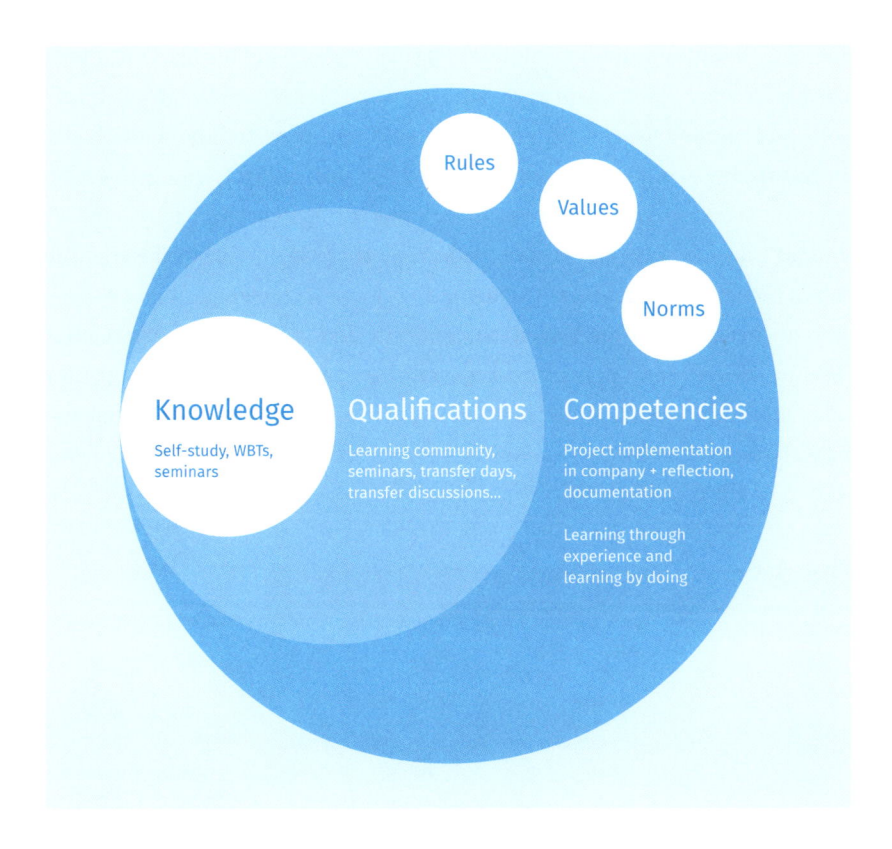

Figure 22. Knowledge, qualifications and competencies in the curriculum. Adapted from Faix and Mergenthaler, 2015, p. 183.

following this concept of education and the personal development process by facing the world and thereby developing their competencies, personalities contribute to the world by their action(s) and individual creativity and are essential for one's own development, the development of society, sciences and arts, economy etc. Due to the high importance of competency development, it has to be recapitulated that competencies comprise knowledge and qualifications. Moreover, competencies imply more, e.g. norms, rules, and values that are internalized and serve as regulators for self-organized actions as a premise to the capability to act in open, uncertain and complex situations (see chapter 3.1.4.4). Based on this understanding of competencies and their relations to knowledge, qualifications, and interiorized rules, values and norms and the comprehensive work of Erpenbeck (2012b) on fostering and development of competencies, Faix and Mergenthaler (2015) have designed an architecture for the development of personality (see Figure 22). Their learning architecture comprises all elements knowledge, qualifications, and competencies.

The latter in turn encompass interiorized rules, values, and norms. Educational contexts were assigned for each of the three elements knowledge, qualifications, and competencies. Thus, knowledge about theories, trends, methods etc. derives from e.g. self-studies, seminars, and / or web-based training. In a next step, the acquired knowledge has to be reflected against the background of student's own context and to be transferred concretely. Through the application of theory and its transfer to concrete, real-world challenges that are complex, uncertain, and open-ended, students traverse a process of experiential learning. Moreover, students must accomplish this autonomously. This process culminates in a reflection and written documentation in order to systematically challenge and foster the student's individual competency development.

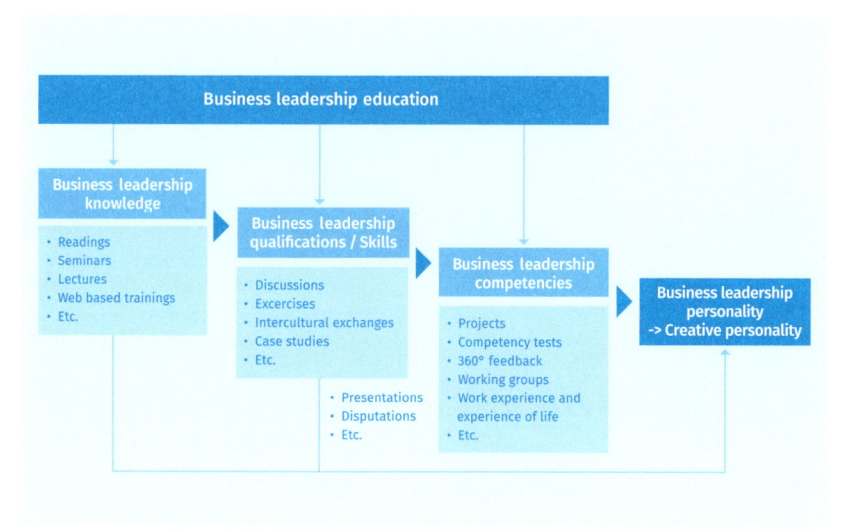

Figure 23. Model for business leadership education. Adapted from Faix et al., 2017b.

Based on this comprehensive architecture for the development of personality, Faix et al. (2017b) have thoroughly deduced a model for business leadership education (see Figure 23). By diligently integrating all elements of knowledge, qualifications / skills, and competencies and their respective educational contexts in the business leadership curriculum, an educational framework is facilitated that enables students to develop the educational ideal that is (creative) personality.

Superior educational ideal and educational goals are the foundation of the business leadership curriculum. Based on the educational ideal and goals, the third principle was developed.

3.2.5.3 Principle 3 – Educational contents

Having the superior educational ideal and goals in mind, which derived from the holistic model of business leadership and contemporary conception of education, the next step is the definition of educational contents (*Bildungsinhalte*) for business leadership curriculum.

As previously outlined, it is not intended to define an ideal curriculum on a detailed level. Consequently, no distinctive content and sequence of and in courses will be delivered. Reasons for this approach are the general principles of academic freedom and unity of research and teaching on one hand and respect for each higher education institution's individual culture and (research) orientation on the other. Moreover, there is no one singular truth and way to determine educational contents for business leadership curricula. Quite the contrary, diversity in curricula and educational contents is considered highly valuable and should be fostered in a global and diverse world. Thus, it has to be clearly pointed out that it is not intended to deliver a standard business leadership curriculum that can be implemented globally to produce streamlined and run-of-the-mill business leaders by enabling them to run the business by executing the fundamentals of business leadership techniques in order to raise profit margins. Rather, both education and business leadership are respectively embedded in a sociocultural context. Each higher education institution's characteristics and each student's unique (personal) potential shall unfold.

Therefore, a rough proportion of technical and functional knowledge versus competency-based aspects within curriculum shall be elaborated, which are necessary for contemporary and future-oriented business leadership education. In order to explain the different approaches further, reference is made to Walterscheid (1998), who explained both approaches, the objectivist and subjectivist educational paradigms, within the context of entrepreneurship education. Thereby, the objectivist educational paradigm was typified as an "old school" (p. 8) approach and the subjectivist educational paradigm as a "modern school" (p. 10) approach that both coexist. The objectivist educational paradigm is characterized by various aspects. Firstly, it is embedded in a material conception of education. Secondly, it is based on the storage of objective knowledge to be transmitted in educational processes. Thirdly, the learner is seen as a "medium of predetermined knowledge" (p. 7), while the teacher is considered a "representative of knowledge" (p. 7), who has to select and structure the knowledge in a way that the learner can easily consume it. Finally, the educational setting has to be detouched from the real living environment; that means to facilitate knowledge consumption in an (artificial) world without disturbances. In contrast, the subjectivist educational paradigm is characterized by different aspects. Firstly, education is conceived in a way that facilitates a subject's individual potentials. Secondly, by means of educational contents, the subjects gain experiences and grow. Educational contents, which represent complex, realistic, and holistic comprised issues, are considered suitable. Thirdly, education has to facilitate the gathering of experiences and assist in the individual processing of these experiences. Finally, within the subjectivist educational paradigm, the educational settings are quite realistic and close to professional life. Based on this subjectivist educational understanding, Bijedić (2013) conceptualized her model of entrepreneurship education that emphasizes the entrepreneurial personality.

Reflecting on the superior educational ideal and educational goals that were elaborated in the first two principles, which were deduced from the holistic model of business leadership and the contemporary conception of education, educational contents have to adapt to this pedagogical architecture. Thus, educational contents of contemporary and future-oriented business leadership education shall comprise all the elements theory, competency-based education, and reflection in a balanced proportion (see Figure 24):

> Theory: Technical and functional knowledge and qualification required to fulfill a business leadership position, comprising at least contents on

- Innovation

- Entre- and intrapreneurship that are basis for innovation

- Management of goals incl. methodologies on goal identification and goal setting procedures etc.

- Case studies

- Leadership knowledge, e.g. organizational behavior, leadership personality, competencies, ethics etc.

- Etc.

> Reality in the meaning of competency-based education that facilitates learners to gather experiences through actions:

- International and intercultural exchanges
- Field trips
- Real-world settings, e.g. internships, work experience, real-world business projects of companies etc.
- Competency tests incl. self-assessment, external assessments, feedback
- Etc.

Based on roots in ancient Greek philosophy (e.g. Socrates), the process of reflection plays an important role in learning (Daudelin, 1996). John Dewey (1859-1952) – a well-known American philosopher and educational reformer – thoroughly described the relationships among experience, reflection, and learning. In his work *How We Think* (Dewey, 1910), reflection is explained as an educational objective and is conceived as a cycle that learners elevate systematically, gathering depth with each turn (White & Guthrie, 2016). Thus, reflection is considered a complex personal cognitive process as the basis of learning and future behavior and action (Boud & Walker, 1991; Daudelin, 1996). It is a normal ongoing process that can be made even more structured and explicit (Boud & Walker, 1991; Grimes, 2015). Considering the nature of reflection, it is unambiguously pointed out in research literature that, while reflection is triggered by external factors, the process of reflection itself happens within an individual's mental self, even though others may assist in the process by e.g. asking questions, listening etc. (Boud & Walker, 1991; Daudelin, 1996). The relationship between reflection and learning is elaborated by Daudelin (1996):

> "Reflection is the process of stepping back from an experience to ponder, carefully and persistently, its meaning to the self through the development of inferences; learning is the creation of meaning from past or current events that serves as a guide for future behavior" (p. 39).

Nevertheless, Boud and Walker (1991) underline the intensity of a reflection process[43], as "it is a complex process in which both feelings and cognition are closely interrelated and interactive. It is an active process of exploration and discovery that often leads to unexpected outcomes" (p. 19).

In the context of this research, reflection is conceived as an intended structured learning process that is directed towards educational goals. It is highly important to incorporate structured reflective thinking in the business leadership curricula to enhance and consolidate the student's experiences and learning of leadership (Grimes, 2015; White & Guthrie, 2016). Various different reflective methods exist that have to be carefully selected and incorporated in curricula due to the respective goals, context, and culture. Regardless of the chosen reflective activities, systematically structured reflection is an essential pedagogical element in business leadership education. Reflection can be roughly categorized[44] in four groups, namely reading, telling, writing, and doing (Eyler, Giles & Schmiede, 1996). Therefore, the following reflective activities represent examples to be integrated in business leadership curricula:

> - Discussions
> - Working groups
> - Peer-Mentoring and Mentoring
> - Coaching
> - Transfer opportunities
> - Written reflection papers
> - Etc.

Based on the educational contents derived from the superior educational ideal and educational goals, the fourth principle was developed and elucidated in the following section.

---

43   For details on the different stages in the reflection process (based on Dewey), please see Daudelin (1996).
44   For more details please see Ash and Clayton (2004); Eyler (2001).

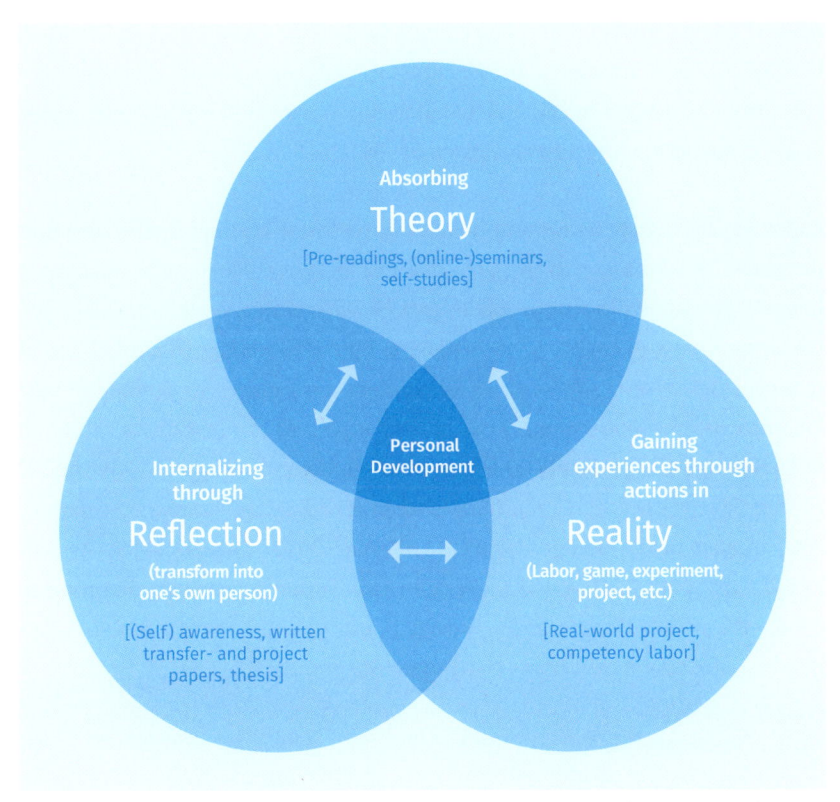

Figure 24. Educational contents of business leadership education. Adapted from Faix et al., 2017b.

3.2.5.4 Principle 4 – Educational methodologies

Educational methodologies specify how teaching and learning could be carried out. In order to shed light on educational methodologies that are best suited for the business leadership curricula in tertiary education, not only the educational ideal, educational goals and the educational contents have to be recapitulated, but also core characteristics for Master's level programs (ISCED level 7) described by UNESCO (2012a) and outlined in chapter 3.2.2.

Following the characteristics provided by UNESCO, it is important in designing Master's programs to define theoretically and / or professionally based content in order to provide knowledge, skills and competencies. Master's programs may comprise a considerable research part. Moreover, it is important to define entry requirements in order to establish a certain level and, in turn, to prepare for any following (doctoral) level.

Against this background of requirements for Master's level programs defined by UNESCO and principles on educational goals, educational goals and the educational contents for business leadership curricula in tertiary education, methodologies emerge almost automatically.

Following the logical considerations of this research, methodologies on a fundamental basis necessarily include academic learning to foster a broad base of knowledge and qualifications / skills (e.g. by self-studies, seminars, web based trainings, case studies etc.). Nevertheless, bulimic learning (*Bulimie-Lernen*) that "creates an environment where students are forced to memorize vast amounts of information with little attention paid to the long-term retention of knowledge and skills necessary to competently practice [a relevant field]" (Zorek, Sprague & Popovich., 2010) is often criticized as a non-contemporary consequence of the Bologna process (Haerder, 2012; Körner, 2015). As criticized earlier, students need more than conventional academic learning to cope with the challenges of an uncertain and unpredictable future in a dynamic environment. Küppers (2010) unerringly stated:

> "Living with the conditions brought about by the knowledge-based society will require a creative approach to ... information and knowledge. To do this, schools and universities must create the corresponding conditions now. In the future, it will be less important for educational institutions to convey knowledge and more important for them to convey a practical approach to knowledge that enables individuals to constructively handle this knowledge." (p. 170)

Thus, along with inquiry-based learning – that is higher education institution's mandate in order to prepare students for succeeding on the academic path – competency-based learning models shall be elucidated.

The term inquiry-based learning encompasses universities' two main scopes – research and learning – that are usually institutionally separated (Wildt, 2009). Although the general principle of unity of research and teaching may be evoked, according to Humboldtian point of view[45] it is primarily conceived as a unity, from whence educational contents emerges and is justified by research. However, although inquiry-based learning is conceived in different and

---

45   For details on "Humboldtianism", please see Bartz (2007).

opposing ways[46], Wildt (2009) points out the common roots of research and inquiry-based learning that is the curiosity to develop new insight. In order to gain new insight, inquiry is an essential element of the practice of science. The basic idea that science learning should adapt to science practice was put forward by Dewey (1964a; 1964b). In the course of time, research in cognitive science revealed the great importance of adequate contexts and activity for learning. Edelson, Gordin and Pea (1999) elaborated the differences between active and passive learning activities.

> "Authentic activities provide learners the motivation to acquire new knowledge, a perspective for incorporating knowledge into their existing knowledge, and an opportunity to apply their knowledge. In contrast to the passive reception of knowledge associated with conventional science learning, inquiry is active. As an authentic scientific practice, inquiry also provides a valuable context for science learning." (p. 393).

Consequently, higher education providers' task is to anchor inquiry-based learning as a systematic process in the curricula. Figure 25, which can also be explained as a systematic cycle for inquiry-based learning, therefore seems to be a suitable basis for a process to be implemented in the business leadership curricula. Sengstag (2001) elaborated various concrete proposals on how to integrate research in teaching, e.g. by thought experiments, work with scientific publications, writing of proposals, learning in and through internships etc. Beyond that, Wildt (2009) has developed a systematic process for inquiry-based learning, which is very similar in its basic idea and philosophy (see Figure 25). The very idea of this process is Dewey's concept of experience that is starting point for the Kolb's experiential learning cycle comprising four phases (Kolb, 1984), as the inner cycle shows. Therein, a learner takes a concrete experience and engages in reflective observation, hereinafter referred to reflection. The process of reflection that is often anteceded by what Dewey (1910) calls "a state of perplexity, hesitation, doubt" (p. 9), consequently may result in new knowledge and abstract conceptualization (see also chapter 3.2.5.3) that were verified in active experimentation. Experiences gained from this rotation are the basis for the next rotation, systematically achieving depth trough each (learning) cycle. The inner experiential learning cycle is

---

[46] For different point of views on inquiry-based learning please see e.g. Huber (1999) and Mittelstraß (1996); for a detailed perspective on opportunities and challenges of inquiry-based learning please see Edelson, Gordin & Pea (1999).

surrounded by the traditional research cycle. Due to many similar steps, the synchronization of the two cycles obviously seems to be possible.

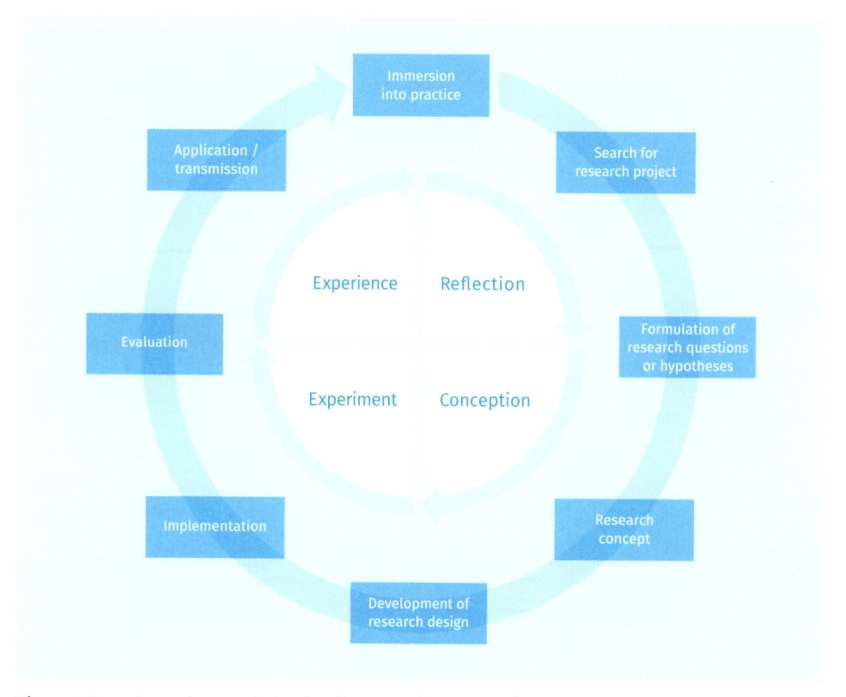

Figure 25. Learning cycle in the format of a research process. Adapted from Wildt, 2009, p. 6.

Irrespective of the choice for an inquiry-based learning process that is best suited to the respective curriculum, the very close proximity and overlap to reflection and competency development process is evident. They are often preceded by what Dewey (1910) calls "a state of perplexity, hesitation, doubt" (p. 9), or by what Erpenbeck (2012b) calls "emotional destabilization", i.e. irritating situations, situations characterized by painful processes or situations that result in reorientation. In other words, it is what Neiman (2014), a contemporary US American philosopher describes in her work *Why grow up*: "It is reason's removal from simple knowledge of reality that allows it to step back and ask why reality is this way rather than that – the condition on creative activity and social change alike" (p. 191).

Hence, a combination of inquiry-based learning and competency-based learning may be a logical consequence. Reviewing research literature reveals that there is no single definition of competency-based education; rather, it has been defined in various ways. According to Le, Wolfe and Steinberg (2014) competency-based education "is an evolving field with no universally shared definition of what makes a model 'competency-based'" (p. 1). Gervais (2016) defined competency-based education (CBE) in a comprehensive way,

> "as an outcome-based approach that incorporates modes of instructional delivery and assessment efforts designed to evaluate mastery of learning by students through their demonstration of the knowledge, attitudes, values, skills, and behaviors required for the degree sought" (p. 2).

Nevertheless, CBE may also be conceived as a kind of umbrella term that embraces various methodologies, leading to competency development such as problem-based learning, project-based learning, work-integrated learning, experience-based learning, action learning etc. It is not aimed at presenting the various methodologies in detail[47]; rather, it is considered relevant to delineate their common denominator for CBE.

Thus, with regard to business leadership education common elements of the aforementioned methodologies under the umbrella of CBE are twofold. Firstly, they aim to promote students' action-oriented learning. Secondly, instruments for students to demonstrate their action-orientation are real-world challenges, i.e. real-world problems emerging from the entrepreneurial and / or scientific environment. In his work, *Projektstudium,* Tippelt (1979) provided sound foundations for the three learning principles crucial in the context of this research, namely exemplary, activity-oriented and inquiry-based learning. He not only formulated theses for action research, but also criteria required for actions as a basis for action research. In order to avoid succumbing to pointless actions, Tippelt (1979) proposes six general criteria for actions within CBE in tertiary education. These six criteria in turn require the learner / researcher to possess knowledge of the empirical-analytical theory of science and allow thinking processes for decision-making. Since Tippelt's work is as topical now as when he wrote it nearly 40 years ago, his six criteria are generalized for this research:

---

47   There is a vast amount of research on several educational methodologies. For details on the variety of educational methodologies mentioned in this chapter, please see e.g. Béchard & Grégoire, 2005; Braßler & Dettmers, 2016; Chin & Chia, 2004; Erpenbeck, 2012b; Faix & Mergenthaler, 2015; Fischer, Müller & Tippelt, 2011; Ganz & Lin, 2012; Gervais, 2016; Gonzo, 1981/1982; Jones, Rasmussen & Moffitt, 1997; Katz-Buonincontro & Ghosh, 2014; Lysø, Mjøen & Levin, 2011; Nabi et al., 2016; Paulson, 2001; Pittaway & Cope, 2007; Schaper, Schlömer & Paechter, 2012; Schneider, 2009; Sirelkhatim & Gangi, 2015; Tippelt, 1979; Vorhees, 2001.

1. Scientific criteria have priority over operational urgencies emerging in practice, e.g. urgency in decision-making.

2. Research based on sound methodologies supersedes the generation of pragmatic knowledge for immediate usage.

3. Sound theoretical foundations and broad information basis supersede the provision of partial and unilateral information ("agitation", p. 168).

4. Scientific standards supersede the effectivity of action. Scientific standards were formulated based on Habermas (in Tippelt, 1979), i.e. consensus within a group (democratic principle), explication, legitimation of information's validity, transparency of research methodologies.

5. The distinctive expertise of learners and / or researchers shall not be neglected.

6. Comprehensibility and transparency in research are limitations for the fifth criterion.

Furthermore, based on distinctive research in the application of real-world challenges in curricula, the following – at least – three distinctive criteria have to be fulfilled:

1. Real-world challenges have to be an integral part of the curriculum; they have to be embedded in the learning process in order to tie in with existing knowledge, experiences and competencies in order to enable students to systematically develop their competencies (Katz-Buonincontro & Ghosh, 2014).

2. Real-world challenges have to be complex, uncertain and open-ended projects that students have to accomplish autonomously (see chapter 3.2.5.2). In order to optimally enable students' learning and competency development within social constructivist pedagogy[48], it is decisive to facilitate a safe learning environment for learners to ask questions, to express themselves freely, to share their thoughts and reflections and to mutually inspire each other (Hamilton, 1996; Porter, 1997). A safe, positive, and motivating learning environment allows students to fail and try again (Chen, 1997; Spitzer, 1998). While students can select and arrange their learning processes with mentors (from e.g. university and / or corporate practice) in a self-organized way within a curriculum's boundaries, instructors have to fulfill the role of a process facilitator responsible

---

[48] For details, please see e.g. Arnold, 2012. When designing social constructivist pedagogy, please also see e.g. Chin & Chia, 2004; Huang, 2002; Ruey, 2010.

for the quality of learning and discussions (e.g. with mentors or peers) (Béchard & Grégoire, 2005; Westera, 1999).

3. Real-world challenges are – from a pedagogical point of view and based on Humboldt – an instrument, i.e. a means to an end for students to transform the world as much as possible according to their own perception. Thereby, students personal and competency development process is initiated, which is a crucial part of Faix's and Kisgen's educational cycle (see Figure 10).

Examples for real-world challenges, wherein actions and competencies may be demonstrated, are:

> Real-world projects that emerge from corporate or scientific practice
> Workplace problems
> Internships
> Experiments
> Labor
> Games
> Etc.

It needs to be pointed out that action-orientation is crucial to stimulate the learning process. It is rooted in Dewey's philosophy that understanding experiences is pivotal in (adult) learning (Dewey, 1938). Moreover, this idea is also put forward by AACSB (2010). In order to develop innovative managers and business leaders, education has to go beyond theories and concepts; rather, practice and feedback are required.

> "When considering the extent to which business schools have done well in developing skills, it must be admitted that many curriculum discussions tend to focus more on content than on pedagogy – even while most management practitioners believe that it is best to learn and develop softer skills through practice with feedback, and through realized opportunities to fail." (AACSB, 2010, p. 23)

Differentiation is required between case studies – widely spread and traditionally used in management and leadership education, especially in MBA programs – and real-world challenges. Due to Mintzberg (2005), and Gosling and Mintzberg (2006), facts and case studies were overvalued, while competency development through experiences is undervalued. Katz-Buonincontro and Ghosh (2014) have clearly pointed out that case studies stop at a theoretical level, e.g. in the form of conceptualization, rather than acting in practice and thereby gaining experiences.

Based on the framework previously outlined, higher education institutions have to incorporate competency-based education in business leadership curricula to enable students to develop their (creative) personalities and their various (business leadership) competencies systematically which, in turn, prepares them for (business) leadership positions. Integration of competency-based education cannot be taken for granted in today's business leadership education in tertiary education (see chapter 4) it is rather– still – an exception. However, according to Mulgan and Townsley (2016), there are various precedents for pedagogy emphasizing real-world problems in medical schools, engineering and other disciplines of education. For exemplary reasons, higher education institutions that have incorporated competency-based education in their curriculum and are closely connected to the context of this research are University of Waterloo / Canada, Maastricht University / Netherlands and Aalto University / Finland. The universities' essential learning models with regard to competency-based education shall be described briefly.

University of Waterloo / Canada has implemented a model of co-operative education, combining both academic education with workplace experiences. According to the university's website[49], 19,000 students are enrolled over three semesters in more than 120 programs across the disciplines Applied Health Services, Arts, Engineering, Environment, Mathematics, Science. The various disciplines do not comprise a distinctive graduate program in business leadership education, but rather two undergraduate Bachelor's degree programs in the broader field of management that are Accounting and Financial Management and Computing and Financial Management. Students participating in this education model, split their time between alternating study and work terms, wherein each of the terms is about four month long. Students have to apply knowledge learned in university on assessed work placements. While curriculum details are not publicly available on the website, the overall program description highlights the combination of Computer Science that uses technology to solve real-world problems with focus on Financial Management. In contrast, program details about courses, sequence of courses, and

---

49   For further details, please see https://uwaterloo.ca.

study sequence of work and study terms are available for the undergraduate Bachelor's degree program in Accounting and Financial Management. Furthermore, the presented underlying learning model (see Figure 26) is aiming to develop knowledge, skills, and professional qualities. Therefore, Figure 26 presents a three-level approach beginning with the understanding of core concepts, followed by applying knowledge and is finally completed by integrating it through courses, experiences of the co-operative workplace experiences, extra-curricular experiences, etc.

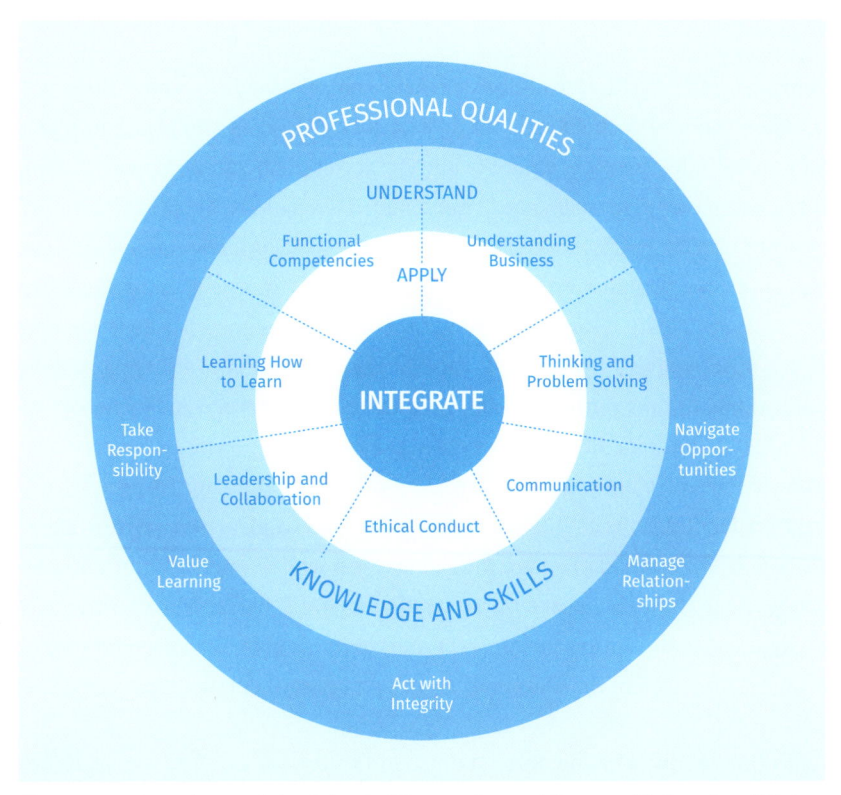

Figure 26. Learning model – School of Accounting and Finance / University of Waterloo. Adapted from the Website https://uwaterloo.ca.

Maastricht University / Netherlands, one of the youngest universities in the Netherlands, with 16,500 students enrolled and 55,000 alumni[50], uses a problem-based learning model in many of the university's degree programs as one of their unique selling propositions. One of the programs using the problem-based learning model is the graduate program Master of Science in

---

50   For further details, please see https://www.maastrichtuniversity.nl.

International Business. In this program, problem-based learning model is described on the website as follows:

> "In small tutorial groups of no more than 15 students, you seek solutions to 'problems' taken from real-world situations. Instructors only give help as it's needed, allowing you to develop independence and problem-solving skills useful to your career. This active, dynamic, and collaborative learning system has one of the highest knowledge retention rates of any instructional method." (https://www.maastrichtuniversity.nl)

However, Maastricht University's problem-based learning model does not provide real-world challenges, as previously defined, as complex, uncertain and open-ended projects students have to accomplish autonomously; rather, it seems to offer discussions on "'problems' taken from real-world situations" that are similar to case studies. Consequently, problem-solving qualification and skills can be enhanced, but this approach may not be grouped together with action-oriented learning and does not promote competency development in the strict sense. Nevertheless, various specializations comprising further educational opportunities are offered in the graduate program Master of Science in International Business. Based on the website's information, real-world experiences were offered through real-world assignments for companies, educational institutions or NGOs, internships as 8-26 week extracurricular activity and a combination of a part-time internship with Master's thesis, wherein the Master's thesis is focused on a topic that emerges from corporate practice. Students have the option (to apply for and) to participate in these educational options; they are not mandatory or an integral part of curriculum.

Aalto University / Finland was established in the year 2010 as a merger between three leading universities in technology, economics, and art and design. It has not only been seen as a flagship project among Finland's higher education and innovation environment but it is also of high importance for the country's holistic approach to innovation (Björklund et al., 2011). Today, Aalto University consists of six schools; 20,000 students are enrolled and around 1,600 students acquire their Master's degrees from Aalto University annually.[51] For exemplary reasons, the focus is on the Aalto University Master's program in Management and International Business due to its close connection to the topic of this research. The program

---

51 For further details, please see http://www.aalto.fi.

"...is a practically grounded and research-based understanding of management and international business. The programme encourages students to cross disciplinary boundaries, engage with tough challenges, connect practice with scholarship, invite creativity, and lead inclusive futures". (http://www.aalto.fi/en)

Degree requirements are 120 ECTS, divided in program studies (84 ECTS), minor studies (24 ECTS) and electives (12 ECTS). The program studies (84 ECTS) comprise common studies (48 ECTS) and specialization studies (36 ECTS). The latter, in turn, include a business development project (6 ECTS) as mandatory element of curriculum. The workload comprises project work in teams (130 - 134 h), classroom contact hours (6 - 8 h), individual work (20 h) and team meetings with facilitator (3 h), aiming to enable students to:

> "identify, analyse and solve real-life business problems from a multi-disciplinary viewpoint
> apply the knowledge and skills gained during their studies to real-life business tasks and challenges
> manage complex projects and work in diverse teams
> present a case report both orally and in writing
> critically reflect on their learning process and outcomes." (https://www.aalto.fi)

According to the module description, the course encompasses "an applied, real-life problem-based project / case that students identify, analyze, and solve in multi-disciplinary teams. It also focuses on developing the students' self-awareness of the key learnings during their studies in the Master's Program" (https://www.aalto.fi). The leading concept of the Aalto University is to encourage student-centered activities, creativity and continuous learning and, among others, challenge traditional teaching boundaries. Anyway, at least 5 % of the Master's program in Management and International Business consists of mandatory real-world challenges.

In addition to degree programs, interdisciplinary "factories" are designed at Aalto University that are health, design and media factory, wherein teams of scholars and students co-operate with companies and communities to develop new products and to search for solutions of health and well-being related problems that cater to the needs from real business and economy. Moreover, new areas of media research and the launch of joint research projects between Aalto University's different schools shall be initiated. Focusing on the innovative approach of Aalto University's design factory (ADF), it is not only described "as a catalyst – a platform for possibilities". Moreover, it is delineated that "experimentation is the art of trying things out in real life" (ADF, 2015, p. 46). Their learning philosophy shall enable students

> "to utilize their disciplinary knowledge effectively in increasingly complex and interdisciplinary environments. They need to step out of their disciplinary silos to efficiently collaborate with people representing a multitude of disciplines and cultures, as well as to adopt a holistic view to confront the challenges presented by the working life." (http://designfactory.aalto.fi)

Therefore, ADF provides an environment, which fosters experiential learning, embracing various elements of learning, e.g. real-world problems, interdisciplinary group work, gathering and evaluation of information and reflection. Moreover, students are considered active knowledge creators, while teachers are seen as facilitators etc. Referring to the manifold elements of learning, it is hardly surprising that they specified this way of learning as "passion based learning". Even if ADF does not lead to an academic degree in tertiary education, it was highlighted in this research due to its innovative character that may inspire the design of business leadership curricula.

Along with the three aforementioned examples, SIBE / Germany provides a holistic approach of competency-based education, wherein students have to accomplish a real-world challenge – emerging from the corporate world – during their Master's program. Approx. 600 students are enrolled and more than 3,500 graduates have passed this education model in Master in Management programs (see chapter 3.1.4.4). SIBE / Germany has incorporated a real-world project as integral part, comprising 50 % of its Experience-Based Curriculum (see Figure 27). Students apply theory, the second 50 % of the curriculum, on corporate real-world challenges, and have the opportunity to gain valuable experiences and future job offers. Due to its integral part of the curriculum, university assess students' scientific performance in written reports (project documentation), whereas employers assess students' performance on workplace.

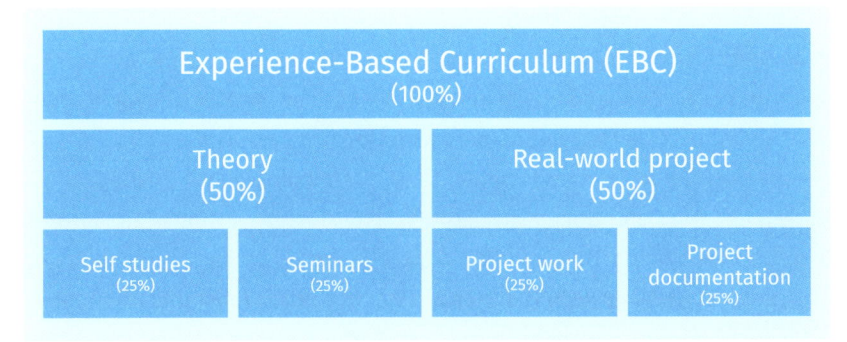

```
┌─────────────────────────────────────────────────────────┐
│           Experience-Based Curriculum (EBC)             │
│                       (100%)                            │
├───────────────────────────┬─────────────────────────────┤
│         Theory            │      Real-world project     │
│         (50%)             │           (50%)             │
├─────────────┬─────────────┼──────────────┬──────────────┤
│ Self studies│  Seminars   │ Project work │   Project    │
│   (25%)     │   (25%)     │    (25%)     │documentation │
│             │             │              │    (25%)     │
└─────────────┴─────────────┴──────────────┴──────────────┘
```

Figure 27.   Ideal course of Experience-Based Curriculum (Formerly called as 'Talent Growth Curriculum'). Adapted from Faix and Mergenthaler, 2015, p. 165.

Thereby, implementing SIBE's EBC means not only to represent all elements of theory, competence-based education and reflection in a balanced proportion in educational contents, but also in educational methodologies (see also Figure 24).

As the different examples and precedents show, competency-based learning incorporating real-world challenges in curricula that meet the appropriate pedagogical requirements are – still – an exception. Moreover, in-depth research is necessary to identify differences and meaning of the promoted methodologies and used pedagogy. Educational methodologies are the centerpiece of curricula that allow to distinguish business leadership programs with focus on knowledge transmission from learner-centered business leadership programs that enables students to develop their individual personality and competencies. Educational methodologies are the centerpiece of curricula that allow separating the wheat from the chaff.

With regard to educational methodologies described in the fourth principle, it is the task of higher education institutions to facilitate the educational settings for inquiry-based and competency-based learning in their business leadership curricula. Therefore, the fifth principle is defined.

3.2.5.5   Principle 5 – Educational settings

For the purpose of this research, educational settings are conceived in a broad sense, referring to the wide variety of settings in which students may learn to embrace e.g. diverse cultures, contexts and physical locations, the ways in which instructors may organize a setting to enable learning and the way students interact with each other. Thus, educational settings aim to facilitate a space and place that students foster and support to construct knowledge, understanding and develop competencies relevant for meaningful and authentic problem solving and action (Wilson, 1998). Based on a sound theoretical basis, Huang (2002) developed social constructivist pedagogy for adult learners in distance education. Due to its relevance and close association with the topic of business leadership, trends and challenges in tertiary (business leadership) education and four principles previously outlined, Huang's basic principles are proposed to be considered in business leadership education in tertiary education in general:

1. Interactive learning: Interaction with instructors and peers is preferred in contrast to engaging in isolated learning in order to foster and stimulate reflection and learning.

2. Collaborative learning: Collaboration is essential to engage in collaborative knowledge construction, learning through social negotiation and reflection.

3. Facilitating learning: It is crucial to provide a motivating, positive, and safe learning environment, in which thoughts may be shared, questions asked and failures allowed (see also chapter 3.2.5.4).

4. Authentic learning: Learning shall be connected with students' real-world problems or work experiences to foster meaningful and authentic knowledge, understanding, and development of competencies.

5. Student-centered learning: Students shall be encouraged to actively create learning processes. Self-directed, autonomous, and individual learning is suitable for e.g. problem solving and experiential learning.

6. High-quality learning: Emphasis is placed on evoking students' critical thinking skills and reflection on their lives, to enable students to analyze, manage and transform information into valuable knowledge based on prior experiences.

Moreover, three educational settings emerging from deductive reasoning are seen to be pivotal and indispensable in order to facilitate contemporary and future-directed business leadership education in tertiary education, allowing students' to thrive in the 21st century. These three educational settings are proposed to be considered in business leadership education in tertiary education, i.e.

1. Real-world setting: Please see in detail fourth principle in previous chapter 3.2.5.4.

2. Technological setting: Technological developments in general and educational technology in particular are in constant state of development. Therefore, technological setting facilitated in tertiary education has to keep pace with technology and play at least a certain role in any offered Master's program. Thus, to propose a minimum criterion for business leadership education, (interactive) online education has to complement face-to-face programs. To prepare for future-oriented business leadership education in tertiary education, the question of how interactive pedagogical and social potentials of online education can be best facilitated for the complete program in the best possible manner, has to be considered and scrutinized (Altbach, Reisberg & Rumbley, 2009; Huang, 2002; Marginson & Wende, 2007; OECD, 2005; Ruey, 2010; Wannemacher & Geidel, 2016).

3. International setting: Globalization and internationalization are common phenomena (Faix et al., 2006). Tertiary education in particular have always been influenced by international trends and operated – at least to a certain degree – in an international context. Nevertheless, global interconnectedness has gained in importance in 21st century (Altbach, Reisberg & Rumbley, 2009; Wannemacher & Geidel, 2016). Therefore, business leadership education in tertiary education has to explicitly facilitate international settings to foster the mobility of students (and scholars and teaching-staff) and contemporary cross-border education in a global world at a governmental, institutional and individual level e.g. by joint- or dual- degree programs, facilitating study abroad, field trips, internships etc.

With regard to educational settings described in fifth principle, it is the task of higher education institutions to facilitate the educational settings in their business leadership curricula to foster and stimulate students to construct knowledge, understanding and develop competencies relevant for meaningful and authentic problem solving and action. In order to evaluate the learning process, the sixth principle is defined.

3.2.5.6 Principle 6 – Evaluation

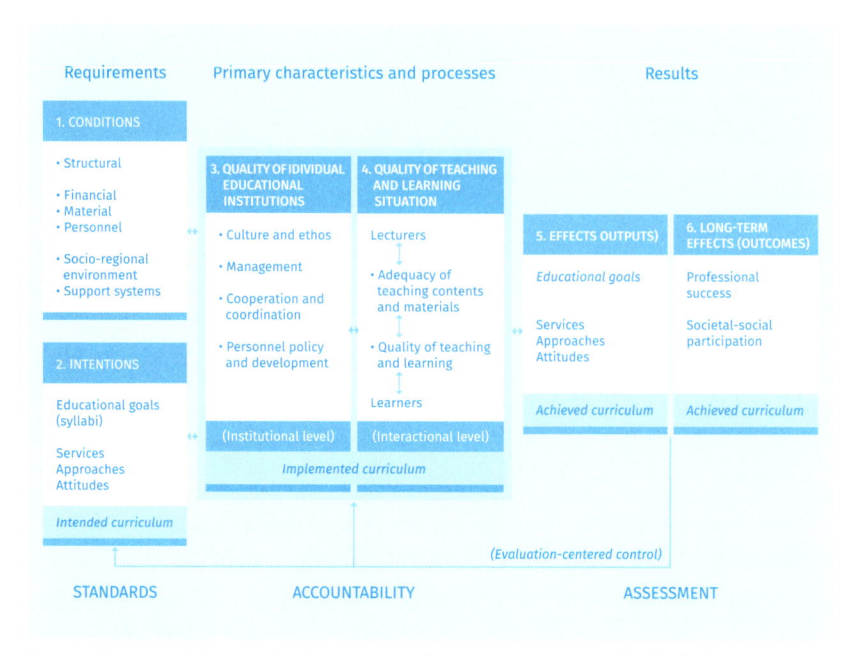

Figure 28. Model on evaluation and quality assurance in the field of education. Adapted from Ditton, 2010, p. 609.

Evaluation gained attention in tertiary education as an essential part of quality assurance. Nevertheless, neither a clear definition nor a general accepted systematization exists among the various approaches (Altbach, Reisberg & Rumbley, 2009; Ditton, 2010). The Joint Committee on Standards for Educational Evaluation (1999) defines evaluation as "systematic analysis of an object's usability or quality" (p. 25). Nevertheless, considering different definitions the purpose-orientation and target-orientation of evaluation can be pointed out as a common denominator (Cronbach, 1972; Kempfert & Rolff, 2005; Schmidt, Hippel & Tippelt, 2010). Furthermore, in order to assess and evaluate quality and success of tertiary education, a variety of stakeholders' interests have to be considered. Ditton (2010) elaborated a comprehensive model on evaluation and quality assurance in the educational context, which is presented in Figure 28. According to this model, the program's intention and goals are crucial compared to the achieved results and long-term outcomes. Based on the program's goals, requirements and resources have to be assured along with institutional aspects, and a program's specific aspects with regard to teaching and learning in order to achieve the program's goals.

Diamond (2008) comprehensively captures the complex phenomenon of evaluations for higher education institutions:

> „In every institution, the final determinant of the quality of the academic program is the performance of its graduates. The degree of success will depend on how well the curriculum is delivered through its courses and other learning experiences provided to students. Every student must have the opportunity to reach and demonstrate every stated basic competency. Carefully articulated learning outcomes must be the basis on which instructional methods are chosen and the criteria by which competency must be measured. The effectiveness of an institution or program and of individual faculty members is then determined by the ability of students to meet these goals." (p. 91)

Schmidt, Hippel and Tippelt (2010) categorized evaluation according to their divergent conceptual use in five dimensions context, input, process, output, and outcome (Schmidt, Hippel & Tippelt, 2010). Furthermore, the authors differentiate evaluation procedures in three levels:

1. Evaluations on the micro level encompass "teaching-learning processes" and "participants' actions" (p. 100).
2. Evaluations on the meso level are resource-oriented (e.g. institutional, personnel-related, faculty resources etc.), research achievements etc. comprising accreditation procedures as well as university and / or program rankings. The latter are considered an instrument "to inform the 'consumers'" (p. 105).[52]
3. Evaluations on the macro level focus on analyzing graduates' transitions and career progress, i.e. the (university) outcome.

For the purpose of this research, the three level-approach elaborated by Schmidt, Hippel and Tippelt (2010) shall be applied to business leadership education in tertiary education. Therefore, it is pointed out:

1. Evaluations on the micro level in business leadership education in tertiary education: Starting points are defined and legitimized educational

---

[52] Rankings are a highly debatable issue. Thus, not only methodological aspects and the dominance and hegemony of the elite Anglo-Saxon research university are questioned but also their use as an instrument for the assessment of research and teaching. For details, please see Marope and Wells (2013); Ordorika and Lloyd (2014); Rauhvargers (2013); Schmidt, Hippel and Tippelt (2010).

goals (see chapter 3.2.5.1), which are embedded in a complex sociocultural context (see chapter 3.2.4). Shuell (1986) underlines instructors' main task "to get students to engage in learning activities that are likely to result in their achieving those outcomes" (p. 429), which in turn refers to constructivist pedagogy. Thus, the focus is not on the traditional and conventional way of knowledge transmission by teachers, rather on construction of knowledge and competency development through students' own (learning) activities. Consequently, outcomes have to be assessed and evaluated based on educational goals defined in advance and encompass both teaching-learning processes and students' performance.

Against this background, higher education institutions have to identify evaluation and assessment strategies best suited to their culture and curriculum design. Following the logical considerations of the initial principles for the curriculum design, it is not intended students to remember and reproduce information. Rather, the focus has to be on the students' rearrangement of information, use of information after accomplishment of reflection and learning process (Zorek, Sprague & Popovich, 2010) along with students' competency development (Schaper, Schlömer & Paechter, 2012). Examples for methods to assess and evaluate students' performance, wherein actions and competencies may be demonstrated are:

> Written papers that demonstrate reflection and learning processes

> Presentations and oral disputations

> Thesis referring to real-world challenges

> Etc.

2. Evaluations on the meso level in business leadership education in tertiary education: Accreditation[53] of programs or / and institutions, a system of quality measurement aiming for quality assurance (Schmidt, Hippel and Tippelt, 2010), is not only inevitable in the USA and post-Bologna Europe, but also a worldwide phenomenon in tertiary education in general as well as business leadership education in tertiary education. As rankings mainly pursue the purpose of consumer information and are not considered an instrument for the quality assessment of research and teaching, they are not taken into account in this context.

3. Evaluations on the macro level in business leadership education in tertiary education: Employment reports – sometimes synonymously referred

---

53 For critical considerations on accreditation, please see Burke & Butler, 2012.

to as career reports – are common practice in order to analyze graduates' transitions and career progress based on student data. An employment report contains structural and statistical student and alumni data. Student data generally reveals acceptance rate, demographical data, work experience (average and range) etc. Alumni data is collected at a particular time after graduation (i.e. three month or three years) and generally provides gender distribution, average age, employment rate, average starting salary, average salary three years after graduation, placement by functional area, sector and position (with or without leadership position), percentage that have founded a business etc. Referring to outcomes based education, employment reports give in-depth insight not only for (potential) students, employers etc. but also for accreditation agencies.

Nevertheless, it has to be pointed out that curriculum design is not completed, but has to be continuously developed and improved due to its integration in sociocultural context (see chapter 3.2.4). Furthermore, along with the six principles for curriculum design elaborated previously, the fundamental question of the funding of tertiary education shall be elucidated. Therefore, the seventh principle is defined.

3.2.5.7 Principle 7 – Financing

Tertiary education is of great importance for the development of individuals, society, innovation and economic development (see chapter 3.2.2). Due to its immense contributions to and benefit for society and economic development, tertiary education has been traditionally conceived as a public asset (Altbach, Reisberg & Rumbley, 2009). Nevertheless, on a transnational level, governmental tax revenues are neither willing nor able to cover rising costs of tertiary education. Salmi and Hauptman (2006) explain this phenomenon by one principal challenge that is the growing demand for tertiary education. The authors not only refer to the increase in student enrolments worldwide, which is generally discussed as massification (see chapter 3.2.2.1). Rather, the authors specify the immense increase in demand for several reasons. Firstly, return on education upon completion of tertiary education is higher when compared to secondary education or less. Secondly, strong social pressures on students to achieve academic degrees in tertiary education can be observed in order to improve prestige and social reputation. Finally, many countries try to promote emerging and relevant disciplines such as engineering, science and information technology. Furthermore, rivaling demands on public resources (e.g. health care, transportation etc.) challenge budget allocations. In summary, rising financial pressures hamper students' access to and success in tertiary education (Johnstone, 2016). Therefore, alternatives to public funding and innovative solutions are needed to finance tertiary education and cope with multitude of challenges.

Various alternatives are already implemented and are a matter of course. Thus, an increase in private higher education can be observed worldwide. Private higher education is usually financed by tuition revenue. In several countries, other financial sources, e.g. student grants or loans, contributions from alumni, corporate or individual donors, or personal wealth of higher education institutions' owner / s, are possible (Altbach, Reisberg & Rumbley, 2009). One alternative to acquire (additional) private resources is the commercialization e.g. of research (Salmi & Hauptman, 2006). Debates on financing tertiary education are ongoing along with evaluation and identification of innovative allocation mechanisms (Johnstone, 2016; Salmi & Hauptman, 2006; Ziegele, 2010). Irrespective of the sources of funds, implications for respective stakeholders have to be thoroughly considered.

Globally ongoing debates on financing tertiary education in general – including the discipline of business leadership education – are of great importance on a supranational, governmental, institutional, corporate, and individual level.

3.2.6   Conclusions

This part of the chapter aimed at answering the first research question of this work. Therefore, in order to elucidate the theoretical foundations of business leadership education in tertiary education for graduates, the essentials of business leadership were elaborated in a first step before light was shed on the pedagogical perspective.

Due to the immense number and variety of definitions and theoretical approaches to leadership, a choice was made. The most prevalent approaches deriving from the discipline of psychology were elucidated. Despite their valuable contributions to leadership research, various strengths and (methodological) shortcomings were outlined. Moreover, it was pointed out that the (traditional) approaches merely reflect a fragmentary instead of a holistic perspective on leadership, failing to measure leaders' performance. Besides, the assessment center belonging to the most popular diagnostic procedures was described. Considering ACs from a positive point of view, the main purpose of ACs may lie in a culture-directed selection of (potential) business leaders when assessors are (higher) leaders. In spite of various improvements, (not all) ACs are able to predict leaders' future job performance. Reliance on only ACs to select future leaders therefore seems to be insufficient, and in many instances, misleading.

Moreover, findings of different disciplines mainly from human ethology and organizational sciences, were compiled due to their high impact on leadership and to obtain a comprehensive overview on the studied topic. Thus, not only humans' leadership behaviors play a vital role in business leadership, but also entrepreneurial leadership.

Due to various external (political, economic, socio-cultural, technological, and legal) influencing factors on (business) environment and with respect to the research topic within the discipline of pedagogics, a contemporary and holistic model of business leadership was developed. This holistic model comprises both the business perspective, i.e. goals and innovations as well as the perspective on the leader's individual personality, i.e. creative personality, business leadership competencies and networks. Moreover, the business leader is not conceived as being isolated, but rather acting in a complex sociocultural context with its multitude of influential factors. Consequently, a holistic definition of business leadership deductively emerged, which is the foundation of this research. Based on the holistic understanding of business leadership, concrete and specific KPIs were defined in order to evaluate (potential) business leaders' performance. Those KPIs are relevant for individuals and organizations in order to select and develop (potential) business leaders and / or to evaluate (current) business leaders. Based on these KPIs it was assumed (hypothesized) that (potential) leader's performance can be better predicted than based on existing (selection) procedures, which has to be tested in future research.

However, although the term *leadership* in this research largely pertains to leadership in the business context, particularly with regard to leadership in business corporations, companies, enterprises, organizations etc., the various aspects and the holistic model of business leadership elaborated can easily be adapted to other domains by considering their specific mission and characteristics.

This contemporary and holistic understanding of business leadership in a dynamic environment laid the foundation for a contemporary humanistic approach on business leadership education in tertiary education deeply rooted in humanistic philosophy. Pivotal goal of this approach is fostering individuals across their entire lifespan to develop their personalities, which is demonstrated by their actions and contributions to nature, other human beings, society, organizations etc. Against this background, the focus was on the segment of tertiary education in general and the discipline of business leadership education in particular and the major trends and challenges both have handle on a worldwide scale. Based on current debates a brand new definition seems to be indispensable in order to design contemporary and future-oriented business leadership education in tertiary education from a pedagogical point of view. To do so, the pedagogical infrastructure for business leadership education in tertiary education that is *curriculum* was examined. Curriculum is conceived as an 'academic plan' that is not static, but rather open-ended in nature. It is experienced by its students and embedded in a dynamic environment and complex sociocultural context with its manifold influencing factors.

Nevertheless, it was not intended to define an ideal curriculum on a detailed level. In contrast, diversity shall be nourished and maintained. Therefore, the general principles of academic freedom, unity of research and teaching and each higher education institution's individual culture and (research) orientation were respected. In order to answer the first research question of this research – how business leadership education in Master's programs for graduates in tertiary education shall be designed –, seven main principles for a curriculum of business leadership education in Master's programs in tertiary education were proposed. The seven principles are deeply rooted in theory and reflect the main questions that have to be answered in a didactic approach. Each of the seven principles was thoroughly elaborated, providing a kind of orientation and guidelines for higher education institutions for curriculum design in business leadership education.

Synthesizing the essential results of curriculum design based on the seven principles proposed, two findings shall be disclosed. Firstly, business leadership education in tertiary education has to focus on student's familiarization with the scientific world on one hand and the individual student's (creative) personality and its competency development on the other. Secondly, a curriculum with its elements – i.e. educational contents, educational methodologies, educational settings, and evaluation – has to ensure a consistent pedagogical infrastructure that nurtures the development of the individual student's business leader personality. Such an infrastructure is characterized by competency-based education. As competency-based education is conceived as an umbrella term, various ways to carry it out are possible. Each higher education institution has to find its own way best suitable for their respective (research) orientation and (institutional) culture.

In a next step, contemporary practice of a sample in business leadership education in tertiary education shall be analyzed in light of the seven principles proposed for the curriculum of business leadership education in tertiary education for graduates.

4. Business leadership education in tertiary education for graduates – Evaluation of exemplary Master's programs

Based on the holistic understanding of business leadership and theoretical foundations of business leadership education in tertiary education for graduates, this chapter focuses on the second research question (chapter 2). An evaluation procedure was chosen in order to answer the second research question, how business leadership education in contemporary tertiary education is practiced in exemplary Master's programs for graduates in the light of the theoretical framework. Therefore, the basic idea of an evaluation procedure elaborated by Ditton (2010) was generalized and applied to this research, in order "to determine the relevant individual factors …, to analyze them in mutual reference to each other and to develop … recommendations for revisions" (p. 608). Thus, a sample of the Master's programs in contemporary tertiary education was evaluated in the light of the theoretical framework.

4.1 Methodology

Figure 29. Evaluation procedures for exemplary Master's programs.

To obtain insight into the Master's programs as they were practiced in contemporary tertiary education information should be aggregated and analyzed following a rigorous systematic evaluation approach based on qualitative research. In order to meet the demands of qualitative research, a comprehensible systematic procedure following strict rules has to be documented (Gläser-Zikuda, 2011). Figure 29 illustrates the overall procedures and the individual phases. After having developed evaluation criteria in a first step, exemplary Master's programs were selected in step two as a basis for systematic data collection in step three. The data were analyzed in step four, finally interpreted, and discussed.

The individual steps are elaborated in the following sections.

4.1.1 Development of evaluation criteria

Based on the theoretical foundations of business leadership education in tertiary education and the proposed principles for curriculum design that were thoroughly developed (chapter 3.2.5), these seven principles shall be the corollary criteria for evaluation of exemplary Master's programs. In order to operationalize the criteria, several didactic components were developed as sub-criteria for each criterion, based on the theoretical foundation in chapter 3.2.5. Consequently, the evaluation criteria and its sub-criteria are as follows:

1. Educational goals: Do educational goals defined by exemplary Master's programs comprise the following elements:

    a. Familiarization of scientific education as general goal in tertiary education;

    b. Five specific educational goals for business leadership education as a whole or as single elements, i.e. personality, competencies, contributions through real-world challenges, goal-setting and achievement, creation and utilization of networks;

    c. If proposed goals cannot be detected, the question of which common or less frequently used goal categories were detected shall be answered.

2. Educational ideal: Did exemplary Master's programs delineate their educational ideal? If yes, is it conform to the educational ideal proposed in chapter 3.2.5.2, i.e. (creative) personality? If not, what is program's educational ideal?

3. Educational contents: Do educational contents provided by exemplary Master's programs meet the minimal criteria proposed in chapter 3.2.5.3 regarding:

    a. Theory: Are courses offered in innovation, entre- / intrapreneurship as the basis for innovation, management of goals, case studies, leadership knowledge?

    b. Reality: Are international and intercultural exchanges (e.g. study abroad), field trips, and real-world settings (internships, work experience and / or real-world projects) provided?

    c. Reflection: Do curricula encompass elements to promote systematic reflection, e.g. discussions, working groups, (peer-) mentoring, coaching, transfer opportunities, written papers, etc.

4. Educational methodologies: Do exemplary Master's programs focus on inquiry-based learning and CBE? Indicators for inquiry-based learning are research projects, research papers, experiments, Master's thesis etc. Indicators for CBE are real-world projects, internships, field trips, international and intercultural exchanges (study abroad).

5. Educational settings: Do exemplary Master's programs facilitate three educational settings proposed for business leadership education in tertiary education:

    a. Real-world setting

    b. Technological setting

    c. International setting

6. Evaluation: What are the evaluation methods for students' performance on the micro level, the meso level (accreditation) and the macro level (employment report)?

7. Financing: How are exemplary Master's programs financed?

The evaluation criteria and its sub-criteria have systematically guided the data collection and the subsequent analysis procedure of exemplary Master's programs selected in the next step.

4.1.2 Selection of exemplary Master's programs

In order to explore the opportunities for business leadership education in tertiary education for graduates, a thorough research of the institutions and programs was inevitable. The number of programs eligible for the evaluation in question was huge worldwide; therefore, a choice had to be made. The prime selection criterion for the institution and program selection were the international rankings. Such rankings for Master's degree programs in the field of management, which are synonymous with business leadership education in tertiary education for graduates, is the ranking of the Financial Times for example, which was considered suitable for the selection procedure, because it is the most established ranking in this special field. Nevertheless, it has to be noted that the rankings paradigm is a highly debatable issue (Marope et al., 2013; Ordorika & Lloyd, 2014; Rauhvargers, 2013; Schmidt, Hippel and Tippelt, 2010). On one hand, rankings provide a relatively simple overview of information on institutions and their programs for decision-making in a highly competitive global market. Even if "rankings are not and should not be used as the sole source of information to guide decisions pertaining to the quality of universities" (Marope et al., 2013, p. 13), they became a prominent performance indicator.

On the other hand, criticism and resistance on rankings are growing not only due to methodological reasons, but also because they underline the dominance and hegemony of the elite Anglo-Saxon research university (Ordorika & Lloyd, 2014), which can also be interpreted as a revelation of US "cultural imperialism" in the sense of Bourdieu and Wacquant (1999). Despite its critical debates, international rankings have been used as a selection tool for exemplary Master's programs due to their function as a paragon for other business schools and their respective programs. It has to be pointed out that, according to the author of this research, the rankings tell nothing about the quality of the program to be examined from a pedagogical point of view, but provides insight to awareness and market acceptance of Master's programs. It is noteworthy to mention here that 12 out of 15 exemplary programs were chosen for further analysis based on the ranking of the Financial Times from the year 2013. The Top 12 study programs from this ranking are included; those, which are jointly associated with the CEMS program[54], have been removed (No. 7). As the United States is considered the benchmark of management training, the top 3 study programs for graduates from the ranking of the U.S. news 2013 were selected in addition to the 12 study programs from the ranking of the Financial Times 2013, wherein US programs are excluded. Table 3 and Table 4 show the list of exemplary programs along with the institutions and countries to which they belong, selected from two rankings, namely Financial Times Masters in management ranking 2013 and U.S. News ranking Best Business Schools 2013[55].

---

54   CEMS (acronym for Community of European Management Schools and International Companies) is a global alliance in management education comprising 30 schools worldwide. CEMS Master in International Management is a joint degree program provided by academic members of CEMS alliance.
55   The rankings are published annually. Although there may be some (minor) shifts in the program's order, the programs chosen as exemplary Master's programs for this research were all among the best-ranked programs within the latest evaluation (Financial Times Masters in management ranking, 2015; U.S. News Best Business Schools, 2016).

No.	Program	Institution	Country	Ranking
1	Master of Arts in Strategy and International Management	University of St. Gallen	Switzerland	1
2	ESCP Europe Master in Management	ESCP Europe	France, UK, Germany, Spain, Italy	2
3	Master of Science in Management	WHU Otto Beisheim School of Management	Germany	3
4	HEC Master of Science in Management	HEC Paris	France	4
5	Master of Science in International Management	Rotterdam School of Management Erasmus University	The Netherlands	5
6	Master in Management	IE Business School	Spain	6
7	Master of Science in Management	ESSEC Business School	France	8
8	Master of Science in Management	Handelshochschule Leipzig, Leipzig Graduate School of Management	Germany	9
9	Master of Science in International Management	Esade Business School at Ramon Llull University	Spain	10
10	Master of Science in Management	Emlyon Business School	France	11
11	Master of Science in Management	Imperial College London Business School	UK	12
12	Master in International Business	Grenoble École de Management, Graduate School of Management	France	13

Table 3. Selected programs of Financial Times Masters in management ranking 2013.

No.	Program	Institution	Country	Ranking
13	MBA	Harvard Business School	USA	1
14	MBA	Stanford Graduate School of Business	USA	2
15	MBA	The Wharton School, University of Pennsylvania	USA	3

Table 4. Selected programs of U.S. News ranking Best Business Schools 2013.

In order to scrutinize the exemplary Master's programs in the light of the evaluation criteria, data was collected systematically.

4.1.3 Data collection

The data was collected from the official websites of the respective institutions and / or program-specific documents available through the official websites between June 1 and June 12, 2014. To note all the significant information from these websites, a data matrix[56] was created on Microsoft Excel, comprising seven main evaluation criteria with its sub-criteria (see chapter 4.1.1) and basic information along a program's life cycle. This helped immensely to organize the vast data related to every program. Subsequently, all details for each criterion and sub-criterion were systematically entered into the data matrix. Some information was not easily available on the website; hence, each university / business school was contacted by email and asked for the missing information. Later, a second and third reminder was sent to the respective institutions for the missing information. Finally, the data matrix was completed. After the information was entered, it was rechecked and revised to obtain information that is more precise regarding the programs and institutions. For in-depth analysis of specific criteria, suitable pages from the websites were investigated in detail to choose the most relevant information based on the criteria. For example, if information about real-world challenges was sought, the webpage that presented the details was searched and the relevant information noted. Relevant data, analyzed in light of the evaluation criteria for each program, are presented in Table 7 - Table 13 along with the template of the data matrix (see Appendix). The following paragraphs explain how the analysis was conducted.

4.1.4 Data analysis

Qualitative research is not only of high importance in social research. Moreover, "[t]he contribution of qualitative research is towards better understanding of the social realities and to shed light upon the processes, meaning patterns and structural features of the issue being studied" (Flick, Kardorff & Steinke, 2004, p. 3). Its broad methodological approach comprises different

---

[56] The data matrix was developed by the author of this research in collaboration with A. Djalali as part of the project "Leadership Education in Tertiary Education", which is a joint research project of the Department of Educational Science at Ludwig-Maximilians-University (LMU) Munich, Germany and Steinbeis School of International Business and Entrepreneurship (SIBE), Germany. The two authors modified the data matrix and conducted the data collection independently due to their individual research objectives. The data collection in the research of A. Djalali was focused on competency development in MBA programs; for details please see Djalali (2017).

ways of analyzing the qualitative data e.g. conversation analysis (Garfinkel, 1967; Goffman, 1983) or grounded theory approach (Glaser & Strauss, 1967). For the purpose of this research, document analysis and qualitative content analysis were considered best suited. In a first step, the data collected in the data matrix were restructured, sorted, and presented in tabular form (Table 7 - Table 13) according to the evaluation criteria and its sub-criteria. Organizing the data will facilitate interpretation, since complexity can be reduced, proportions of programs that fulfill or do not fulfill the criteria can be detected, similarities and differences between theory and practice can be uncovered, and clear results can be retrieved. This first step directed the qualitative content analysis. Content analysis was conducted in a second step for in-depth analysis of crucial aspects (e.g. the institution's understanding of a 'real-world project') being studied in this research since the procedure of the data analysis is "transparent, intelligible, easy to learn and readily transferable to new research questions" (Flick, 2009, p. 269).

4.1.4.1 Document analysis

As the analyzed data belonged to internet-based documents created from official websites of the respective institutions, it is necessary to understand the concept of document analysis. Document analysis involves a systematic procedure to evaluate and review documents. These documents can be either in a printed or electronic (computer-based and internet transmitted) form. Document analysis further focuses on the examination and interpretation of data as in any other qualitative data analysis, thus helping to understand the meaning of the collected data (Corbin & Strauss, 2008). Documents contain text information (words) that has been collected by the researcher without any alteration (Bowen, 2009). Document analysis seems to be closely applicable to qualitative case studies – studies that describe a single phenomenon, event, program, or organization in detail (Stake, 1995; Yin, 1994). It was also pointed out that "Documents of all types can help the researcher uncover meaning, develop understanding, and discover insights relevant to the research problem" (Merriam, 1988, p. 118).

The advantages of document analysis are:

1. Availability and efficiency: Recently, documents are available in the public domain, as the use of internet has increased incredibly. They are mostly obtained without the author's permission. Thus, there is easy access to a lot of valuable information. It therefore involves data selection rather than data collection (Bowen, 2009).
2. Cost effectiveness: It is less expensive than other qualitative methods as the data is normally already collected in documents (Bowen, 2009).
3. Coverage – Documents possibly cover a long span of time, events and many situations or settings (Yin, 1994).

The procedure of qualitative content analysis – one of the classical approaches of analyzing textual data, e.g. interview data or media data (Bauer, 2000) – conducted for crucial aspects being studied in this research shall be presented in the following paragraph.

4.1.4.2 Content analysis

Content analysis typically involves categorization, then organizing the data as per the created categories and furthermore refining the data based on the categories (Flick, 2009). For the purpose of systematic text analysis and to reduce the material (Flick, 2009; Gläser-Zikuda, 2011), Mayring (2000, 2004) developed a qualitative content analysis procedure comprising various techniques. Basic principle of this procedure is to sustain the advantages of the qualitative content and allow the content to be transformed into progressive steps leading to in-depth analysis. Following the rules of Mayring (2000), the qualitative content analysis was carried out systematically adapting the clear structure of Shah (2014) as described below:

1. Content of analytical units: Transformation of the vast data into smaller units was conceived to be the first step. Theoretical foundation, pre-conceived evaluation criteria and sub-criteria decided which text will be included in the next step. This process is also popularly known as 'data reduction'. Subsequently, the reduced data was scanned for repeated ideas. Paraphrasing technique was implemented to transform the text units into precise and clear statements. In some cases, due to the length of the text,

it was divided into smaller text chunks, which were converted into statements. Therefore, it may appear that more statements belong to one code. The clear statements that emerged from the earlier step were assigned to suitable codes, considering the suitability more than one code was assigned to the statement.

2. Code development: In a second step, a coding scheme was developed for the data analysis according to the procedure of inductive code development. The inductive approach was employed to the codes obtained from the text units. Inductive codes were defined according to the textual units based on the evaluation criteria and its sub-criteria, and the statements relevant to the definitions were allotted relevant codes. Table 5 illustrates how the coding was carried out. MAXQDA-plus®, a computerized software, was used to organize the data and carry out the coding. The software proved to be beneficial and made the coding process easy and traceable. The text units were allotted appropriate categories and codes, keeping in mind the evaluation criteria and sub-criteria. Further analysis involved the reconsideration of allotted codes. Depending on the proximity between codes and categories, the greater the proximity, the easier the clustering of codes into categories.

Category / code	Definition	Statements	Coding rules
Leadership / leadership approach	How is leadership taught to students	"To develop leaders who act with a deeper understanding of themselves, their organizations, and their communities, and contribute positively to the growth of each." (Statement 15) MBA at The Wharton School, University of Pennsylvania / USA.	Statements that define leadership approach
Practical learning / Project	Information regarding project	"Consulting Project: To analyze a real consultancy problem, apply their knowledge from other courses to solve a real consultancy problem, integrate theoretical knowledge with practical skills relevant to industry." (Statement 16) Master of Science in Management at Imperial College London Business School / UK	Relevant project information about duration, definition etc.

Table 5. Example of the process of coding according to the coding system.

3. Review of coded statements and revision of codes: In the third step, following the clustering of codes into categories, the software organized the coded statements for all the 15 programs. The process can simply be referred to as 'retrieval'. Exporting the retrieved statements into an Excel sheet further eased the analysis procedure. The further analysis steps involved the elimination of superfluous codes, rechecking whether the statements were allotted correct codes, and keeping track of the numbers generated automatically by the software.

4. Qualitative interpretation: For the interpretation of the statements, their clusters were facilitated by the retrieval process, e.g. by program or country group. Such retrieval and sorting of statements according to codes led to the exploration of similarities and differences within and between the involved programs and country-groups. Specific codes were allotted to the retrieved statements and, as a next step, they were regrouped as per the evaluation criteria and sub-criteria. This entire coding system together with the statements was visualized to examine the Master's programs and thus carry out the evaluation procedure according to the criteria and sub-criteria.

5. Content Analysis Results: Following the steps mentioned above and considering the vastness of data, it was decided to focus only on the most relevant information. Table 6 shows the results deliberately chosen from content analysis, i.e. four main codes, which consisted of several sub-codes. Seven sub-codes contributed to understanding the main codes. As mentioned earlier, clear statements were formulated that described each sub-code. A total number of 135 statements resulted from the content analysis.

Main code	Sub-code	Statements
1. Leadership	Leadership approach	25
2. Educational goal	Educational goal	17
3. Pedagogical approach	Pedagogical approach	40
4. Practical learning	Project	12
	Internship	12
	Study abroad	20
	Field trip	9

Table 6. Overview of main codes and sub-codes and the number of statements.

4.1.5 Interpretation and discussion

The content analysis interpretation has to answer the questions, whether and how the exemplary Master's programs fulfill the evaluation criteria and its sub-criteria.

Before delving into the curriculum design, it is worth introducing the overall framework in which the programs (and institutions) operate. To consider the overall framework of the exemplary programs, there was also the possibility of comparing the programs in Europe and the USA. The data analysis showed that the programs in Europe and the USA had some similarities as well as differences that shall be presented briefly in terms of the five aspects of program duration, admission requirements, student profile, class size and, ultimately, the overall leadership approach.

One of the considerable aspects of the framework put forth by the different institutions is the program duration (see Table 13). The standard program duration differed throughout Europe. Many institutions specified the course duration, ranging from 10 months to a maximum of 48 months, while the American programs had a standard duration of 24 months.

The second aspect of the framework was the various admission requirements for the Master's program. Please note that these requirements are besides the copies of all degrees, diplomas, copies of attendance in earlier courses etc. The basic requirement for securing admission was the first degree or a qualifying academic degree. All the schools mentioned that a Bachelor's or equivalent degree was a pre-requisite. The age requirement specified by four institutions in Europe, namely Emlyon Business School, ESSEC Business School, HEC Paris, and ESCP (including 5 campuses in Europe) was that the applicant should not be older than 30 years at the time of application, whereas none of the American schools mentioned any age requirement. Prior work experience was also an important factor in the admission requirements. Most European institutions did not consider prior work experience mandatory for admission to the respective university, except for the University of WHU Otto Beisheim School of Management (5 months), and Leipzig Graduate School of Management (3 months). The American universities, on the other hand, did not mention mandatory work experience in order to be admitted to a course. Further requirements were the tests namely GMAT (Graduate Management Admission

Test) and TOEFL (Test of English as Foreign Language). All schools mentioned these two types of tests as important factors for securing admission; although not all schools considered these tests mandatory to secure admission for the respective Master's course. There were differences in the GMAT score requirements across the schools. Some schools did not require this test at all, whereas others deemed it mandatory. For universities / business schools, which considered GMAT mandatory, the scores ranged from 600-730. A similarity was seen in the TOEFL IBT (Internet Based Test) score. All schools mentioned TOEFL IBT scores, which ranged from 95-110. Lastly, language requirement also played an important role. English being a global language and the orientation of all Master' programs being international, it was essential according to the universities / business schools that the applicants were well versed in the English language. It was important that students were able to follow the courses, because the medium of instruction for all the programs was English, either for the complete program or for part of the program. There were also options of attending language courses in other native languages, such as Spanish in Spain, German in Germany, French in France etc.

Another aspect of the educational framework was the student profile. It was considered important, because the percentage of female candidates and the percentage of international students show the cultural diversity and global approach of the universities / business schools. All schools had a considerable percentage of female candidates ranging from 39 %-47 %.

The class size differed greatly in European and American programs. The European institutions had enrolled students ranging from 54 to 560; while the American universities had a greater number of students, ranging from 400-916. The percentages of international students were much higher in European institutions compared to American universities. The program at University of St. Gallen had a maximum of 87 % of international students in the European section, compared to the MBA program at Stanford Business School, which, at 41 %, had the highest percentage of international students among the three American programs.

Finally, the overall document-based content analysis showed that leadership seemed to be quite an important topic among many schools that were chosen for the analysis. For clear understanding, the relevant text was coded as *leadership approach*. Each school has its own unique approach towards leadership.

Leadership curriculum is also designed based on this approach. Some specific statements from a few schools are presented below to describe the state of art in leadership in schools ranging from functional knowledge approach to an approach aiming at students discovering their individual strengths and weaknesses as a leader personality:

> "The leadership course considers what kind of leader you want to be, what kind of leader you are, and how to align your leadership behaviour with your leadership goals. You will have an opportunity to lead your squad and in doing so to discover your strengths and challenges as a leader. You will receive feedback about your approach to leadership and you will have the opportunity to try out new skills and tools."
>
> *(Statement 15) MBA at Stanford Graduate School of Business / USA*

> "The leadership course focuses on enabling students to understand their leadership journeys and their crucibles through framing their life stories and experiences to date. Third goal is to understand why leaders lose their way and the self-awareness needed to avoid derailment. Fourth goal is to gain clarity about their leadership principles, values, and ethical boundaries, and how they will respond under pressure when severely challenged. Fifth goal is to understand what is motivating them, both extrinsically and intrinsically, and to find leadership paths that will enable them to utilize their motivated capabilities. Sixth goal is to explore how to build support teams and lead an integrated life. Lastly, to understand the purpose of their leadership and to create a Personal Leadership Development Plan to guide them throughout their lives."
>
> *(Statement 16) MBA at Harvard Business School / USA*

> "Leadership perspective means technical know-how and an excellent understanding of management concepts are only one side of the coin. The ability to apply, implement and communicate the know-how is the other side. Courses in economics and leadership skills as well as practical experience enable students to understand, assess and lead complex decision-making processes and establish new values in management."
>
> *(Statement 15) Master of Science in Management at HHL, Leipzig Graduate School of Management / Germany*

"Since leaders are made, not born, it is important to establish as early as possible a reflective understanding for the fundamentals and crucibles of leadership. Effective and responsible leadership requires leaders who are aware of the context in which they lead, the purpose of their leadership project, their stakeholders, their responsibilities, limitations and strengths, as well as the challenges and dilemmas they may encounter. In other words, they need to demonstrate self-awareness and awareness of others, that is, of followers as stakeholders. In addition, leaders need to know how and where to grow - and how they can help others to grow and become leaders in their own right."

(Statement 15) Master of Science in International Management at Esade Business School at Ramon Llull University / Spain

"The University of St. Gallen aspires to instill in its students competencies in the following key areas:· Leadership Skills to develop problem-solving competence and solution-oriented approaches to diverse situations that may arise both during studies as well as in their professional careers.· Critical Thinking and Cultural Awareness to think systematically and methodically about intellectual problems and cultural questions.Courses of this type are intended to promote critical thinking by introducing the thought processes and interpretative strategies that are characteristic to this field."

(Statement 15) Master of Arts in Strategy and International Management at University of St. Gallen / Switzerland

Thus, the state of art of framework for business leadership education in tertiary education for graduates has been explained by presenting some similarities that emerged during the content analysis. Furthermore, the statements presented so far provide a clear idea about the differences that lie between the European and American institutions.

4.1.5.1 Educational goals

Considering the educational goals defined by exemplary Master's programs, the criteria as defined in chapter 4.1.1 have to be evaluated:

1. Do educational goals defined by exemplary Master's programs comprise the following elements:

    a. Familiarization of scientific education as general goal in tertiary education.

    b. Five specific educational goals for business leadership education as a whole or as single elements, i.e. personality, competencies, contributions through real-world challenges, goal-setting and achievement, creation and utilization of networks.

2. If proposed goals cannot be detected, the question of which common or less frequently used goal categories were detected shall be answered.

In order to obtain clear results to the first aspect, the relevant data were organized in order to uncover similarities and differences between theory and practice and to detect proportions of programs that fulfill or do not fulfill the criteria. Qualitative content analysis was conducted. This systematic procedure was used to obtain a better understanding of the evaluated topic.

Nevertheless, educational goals for the 15 exemplary Master's programs were not readily available on the website, but the various subpages or program specific documents available through the official websites had to be searched, e.g. study and examination regulations, program brochures etc. Furthermore, no standard headline (e.g. educational goals) can be found; rather, the relevant information was subsumed to the topics of e.g. program objectives, program's aims, program's mission etc. For reasons of unambiguousness, the term 'education goals' is used in the following descriptions. The retrieved educational goals for each program are presented in Table 7. Although (sometimes) hard to find, each institution has defined education goals for the respective programs.

No.	Program at Institution / Country	Educational goal
1	Master of Arts in Strategy and International Management at University of St. Gallen / Switzerland	Our mission is to provide our students with the necessary expertise and competencies in the field of management and to prepare them for a successful career. We enable our students to cope with complex managerial challenges based on a profound strategic understanding, to think and act internationally and to take on an integrative and interdisciplinary approach when dealing with general management issues. We also want our students to be able to initiate and conduct research of high managerial relevance and follow through business projects guided by the highest professional standards.
2	ESCP Europe Master in Management at ESCP Europe / France, UK, Germany, Spain, Italy	> Develop in-depth knowledge of management topics and the business world > Build and test your career plans through specialised course options and in-company experience > Strengthen your ability to live and work in a highly multicultural and international environment > Broaden your horizons by studying alongside students from a vast range of backgrounds, such as business management, economics, engineering and social sciences > Learn through practical applications with case studies, field projects and internships > Prepare to take on major responsibilities in tomorrow's economic environment by developing a personal vision of the globalised economy
3	Master of Science in Management at WHU Otto Beisheim School of Management / Germany	WHU Learning Goals: > Discipline-specific knowledge and competence > Management-specific skills > Understanding global business environment > Teamwork and responsibility > Critical thinking and problem-solving skills > Managerial and entrepreneurial practice
4	HEC Master of Science in Management at HEC Paris / France	Students are trained to become decision-makers, while focusing on the academic specialization that they choose in light of their professional goals. With the diversity of courses and specializations available, students develop expertise in several areas of business administration, shape their career plans and also prepare their entry into the business world through company internships.
5	Master of Science in International Management at Rotterdam School of Management Erasmus University / The Netherlands	The degree programme is intended to impart scientific knowledge, skills and insight in the area of international management in such a way that the graduate is capable of scientific and socially responsible professional practice in this area, and is qualified to take any desired advanced programme and to become, among others a scientific researcher.

6	Master in Management at IE Business School / Spain	IE Business School has designed the Master in International Management as an innovative and international business program for high performing individuals. We help students develop an entrepreneurial mindset and a strong foundation of management skills to succeed in a dynamic, global, and diverse business environment.
7	Master of Science in Management at ESSEC Business School / France	The flexible nature of the curriculum allows students to combine academic content, professional and international experiences. Students build their own curriculum as they wish, combining work and study, in France and abroad. The objective of the personalized curriculum is to progressively nurture the personal and professional development of each student. Each student is accompanied by a tutor until graduation to help him / her make the best choices for his / her projects.
8	Master of Science in Management at Handelshochschule Leipzig (HHL), Leipzig Graduate School of Management / Germany	It is the objective of the Master's study course to acquire basic scientific knowledge and abilities, which are required to cope with these tasks. These include in particular the following abilities and knowledge of: a) Recognizing and analyzing operational overall coherences as well as interdependencies between the areas of activity of a company. b) Recognizing and solving structured and non-structured economic problems as well as communicating problem solutions. c) Grasping and assessing international and macro-economic events and developments and turning their effects into decisions. d) Ability to work in a team; social competence and target orientated leadership conduct.
9	Master of Science in International Management at Esade Business School at Ramon Llull University / Spain	Programme objectives. By the time you graduate, you will have learned how to: > Embrace complexity, including how it frames the cultural, economic and political context, how it affects business practice, and how it can be managed. > Identify global issues and problems in relation to companies, and integrate them into core business policies and activities. > Construct a systemic understanding of a company and manage the paradoxes inherent to international operations, such as local-versus-global or conflicting stakeholder demands. > Acquire analytical skills and critical thinking, challenge assumptions, and understand the value of intangible assets. > Develop the competencies necessary to implement global strategies in the different functional areas of a company such as operations, organization, marketing and finances.

10	Master of Science in Management at Emlyon Business School / France	The MSc in Management programme's mission is to train students through educational knowledge, as well as to accompany them throughout their personal and professional development. We chose to put students' education and their professional project at the heart of their learning experience.
11	Master of Science in Management at Imperial College London Business School / UK	The programme aims to provide a one-year programme in management that will equip students with the knowledge and skills to effectively manage and lead in private, voluntary and public domains, or to pursue further academic study (doctoral research). Students who complete the programme successfully will be able to: 1) demonstrate relevant knowledge of organisations, and their role in pursuing sustainable business in the context in which they operate and how they are managed in compliance with codes of ethics and Corporate Social Responsibility; 2) apply analytical and problem solving techniques to the decision making process in real-life business contexts and present their analysis in a professional and persuasive manner; 3) use interdisciplinary knowledge to develop a holistic view of business management challenges and cross-subject skills to propose relevant solutions; 4) demonstrate they have obtained a set of personal development and lifelong learning skills applicable to the international business environment
12	Master in International Business at Grenoble École de Management, Graduate School of Management / France	The mission of the Master in International Business program is to provide employers worldwide with intercultural aware graduates who have developed key skills and competencies in international business and management.
13	MBA at Harvard Business School / USA	Harvard Business School invites students in. Into two years of leadership practice immersed in real-world challenges. Into a diverse community of colleagues and faculty reflecting a world of talents, beliefs, and backgrounds. Into an intense period of personal and professional transformation that prepares you for challenges in any functional area – anywhere in the world. To experience the HBS MBA is to go inside the issues that matter – and to reach inside yourself for the strength, skills, and confidence you will develop to face them. In every case, class, event, and activity, you are asked not only to study leadership, but to demonstrate it. Each day at HBS begins with one question: "What will you do?" Because that's the truest way to prepare you for the larger question that matters most, here and in your career beyond our campus: "What difference will you make in the world?

14	MBA at Stanford Graduate School of Business / USA	Stanford Graduate School of Business empowers you to act – to take steps that will change the world. Our programs develop insightful leaders. Our students are not afraid of making mistakes; they fear only missed opportunities. Our alumni are insightful, passionate professionals who are never satisfied with the status quo. Instead, they choose to employ their knowledge, talent, and ideas to create change.
15	MBA at The Wharton School, University of Pennsylvania / USA	Why Wharton? Because you'll be stretched, pushed and, ultimately, transformed. Our challenging, flexible program – driven by the best minds in business education – unleashes your potential, giving you the confidence and skills to lead anywhere in the world.

Table 7. Educational goals defined by selected Master's programs. Individual educational goals adapted from institution's official website or documents available through website. Data retrieved from June 1 to June 12, 2014.

Clustering the programs according to the question whether the programs' defined goals comprise different elements proposed, the following results can be reported (see Table 8):

> Three of 15 exemplary programs explicitly outline students' familiarization of scientific education that was proposed as a kind of umbrella purpose. The three programs are no. 1, no. 5, and no. 11.

> The proposed educational goals for business leadership education in Master's programs in tertiary education for graduates developed in chapter 3.2.5.1. cannot be found in any of the programs as a whole; rather, single elements of the proposed goals were detected.

> The term "personality" was not explicitly retrieved; rather, three of 15 remaining exemplary programs aim to promote personal development. The three programs are no. 7, no. 10, and no. 11.

> Five of 15 exemplary programs explicitly outline competency development, of which three programs refer to competency in a broad sense (no. 1, no. 9, and no. 12). The remaining two programs refer to discipline-specific knowledge and competence (no. 3) or social competence (no. 8). How the institutions conceive the term competency or competence requires an in-depth analysis.

> Real-world challenges in a broad sense were outlined in educational goals by five of 15 programs (no. 1, 2, 7, 10, and 11). The programs use different terms and different contexts. For an in-depth analysis of real-world setting, please see chapter 4.1.5.5.

> Setting personal or professional goals and achievement of (self-set) goals and creation and utilization of valuable networks cannot be found in any of the programs.

No.	Program at Institution / Country	Familiarization to scientific education	Personality	Competency development	Contributions through real-world projects	Goal setting and achievement	Creation and utilization of networks
1	Master of Arts in Strategy and International Management at University of St. Gallen / Switzerland	yes	no	yes	yes	no	no
2	ESCP Europe Master in Management at ESCP Europe / France, UK, Germany, Spain, Italy	no	no	no	yes	no	no
3	Master of Science in Management at WHU Otto Beisheim School of Management / Germany	no	no	(yes)	no	no	no
4	HEC Master of Science in Management at HEC Paris / France	no	no	no	no	no	no
5	Master of Science in International Management at Rotterdam School of Management Erasmus University / The Netherlands	yes	no	no	no	no	no
6	Master in Management at IE Business School / Spain	no	no	no	no	no	no
7	Master of Science in Management at ESSEC Business School / France	no	yes	no	yes	no	no
8	Master of Science in Management at Handelshochschule Leipzig (HHL), Leipzig Graduate School of Management / Germany	no	no	(yes)	no	no	no
9	Master of Science in International Management at Esade Business School at Ramon Llull University / Spain	no	no	yes	no	no	no
10	Master of Science in Management at Emlyon Business School / France	no	yes	no	yes	no	no

11	Master of Science in Management at Imperial College London Business School / UK	yes	yes	no	yes	no	no
12	Master in International Business at Grenoble École de Management, Graduate School of Management / France	no	no	yes	no	no	no
13	MBA at Harvard Business School / USA	no	yes	(yes)	yes	(yes)	(yes)
14	MBA at Stanford Graduate School of Business / USA	no	no	no	no	no	no
15	MBA at The Wharton School, University of Pennsylvania / USA	no	no	no	no	no	no

(yes) – not explicitly conceived but to be conceived analogously

Table 8. Elements of proposed goals in selected Master's programs goal definition based on criteria defined in chapter 3.2.5.1. Data retrieved from institution's official website between June 1 to June 12, 2014.

As proposed goals (chapter 3.2.5.1) cannot be found as a whole, and only single elements were detected in different programs, the question of which other or further elements were defined in educational goals emerges.

Three different categories resulted from the qualitative content analysis. Firstly, the educational goals had a global approach, meaning that international opportunities for students were either mandatory or highly encouraged by the programs. Furthermore, imparting knowledge and skill development of students were of highest importance, which is what almost half of the exemplary programs focused on. Nevertheless, it has to be noted that the term 'skills' may also be used in the meaning of competencies (see chapter 3.1.4.4). A more detailed analysis is proposed to obtain in-depth insight. Some selected education goals are presented in the following section according to the three categories of global approach, knowledge, and skill development:

> "IE Business School has designed the Master in International Management as an innovative and international business program for high performing individuals. We help students develop an entrepreneurial mindset and a strong foundation of management skills to succeed in a dynamic, global, and diverse business environment."
>
> *Master in Management at IE Business School / Spain*

"It is the objective of the Master's study course to acquire basic scientific knowledge and abilities, which are required to cope with these tasks. These include in particular the following abilities and knowledge of:
a) Recognizing and analyzing operational overall coherences as well as interdependencies between the areas of activity of a company.
b) Recognizing and solving structured and non-structured economic problems as well as communicating problem solutions.
c) Grasping and assessing international and macroeconomic events and developments and turning their effects into decisions.
d) Ability to work in a team; social competence and target orientated leadership conduct."

Master of Science in Management at Handelshochschule (HHL) Leipzig, Leipzig Graduate School of Management / Germany

"The degree programme is intended to impart scientific knowledge, skills and insight in the area of international management in such a way that the graduate is capable of scientific and socially responsible professional practice in this area, and is qualified to take any desired advanced programme and to become, among others a scientific researcher."

Master of Science in International Management at Rotterdam School of Management Erasmus University / The Netherlands

To summarize, educational goals set by institutions for their respective programs, which were presented exemplarily in this research, not only use a heterogeneous terminology and presentation, but also focus on heterogeneous aspects. (Creative) personality elaborated not only as pivotal educational goal (chapter 3.2.5.1) but also as a superior educational ideal is hardly found. Competency development and mastering real-world challenges were defined by a minor proportion of programs, while goal setting and achievement as well as creation and utilization of valuable networks were not explicitly outlined in any of the exemplary programs. In consequence, it does not mean that programs fail to comprise these elements, but they were at least not prioritized and not a part of the educational goals. In contrast, knowledge- and skill-oriented educational goals were prevalent. Although graduates' employability is of great importance, the program orientation is proposed to be critically reflected by various stakeholders (e.g. policy-makers, higher education institutions, individuals / students etc.) from a humanistic and pedagogical aspect.

4.1.5.2 Educational ideal

All official websites, materials, and program-specific documents available through official websites were researched along with a target-oriented search of key words through internet search engines in order to identify the respective educational ideal of exemplary Master's programs. Despite an intense and thorough search procedure, an educational ideal was not found for any of the programs. Therefore, it is proposed for higher education institutions to either make the educational ideal accessible for their study programs if it already exists (e.g. in internal documents) or – if an educational ideal does not yet exist – to reflect on and elaborate an educational ideal best suited to the higher education institutions' (and programs') culture and (educational) philosophy.

4.1.5.3 Educational contents

While an educational ideal was not found for any of the exemplary Master's programs, and educational goals were difficult to identify, educational contents were easily accessible for all programs on official institutions' websites. It seems to be common to promote the specific orientation, focus and – partly – differentiation of institutions and programs, e.g. from other higher education institutions and programs, in order to attract potential students. Thereby, in almost all programs – apart from Master in International Business at Grenoble École de Management, Graduate School of Management / France – curricula are distinguished in core curriculum that is mandatory for every student and electives or specialization, allowing students to choose from a broad spectrum of courses and to individualize the curriculum. Considering the overall similarities between the programs, research reveals that the focus was on at least the mandatory part of curricula in the context of international management in the fields of financial management, strategy, and marketing.

Nevertheless, delving into educational contents, the question of whether contents provided by exemplary Master's programs in either core curriculum or electives or specialization comply with the minimal proposed criteria (chapter 3.2.5.3), shall be answered regarding:

1. Theory: Are courses offered in innovation, entre- / intrapreneurship as a basis for innovation, management of goals, case studies, and leadership knowledge?
2. Reality: Are international and intercultural exchanges (e.g. study abroad), field trips, and real-world settings (e.g. internships, work experience and / or real-world projects) provided?
3. Reflection: Do curricula encompass elements to promote systematic reflection, e.g. discussions, working groups, (peer-) mentoring, coaching, transfer opportunities, written papers, etc.

In order to obtain clear results to the first aspect, the relevant data were organized to uncover similarities and differences between theory and practice and to detect proportions of programs that fulfill or do not fulfill the criteria. The following results can be reported (see Table 9 and Table 10):

1. Theory:

    a. Courses on the topic of innovation are provided by eleven of 15 exemplary programs, wherein five programs offer it as mandatory part of the curriculum and in the remaining six, students may choose during the elective, or specialization part of curriculum. Curricula of four programs do not comprise courses on innovation.

    b. Courses on entrepreneurship were offered by almost all programs, either as mandatory part of the core curriculum (4) or as optional part in electives or specialization of the curriculum (10). Only one program does not offer courses on entrepreneurship.

    c. Courses on leadership knowledge, e.g. organizational behavior, leadership personality, competencies, ethics etc. were also provided by almost all programs. In the curricula of eleven programs, it is mandatory to attend courses on leadership; in seven of the 11 programs, leadership can be additionally chosen in the elective or specialization part of the curriculum. In two programs, leadership is generally part of the optional elective or specialization curriculum. In curricula of two programs leadership as a topic is not provided as part of the curriculum.[57]

---

57 The data refer to June 2014. Since curricula are dynamic in nature, visiting the website in August 2016 for actual information revealed, that one of the two curricula that formerly did not provide courses on leadership knowledge as part of curriculum recently have integrated it in the optional part of curriculum, students can choose from (WHU/Germany).

d. Courses on the management of goals were not provided by any of the programs, at least it is not explicitly outlined in exemplary programs' curricula; this does not mean that the content is not available in any of the other courses offered, at least on a small scale. Therefore, syllabi have to be checked in detail.

e. Case studies[58] are an integral part of all curricula and are put forth by institutions, e.g. according to Harvard Business School; 500 cases were read by each student during the two-year MBA program.

No.	Program at Institution / Country	Innovation	Entre- (and / or intrapreneurship)	Goals**	Leadership***	Case studies
1	Master of Arts in Strategy and International Management at University of St. Gallen / Switzerland	no	yes (O)	no	yes (M)	yes
2	ESCP Europe Master in Management at ESCP Europe / France, UK, Germany, Spain, Italy	yes (O)	yes (O)	no	yes (O)	yes
3	Master of Science in Management at WHU Otto Beisheim School of Management / Germany	yes (O)	yes (O)	no	no	yes
4	HEC Master of Science in Management at HEC Paris / France	no	yes (O)	no	yes (M)	yes
5	Master of Science in International Management at Rotterdam School of Management Erasmus University / The Netherlands	no	yes (O)	no	yes (M + O)	yes
6	Master in Management at IE Business School / Spain	yes (M)	yes (M)	no	yes (M)	yes
7	Master of Science in Management at ESSEC Business School / France	yes (O)	yes (O)	no	yes (M + O)	yes
8	Master of Science in Management at Handelshochschule Leipzig (HHL), Leipzig Graduate School of Management / Germany	yes (O)	yes (M)	no	yes (M)	yes

---

58 Critical on case studies, please see Mintzberg (2005); Gosling and Mintzberg (2006).

9	Master of Science in International Management at Esade Business School at Ramon Llull University / Spain	yes (O)	yes (O)	no	yes (O)	yes
10	Master of Science in Management at Emlyon Business School / France	no	yes (M)	no	no	yes
11	Master of Science in Management at Imperial College London Business School / UK	yes (M)	yes (O)	no	yes (M + O)	yes
12	Master in International Business at Grenoble École de Management, Graduate School of Management / France	yes (M)	no	no	yes (M)	yes
13	MBA at Harvard Business School / USA	yes (O)	yes (M)	no	yes (M + O)	yes
14	MBA at Stanford Graduate School of Business / USA	yes (M)	yes (O)	no	yes (M + O)	yes
15	MBA at The Wharton School, University of Pennsylvania / USA	yes (M)	yes (O)	no	yes (M + O)	yes

* Minimal criteria for theoretical content defined in chapter 3.2.5.3. are: technical and functional knowledge and qualification that is required to fulfill a business leadership position, comprising at least contents on a) innovation, b) entre- and intrapreneurship that are basis for innovation, c) management of goals [...], d) cases studies, e) leadership knowledge etc.

** Courses in management of goals (incl. methodologies on goal identification and goal setting procedures) were not explicitly outlined in curricula of selected Master's programs; this does not mean that the content is not available in any other courses offered at least on a small scale. Therefore, syllabi has to checked in detail.

*** Courses on leadership knowledge are e.g. leadership, organizational behavior, ethics, competencies etc.

M – Mandatory part of core curriculum; mandatory for every student

O – Optional part of elective (or specialization) part of curriculum; it is not mandatory part of curriculum

Table 9. Educational contents of selected Master's programs based on minimal criteria for theory defined in chapter 3.2.5.3*. Data retrieved from institution's official website between June 1 to June 12, 2014.

2. Reality:

    a. International and intercultural exposure (e.g. by study abroad) is an integral part of all exemplary Master's programs. This further underlines the international orientation of all Master' programs (see also chapter 4.1.5.5).

    b. One way to facilitate real-world impressions and company insight are field trips. Seven of 15 exemplary programs offer field trips; in three of the programs, students can attend optionally.

    c. Of high importance for CBE are real-world settings. As there is no clear terminology, the term real-world setting is used comprising e.g. internships, work experience and real-world projects in companies / organizations. The actions and competencies of students can be demonstrated in real-world settings. All 15 schools offer an opportunity for real-world exposure by conducting a project in a company. Many institutions made the real-world setting mandatory for students (9); while some kept it optional (6). In programs, where real-world settings and field trips are only optional, it may occur that students, who do not select either a field trip or a real-world setting, consequently fail to obtain any real-world exposure for the duration of the Master's program. This may be the case in two American MBA programs (Stanford Graduate School of Business and Wharton Business School at University of Pennsylvania). Furthermore, the duration and intensity of the offered real-world settings vary immensely. For in-depth analysis of real-world settings, please see chapter 4.1.5.4.

3. Systematic reflection is provided in all curricula of exemplary programs. In the process, different ways to demonstrate reflection are chosen and all examples proposed in chapter 3.2.5.3 (discussions, working groups, (peer-) mentoring, coaching, transfer opportunities, written reflection papers) were mentioned and used frequently by the programs.

To summarize, considering the theoretical aspect of educational contents, courses in innovation, entrepreneurship, and leadership knowledge are widely provided in curricula of exemplary programs – at least in the optional part of the curricula. Nevertheless, it shall be proposed to integrate these elements as a standard in the mandatory part of the curriculum, as case studies are an

No.	Program at Institution / Country	Reality			Reflection
		International / intercultural exposure	Field trip	Real-world setting (for details: Table 11)	
1	Master of Arts in Strategy and International Management at University of St. Gallen / Switzerland	yes	no	yes	yes
2	ESCP Europe Master in Management at ESCP Europe / France, UK, Germany, Spain, Italy	yes	no	yes	yes
3	Master of Science in Management at WHU Otto Beisheim School of Management / Germany	yes	yes	yes	yes
4	HEC Master of Science in Management at HEC Paris / France	yes	no	yes (O)	yes
5	Master of Science in International Management at Rotterdam School of Management Erasmus University / The Netherlands	yes	no	yes	yes
6	Master in Management at IE Business School / Spain	yes	yes	yes	yes
7	Master of Science in Management at ESSEC Business School / France	yes	no	yes	yes
8	Master of Science in Management at Handelshochschule Leipzig (HHL), Leipzig Graduate School of Management / Germany	yes	no	yes	yes
9	Master of Science in International Management at Esade Business School at Ramon Llull University / Spain	yes	yes	yes (O)	yes

10	Master of Science in Management at Emlyon Business School / France	yes	yes (O)	yes	yes
11	Master of Science in Management at Imperial College London Business School / UK	yes (O)	yes (O)	yes (O)	yes
12	Master in International Business at Grenoble École de Management, Graduate School of Management / France	yes	no	yes (O)	yes
13	MBA at Harvard Business School / USA	yes	yes	yes	yes
14	MBA at Stanford Graduate School of Business / USA	yes	no	yes (O)	yes
15	MBA at The Wharton School, University of Pennsylvania / USA	yes	yes (O)	yes (O)	yes

International and intercultural exchange – e.g. study abroad

Field trip – company visits

Real-world setting – it comprises any form of students' exposure to real-world working experience; since no standard term exists, the term real-world setting is used comprising e.g. internships (work experience, projects etc. In real-world settings students' actions and competencies may be demonstrated

Reflection – systematic structured reflection e.g. discussions, working groups, (peer-) mentoring, coaching, transfer opportunities, written reflection papers, etc.

O - Optional part of elective (or specialization) part of curriculum; it is not mandatory part of curriculum

Table 10. Educational contents of selected Master's programs based on minimal criteria for reality and reflection as defined in chapter 3.2.5.3 and 3.2.5.4. Data retrieved from institution's official website between June 1 to June 12, 2014.

integral part of all programs. Regarding the CBE-aspect of educational contents, it was granted matter of course that all programs provide international and intercultural exposure. In addition, field trips are prevalent and all 15 schools offer an opportunity for real-world exposure to conduct (a) project(s) in (a) company / companies. Nevertheless, duration and intensity of real-world projects vary immensely (see chapter 4.1.5.4). It shall be proposed to integrate them as a fundamental and as an intense part of the mandatory curriculum, as it facilitates learners to obtain experiences through actions and can best be supported by the systematic reflection procedures already anchored in all exemplary Master's programs.

4.1.5.4 Educational methodologies

Based on theoretical roots, inquiry-based learning and CBE were proposed to be educational methodologies for business leadership education in tertiary education. Therefore, the question whether or not the exemplary Master's programs focus on inquiry-based learning and CBE has to be answered. In order to evaluate programs, indicators for both methodologies were defined. Thus, the strongest indicator for inquiry-based learning is the Master's thesis, wherein students demonstrate the ability to conduct considerable individual research in a restricted time limit etc. Strongest indicator for CBE is real-world setting.[59] Based on theoretical roots, educational content was defined comprising the parts theory, reality, and reflection in a balanced way (see chapter 3.2.5.3). Consequently, the proportion of reality encompasses 33 %. Reality was proposed to comprise e.g. international and intercultural exchanges, field trips and real-world-settings of which real-world settings are of highest importance for business leadership education in tertiary education as therein students can demonstrate their actions and competencies and learn to take responsibility for consequences. Due to its high importance, the proportion of real-world settings was proposed to represent 20 % of the total curriculum.

Based on these criteria, data were analyzed for the educational methodologies of inquiry-based learning and CBE. In order to obtain clear results to the first aspect, the relevant data were organized to uncover similarities and differences between theory and practice and to detect proportions of programs that fulfill or do not fulfill the criteria. The following results can be reported (see Table 11):

1. Inquiry-based learning: Master's thesis is required in ten of 15 exemplary programs. In one of the ten programs (no. 9), students may choose from one of the three options: in-company project, Master's thesis, or business plan. The analysis revealed that the Master's thesis' proportion of the total curriculum differed across the programs, ranging from 11.7 % (no. 9) up to 37.5 % (no. 12). Five out of 15 programs did not require a Master's

---

[59] As there is no clear terminology, the term real-world setting is used – as determined in chapter 4.1.5.3 – comprising e.g. internships, work experience and real-world projects in companies/organizations. Students' actions and competencies can be demonstrated in real-world settings.

thesis. These include all three American programs (no. 13-15) along with two European programs (no. 6 and 11), where final exams were conducted, e.g. as presentation before a jury panel (no. 6) or case-based exams, wherein students have to read cases and write an essay (no. 12).

2. Competency-based education: As outlined previously (chapter 4.1.5.3), all 15 programs offer an opportunity to obtain real-world experiences, e.g. to conduct a project in a company. Many institutions made the real-world setting mandatory for the students (9); some kept it optional (6). Even though the following aspect was elucidated in chapter 4.1.5.3, it has to be repeated due to its relevance. In programs, where real-world settings and field trips are only optional, it may occur that students that do not choose either a field trip or a real-world setting, and consequently do not experience any real-world exposure during the term of the Master's program. Furthermore, the duration and intensity of the offered real-world settings vary immensely, ranging from 1 % of total curriculum (no. 13) up to 75 % (no. 7). Considering the proposed proportion of real-world settings to be 20 % of total curriculum, only five of 15 programs meet the demands (no. 2, 4, 7, 10, and 12). Only three of the five programs made real-world setting mandatory for their students (no. 2, 7, and 10), while they are optional in two programs (no. 4 and 12). When comparing the programs by country, it was observed that German programs (no. 3 and 8) and American programs (no. 12-15) were allotted minimum importance compared to – notably – the French programs (no. 2, 4, 10, and 12) that considered real-world settings to be of high importance. At least for the German programs, the results seem – ostensibly – surprising. Nevertheless, while professional dual education is deeply rooted in Germany, tertiary education is mostly academic in its nature. In contrast, results for American programs underline the high importance of case studies examined in business leadership education in tertiary education.

While inquiry-based learning is reasonable practiced in most of the exemplary Master's programs, only a small part of the programs meet the demands of competency-based education. Clearly spoken, only the three programs that made real-world settings a mandatory part of the curriculum strictly facilitate students' development for business leadership competencies. Nevertheless, if most programs do not focus on competency-based education, the question of how exemplary Master's programs describe their pedagogical approach arises.

No.	Program at Institution / Country	Master's thesis as strongest indicator for inquiry-based learning (in ECTS and in % of total curriculum workload)	Real-world setting ≥ 20 % of curriculum as strongest indicator for competency-based education (in ECTS and in % of total curriculum workload)
1	Master of Arts in Strategy and International Management at University of St. Gallen / Switzerland	yes (18 ECTS = 20 %)	yes (10 ECTS = 11.1 %)
2	ESCP Europe Master in Management at ESCP Europe / France, UK, Germany, Spain, Italy	yes (n.a.)	Yes (n.a. – 39 weeks – ca. 48.8 %)
3	Master of Science in Management at WHU Otto Beisheim School of Management / Germany	yes (25 ECTS = 20.8 %)	Yes (5 ECTS = 4.2 %)
4	HEC Master of Science in Management at HEC Paris / France	yes (20 ECTS = 16.7 %)	yes (O) (ECTS n.a. – if chosen: 12 months between year 1 and year 2 = 40 %)
5	Master of Science in International Management at Rotterdam School of Management Erasmus University / The Netherlands	yes (20 ECTS = 22.2 %)	yes (15 ECTS = 16.7 %)
6	Master in Management at IE Business School / Spain	no	yes (n.a. – 1 week = ca. 2 -3 %)
7	Master of Science in Management at ESSEC Business School / France	yes (n.a.)	yes (n.a. – 18 months = 37.5 - 75 %)
8	Master of Science in Management at Handelshochschule Leipzig (HHL), Leipzig Graduate School of Management / Germany	yes (15 ECTS = 12.5 %)	yes (5 ECTS – 4.2 %)
9	Master of Science in International Management at Esade Business School at Ramon Llull University / Spain	yes (O) (if chosen: 7 ECTS = 11.7 %)	yes (O) (if chosen: 7 ECTS = 11.7 %)

10	Master of Science in Management at Emlyon Business School / France	yes (15 ECTS = 12.5%)	yes (ECTS n.a. - 12 months = 33.3 – 50%)
11	Master of Science in Management at Imperial College London Business School / UK	no	yes (O) (ECTS n.a. - 5 weeks = ca. 10%)
12	Master in International Business at Grenoble École de Management, Graduate School of Management / France	yes (45 ECTS = 37.5%)	yes (O) (ECTS n.a. – if chosen: 12 months = 50%)
13	MBA at Harvard Business School / USA	no	yes (1 week – ca. 1%)
14	MBA at Stanford Graduate School of Business / USA	no	yes (O) (if chosen: at least 4 weeks – ca. 4%)
15	MBA at The Wharton School, University of Pennsylvania / USA	no	yes (O) (if chosen: 6 -12 weeks = ca. 6-12%)

n.a. – not available

O – Optional part of elective (or specialization) part of curriculum; it is not mandatory part of curriculum

Table 11. Educational methodologies of selected Master's programs according to chapter 3.2.5.4. Data retrieved from institution's official website between June 1 to June 12, 2014.

For in-depth analysis of this aspect, qualitative content analysis was conducted. The additional content analysis complements the results previously outlined and provides a better understanding of the evaluated topic.

Analyzing the pedagogical approach helped to understand the pedagogical concept and the methodologies used in the programs. Thus, each institution had a clear pedagogical approach. Some statements that depict the pedagogical concept are as follows:

> "The general management curriculum rests on a foundation of social science principles and management functions, tailored to each student's background and aspirations. Interdisciplinary themes of critical analytical thinking, creativity and innovation,

and personal leadership development differentiate the Stanford MBA experience. Each MBA student undertakes a global experience to provide direct exposure to the world's opportunities."

(Statement 20) MBA at Stanford Graduate School of Management / USA

"A holistic education: more than just theory consists of 5 elements: 1) Leadership perspective, 2) Integrated management, 3) Combining theory and practice, 4) International experience, 5) Individual attention. Combining theory and practice means: At HHL, preparing the theoretical background is just the starting point. A successful career in a leadership position requires theory testing experience: theory becomes tangible through case studies and field (consulting) projects. Back in the classroom, our experts share their knowledge and state-of-the-art research with the managers of tomorrow. Individual attention means: Along with the theoretical and methodical framework, HHL offers you efficient and exemplary learning conditions".

(Statement 19) Master of Science in Management at HHL Leipzig Graduate School of Management / Germany

Furthermore, each institution mentioned the various methodologies that were used. The following statements uncover those methodologies:

"Teaching methods for MBA include Lecture & Discussion, Case, Experiential, Simulation, Labs, Feedback & Coaching, Leadership Design, Gust Speakers, Role Play, Global Immersion."

(Statement 20) MBA at Stanford Graduate School of Management / USA

"The Harvard MBA teaches you to learn how to make decisions in the face of conflicting data, complex politics, and intense time and fiscal pressures – then defend your choices among peers as motivated and intelligent as you are. That's exactly what you'll do at HBS, not once but many times over through two years of in-depth, case-method learning and a hands-on Field Immersion Experiences for Leadership Development (FIELD) course that puts leadership into practice through teamwork, personal reflection, global immersions, and hands-on experience designing and launching a micro business."

(Statement 25) MBA at Harvard Business School / USA

"The Master course challenges you academically, culturally, and personally. One gains international as well as practical experience which is crucial for a career in management. One also learns beyond the classroom by getting involved in one of WHU's numerous student clubs. The program content combines academic rigor with practical relevance. Students also get an exposure to the real world of business through internships in Germany or abroad."

(Statement 20) Master of Science in Management at WHU Otto Beisheim School of Management / Germany

"Innovative pedagogy based upon case studies, instruction from visiting executives and ESCP Europe's partnerships with leading companies ensure the link between in-class theory and the reality of the business world. The integrated internship is a key aspect in this approach".

(Statement 20) ESCP, Europe, Management.

In contrast to competency-based education, many schools focus on imparting functional management knowledge and skills to teach their students. Thus, theory-oriented courses and various (practical) activities were implemented by institutions.

4.1.5.5 Educational settings

Based on theoretical roots, three educational settings were proposed for business leadership education in tertiary education (see chapter 3.2.5.5). Therefore, the question of whether the exemplary Master's programs facilitate these three educational settings proposed – 1. real-world setting, 2. international setting and 3. technological setting – has to be answered.

In order to obtain clear results to the first aspect, the relevant data were organized in order to uncover similarities and differences between theory and practice and to detect proportions of programs that fulfill or do not fulfill the criteria. For in-depth analysis, the qualitative content was examined. This systematic procedure was used to obtain a better understanding of the evaluated topic.

1. Real-world setting

As elaborated previously, all 15 schools offer real-world settings to gain real-world experiences (see chapter 4.1.5.4 and Table 11). Many institutions made the real-world setting mandatory for the students (9); some kept it optional (6). Nevertheless, the duration and intensity of the real-world settings offered vary immensely, ranging from 1 % of the total curriculum (no. 13) up to 75 % (no. 7). Furthermore, in case of optional real-world settings, it may occur that students, who do not choose this option, consequently do not obtain any real-world exposure during the Master's program. Considering the proposed proportion of real-world settings at 20 % of total curriculum, it was detected that only the three programs that made real-world settings as mandatory part of the curriculum, meet the demands, and strictly facilitate student's competency development for business leadership competencies. Nevertheless, due to the immense differences in duration and pedagogical approach, a detailed analysis was conducted on internships / work experience and real-world projects to better understand the institutions' intentions. The two ways to facilitate real-world settings and the relevant statements that describe them is presented in the following section.

A real-world project was observed to be quite popular among most higher education institutions. Some similarities were observed during the content analysis. According to the universities / business schools that provided this opportunity, the general aim of a project was to give hands-on experience to students by working in a company and combining theory and practice. The projects were not only beneficial for the respective students, but also for the companies. The analysis revealed that such projects also helped companies to resolve practical business issues and students in their personal development, as the following statements show:

> "Teams of international students work intensively on a consultancy project for a company or institution, supervised by coaches from the university and the company. Students are expected to respond professionally to a real-world management problem, and to learn from working together in multidisciplinary and culturally heterogeneous groups."
>
> *(Statement 9) Master of Science in International Management at Rotterdam School of Management Erasmus University / The Netherlands*

"SIMagination Challenge: An innovative approach to spur advanced learning in initiating and sustaining a positive impact for unmet social needs, the SIMagination Challenge is a course that allows for meaningful experiences and insights regarding the realization of sophisticated international projects. This collaborative course includes various events and workshops which enable students to blend individual and collective learning and development, and sharpen their strategic thinking, team skills, and applied global leadership ethics and effectiveness."

(Statement 17) Master of Arts in Strategy and International Management at University of St. Gallen / Switzerland

A major difference observed was that some schools encouraged the students to conduct the projects in a foreign country. Such projects were called overseas projects for the purpose of the content analysis. In 4 of 15 schools, students had the opportunity to conduct the project either at an international partner university or an international campus of their host university / business school.

"The project may require the students to go to corporate sites overseas."

(Statement 16) Master of Science in Management at Imperial College London Business School / UK

"Global Management Immersion Experience (GMIX): Gain hands-on global management experience by living and working in another country."

(Statement 15) MBA at Stanford Graduate School of Business / USA

"Consulting projects at Emlyon (not mandatory) are a part of the international learning in Asia."

(Statement 16) Master of Science in Management at Emlyon Business School / France

"Students initiate projects around the globe, first by carefully identifying and analysing social needs and then by developing effective and lasting solutions to address these challenges in the long-term. The course includes topics such as team diversity, strategy execution, and social impact, which in combination address the key development needs of leaders in the 21st century."

(Statement 20) Master of Arts in Strategy and International Management at University of St. Gallen / Switzerland

The analysis revealed that, along with real-world projects, mandatory internships are a popular way to facilitate real-world settings either locally or internationally. In some cases, the internships were combined with real-world projects and opportunities to study abroad. The purpose of the internships was viewed differently by each institution. The following statements will shed light on the differences:

> "Students are encouraged to seek out an in-company internship and to base their final management projects in the companies where they have found the internship."
>
> *(Statement 18) Master in International Business at Grenoble École de Management, Graduate School of Management / France*

> "At HEC between Master Cycle 1 and Master Cycle 2, students have the opportunity to take a gap year and gain work experience in business."
>
> *(Statement 19) HEC Master of Science in Management at HEC Paris / France*

> "Professional Experience: Students must complete a minimum of eighteen months of work experience during the program which can take the form of internships, apprenticeship program and entrepreneurial projects."
>
> *(Statement 20) Master of Science in Management at ESSEC Business School / France*

> "During M.Sc. in Management program, students must build work experience for a minimum of 12 months. For most participants, this experience will consist of two internships; option of an international internship is available."
>
> *(Statement 18) Master of Science in Management at Emlyon Business School / France*

> "SIM International Project: Each student is required to engage in a challenging international internship that should be independently defined, planned, initiated, successfully completed, and reflected upon."
>
> *(Statement 19) Master of Arts in Strategy and International Management at University of St. Gallen / Switzerland*

Based on the deepened understanding of real-world setting that is combined with international setting in many institutions, the latter shall be shed light on in detail.

2. International setting

As mentioned earlier, all the schools had a global focus and encouraged their students to conduct projects or internships in a foreign country. Broadening the horizons was the prime focus of the schools. Therefore, the study-abroad opportunities were analyzed in detail. Some universities made it compulsory for students to travel abroad for studying. Nine of 15 schools had mandatory study abroad opportunities for students. A similarity of such study abroad opportunities was observed across all schools. Studying abroad for a few weeks / months or with an entire term would give the students a chance to experience the culture and economic aspects of a foreign country. A few differences were also noted. The duration of studying abroad was different for each institution. In case of American universities only one school Harvard Business School mentioned that the study abroad opportunity is 1 % of the curriculum. In case of European institutions, the duration is longer e.g. 25 % for WHU Otto Beisheim School of Management, 33.3 % for Rotterdam School of Management Ersamus University, 25 % HHL Leipzig Graduate School of Management etc. The following statements depict the purpose of the study abroad opportunity and differences that lie between the institutions:

> "Global Study Trips: Develop a meaningful, on-the-ground perspective of the business, political, and social climates within a country during a Global Study Trip, Prior to the trip, you'll hear from and host speakers on topics such as macroeconomic policy or political history and facilitate discussions on history, culture, and business etiquette. You'll travel with about 30 classmates and a faculty advisor and have unprecedented access to business, government, and non-profit leaders with whom you'll explore the complexities of global management."
>
> *(Statement 22) MBA at Stanford Graduate School of Business / USA*

> "Field Immersion Experiences for Leadership Development (FIELD) course to work on a product or service idea in emerging markets for a weeklong immersion.
>
> *(Statement 27) MBA at Harvard Business School / USA*

"It is the objective of a term abroad to introduce students to general and specialist experiences about the way of living and working in other countries. The knowledge of foreign languages should be deepened too. Thereby, the continuous internationalization of economy and society will be appropriately taken into account in the study course. The possible content of a study course abroad will be established separately for each partner university in accordance with its curriculum."

(Statement 20) Master of Science in Management at HHL, Leipzig Graduate School of Management / Germany

"Short exchange program: the September intake has the opportunity to take part in it with London Business School (LBS). The exchange complements the program's academic experience, while providing the opportunity to network with peers and faculty from another reputed institutes and to engage with prominent leaders from UK and from around the world."

(Statement 21) Master in Management at IE Business School / Spain

"International Immersion: students of the MSc in Management will be required to spend at least 6 months in a country other than their home country."

(Statement 16) Master of Science in Management at Emlyon Business School / France

Some schools expected a final written report about the study abroad experience. Two institutions in Europe (Imperial College London Business School / UK and Grenoble École de Management, Graduate School of Management / France) and two institutions in the USA (The Wharton School, University of Pennsylvania and Stanford Graduate School of Business) demanded written reports. Furthermore, it is popular across European universities that offered study abroad opportunities to also pursue double degrees. Considering the international setting that was described, it can be summarized in three main aspects. Firstly, it is observed that institutions prefer to combine real-world and international setting. Secondly, various possibilities were shown, how universities / business schools facilitate international settings and finally, international setting is a matter of course in contemporary business leadership education in tertiary education.

Against this background, technological setting shall be examined.

3. Technological setting

The overall document-based content analysis revealed that none of the exemplary Master's programs conducted sessions of core, elective or specialization courses online. In contrast, the presence of the students in the classroom considered very important by all the exemplary programs. Digital media are not neglected, but are widely seen as a tool that supports learning, as the following statement shows:

> "In addition to class discussions, you will have access to multimedia simulations, case studies, hands-on workshops, industry visits, and the opportunity to listen to eminent business leaders. In the case method each area of business is studied using practical cases, most of which deal with real problems that may arise in any type of company. Cases are first prepared individually, then in groups before being discussed in class under the guidance of the professor. In interactive learning we put a wide range of multimedia tools at our students' disposal: simulators, interactive graphics, videos and podcasts, as well as completely interactive case studies and technical notes. This innovative use of media supports different learning styles and makes content easier to absorb for all types of learners."
>
> *(Statement 20) Master in Management at IE Business School / Spain*

Considering trends and challenges in the segment of tertiary education in general and in business leadership education in particular (chapter 3.2.2), along with digitization as a major driver in the VUCA-world, the results were surprising. It may be assumed that tomorrow's model of business leadership education in tertiary education will look different.

4.1.5.6 Evaluation

Based on theoretical roots, evaluation methods were proposed for business leadership education in tertiary education (see chapter 3.2.5.5). Therefore, the question of what are the evaluation methods on the micro level for students' performance, on the meso level (accreditation) and on the macro level (employment report), has to be answered. In order to obtain clear results, the relevant data was organized to uncover similarities and differences between theory and practice, and to detect proportions of programs that fulfill or do not fulfill the criteria.

Considering the evaluation methods on the meso and macro level, i.e. accreditation and employment report, information along with application procedures, curricula contents and ranking information belong to the information mostly available on the institution's official websites. Higher education institutions are generally proud to present their 'seal of approval' granted by accreditation agencies for quality assurance on all available (marketing) information. Along with the information of the employment report on alumni, career progress information on accreditation are of high importance to recruit applicants.

The analysis revealed that 12 of 15 institutions, apart from three European business schools (University of St. Gallen / Switzerland, WHU / Germany and Grenoble Graduate School of Management / France), have an employment report (see Table 12). Furthermore, all institutions received accreditation. AACSB is the most favored accreditation agency for all business schools analyzed in this research. All European business schools analyzed in this research have two or more 'seals of approval', with EQUIS being prevalent. Eight of the 12 European business schools have received three accreditations, one business school even five. Thus, these distinct results show the importance of the evaluation methods, accreditation[60] and employment report, on the meso and macro level.

Along with evaluation methods on the meso and macro level, evaluation methods on the micro level, i.e. students' performance are examined. In contrast to information of programs' Master's thesis or final exams, which is easily available on the institutions' official websites, information on evaluation methods during Master's programs are scarce in case of almost half of the analyzed programs. Thus, some schools provide some information on their websites, some schools provide all information, i.e. syllabi, and study and examination regulations that are easily accessible through the institutions' websites and some information fail to provide any information on evaluation methods for student's performance. Nevertheless, considering the information available it becomes evident that business schools use a mix of various evaluation methods encompassing written tests, case analysis, essays, reports, business plan documents and pitch, presentations and active participation. Evaluation

---

60 For critical considerations on accreditation, please see Burke & Butler, 2012.

methods referred to by analyzed business schools mostly require students to rearrange the learned information or problem-solving techniques. Nevertheless, this is congruent with the results of the content analysis on pedagogical approach and educational methodologies presented earlier. As educational methodologies focus on teaching management-relevant knowledge and skill development, the defined evaluation methods are obviously consistent with and complement the programs' educational methodologies. In contrast, the analysis detects that only a minor proportion of programs emphasized competency-based education, wherein actions and competencies are demonstrated to foster "outcome-based approaches to student learning" (Altbach, Reisberg & Rumbley, 2009, p. 119) (see chapter 3.2.5.6). Consequently, evaluation methods consistent with competency-based education are (still) neglected in analyzed programs.

No.	Program at Institution / Country	Employment Report	Accreditation				
			AASCB	AMBA	EQUIS	FIBAA	Other
1	Master of Arts in Strategy and International Management at University of St. Gallen / Switzerland	no	yes	no	yes	no	no
2	ESCP Europe Master in Management at ESCP Europe / France, UK, Germany, Spain, Italy	yes	yes	yes	yes	no	no
3	Master of Science in Management at WHU Otto Beisheim School of Management / Germany	no	yes	no	yes	yes	no
4	HEC Master of Science in Management at HEC Paris / France	yes	yes	yes	yes	no	no
5	Master of Science in International Management at Rotterdam School of Management Erasmus University / The Netherlands	yes	yes	yes	yes	no	yes (+2)
6	Master in Management at IE Business School / Spain	yes	yes	yes	yes	no	no
7	Master of Science in Management at ESSEC Business School / France	yes	yes	no	yes	no	no

8	Master of Science in Management at Handelshochschule Leipzig (HHL), Leipzig Graduate School of Management / Germany	yes	yes	no	no	no	yes (+1)
9	Master of Science in International Management at Esade Business School at Ramon Llull University / Spain	yes	yes	yes	yes	no	no
10	Master of Science in Management at Emlyon Business School / France	yes	yes	yes	yes	no	no
11	Master of Science in Management at Imperial College London Business School / UK	yes	yes	yes	yes	no	no
12	Master in International Business at Grenoble École de Management, Graduate School of Management / France	no	yes	yes	yes	no	no
13	MBA at Harvard Business School / USA	yes	yes	no	no	no	no
14	MBA at Stanford Graduate School of Business / USA	yes	yes	no	no	no	no
15	MBA at The Wharton School, University of Pennsylvania / USA	yes	yes	no	no	no	no

Table 12. Evaluation methods of selected Master's programs on the macro and meso level according to chapter 3.2.5.6. Data retrieved from institution's official website between June 1 to June 12, 2014.

4.1.5.7 Financing

Students have to pay study fees for all of the exemplary Master's programs. Study fees for each program were gathered from the official websites of the programs. Amount of study fees differ immensely. A well-known difference exists between European and American programs, as the fees for the latter are many times higher than for European programs. Although there may be other traditions and financing opportunities, increasing students' debts and value-for-money programs are generally a highly debatable issue in USA (see chapter 3.1.4.4). Study fees for each of the exemplary programs are presented in Table 13.

No.	Program	Institution / Country	Program duration in months (ECTS)*	Study fees / total for locals in local currency**	Study fees / total for locals converted in EUR***
1	Master of Arts in Strategy and International Management	University of St. Gallen / Switzerland	18 (90 ECTS)	1,426 CHF	1,168 EUR
2	ESCP Europe Master in Management	ESCP Europe / France, UK, Germany, Spain, Italy	24 (120 ECTS)	24,400 EUR	24,400 EUR
3	Master of Science in Management	WHU Otto Beisheim School of Management / Germany	17-21 (120 ECTS)	22,000 EUR	22,000 EUR
4	HEC Master of Science in Management	HEC Paris / France	18 (120 ECTS)	24,400 EUR	24,400 EUR
5	Master of Science in International Management	Rotterdam School of Management Erasmus University / The Netherlands	18 (90 ECTS)	1,906 EUR	1,906 EUR
6	Master in Management	IE Business School / Spain	10 (120 ECTS)	32,200 EUR	32,200 EUR
7	Master of Science in Management	ESSEC Business School / France	24-48 (120 ECTS)	30,000 EUR	30,000 EUR
8	Master of Science in Management	Handelshochschule Leipzig (HHL), Leipzig Graduate School of Management / Germany	21-24 (120 ECTS)	25,000 EUR	25,000 EUR
9	Master of Science in International Management	Esade Business School at Ramon Llull University / Spain	12 (60 ECTS)	24,750 EUR	24,750 EUR
10	Master of Science in Management	Emlyon Business School / France	24-36 (120 ECTS)	26,000 EUR	26,000 EUR

11	Master of Science in Management	Imperial College London Business School / UK	12 (90 ECTS)	24,100 GBP	29,678 EUR
12	Master in International Business	Grenoble École de Management, Graduate School of Management / France	24 (120 ECTS)	19,200 EUR	19,200 EUR
13	MBA	Harvard Business School / USA	24	117,750 USD	86,988 EUR
14	MBA	Stanford Graduate School of Business / USA	24	123,750 USD	91,421 EUR
15	MBA	The Wharton School, University of Pennsylvania / USA	24	136,420 USD	100,871 EUR

* ECTS are important to compare workload in Bologna region. Workload in the USA is defined in credits (e.g. semester credits (CRS)). Total workload for MBA programs in USA is not strictly defined. Therefore, a total workload in MBA programs may vary due to different universities / business schools and the electives / specialization students' choose.

** For the total period of study; in some programs study fees for foreigners are more expensive; study fees for programs in USA (no. 13-15) refer only to tuition not total costs; for more details, please see official program websites.

*** For the reason of comparability local currency was converted in EUR on June 12th, 2014 using https://www.oanda.com.

Table 13. Study fees for selected Master's programs. Data retrieved from institution's official website between June 1 to June 12, 2014.

According to alumni career progress – that is generally proven by average salary three years after graduation and is a common indicator in rankings and higher education institutions' marketing activities – salaries from US (top) universities usually exceed those from the European market. Nevertheless, as previously outlined, global debates on financing tertiary education are ongoing and of great importance, especially with regard to the evaluation and identification of innovative allocation mechanisms (see chapter 3.2.5.7).

4.1.6 Limitations and future research

The evaluation of exemplary, deliberately selected Master's programs is based on criteria thoroughly developed and rooted in strong theoretical foundations. Therefore, the evaluation procedure provides deep insight into the curriculum design of exemplary Master's programs and uncovers its nucleus. Nevertheless, as with any research, the discussions in this research have some limitations and generate questions for future research. First, as a common phenomenon for any exemplary research and due to a limited and not representative sample within this research, the results may not be generalized for all Master's programs in Management education – which is synonymously for business leadership education – in tertiary education. Furthermore, information was – at least partly – difficult to obtain and was mainly based on official institutions' websites and / or program-specific documents available through official websites, which, in turn, are created for profiling and promotion. Although it may be assumed (hypothesized) that main findings of this research will not change – at least not significantly, future research could focus on a larger scale, using mixed-method approaches. Thus, a combination of quantitative research with qualitative data (e.g. expert interviews) is highly recommended, as the latter is indispensable in order to obtain meaningful representative results.

4.2 Conclusions

This part of the chapter is aimed at answering the second research question of this work. Therefore, based on a holistic understanding of business leadership and sound theoretical foundations of business leadership education in tertiary education for graduates, exemplary Master's programs in contemporary tertiary education were evaluated in light of the theoretical framework. A comprehensible systematic evaluation approach following strict rules was carried out to meet the demands of qualitative research. Exemplary Master's programs in management for graduates were selected in a systematic procedure and evaluated based on seven evaluation criteria and its sub-criteria. These seven evaluation criteria and its sub-criteria are deeply rooted in theory. They reflect the seven principles proposed earlier for curriculum design in business leadership education in tertiary education for graduates. Based on the defined evaluation criteria and its sub-criteria, the data was collected from the official websites of the respective institutions and / or program-specific documents available through the official websites, following the procedure of document analysis. In order to obtain clear results, a document-based content analysis was considered best suited. In a first step, the relevant data was organized in order to reduce complexity, uncover similarities and differences between theory and practice, and detect proportions of programs that fulfill or do not fulfill the criteria and obtain clear results. A content analysis was carried out for in-depth analysis of crucial aspects studied in this research (e.g. institution's understanding of 'real-world project'). This systematic procedure was used to obtain a better understanding of the evaluated topic.

Considering the detailed analysis and its results, it may be concluded that each program meets high quality demands demonstrated through at least one 'seal of approval' granted by AACSB. Moreover, each program has a distinct orientation providing a highly attractive educational opportunity. Nevertheless, synthesizing the essential results of the evaluation procedure, two findings are established. Firstly, exemplary Master's programs in the field of business leadership education for graduates focus on imparting functional management knowledge and development of management qualifications / skills in order to increase students' employability. Secondly, this educational approach is diametrically opposed to the earlier findings of this research. Hence, (creative) personality was revealed as the superior educational ideal promoted through competency-based education.

Conclusively, the research provided insight into the status quo of business leadership education in tertiary education and helped to uncover conflicting results between theory and practice. Finally, conducting the evaluation procedure based on defined evaluation criteria and its sub-criteria, which reflect the seven principles proposed for curriculum design in business leadership education in tertiary education, clearly uncovers the pedagogical nucleus of a program. Getting such clear results and thereby revealing such distinctive leverages for change means conversely that the seven principles for curriculum design are scientifically confirmed for curriculum design in business leadership education in tertiary education.

5. Conclusions Part 2

The principal purpose of this part was to introduce the principles of business leadership education in tertiary education for graduates based on a thorough literature review. Therefore, it was indispensable to obtain an overview on the meaning of business leadership. Furthermore, the research aimed at uncovering how business leadership education in tertiary education is practiced in exemplary Master's programs for graduates in light of the theoretical approach. Two pivotal research questions directed the design and implementation of this chapter. The chapter was structured in two parts. Theoretical foundations of business leadership education in tertiary education for graduates were scrutinized in a first part, based on thorough literature review; subsequently, exemplary contemporary Master's programs were evaluated in light of the theoretical framework in the second part.

Therefore, in the first part of this chapter, the most prevalent approaches to leadership were elucidated. As an immense number and variety of definitions and theoretical approaches to leadership exist, a choice was made. Hence, the most prevalent approaches deriving from the discipline of psychology were elucidated. Despite their valuable contributions to leadership research, various strengths and (methodological) shortcomings were outlined. Moreover, it was pointed out that the (traditional) approaches reflect merely a fragmentary instead of a holistic perspective on leadership, failing to measure leaders' performance. Besides, the assessment center that belongs to the most popular diagnostic procedures was described. Considering ACs from a positive point of view, the main purpose of ACs may lie in a culture-oriented selection of (potential) business leaders when assessors are (higher) leaders. In spite of various improvements, (not all) ACs are able to predict leaders' future job performance. Reliance on only ACs to select future leaders therefore seems to be insufficient and in many instances misleading.

Moreover, findings of different disciplines mainly from human ethology and organizational sciences were compiled due to their high impact on leadership and to obtain a comprehensive overview on the studied topic. Thus, not only personal leadership behavior, but also entrepreneurial leadership plays a vital role in business leadership.

Due to various external (political, economic, socio-cultural, technological, and legal) influencing factors on (business) environment and with respect to the research topic in the discipline of pedagogics, a contemporary and holistic model of business leadership was developed. This holistic model comprises both the business perspective, i.e. goals and innovations as well as the perspective on the leader's individual personality, i.e. creative personality and business leadership competencies. Moreover, the business leader is not perceived as being isolated, but rather as acting in a complex sociocultural context with its multitude of influential factors.

This contemporary and holistic understanding of business leadership in a dynamic environment laid the foundation for a contemporary humanistic approach on business leadership education in tertiary education, deeply rooted in humanistic philosophy. Pivotal goal of this approach is fostering individuals throughout their entire life to develop their personalities, which is demonstrated by their actions and contributions to nature, other humans, society, organizations etc. Against this background, the segment of tertiary education in general and the discipline of business leadership education in particular were examined; both have to cope with major trends and challenges on a global scale. Based on current debates, a brand new definition seems to be inevitable in order to design contemporary business leadership education in tertiary education from a pedagogical point of view. To do so, the pedagogical infrastructure for business leadership education in tertiary education, the *curriculum,* was examined.

Nevertheless, it was not intended to define an ideal curriculum on a detailed level. On the contrary, diversity is nourished and maintained. Therefore, the general principles of academic freedom, unity of research and teaching and each higher education institution's individual culture and (research) orientation were respected. In order to answer the first question of this research – how business leadership education in Master's programs for graduates in tertiary education shall be designed –, seven main principles were proposed for a curriculum of business leadership education in Master's programs in tertiary education. The seven principles are deeply rooted in theory and reflect the main questions that need to be answered with a didactic approach. They are conceived to serve as a kind of orientation and guidelines for curriculum design in business leadership education in tertiary education for graduates.

Synthesizing the essential results of curriculum design based on the seven proposed principles, two findings are established. Firstly, business leadership education in tertiary education has to focus on the student's familiarization with the scientific world on one hand, and the individual student's (creative) personality and its competency development on the other. Secondly, curriculum with its elements – i.e. educational contents, educational methodologies, educational settings, and evaluation – therefore has to facilitate a consistent pedagogical infrastructure that nurtures development of the individual student's business leader personality. Such an infrastructure is characterized by competency-based education. As competency-based education is conceived as an umbrella term, various implementations are possible. Each higher education institution has to find its own way best suited for its respective (research) orientation and (institutional) culture.

Based on the theoretical foundations, the second part of this chapter aimed at answering the second research question of this work. Therefore, based on a holistic understanding of business leadership and sound theoretical foundations of business leadership education in tertiary education for graduates, exemplary Master's programs in contemporary tertiary education were evaluated based on seven evaluation criteria and its sub-criteria in the light of the theoretical framework. A comprehensible systematic evaluation approach following strict rules was carried out to meet the demands of qualitative research. Considering the detailed analysis and its results, it can be concluded that each program meets high quality demands demonstrated through at least one 'seal of approval' granted by AACSB. Moreover, each program has a distinct orientation, providing a highly attractive educational opportunity. Nevertheless, synthesizing the essential results of the evaluation procedure yielded two findings. Firstly, exemplary Master's programs in the field of business leadership education for graduates focus on imparting functional management knowledge and development of management qualifications / skills in order to foster students' employability. Secondly, this educational approach is diametrically opposed to the earlier findings of this research. Hence, (creative) personality was revealed to be the superior educational ideal fostered through competency-based education.

However, the results of this chapter perfectly match Kellerman. Kellerman, a contemporary American scholar in public leadership, stated in her work *The End of Leadership* "The reason is that I`m uneasy, increasingly so, about leadership in the twenty-first century and the gap between the teaching of leadership and the practice of leadership" (Kellerman, 2012b, p. XIII).

As the findings of this chapter demonstrate, it is urgently required to redesign business leadership education in tertiary education for graduates to equip tomorrow's business leaders with the competencies, which they need to cope with the challenges of the VUCA-world in the 21st century, to facilitate a pedagogical infrastructure that nurtures students' development of a (creative) personality.

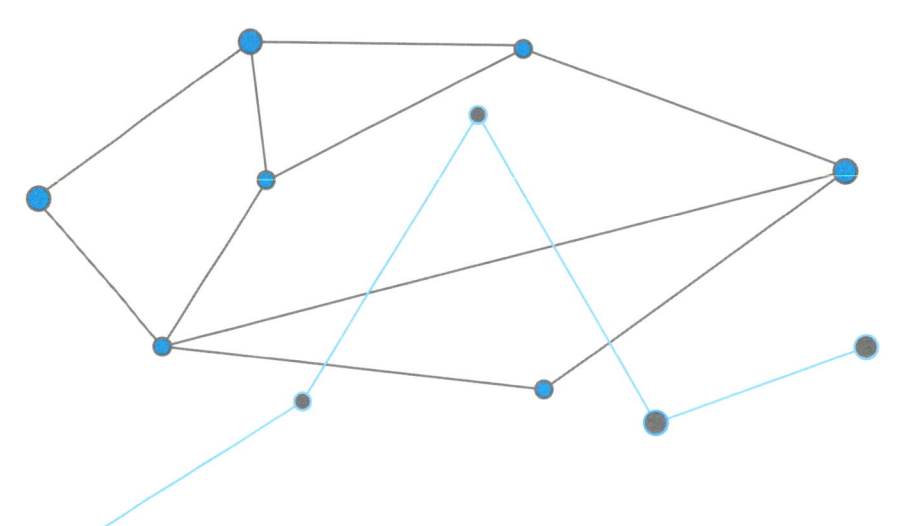

Part 3: Delphi-based scenario study: Business leadership education in tertiary education for graduates in the year 2030

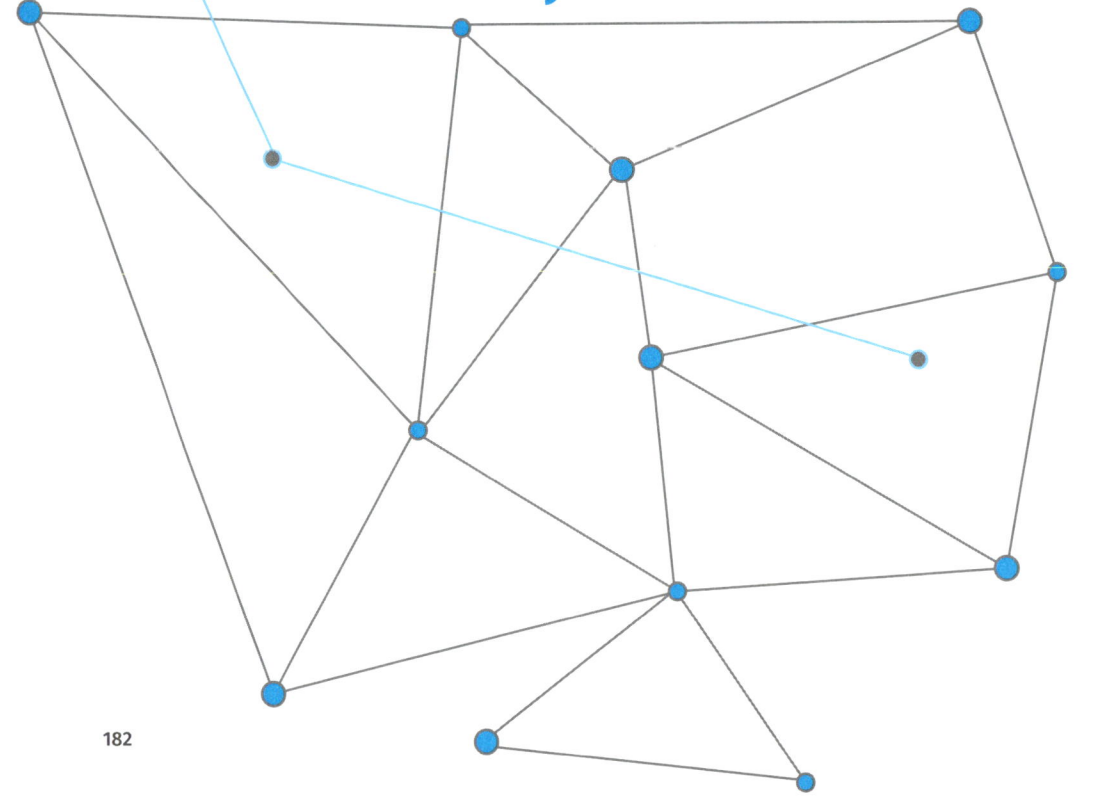

1. Aim of research

Based on the analysis of current situation and framework of business leadership education in tertiary education and the gap between theory and practice shown in previous chapters, objectives for future business leadership education in tertiary education for graduates have to be identified as step four of the overall research design and process (Part 1, Chapter 4).

As mentioned earlier one of the major leadership tasks is setting goals in the present to ensure the organization's future. In the short-term, forecasting can be a suitable option to support decision-making due to a high degree of predictability. As a basic principle in the process of setting objectives and decision-making and the subsequent strategy process it can be stated that the further the future horizon, the greater the dynamic of a system, the higher the degree of uncertainty and the lower the degree of predictability. This principle is shown in Figure 30. Information about the future either does not exist or is incomplete and a multitude of driving forces impact on the future. Moreover, those influencing factors are interdependent in a complex way (Rikkonen, Kaivo-oja & Aakkula, 2006). Hence, the probability of structural changes, which may create a trend break, increases in the long-term. Uncertainty and the possibility of structural changes increase in the central zone of Figure 30, so that the basis for decisions about the future can be enlarged by developing scenarios for multiple future settings due to broader information (Graf & Klein, 2003; Heijden, 2005). This is necessary to be prepared for the future and to be able to create a future based on comprehensive alternatives in a conscious way since there is no one-and-only predictable future.

According to the relevant perspective of the World Future Society (WFS), a prospect of the future has to be manifold and to consider the principle "3P plus 1W". Following this principle, a probable (P), preferable (P) and possible future (P) plus one surprising wildcard (W) have to be provided (WFS; WFS, 2002).

To be prepared for the future of business leadership education in tertiary education for graduates, the aim of research is the definition of goals for the year 2030 and the creation of different future alternatives. Thereby, according to Godet (2001), a proactive attitude to meet the futures perspectives should be adopted. Scientific studies clearly prove the positive effect of strategic foresight and scenario planning on e.g. corporate performance (Phadnis et al., 2015; Phelps, Chan & Kapsalis, 2001; Visser & Chermack, 2009).

Since scenarios are claimed to provide multiple plausible futures, and thereby serve as a basis for decision-making (Keough & Shanahan, 2008; Schoemaker, 1995), the scenarios of this research should support the main stakeholder groups of business leadership education in tertiary education in their decision-making process. A scenario in this context contains a rough proportion of technical and functional management versus personality and leadership aspects in education. The scenarios in this context will not illustrate market-relevant trends such as branding etc. for providers of tertiary education (universities / business schools). Quality, accreditation, and ranking issues shall also not be discussed separately, due to the presumption that those aspects can be taken for granted in successful providers in the year 2030. In order to enhance the quality and validity of scenarios, Delphi-based scenario development was proposed.

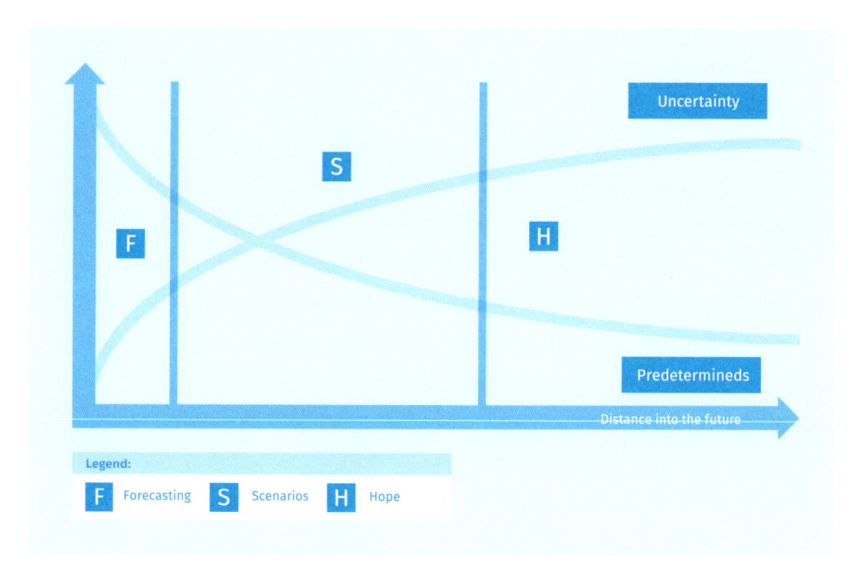

Figure 30.   The balance of predictability and uncertainty in the business environment. Adapted from Heijden, 2005, p. 98.

Furthermore, this research should contribute to further improve and continuously develop business leadership education in tertiary education to become state of the art.

2. Formulation of research questions

In order to deal with the defined aim of research, it is imperative to formulate relevant and concrete research questions. Based on the thorough knowledge gained from integrated scenario and Delphi approach, the following research questions guide the design and implementation of this study:

1. How do experts assess (the) projections for business leadership education in Master in Management programs in tertiary education for the year 2030 according to their estimated probability of occurrence (EP) (scale 0-100 %), desirability (D) (5-point Likert scale) and impact (I) (5-point Likert scale), and how do they support their quantitative evaluations for the three dimensions?
2. Which scenarios and wildcard(s) can be developed for business leadership education in Master in Management programs in tertiary education for the year 2030, based on the quantitative and qualitative data of this (real-time) Delphi study?

3. Methodology: Framing of Delphi-based scenario study

3.1 Principles of scenario planning

Along with other early forecasting approaches scenario method was developed in the 1960s at RAND corporation, one of the oldest think tanks in the USA by Herman Kahn, "the father of modern scenario planning" (Nowack, Endrikat & Guenther., 2011, p. 1603) and his research team, which has subsequently further developed and shaped this approach. During the following years, the scenario technique emerged increasingly, particularly in the work of Royal Dutch Shell, who was interested in this approach due to an increase of planning failures based on forecasts. Pierre Wack introduced and further refined a scenario approach in Royal Dutch Shell based on Kahn's philosophy (Heijden, 2005; Fink & Siebe, 2011; Gausemeier, Fink & Schlake, 1996). In the meantime, scenario method found its way in many different disciplines and industries. Subsequently a variety of scenario analysis and methodological research were published, e.g. for government planning, health care, tourism, logistics, supply chain management etc. (De Mooij & Tang, 2003; Gracht & Darkow, 2010; Markmann, Darkow & Gracht, 2013; Rikkonen, 2005; Solnet et al., 2015). With regard to the field of this research, which is educational sciences, there were also various publications, e.g. for professional training (Becker & Gracht, 2014), tertiary education in general (CERI, 2008[61]; Gregersen, 2011) and the specific field of management education in tertiary education (Thomas et al., 2014). However, the latter provide a general overview on the future of management education.

As a result of browsing literature on scenario method it can be stated that there is no one and only concept; rather, numerous definitions and approaches can be found. This is why Mietzner and Reger (2004) conclude that the "term scenario describes a fuzzy concept that is used and misused, with various shades of meanings" (p. 4). In their review of Delphi-based scenario studies, also Nowack, Endrikat and Guenther (2011) state that "each author has his own approach and designates the steps to his preference" (p. 1606). To present some examples of definitions for scenarios, the following were retrieved from literature.

According to Kahn and Wiener (1967), scenarios are "hypothetical sequences of events, built in the intent of attracting attention to causal processes and points of decision" (p. 6). Godet (1987) defines scenarios as "a description of a future situation together with the progression of events leading from the base situation to the future situation" (p. 21). A similar definition is used by Gausemeier, Fink and Schlake (1996). In addition, they expect scenarios to be "based on a complex network of influencing factors" (p. 90). Based on previous research of Gausemeier, Fink and Schlake (1996) and Heijden (2005), Markmann, Darkow and Gracht (2013, p. 1822) and Gracht & Darkow (2010, p. 47) defined scenarios as "internally consistent, plausible, and challenging narrative descriptions of possible situations in the future, based on a complex network of influencing factors". It must be noted that scenarios do not play any role in getting the future "right", nor do they serve as tools for probabilistic prediction (Chermack & Swanson, 2008). Therefore, the term scenarios is typically used in the plural since the basic principle of this approach is to develop multiple plausible futures (Rikkonen, Kaivo-oja & Aakkula, 2006). Consider-

---

61 For details, please see Part 2, chapter 3.2.2.1.

ing alternative images and perspectives of potential future situations helps to understand and deal with uncertainties and therewith prepare – different options for – decision-making (Heijden, 2005; Keough & Shanahan, 2008).

Along with various definitions, there are also different and multiple ways to categorize scenarios. Mietzner and Reger (2004) state that the "different classifications of scenarios in the research process are not investigated at all" (p. 52). The most relevant categorization for this research is the distinction between exploratory or descriptive scenarios and normative or anticipatory scenarios. Exploratory or descriptive scenarios are characterized as future-oriented, beginning at a certain point in a current situation, leading to alternative possible futures by answering the questions "what if" and "what can happen". They are rather based on qualitative information. In contrast, normative or anticipatory scenarios describe probable and preferable futures. They were designed as looking back from the possible event and consider the question of how the anticipated (or, conversely, feared) state can be reached (Gausemeier, Fink & Schlake, 1996; Godet, 2000).

According to the logic of science, inductive and deductive approaches are two methodological ways of developing scenarios along with abductive and incremental approaches, which are also referred to (Peirce, 1878; Heijden, 2005).

In the inductive method a general conclusion is based on experiences or experimental evidences, which allows the scenarios to be built systematically wherein the structure of the scenarios materializes on its own (Heijden, 2005). The inductive approach is not a highly planned method, but rather depends upon the continuing discussions of an expert group regarding appropriate scenarios until they reach a consensus. The consensus-building process can be supported by the Delphi method, which is characterized by its iterative procedure. Two possible alternative paths can be distinguished in the inductive approach. Firstly, distinctive scenarios can be brainstormed in an expert group. Secondly, an "official future" can be agreed upon within an expert group, which subsequently searches for influences that can have an effect on that official future which substantially varies from that route (Schwartz & Ogilvy, 1998, p. 61 f.). Using the inductive approach, Heijden (2005) points out a natural tendency, developing scenarios in a polarizing mode of good versus bad or favorable versus unfavorable. Since it is a basic principle of the scenario-based planning methodology to consider all scenarios as equally plausible, polarization significantly weakens the value of the scenarios. He furthermore highlights plausibility and internal consistency as acceptable criteria for effective results.

On the other hand, a specific conclusion is drawn logically and necessarily from general premises in the deductive approach. Therefore, in a first step, an overall structure in the data has to be identified as a framework for the scenarios to be developed. Based on a principle structure of scenarios and their dimensions (e.g. future horizon), the scenarios have to be supplemented with (new) data if required and described in a storyline. The deductive approach implies grouping the data hierarchically, clustering, testing the clusters on mutual interdependence and internal consistency, prioritizing (e.g. impact) and selecting the most important topics as structuring dimensions (Heijden, 2005). Delphi studies are also useful in evaluating uncertain events. The estimations by experts help to focus on the most relevant and most uncertain topics to create scenarios (Rikkonen, 2005; Heijden, 2005). According to Heijden (2005), the deductive approach is not only the most analytical, but also "offers the best opportunity to explore widely in areas where the thinking would not otherwise penetrate, and it has a strong outside-in emphasis" (p. 253).

Several advantages for the application of scenario approach have been highlighted in literature. Ranking first is that the scenario approach describes multiple futures instead of predicting one future as accurately as possible (Schoemaker, 1995; Markmann, Darkow & Gracht, 2013; Keough & Shanahan, 2008). Hirsch, Burggraf and Daheim (2013) underline the contribution of scenario method and other foresight techniques to long term planning in a manner, which reduces complexity and focus on future challenges and potentials. Besides, one of the main features of scenario planning is the possibility to include disruptions, weak signals, or unexpected events in long-term thinking (Hirsch, Burggraf & Daheim, 2013; Nowack, Endrikat & Guenther, 2011). Applying scenario approach in organizations can also improve communication to deal with future issues (Heijden, 2005) and to communicate messages within the organization, e.g. a need for fundamental change (Schoemaker, 1995). Furthermore, scenarios help to stimulate actions rather than staying theoretical when addressing specific issues (Lizaso & Reger, 2004). Due to the multiple definitions and approaches mentioned above, scenario planning is flexible enough to be adjusted to the specific context and is highly participative (Hodgkinson & Wright, 2002; Korte & Chermack, 2007).

However, several shortcomings of the scenario method have been discussed in literature. These included the time-consuming aspect, was pointed out by Rikkonen, Kaivo-oja and Aakkula (2006), as well as the fact that scenarios can be affected by biases (Schoemaker, 1995). In contrast to the flexible way of usage, which has been described as an advantage, Keough and Shanahan (2008) comment that scenario-planning literature does not provide proper guidance for the usage of scenario-building models. There are only few guidelines for the practical utilization of existing models. According to Ricard and Borch (2011) scenarios are too distant to support strategy development. Overall, a careful and disciplined investigation is required to be able to learn about scenario planning (Chermack & Swanson, 2008).

To overcome the weaknesses (of the individual approaches) and to enhance the quality and validity of the scenarios a multi method approach was used in this research. Following the clear recommendations by different researchers, Delphi-based scenario development was applied (Nowack, Endrikat & Guenther, 2011; Rikkonen, 2005; Solnet et al., 2014; Gracht & Darkow, 2010), in which a reasonable number of relevant stakeholders can participate, and deep knowledge can be gained (Rikkonen, Kaivo-oja & Aakkula, 2006). The combination is not only possible because the Delphi procedures are easy to incorporate into the scenario development process, but rather useful for the purpose of quality. The Delphi study provides valuable, valid, and reliable data for the creation of scenarios (Gracht & Darkow, 2010) and furthermore enhances the creativity, credibility and objectivity of scenarios (Nowack, Endrikat & Guenther, 2011).

3.2 Study design and procedures

To obtain insights in the research topic of business leadership education in tertiary education, expert information and knowledge should be aggregated and analyzed following a rigorous systematic research approach.

As demonstrated above, numerous definitions and approaches for scenario-planning can be found in literature. Furthermore, Keough and Shanahan (2008) state a lack of standardized process for scenario planning. Subsequently, the number of steps involved in scenario planning process differs considerably from model to model (Keough & Shanahan, 2008; Nowack, Endrikat &

Guenther, 2011). For example, Phelps, Chan and Kapsalis (2001) presented a 4-step-model, while Schoemaker's model comprises ten steps (Schoemaker, 1995). Keough and Shanahan (2008) carefully conclude on basis of their analysis that "scenario planners should not rely on one specific method" (p. 172). Based on the possible combinations of Delphi technique and scenario approach analyzed in literature (Kinkel, Armbruster & Schirmeister, 2006; Nowack, Endrikat & Guenther, 2011) and successfully completed Delphi-based scenario studies (e.g. Becker & Gracht, 2014; Markmann, Darkow & Gracht, 2013; Solnet et al., 2014; Gracht & Darkow, 2010), a suitable overall process to carry out the Delphi-based scenario study in this research was developed and applied.

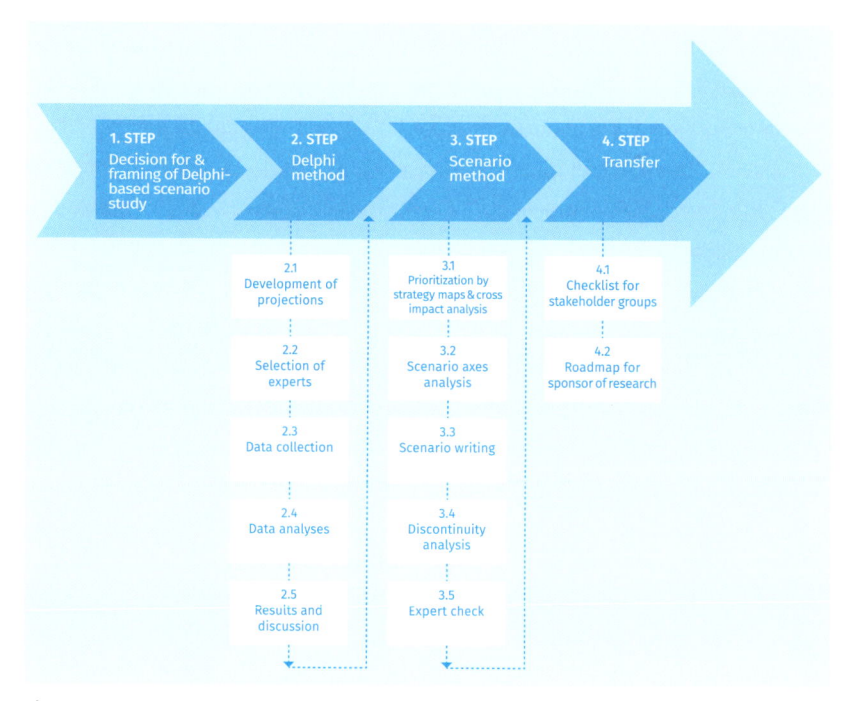

Figure 31. Process of Delphi-based scenario study.

Figure 31 illustrates the overall procedures and the individual phases of scenario development, and the way in which the Delphi method was integrated in this process. After having reached the decision for the Delphi-based scenario study in a first step as described in this section, Delphi method was performed in step two as basis for the subsequent scenario method in step three. The Delphi process in this research is based on the classical procedure from the RAND Corporation, which is not only recognized and accepted (Dalkey,

1969), but also applied in various research articles (e.g. Markmann, Darkow & Gracht, 2013; Gracht & Darkow, 2010). The Delphi process consists of five steps. In a first step, projections were developed in workshop sessions with selected experts based on previous results of this research work. In a second step, appropriate experts were carefully selected in order to ensure validity and reliability (Spickermann, Zimmermann & Gracht, 2014; Warth, Gracht & Darkow, 2013). In a third step, the real-time Delphi survey was conducted to collect data following a pre-test. The quantitative and qualitative data were analyzed in step four in order to identify the contribution of the survey in the field of research and to create a basis for the scenario development process. Finally, the results were presented and discussed. On basis of the results of the Delphi survey, scenario method was performed in five steps based on different methods of futures studies to ensure validity of results. Therefore, the results of the Delphi survey were prioritized by means of portfolio analysis, cross impact analysis and scenario axes analysis before scenario writing, discontinuity analysis and a final expert check. Finally, scenario transfer in step four prepares decision makers to apply theoretical results in their individual practice, based on a checklist for stakeholder groups and a roadmap for the sponsor of this research. The roadmap can be transferred to any institution of (higher) education.

As the Delphi study is important and impacts on the quality and validity of the scenarios, a brief introduction in the Delphi method is presented in the following section before the four steps are described in detail.

4. Delphi method

4.1 Principles of the Delphi method

During the years 1950-60, the Delphi method was also used by researchers of the RAND Corporation in the USA. They used this method to record expert opinions about the future of certain fields of study, and to examine long-range trends. According to Ziglio (1996), "the Delphi method is intended to structure and detail the expansive information for which there is some evidence (but not yet knowledge) in an attempt to achieve informed judgement and decision-making. There is no attempt to gain the "truth", as the founders of the Delphi method realized that truth is relative (Stone Fish & Busby, 1996)" (Dawson & Brucker, 2001, p. 126).

The most common, and in Delphi research accepted, definition of the Delphi technique is that of Linstone and Turoff (1975); "Delphi may be characterized as a method for structuring a group communication process so that the process is effective in allowing a group of individuals, as a whole, to deal with a complex problem" (p. 3). "As Turoff & Hiltz (1996) have made it clear that Delphi method does not posit to predict future related events, it does not aim to generate quick solutions, it also does not aim to reduce the need for long discussions, in a group setting it also does not quantify human judgement" (Dawson & Brucker, 2001, p. 126-127). According to Turoff and Hiltz (1996), "The Delphi method is a communication structure aimed at producing detailed critical examination and discussion, not at forcing a quick compromise. Certainly, quantification is a property of the method, but only in so far as it serves the goal of quickly identifying agreement and disagreement in order to focus attention on significant issues" (p. 56-57). One of the potential outcomes of this process is to achieve consensus among experts (Dawson & Brucker, 2001; Fletcher-Johnston, Marshall & Straatman, 2011), and measurement of consensus is a valuable element of data analysis and data interpretation (Gracht, 2012). Nevertheless, primary goal of the Delphi technique is not necessarily to reach consensus, since dissent is equally a valuable result for further interpretation (Linstone & Turoff, 1975; Linstone & Turoff, 2011; Steinert, 2009; Tapio, 2003; Turoff, 1970).

The use of the Delphi method is prevalent for areas that are scarcely researched, or to direct the formulation of policy or development of theoretical models (Linstone & Turoff, 1975; Stone Fish & Busby, 1996). The principal components of the Delphi method comprise the experts, multiple rounds of data collection, controlled feedback, anonymity of responses and statistical analysis (Dalkey, 1969), which "make the Delphi technique a highly efficient and methodologically robust survey tool" (Spickermann, Zimmermann & Gracht, 2014, p. 106). In a traditional Delphi study, experts participate in an open-ended questionnaire using the Likert scale. Upon requirement, participants may be encouraged to justify their ratings and consider differing points of view of other participants. The rating process is usually carried out until consensus is reached or it can be concluded that it cannot be reached (Linstone & Turoff, 1975; Doughty, 2009; Dawson & Brucker, 2001).

Linstone and Turoff (1975) and Ziglio (1996) recommend the following three aspects prior to conducting a Delphi study:

1. It is important that the researcher identifies supplementary group communication processes which could be suitable for the study in question, and establish justification for the use of the Delphi over other techniques.
2. It is vital that the researcher knows the "experts" on the topic being researched and can identify ways to access these participants.
3. Equally important is that the researcher can estimate the kind of results the study will produce by engaging these experts utilizing the Delphi method.

Because Delphi studies do not claim representativeness of a population (e.g. Hussler, Muller & Rondé, 2011), the selection of a sample plays a central role for the strength and validity of the Delphi method (Clayton, 1997; Häder, 2009). The consideration of experts or panel members should be based on their success and knowledge in the specific area of study, which will lead to their valid contribution (Powell, 2003). To also yield wide-ranging and robust results, a diverse group of experts referred to as panel with different opinions on the same topic, varied skills, and various perspectives on the topic of study is essential (Murphy et al., 1998; Wester & Borders, 2014). Beyond the variable of expertise, additional panel selection variables should be included to ensure survey precision by a diverse and heterogeneous[62] panel (Hussler, Muller & Rondé, 2011). In order to obtain divergent opinions and to increase the number of varying responses, Rauch (1979) opines to include relevant stakeholders instead of experts, as is the case in a conventional Delphi study, and Hussler, Muller and Rondé (2011) suggest the inclusion of non-experts in Delphi studies. It can be stated that there are various opinions regarding panel composition and "generally accepted sampling and selection procedures are missing" (Steinert, 2009, p. 293).

The major weakness noted is panel mortality (De Leeuw, 2001), also referred to as panel attrition (Snow & Tebes, 1992), which is a form of partial non-re-

---

62 The terms "diverse" and "heterogeneous" are used synonymously "as a mixture of several dimensions rather than as a single dimension" (Spickermann, Zimmermann & Gracht, 2014, p. 117).

sponse, a type of missing data where "all the data are missing after a certain point in the questionnaire" (De Leeuw, 2001, p. 149). The Delphi method runs the risk of falling victim to the 'band wagon effect'. It is probable that leading personalities can unjustifiably influence the other member experts (Chung & Ferris, 1971), thus causing them to agree with such influential experts in spite of having contrary opinions on the same issue. Research shows that there is a tendency for Delphi experts to match their ratings based on false information, if they are given vague or imprecise feedback between iterations (Francis, 1977; Scheibe, Skutsch & Schofer, 1975). Moreover, the Delphi method is criticized due to lack of statistical reliability in quantitatively explaining forecasting results and must therefore be considered "as an explorative research tool" (Steinert, 2009, p. 293).

4.2 Real-time Delphi approach

The conventional Delphi method involves paper-pencil questionnaires, which are usually administered by mail. The real-time (RT) Delphi is a latest development (Gordon & Pease, 2006). In RT Delphi, a chosen panel of experts is encouraged to access a web-based questionnaire. As the experts rate the questions online, the mean and other relevant statistical values are automatically generated and updated on the web page. It is also possible to view the justification comments given by the experts for immediate feedback in real-time. Panelists are motivated to visit the site several times during the specified period. Gordon and Pease, the developers of RT Delphi method, refer to it as "round-less" method, as it has an advantage over the classical Delphi method due to not being carried out in various rounds. The responses can be collected in a single round (Geist, 2010). Once the participants revisit the website for the Delphi study, they can view their own responses along with the input of other participants.

As the study functions in real-time, they also view the updated distributions, averages (means), medians, and comments of other panelists describing the reasons for their opinions (Gordon & Pease, 2006). RT Delphi proves to be advantageous as it works in "real time", during which experts can participate at their convenience (Geist, 2010). The RT Delphi design is applicable to both the synchronous and asynchronous approaches. RT Delphi works well if the panel size is small and if speedy completion is required. RT Delphi is an equally efficient way of data collection if the panel is asynchronous, wherein the panel is large, and more time is at hand (Gordon & Pease, 2006). Multiple RT Delphi surveys have been successfully conducted after its development by Gordon & Pease (2006) (e.g. Becker & Gracht 2014; Gnatzy et al., 2011; Markmann, Darkow & Gracht, 2013; Steinert, 2009; Warth, Gracht & Darkow, 2013).

Having thoroughly weighed the advantages and disadvantages discussed above, RT Delphi was chosen for the current research topic, as it is a "roundless" (Gordon & Pease, 2006) and efficient way of data collection with a possibility of immediate feedback, and its asynchronous approach proved to be adequate criteria to streamline the survey process across a global panel. This is supported by Förster and Gracht (2014) as they affirm that the experts are given a direct feedback in the RT Delphi survey, and closing the survey does not depend on achievement of consensus or stagnation but rather on a preset time span. Zipfinger (2007) and Gnatzy et al. (2011) have compared conventional and RT Delphi studies and confirmed that results gained from both the types of Delphi studies reveal no differences. The innovative RT Delphi method rather has advantages over the conventional Delphi method by minimizing the complexity involved in the conventional Delphi method and adding to the validity and usefulness of this innovative approach. Choosing this approach, data validity should be enhanced by reducing research fatigue and panel mortality (Markmann, Darkow & Gracht, 2013; Spickermann, Zimmermann & Gracht, 2014; Warth, Gracht & Darkow, 2013).

Aim of this explorative cross-country RT Delphi study is to generate new information and insights in the future of business leadership education of a heterogeneous expert sample in order to cover as many world views as possible. The opinions of the cross-country RT Delphi survey will serve as a strong foundation in creating robust scenarios for business leadership education in tertiary education for graduates for the year 2030.

4.3 Delphi procedures

Figure 31 illustrates the individual steps of the Delphi method, which are described in detail in the following sections.

4.3.1 Development of projections

Since previous research has accentuated the importance of systematically developing projections for the successful implementation of the Delphi survey (Loveridge, 2002; Spickermann, Zimmermann & Gracht, 2014; Warth, Gracht & Darkow, 2013), a structured procedure for projection development was realized to determine the factors expected to affect the future of business leadership education in tertiary education for graduates. Based on the results of previous Part 2 of this research accompanied with intense literature research, the RT Delphi projections were systematically developed in three workshop sessions with four experts.

According to Freeman's stakeholder approach (Freeman, 1984 / 2010), four main stakeholder[63] groups were identified for business leadership education in tertiary education. The four stakeholder groups are 'providers' referring to universities / business schools, 'participants / learners' referring to students, 'purchasers' referring to employers / companies (i.e. business corporations, companies, enterprises, organizations etc.) and 'politics' referring to policy making and politicians' views; they are necessary to set the framework for tertiary education. One expert for each stakeholder group was considered as a representative in the workshop sessions to obtain a holistic view on the topic. Thus, a team of four experts played a crucial role in the development of projections.

Based on a presentation of the previous results of this research for each of the four stakeholder dimensions possible factors were identified that might influence the future of business leadership education in tertiary education in a first workshop session. Consequently, the initial results were further clustered, refined, and prioritized in a second workshop session, resulting in a list of relevant key factors. Identifying key factors to develop projections was particularly challenging due to the multiple stakeholders involved and the

---

[63] Freeman (1984/2010) defines stakeholders as "groups or individuals that can affect, or are affected by, the accomplishment of organizational purpose" (p. 25).

complex topic in a global dimension. In a next step, the relevant key factors were precisely formulated. Due to redundancies and a potential lack of clarity, the preliminary set of projections was refined. After the elimination of two projections, a final set of 16 projections emerged.

Following methodological rules in projection development is an important part in the Delphi design to ensure validity and reliability. Therefore, the criteria of concise formulation, non-ambiguity, and number of words have to be considered (Loveridge, 2002; Salancik, Wenger & Helfer, 1971). At the same time, it was ensured that the phrasing of the projections was not too brief to exclude the risk of participants arriving at different interpretations, which was important for projections 5, 10, 14 and 15. Reduction to the most important factors on one hand and assurance of a holistic view on the research topic on the other is also a necessary and logical step in the Delphi design to increase willingness in the participants to answer and thus influence response rate and accurateness (Warth, Gracht & Darkow, 2013). Furthermore, according to Gnatzy et al. (2011), each projection must be introduced by the future horizon, namely 2030, for the purpose of validity. "Thus, with every new projection the experts are mentally taken further into the future" (p. 1683).

The time horizon of 2030 for all the projections was adopted not only to shelve operational urgencies, but also to evoke experts' long-term thinking and thus generating the basis for further scenario development process. Schwartz (1996) emphasizes opting for a long-term perspective in scenario planning to get the most from it. Reorganizing educational systems implies long decision-making processes, long phases of implementation and long-term effects. As a long-term implementation procedure in the educational system, the Bologna process can be mentioned exemplary, where many differences among the countries are still evident according to the European Commission (2015). Considering the creation of future-oriented educational systems in the year 2030, the decisions for change and initial actions have to be made in the present.

Table 14 presents the final set of 16 projections based on Part 2 of this research along with a selection of the underlying literature.

	No.	Key factor	Underlying literature (selection)	Projection
Perspective of providers (universities)	1	Personality & leadership competencies	Bijedić, 2013; Braukmann, Bijedic & Schneider, 2008; Faix, Rütter & Wollstadt, 1995; Faix & Mergenthaler, 2015; James, 2009	In 2030, Master in Management programs tend to focus on personality and leadership competencies rather than impart (functional) knowledge.
	2	Educational setting & development of competencies	AASCB, 2010; Erpenbeck, 2012a / 2012b; Faix & Mergenthaler, 2015; Gellman, 2016*	In 2030, Master in Management programs take place both on campus and in companies in equal measure.
	3	E-learning	Bailey et al., 2011; Becker & Gracht, 2014; Halarnkar & Kulkarni, 2013; NMC, 2015; OECD, 2005; Ullmo, 2013; UNESCO, 2012b	In 2030, advanced digitization (Web 2.x) has completely transformed business leadership education in tertiary education.
	4	Individualization	Becker & Gracht 2014; Devine, 2013; Friebel et al., 2000; Klovert, 2015; Lohmann, 2003	In 2030, business leadership education in Master in Management programs for graduates is highly individualized and custom-tailored.
	5	Allocation to schools	Bijedić, 2013; Drucker, 2010; Gagliardi & Czarniawska, 2006	In 2030, Master in Management programs are no longer part of Business Schools but rather a part of Schools of Education or Schools for Social Sciences due to changed requirements for leaders, managers and talents.
Perspective of participants (Students)	6	Requirements for leadership positions	Becker & Gracht, 2014; IBM, 2010; IBM, 2010a / 2010b / 2012a / 2012b / 2016*; Regnet, 2014, Weber, 2007	In 2030, requirements for leaders, managers, and talents have changed fundamentally compared to 2015.
	7	Entre- & Intrapreneurship as a basis for innovations	Bijedić, 2013; Braukmann, Bijedic & Schneider, 2008; Faix & Mergenthaler, 2015; Huynh, 2007; Karmarkar, Chabra & Deshpande, 2014; Rosenstiel & Comelli, 2003; Schumpeter 1911 / 2008; Weber, 2007	In 2030, intrapreneurship and entrepreneurship as well as innovations are highly important parts of Master in Management programs compared to management related themes.

	#	Topic	References	2030 Scenario
rowspan Perspective of purchasers (employers / companies)	8	International internships & development of competencies	Altbach, Reisberg & Rumbley, 2009; Faix et al., 2006; UNESCO, 2015; Wannemacher & Geidel, 2016*	In 2030, gaining leadership related experiences in an international work environment will be more important compared to theoretical management knowledge.
	9	Transfer of knowledge by "real-world projects"	AASCB, 2010; Erpenbeck, 2012a / 2012b; Faix & Mergenthaler, 2015; Gellman, 2016*	In 2030, students are realizing "real-world projects" within companies by transferring knowledge as a mandatory and integrated part of their Master in Management programs.
	10	Return on Education (ROE)	Bailey et al., 2011; Becker & Gracht, 2014; Bouroujerdi & Wolf, 2015	In 2030, companies and students demand a measurable and comprehensible verification of the benefits of business leadership education of Master in Management programs from universities as "return on education" provided by these universities.
	11	Transformation of working environment & working conditions	Priddat, 2013; Weber, 2007	In 2030, the labor market has transformed. Therefore, project-based work and collaboration with freelancers has increased.
	12	International and intercultural experiences	Altbach, Reisberg & Rumbley, 2009; Faix et al., 2006; IBM, 2010; IBM, 2010a / 2010b / 2012a / 2012b / 2016*; Wannemacher & Geidel, 2016	In 2030, companies and students demand Master in Management programs, which are organized globally.
	13	Corporate universities	Gebauer, 2007; Hovestadt & Beckmann, 2010; Wimmer, Emmerich & Nicolai, 2002	In 2030, enterprises have their own state-recognized degree-awarding corporate universities as an important success factor for competitiveness.
Perspective of politics	14	International student mobility & recognition of degrees	Altbach, Reisberg & Rumbley, 2009; UNESCO 2015; Verbik & Lasanowski, 2007; WEF, 2010	In 2030, an international agreement for recognition of degrees in tertiary education is enacted to promote student mobility among different fields of study, institutions and nations in a global world.

	15	Funding of tertiary education	Altbach, Reisberg & Rumbley, 2009; Johnstone, 2016*; Lohmann, 2003; OECD 2015; Salmi & Hauptman, 2006; Ziegele, 2010	In 2030, business leadership education in Master in Management programs for graduates is rather financed by companies, the private-sector or participants (students) themselves than public funded.
	16	Duration of Master's programs	based on analysis Part 2, Table 13 and subsequent expert discussions in workshops	In 2030, most of the offered Master in Management programs for graduates can be completed in one year.

* References of 2016 were added to the table after the projections were developed and surveyed due to the high relevance.

Table 14. Key factors and literature for development of final set of projections.

4.3.2 Selection of experts

The creation of an appropriate and well-selected panel of experts (Häder, 2009) is critical to the strength and validity of any Delphi study (Clayton, 1997) as well as the reliability of Delphi research results (Warth, Gracht & Darkow, 2013). The researcher is free to create criteria for the inclusion of an "expert" (Doughty, 2009). Wilhelm (2001) suggested that the purpose and context of the study explicitly govern the standards from which panelists are chosen. He further recommended that the participants' motivation should be considered as a significant point while choosing panelists; further pointing out that the panelists must have a deep interest in the subject matter and topic being researched. Scheele (1975) suggested the panel should be broadly based in order to develop a "contextual mapping that would describe the society's response to any complex issue" (p. 60). He also put forward the fact that a split panel comprising of scholars and practitioners may be instrumental in the success of the Delphi study (Doughty, 2009).

It is worth mentioning that the literature reveals variances regarding the use of the Delphi technique and only a small amount of researchers use a uniform method (Chien, Cook & Harding, 1984; Keeney, Hasson & McKenna, 2001). There are not only various opinions regarding the panel composition as discussed above, but also differences of opinions regarding the size of the panel necessary to conduct a Delphi study. It is suggested that the researcher can decide on the size (Skulmoski, Hartmann & Krahn, 2007); although Clayton (1997) advised that it is appropriate to engage between 15 and 30 experts from a heterogeneous population. Furthermore, Wilhelm (2001) directs our attention to the fact that Ziglio (1996) and Linstone and Turoff (1975) believed a panel of 10 to 15 participants also has the potential to yield good results.

Since there are different opinions for panel size in literature, the aim of this Delphi survey was to include at least 100 experts, which is also recommended by Warth, Gracht and Darkow (2013). Assuming a response rate of 12-15 %, a total number of 700 to 900 experts should be targeted in order to compile different opinions for future business leadership education in tertiary education.

Having the aim of research for this RT Delphi survey in mind, the panelists were chosen according to pre-defined criteria. Representatives of the four main stakeholder dimensions, which were identified for business leadership education in tertiary education, were defined as part of the panel. Therefore, next to representatives of providers (business / schools), purchasers (companies / employers) and politics, participants / learners (students) were also included in the panel as they are mostly affected by the changes in business leadership education in tertiary education. Furthermore, the panelists were chosen according to their current management level, academic background respective education, job specialization, field of work and publications. With the aim of exploring heterogeneous, opposing viewpoints and gaining futuristic results for business leadership education in tertiary education in a global world, experts from various countries were selected. Intensive desk research was conducted and the existing contacts of SIBE with respect to universities and industries in an international context were targeted. For the panelists in USA, China and Brazil, renowned research universities and industrial organizations cooperating with SIBE were requested to suggest suitable experts according to the defined selection criteria.

Ultimately, 762 experts were identified who met these criteria. The selected candidates were informed by either email, telephone, Skype or contacted personally and invited to be a part of an expert panel and participate in this RT Delphi study.

4.3.3 Data collection

After an extensive search on the web and recommendations by experts, nine different ways to conduct RT Delphi were identified and checked for usability. After having tested two different options, it was decided to use the Calibrum™ software for conducting the current RT Delphi study. The criteria for the selection of Calibrum™ software were user-friendliness and the professional feedback of statistics of group opinions and experts' comments. Calibrum™ made it very convenient for the international experts to participate in real time. The software also kept track of the progress of responses and sent reminders to experts to improve the response rate.

To discover ambiguity and a potential lack of clarity the respondents may be confronted with when participating in the survey, and to ensure face validity, accuracy of content and plausibility (Bradburn, Sudman & Wansink, 2004; Dillmann, 2007; Spickermann, Zimmermann & Gracht, 2014), nine experts belonging to four different stakeholder groups for business leadership education in tertiary education were consulted to run a pre-test after setup of Calibrum™ software. The feedback of the pre-test panel resulted in minor revisions of the projections leading to improvements and later successful implementation of the RT Delphi survey.

All 762 identified experts were invited to participate in the cross-country RT Delphi survey. They received an invitation email which briefly described the Delphi study and contained the hyperlink to be accessed in order to participate in the survey. In line with Gnatzy et al. (2011), primary conditions were set by four experts representing the four stakeholder groups to ensure that feedback was received by the first few experts. The research by Gnatzy et al. (2011) showed that the ultimate findings were not influenced by the initial circumstances.

Following the state of the art in the RT Delphi process (Gnatzy et al., 2011; Steinert, 2009), the experts were provided with an anonymous individual link to ensure that their opinion and all entries were kept anonymous, reducing possible bias. "Usually, the participating experts remain anonymous and any coordination between them is prohibited. That way, a "dominant expert" in terms of reputation or communication / persuasive skills is prevented to influence the approximations and discussions overly (Bandwagon-effect, Halo effect)" (Steinert, 2009, p. 292).

For a clear understanding of how data was collected in this RT Delphi survey, the details are explained in the section below:

1. Background and aim of research as well as notes for the used terms were presented at the beginning of the RT Delphi survey.
2. The experts' task was presented very clearly. They were asked
   > to rate the probability of occurrence of each key Delphi projection
   > to rate the desirability of this occurrence and
   > to rate the impact on business leadership education in case of this occurrence
   > to provide reasons and comments for their answers wherever necessary. They were told that their reasons and comments are a valuable contribution for the clarification of the given ratings.
3. The experts were encouraged to revisit the Calibrum™ website to view the responses of other experts and change or add their comments, if necessary.
4. The rating scale for probability was set as an 11-unit scale from 0 % to 100 %. The rating scale for desirability was chosen to be a five-point Likert scale wherein 1 was very low desirability and 5 was very high desirability; the rating scale for impact was also a five-point Likert scale wherein 1 was very low impact and 5 was very high impact. As the panel had different international backgrounds, English was not expected to be their first language. The Likert scale was adapted to suit the international panel. When responding to a Likert-type scale, respondents typically specify their level of agreement or disagreement on a symmetric agree-disagree scale for a series of statements. Thus, the scale captures the intensity of their feelings for a given item (Burns & Burns, 2008). For the purpose of effective data collection and clear understanding of the international panel regarding the projections it was decided to include a negative rating "not desirable" and "no impact" for all the sixteen projections. Research shows that a Likert-type scale is a bipolar scaling method, which measures either positive or negative response to a statement. If necessary, the middle option of "Neither agree nor disagree" is removed. This is referred to as a "forced choice" method, since the neutral option is removed (Allen & Seaman, 2007).

It was an important step in data collection as the purpose of a RT Delphi survey is to collect clear opinions of experts and the clear opinions further aid in creating future based scenarios. The usual Likert-scale options e.g. "very low", "low", "undecided", "high" and "very high" measures the intensity as reported before. If the experts choose the option "not desirable" or "no impact" for a specific projection, there is a clear conclusion that the experts do not wish this projection to be a reality in the future or a specific projection will have no impact of business leadership education. Such a clear conclusion would not have been possible if the conventional Likert scale (which does not have a clear negative option) had been used. Additionally, the option of "undecided" is not applicable for the current RT Delphi study, because it does not contribute to the results. It should be noted that the option "not desirable" or "no impact" was placed in the center of the rating scale to balance the scale. This is further supported by Armstrong (1987), who demonstrated that the neutral option seems to be a convenient option when a respondent is unsure. He further reported negligible differences between the use of "undecided" and "neutral" as the middle option in a 5-point Likert scale. Thus, adapting the Likert scale by using a negative option for the current study is justified.

Each expert who participated in the RT Delphi study considered the following for each projection.

1. The expert could review his / her own comment. The expert could revisit and change the comment or add text after viewing other experts' comments and ratings.
2. Then the expert could view consensus and dissent respectively. Consensus or dissent was displayed in percentage along with group stability in percentage, number of invited experts, number of actual responses and lastly the number of revisions for that specific projection.
3. The expert could view the histogram of the ratings given by all experts to understand how the specific projection is rated by other experts.
4. Finally, the experts could view the comments made by other experts.

The option of saving the survey responses was made available to the experts, to provide them with the opportunity to reconsider any specific projection and could complete the survey later. The experts could access their survey repeatedly via the same personalized hyperlink. The Calibrum™ software was extremely user-friendly and it was possible for the experts to rate and view the responses of other experts simultaneously. Thus, building consensus and dissent for each projection was statistically controlled and generation of statistical information such as mean, agreement or disagreement could be viewed in real-time. This made it very convenient for the experts to view and edit their opinions, thereby causing the *"Delphi"* effect to take place.

It was estimated that the data collection process would last for four to six weeks. After the invitation email, including a deadline to complete the survey was sent, the first email reminder was sent on the 14th day after the start date. While checking the responses from time to time, a second reminder email was sent on the 21th day. In between, the participants who had completed the survey, were reminded to revisit and review other opinions and change their own if they wished. The experts were assured that the results of the Delphi study would be shared with them after the analysis was carried out.

Stakeholder groups of business leadership education in tertiary education	Invitations	Participants	Response rate (%)
Providers: universities / business schools	180	33	18.33
Participants / learners: students	38	12	31.58
Purchasers: employers / companies	491	50	10.18
Politics	53	10	18.87
Experts / total	762	105	13.78

Table 15. Panel invitations and participants according to stakeholder groups.

Overall, 105 of the 762 invited experts (13.78 %) participated in the study, of which 33 (31.43 %) were from universities / business schools, 12 (11.43 %) were students, 50 (47.62 %) came from employers / companies and 10 (9.52 %) from politics and related associations (Table 15). The overall response rate of 13.78 % is acceptable because Delphi surveys do not claim representativeness, which is comparable to any other expert based research methodology (Hussler, Muller & Rondé, 2011; Spickermann, Grienitz & Gracht, 2014).

The employers' / companies' share included representatives from 16 different industries. Participants were based in 13 different countries. Figure 32 shows that 87 % of the participants were located in five countries (Germany (58 %), USA (11 %), China (7 %), Brazil (7 %) and India (4 %)). The remaining 13 % of participants were located in eight different countries, ensuring a global view and different perceptions of business leadership education in tertiary education for graduates.

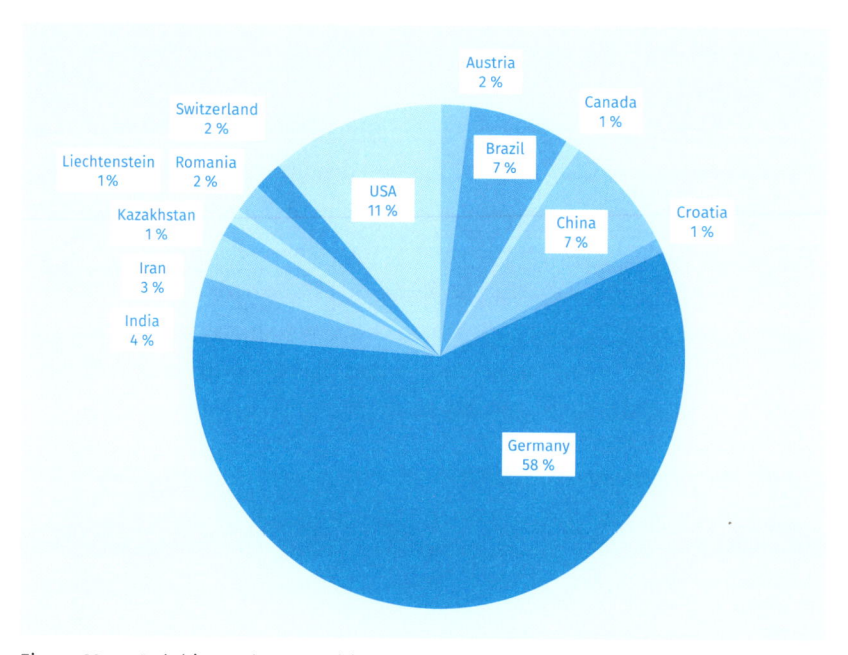

Figure 32.　Delphi panel composition according to countries (n=105).

Participants belonged to six different age groups, with almost one quarter (24 %) of the participants being 55 years and over (Table 16), who exhibit comprehensive experience.

Furthermore, adding the six groups leader of team, director, C-suite-level, assistant professor, professor and president / dean, at least 78 (74 %) of the participants held a leadership position (Table 17). 14 (13 %) participants are responsible for more than 100 employees. Nearly one third (31 %) of the participants (33) work in companies with 2,000 or more employees and 16 of them in companies with 10,000 or more employees. 77 (73 %) of the participants are male, 28 (27 %) are female.

Including such a heterogeneous composition of experts due to cultural and professional backgrounds in the RT Delphi panel for business leadership education for graduates in Master in Management programs in tertiary education, it is possible to achieve not only a multi-stakeholder view on the research topic but also stimulate a controversial discussion among experts. "Diversity in a panel proves to be beneficial for obtaining useful results in several ways: the advice comes from multiple independent sources; the panelists have different skills and points of view." (Förster & Gracht, 2014, p. 216) Above all, the panel size exceeded the minimum recommended number of Delphi participants, which, according to Markmann, Darkow and Gracht (2013), further underlines "the quality and robustness of the survey results due to the higher number of incorporated perspectives" (p. 1822).

Total	105	100 (%)
18-24	2	1.90
25-34	21	20.00
35-44	36	34.29
45-54	21	20.00
55-64	16	15.24
65 and above	9	8.57

Table 16. Delphi panel composition according to age groups.

Total	105	100 (%)
Student (potential future leader)	12	11.43
Employee without leadership position / role	6	5.71
Project manager	3	2.86
Leader of team / division	14	13.33
Director	25	23.81
C-suite-level	14	13.33
Assistant Professor	4	3.81
Professor	17	16.19
President / Dean of University	4	3.81
Other	6	5.71

Table 17. Delphi panel composition according to position within organization.

4.3.4 Data analyses

The Delphi research method "is a flexible research technique well suited when there is incomplete knowledge about phenomena" (Skulmoski, Hartmann & Krahn, 2007, p.12). Conducting a Delphi study generates an extensive amount of quantitative and qualitative data, which has to be analyzed thoroughly. Due to previous research on multiple Delphi studies, "no two Delphi studies are the same" (Skulmoski, Hartmann & Krahn, 2007, p.12). Skulmoski, Hartmann and Krahn (2007) furthermore highlight that Delphi "is not just a quantitative method, but works very well in qualitative research. […] There are many varieties of Delphi ranging from qualitative to quantitative, to mixed-method Delphi" (p.12). As this RT Delphi study involves both quantitative and qualitative methods of data collection, it was self-evident to analyze both methods according to the aim of research and to answer the defined research questions.

4.3.4.1 Quantitative data analysis

In a first step, the quantitative data of experts' assessments for estimated probability, desirability and impact were analyzed for each of the sixteen projections. The arithmetic mean served as a general basis for quantitative evaluation. It shed light on the expected future development of the surveyed projections. In addition, the interquartile range (IQR), which measures dispersion for the median and consists of the middle 50 % of the provided evaluations, was calculated. Therefore, the smaller the range, the lower the dispersion of the data and, in case of Delphi studies, the higher the consensus (De Vet et al., 2005). The IQR "is a frequently used measure in Delphi studies, and it is generally accepted as an objective and rigorous way of determining consensus" (Gracht, 2012, p. 1531). The criteria for consensus are defined in line with previous research of Gracht (2012). Thus, consensus is reached when the IQR is no greater than 2 units on an 11-unit-scale[64] (Scheibe, Skutsch & Schofer, 1975), or rather 1 or less for 5-unit-scales (Rayens & Hahn, 2000; Raskin, 1994). Furthermore, the convergence rate was measured in order to study whether the standard deviation (SD) of the initial assessments decreased

---

64 Research literature defines that consensus is reached when the IQR is no greater than 2 units on a 10-unit-scale (Scheibe , Skutsch & Schofer, 1975). Specific definition for consensus indicated by the IQR value on an 11-unit scale was not found in research literature. Thus, it was decided to adapt the indicator for consensus of the 10-unit-scale (IQR no greater than 2 units), which is in line with e.g. Becker and Gracht (2014).

compared to the final assessments. This aspect reveals whether the group communication process equals a consensus building process among experts and led to the harmonization of different assessments. Negative convergence values in this case mean convergence.

4.3.4.2 Qualitative content analysis

Due to the large number of comments recorded, the heterogeneity and the high expertise of the expert panel the extensive amount of qualitative data were analyzed in a second step. For the purpose of systematic text analysis, Mayring (2000, 2004) has developed a qualitative content analysis procedure comprising various techniques. Basic principle of this procedure is to sustain the advantages of the qualitative content and allow the content to be transformed into progressive steps leading to in-depth analysis. Following the rules of Mayring (2000) the qualitative content analysis was carried out systematically adapting the clear structure of Shah (2014) as described below:

1. Content analytical units: In order to structure the extensive amount of data from the RT Delphi survey, each projection was analyzed separately. The text units comprised the actual comments provided by the panel of experts. These comments were grouped systematically for each projection by the Calibrum™ software. Some comments that were unclear or seemed to have no relevance to the projection were marked as "irrelevant". This helped to concentrate on the useful and relevant comments. Redundant ideas observed in the comments were also marked. In some cases, due to the length of the comment, it was divided into smaller text chunks, which were converted into statements. Therefore, it may appear that more comments belong to one code. In the following procedure, these comments were allocated specific codes. It is possible that one comment had more than one assigned code.

2. Code development: In a second step, a coding scheme was developed for the data analysis following the procedure of inductive code development. Applying the inductive approach, the codes were derived from the text units. Inductive codes were defined according to the textual units based on research questions. The textual data material is systematically clustered to these definitions. MAXQDA-plus®, a computerized software, was used to organize the data and carry out the coding. The software proved to be beneficial and made the coding process easy, transparent and repro-

ducible. The relevant text units were allocated the defined codes following the research questions. A revision of codes was conducted in an iterative way during process of analysis. Many text units that described entirely the nature of each code were subsumed under every code. To conform to the reliability standards an inter-rater reliability was calculated for the coding system specifically developed for the content analysis for the RT-Delphi survey data mainly collected as 'expert comments'. The expert comments, which were clustered under 16 projections were analyzed qualitatively in two ways. In a first step, two pairs of projections were randomly chosen to carry out the code correlation. MAXQDA-plus® allowed an easy calculation of inter-rater rating. In case of the first pair of projections, $r = .77$, which means the codes for rater 1 and rater 2 matched up to 77 % codes. In case of the second pair of projections, $r = .94$, implying that 94 % codes matched between both raters. The higher correlation was considered for further analysis. Cohen's kappa was carried out through a computer program StatsToDo. The kappa score was $\kappa = .73$, which states that there is considerable agreement between raters (Viera & Garrett, 2005). Thus, it can be inferred that the inter-rater correlation and Cohen's kappa support the development of code system positively.

3. Review of coded statements and revision of codes: After all comments of 16 projections were clustered to specific codes, the coded segments were retrieved with the help of the software MAXQDA-plus® and in the next step transferred to Excel. This process facilitated the review process for each statement, the assigned codes to each statement and if the projections were clustered as per the appropriate code. This review process also resulted in the removal of redundant codes. Each comment was allocated a unique number by the software MAXQDA-plus® during the retrieval process. This process allows tracking the document from which the statement originally emerged.

4. Qualitative interpretation: The process of classification of retrieved statements as per the projections further simplified the process of selection of suitable comments for each projection. The classification also played an important role in the interpretation of comments on three levels. First aspect of selection of coded comments was the exactness of a comment, which displayed a reason for the occurrence (also no occurrence), desirability (no desirability), and impact (no impact) of the specific projection. The second aspect of the selection of comments was the category of the expert according to the stakeholder groups (providers (universities / business schools), participants (students), purchasers (employers / companies), and politics). The idea was to include perspectives of experts

from each stakeholder group in order to represent balanced findings and to avoid representation of only one or two groups. The third aspect of selection is the nationality of experts. The data revealed a variety of comments from a diverse panel. The comments of experts belonging to different countries were purposefully chosen to interpret each projection in a balanced manner. This was helpful to elucidate similarities within and differences between the perspectives of experts. The retrieved statements were clustered under specific codes. Furthermore, these codes were grouped according to the research questions. The relevant codes as well as the specific statements that defined those codes were conjointly used to answer the research questions. Once the appropriate comments were chosen, they were grouped under two criteria: "pro" comments and "contra" comments. The comments that largely supported the projection were considered as "pro" and those that did not support the projection and provided different aspects related to the projection were considered as "contra" statements. The "contra" statements were even more important as they revealed related facets of the projection, which played an important role in interpretation of results.

According to Rikkonen, Kaivo-oja and Aakkula (2006), quantitative data analysis has preceded over qualitative data in conventional Delphi studies. However, qualitative data is gaining importance in recent years. As this RT Delphi study involves two methods of data collection that is quantitative and qualitative, it was imperative to interpret these methods separately as well as together. Therefore, initially separate interpretations of each method were reported and an integrated overview of both methods was ultimately elaborately explained, as these methods together either support the projection, provide less support to the projection or provide conflicting results, which uncover various features of the projections, that would have been lost if only one method had been employed. Inferentially, employing two methods of analysis was a demanding task, nevertheless, this shall essentially serve the prime purpose of the RT Delphi study, which is to build scenarios for business leadership education in tertiary education for graduates based on these 16 projections.

4.3.5 Results and discussion

4.3.5.1 Overview

In order to gain a general overview of the RT Delphi survey results, the key characteristics are illustrated in the following Table 18. A final set of 16 projections covering the four stakeholder dimensions for business leadership education in tertiary education was presented to a heterogeneous panel possessing cultural and professional backgrounds to enhance a constructive discussion among experts. After data collection within a period of five weeks, responses of 105 participants (response rate 13.78 %) allowed to incorporate multiple experts' perspectives while interpreting the expert opinions for the projections. The average number of panel logins was 2.26, which equals "the number of survey rounds in which the panelists participated" (Förster & Gracht, 2014, p. 220).

Projections	Set of 16 projections concerning 4 strategic perspectives (providers = universities / business schools; participants / learners = students; purchasers = employers / companies & politics) of stakeholders on business leadership education in tertiary education
Panelists	105 experts from 13 countries and 16 industries related to business leadership education in tertiary education.
	Stakeholder groups: 31.43 % providers (universities / business schools); 11.43 % participants (students); 47.62 % Purchasers (employers / companies); 9.52 % politics (policy making, politicians)
	Age groups: 6 different age groups; 24 % are 55 years and above
	Position within company: At least 74 % of the participants hold a leadership position
	Gender: 77 male (73.33 %), 28 female (26.67 %)
Response rate	13.78 % (762 experts invited; 105 experts' responses)
Sample period	September 2nd 2015 - October 7th 2015 (5 weeks)
Average number of logins	2.26
Number of written comments [total / per person]	1,255 / 12
Supportive comments ("pro")	631
Unsupportive comments ("contra")	412
Average IQR of probability ratings	30

Table 18. Panel information – general overview.

The majority of comments were provided after the first login. In total, this international experts' panel provided 1,255 written comments in order to justify their quantitative estimations, which underlines the participants' high interest in the topic as well as in a multi-faceted discussion in a global context. The comments were systematically analyzed with qualitative content analysis. 631 comments were grouped as supportive comments ("pro") and 412 were grouped as unsupportive comments ("contra"). Finally, the average IQR is 30 for expected probability, which is the indicator for consensus measurement for the 16 surveyed projections on average. It demonstrates a high degree of dissent, as the range for consensus on a 11-unit-scale is no larger than 2. It implies that the panelists have different assessments of the future.

Based on the general overview, the quantitative database was analyzed to reveal the future trend of business leadership education. Table 19 summarizes the relevant statistics. Mean values were calculated of the experts' assessments of estimated probability of occurrence (EP), desirability (D) of occurrence and impact (I) on business leadership education. The values represent the opinions of the surveyed stakeholders and thus reflect their perceptions of the surveyed projections. It was stated that

> "... the reported values may not be considered separately. Their conjoint reflection is necessary ... A high probability value of a projection, for instance, together with a quite low impact value would make the respective projection rather irrelevant for consideration. On the other hand, a high impact value of a probable projection would convey the relevance of the underlying factor and consequently cause an in-detail examination." (Markmann, Darkow & Gracht, 2013, p. 1824)

Altogether, experts' ratings for impact are high. As Table 19 shows, mean values for 14 out of 16 impact assessments vary between M = 3.7 and M = 4.32, which is high impact on business leadership education. Only two of 16 ratings (projections 5, 13) are M = 3.24 or M = 3.43, which is medium impact. Likewise, experts' assessments for desirability are relatively high. For 12 out of 16 projections, desirability mean values range between M = 3.51 and M = 4.39, which demonstrates high desirability. Only for four desirability estimations (projections 5, 13, 15, 16), the mean values vary between M = 2.7 and M = 3.25, which expresses that those four projections are of low desirability according to the experts. In addition, most of the projections have an estimated probability of occurrence of more than 50 %. For 12 out of 16 projections, the probability of occurrence values varies between 54.1 % and 73.0 %. According to other Delphi studies expected probability is high when EP is above 60 % (Gracht & Darkow, 2010). Consequently, for 9 out of 16 projections the values are above 60 %. The values shed light on "which of the topics are expected to gain importance in the future" (Markmann, Darkow & Gracht, 2013, p. 1824). The consistently high values demonstrate the high relevance of the developed projections and are an indicator "that the *a priori* formulation and selection of projections have accurately taken place" (Gracht & Darkow, 2010, p. 52).

	No.	Projections for the year 2030	EP statistics			D statistics		I statistics	
			EP (mean)	IQR	Con	D (mean)	IQR	I (mean)	IQR
Perspective of providers (universities)	1	In 2030, Master in Management programs tend to focus on personality and leadership competencies rather than impart (functional) knowledge.	62.76 %	30	4.81 %	3.99	0	4.02	0
	2	In 2030, Master in Management programs take place both on campus and in companies in equal measure.	54.10 %	40	1.94 %	3.87	0	4.01	0
	3	In 2030, advanced digitization (Web 2.x) has completely transformed business leadership education in tertiary education.	61.00 %	30	4.18 %	3.6	1	3.84	2
	4	In 2030, business leadership education in Master in Management programs for graduates is highly individualized and custom-tailored.	54.9 %	40	1.75 %	3.75	2	3.97	1

Perspective of participants (students)	5	In 2030, Master in Management programs are no longer part of Business Schools but rather a part of Schools of Education or Schools for Social Sciences due to changed requirements for leaders, managers and talents.	30.28%	30	-0.96%	2.7	2	3.24	2
	6	In 2030, requirements for leaders, managers, and talents have changed fundamentally compared to 2015.	59.1%	40	-1.57%	3.51	1	3.93	1
	7	In 2030, intrapreneurship and entrepreneurship as well as innovations are highly important parts of Master in Management programs compared to management related themes.	70.40%	30	-0.43%	4.25	1	4.32	1
	8	In 2030, gaining leadership related experiences in an international work environment will be more important compared to theoretical management knowledge.	73.00%	30	5.45%	4.16	1	4.27	1
	9	In 2030, students are realizing "real-world projects" within companies by transferring knowledge as a mandatory and integrated part of their Master in Management programs.	68.10%	40	0.62%	4.39	1	4.22	1

Perspective of purchasers (employers / companies)	10	In 2030, companies and students demand a measurable and comprehensible verification of the benefits of business leadership education of Master in Management programs from universities as "return on education" provided by these universities.	60.90%	30	0.26%	*3.69*	1	3.83	2
	11	In 2030, the labor market has transformed. Therefore, project-based work and collaboration with freelancers has increased.	70.19%	30	0.09%	*3.52*	1	3.94	1.75
	12	In 2030, companies and students demand Master in Management programs, which are organized globally.	70.20%	30	-1.33%	*4.06*	1	4.1	1
	13	In 2030, enterprises have their own state-recognized degree-awarding corporate universities as an important success factor for competitiveness.	46.80%	40	-0.58%	*2.82*	2	3.43	1
Perspective of politics	14	In 2030, an international agreement for recognition of degrees in tertiary education is enacted to promote student mobility among different fields of study, institutions and nations in a global world.	60.40%	30	-0.15%	*3.99*	1	4.02	1

15	In 2030, business leadership education in Master in Management programs for graduates is rather financed by companies, the private-sector or participants (students) themselves than public funded.	59.00%	20	-3.00%	3.25	2	3.73	1
16	In 2030, most of the offered Master in Management programs for graduates can be completed in one year.	48.20%	40	-0.17%	2.73	2	3.7	1

Legend: EP = Estimated probability of occurrence (0-100%); IQR= Interquartile range; Con (SD) = Convergence of opinion (variation of standard variation: negative values equals convergence); D = Desirability of occurrence (1 = very low, 5 = very high); I = Impact in case of occurrence (1 = very low, 5 = very high).

Note degree of consensus / dissent: Italic numbers indicate that consensus among experts was achieved; i.e. for EP IQR ≤ 25 equals consensus, for D and I respectively IQR ≤ 1 equals consensus.

Table 19. Quantification of projections (n=105).

Furthermore, the convergence rate was measured in order to study whether the standard deviation (SD) of the initial assessments decreased compared to the final assessments and conclusively whether experts' assessments matched their own opinions considering the several changes in the comments by the experts after viewing others' opinions. The results show negative convergence values for 8 out of 16 projections. This result can be interpreted as a consensus building process taking place, which led to a moderate harmonization of the estimated probability of occurrence. For the remaining eight projections, divergence was achieved which means that participants further intensified their experts' opinions. This conclusion is also supported by the strong dissent in probability assessments. As defined according to former Delphi studies, consensus is reached when the IQR ≤ 25 for EP. Thus, consensus could be achieved for 1 out of 16 projections, which is projection 15 (funding of business leadership education in tertiary education). Altogether, the Delphi process showed a strong degree of dissent for 15 out of 16 projections. Such results imply that there are controversial opinions among the experts regarding the estimated probability. As it is the aim of traditional Delphi studies to achieve consensus and "to minimize the variance between expert opinions" (Steinert, 2009, p. 297), the aim of this cross-country RT Delphi survey was to explore and to cover as many worldviews as possible on the surveyed topic. Therefore, different perspectives and perceptions of four different stakeholder groups possessing different cultural and professional backgrounds were incorporated in the panel with the aim "to yield robust decision-making" (Markmann, Darkow & Gracht, 2013, p. 1826) for the future of business leadership education in tertiary education.

While conducting a conjoint analysis, it was detected conversely that IQR results are showing high consensus for desirability and impact (IQR ≤1) for most of the projections. For 12 out of 16 projections' impact assessments, strong consensus could be achieved; IQR shows strong dissent only for the remaining four impact ratings (projections 3, 5, 10, 11). Similar results can be observed for desirability ratings. Strong consensus could be achieved for 11 of 16 projections' desirability assessments. For the four above mentioned desirability ratings with the lowest results (projections 5, 13, 15, 16) and for projection 4 additionally experts have controversial opinions since there is strong dissent.

As a conclusion for quantitative analysis, the consistently high values for estimated probability, desirability and impact can be evaluated as a quality criterion for the relevance and importance of the developed projections. In 50 % of the projections, a consensus building process can be detected by analyzing the negative values for convergence rate, whereas participants further expressed their experts' opinions in 50 %. Those results are also supported by the values for IQR, which show strong dissent for all but one projection, while IQR results are showing high consensus for desirability and impact assessments. "By its nature, dissent is more likely to be associated with projections for which the future development is still difficult to assess." (Gracht & Darkow, 2010, p. 52)

Although there seems to be a trend in recent research articles (e.g. Ecken, Gnatzy & Gracht, 2011; Warth, Gracht & Darkow, 2013) on Delphi studies to conduct inferential statistics and the corresponding statistical tests to explain certain assumptions (e.g. desirability bias) or dissent, as a precaution it should be noted that the results of this RT Delphi survey were analyzed under holistic considerations. Fostering a holistic view on business leadership education in tertiary education, each of the four stakeholder groups is an essential and indispensable part of this education in the present and the future. More than this, the four stakeholder groups were analyzed under equal conditions, irrespective of the gender. Moreover, it was determined to analyze a global panel as a total. On one hand, the sample size of some countries does not allow further statistical tests due to the limited number of cases. Analyzing according to country groups will not provide further insights. On the other hand, business leadership education for graduates in Master in Management programs in tertiary education in the year 2030 was analyzed on a global perspective.

The 16 projections were, however, of particular interest for more profound analysis using quantitative and qualitative analysis methods. Concerning the content, the 16 projections are allocated to the four stakeholder dimensions for business leadership education in tertiary education. Each stakeholder dimension is briefly introduced, followed by a presentation of the relevant projections according to the principle of Becker and Gracht (2014). Therefore, each of the projections was analyzed thoroughly, using a homogenous structure. This homogeneous three-step structure comprises preliminary notes showing underlying literature and current state of discussion, followed by experts' opinions showing quantitative and qualitative results and finally a conclusion. Each of the four stakeholder dimensions concludes with a summary.

4.3.5.2 Stakeholder dimension providers (universities / business schools)

Business leadership education for graduates in Master in Management programs in tertiary education is provided by public and private universities and within universities, traditionally by their business schools. The origins of this field of studies are located in the USA and can be considered a consequence of industrialization, mass manufacturing and the need for management. "Wharton, set up in 1881 in the University of Pennsylvania, was the first business school in the United States." (Canals, 2011a, p. 4) Thus, the history of business schools and management education is a relatively recent development compared to other traditional fields of studies, such as philosophy for example. The economic growth during the second half of the twentieth century was accompanied by an increase of business schools in the USA and, later, in Europe (Canals, 2011a). In the meantime, business schools and business leadership education emerged all over the world in different models with differences in framework, admission requirements, curricula, teaching and learning objectives, didactics, exams and so on. As a result, the global market for this field of study is quite complex. Focusing exemplarily only on the German market, 1,435 Master's programs in the field of management were offered in the year 2016 (Hochschulkompass, 2016). Not only because of the overwhelming and complex offers of Master's programs in the field of management worldwide, but business leadership education in tertiary education has to be examined from a future perspective, also because of the criticism expressed on business schools due to the financial and banking crisis in the year 2008 (The Economist, 2013).[65] It was discussed controversially whether business schools should "bear some blame" (James, 2009) that graduates of (MBA) programs hold decisive leadership positions but are not (sufficiently) aware of business ethics and unable to create a sustainable and ethical valuable business culture (Businessweek, 2008; James, 2009; Sheridan, 2009). Furthermore, due to multiple influencing factors such as globalization, digitization etc., the transformation of the working environment on one hand and changed requirements for business leaders to cope with the future on the other (IBM, 2010 & 2012a / b; Regnet, 2014; Weber, 2007) may affect business leadership education in tertiary education. Consequently, providers of business leadership education in tertiary education have to scrutinize and rethink their educational goals, educational contents, educational methodologies and educational settings. As initially noted, market-relevant trends such as branding etc. as well as quality, accreditation, and ranking issues are not a part of this research due to the educational focus as well as the presumption that those aspects can be taken for granted in successful providers in the year 2030. It is imperative to explore the future of business leadership education in tertiary education considering the above-mentioned developments. Therefore, projections 1-5 were developed and surveyed within this rubric.

4.3.5.2.1 Projection 1 – Personality & leadership competencies

Preliminary notes

In times of rapidly changing environments and accelerated uncertainty, not only employers demand for "innovative and socially-conscious graduates" (Lewington, 2016), but also universities / business schools around the globe are challenged to educate according to one of the main goals of Catholic University: producing "mature and competent personalities who are capable of

---

[65] For more details, please see Part 2, Chapter 3.2.2.2.

committing themselves with generosity to new national and international scenarios" (Parolin, 2016). Furthermore, Becker and Gracht (2014) underline that "while the relevance of professional competencies remains constant, requirements for social, personal and methodical competencies of leaders were increased" (p. 50).[66]

Therefore, the focus of Master in Management programs in tertiary education was of prime interest. The first projection was formulated to find out if such programs would focus on personality and leadership competencies rather than functional knowledge in the year 2030.

Experts' opinions

The estimated probability (EP) that, in 2030, Master in Management programs will tend to focus on personality and leadership competencies rather than impart functional knowledge is 62.8 %. Desirability (D) $M = 3.99$ and impact (I) $M = 4.02$ are quite high (Table 20). The interquartile range (IQR), which is the measurement of consensus for this RT Delphi survey, confirms a considerably high degree of dissent regarding EP. This shows that the panelists have different assessments of the projection, even though the overall EP is relatively high. In contrast, for desirability and impact in case of occurrence, the IQR ranges show that a high consensus was achieved between the experts.

A qualitative examination of the valuable comments noted by the experts revealed that 12 experts have revised their answers 20 times in total for the EP. 7 of 12 confirmed their first choice in completely different ranges of the 11-unit scale: 1 of 12 rated the EP higher than before (from 70 % to 80 %) and 4 of 12 finally rated EP lower than in their first choice and decreased the EP between 20-60 %. Only 5 final revisions revealed that the opinions of experts show no tendency towards the mean. Inferentially, the experts continue to have the same ultimate opinion in spite of several revisions. This conclusion is also supported by the 4.81 % divergence of opinion.

---

66   For details, please see Part 2, chapters 3.1.4.3 and 3.1.4.4.

No.	Projection for the year 2030
1	In 2030, Master in Management programs tend to focus on personality and leadership competencies rather than impart (functional) knowledge.

EP statistics			D statistics			I statistics	
EP (mean)	IQR	Con	D (mean)	IQR		I (mean)	IQR
62.76%	30	4.81%	3.99	0		4.02	0

Legend: EP = Estimated probability of occurrence (0-100%); IQR= Interquartile range; Con (SD) = Convergence of opinion (variation of standard variation: negative values equals convergence); D = Desirability of occurrence (1 = very low, 5 = very high); I = Impact in case of occurrence (1 = very low, 5 = very high).

Note degree of consensus / dissent: *Italic numbers* indicate that consensus among experts was achieved; i.e. for EP IQR ≤ 25 equals consensus, for D and I respectively IQR ≤ 1 equals consensus.

Table 20. Statistical data for projection 1 (n=105).

The experts provided 127 written comments in total. There were 53 comments for EP, 34 comments for D and 40 comments for I (Table 21). The analysis also revealed 56 comments, which support the future trend that Master in Management programs will focus on leadership competencies rather than functional knowledge, which shall be referred to as "pro" comments. A total number of 17 comments were found to be unsupportive of this specific future trend, which shall be referred to as "contra" comments.

Projection for the year 2030	1 (Personality & leadership competencies)
Number of comments (total)	127
Number of comments (sub-questions 1.1, 1.2, 1.3)	53, 34, 40
Supportive comments ("pro")	56
Unsupportive comments ("contra")	17

Table 21. Details of comments for projection 1.

To understand the future implications for a focus change in Master in Management programs from mere functional knowledge to leadership and competencies of prospective leaders, it is important to analyze quantitative and qualitative results together. The quantitative results show that it is uncertain that such a trend will occur in the year 2030. The results further show the desirability of such a trend to become a reality and that it would have a high impact on how the curriculum for business leadership is designed and how business leadership as a topic will undergo changes in tertiary education. The qualitative content analysis displayed support to this fact. In spite of the fact that there were more supportive statements (56) noted for this projection than unsupportive comments (17), the highest number of contra comments were shown for estimated probability supporting the dissent shown in quantitative results for EP and consensus shown for D and I. This means that the diverse expert panel had differences of opinions regarding the probability of such a trend to become a reality in the year 2030. They agreed, however, that such a trend would be highly desirable and would have a high impact on business leadership education.

Some relevant comments were chosen to support the quantitative results of the first projection. These comments were firstly selected according to the exactness displayed in the specific comment, secondly according to the category of experts and thirdly according to the nationality of the expert. For projection 1, the selective comments presented in Table 22 display the perspectives of three groups of experts namely universities / business schools, companies / CEOs and students. Please note that no comments were mentioned by the fourth type of experts namely politics / associations for this specific projection.

The selected expert comments belonging to Germany and USA highlight the importance of leadership and competencies in the future. The personality of a leader, according to a German expert, plays an important role and a leader with personality is more desirable than a technocratic manager. Another German expert points out that the role of a leader is to balance both sides, knowledge and personality, as these are essential for success of the business.

While considering the supportive comments, it is also worth taking into account the differences in opinions displayed by the experts. Many experts highlight the importance of functional knowledge. The selected comments in Table 22 show that an American and an Indian expert believe that it would be difficult for universities to part from functional knowledge and that such knowledge should not be disregarded. Another German expert considers this projection a paradox because, on one hand, it is essential that universities focus more on leadership in the future; on the other hand, basic knowledge is equally essential according to him. A Brazilian expert comments that leadership education is a mere tool provided to students; whether they use it for themselves rather depends on influential examples around them than on courses conducted in classes.

Pro comments	Contra comments
EP - "While there is likely to be a need for basic foundation for functional knowledge, individual characteristics and leadership competencies will cross over diverse areas and range will be addressed much more greatly in future." *Universities / Business Schools, USA*	EP - "Although I believe the statement to be truer than 50% that I posted, my experience is still that Universities will have a difficult time moving away from functional knowledge." *Universities / Business Schools, USA*
EP - "Changes in education need a long time, but the companies hopefully will demand such Master's programs, because personality and leadership competences are most important in the future." *Student, Germany*	EP - "Although the emphasis will be on leadership, the functional knowledge cannot and should not be disregarded." *Universities / Business Schools, India*
D - "Leader's and executives with personality are in principle much more successful and therefore much more desirable than technocratic manager." *Companies / CEOs, Germany*	D - "I tend to say on the one hand, that universities were and should be the bearer and keeper of knowledge. On the other hand, I tend to say, that the education of leaders were and should be not be based mainly on knowledge but on the development of competencies and personality. So I find myself in a paradox, because I like the idea of putting personality in the heart of the education of leaders but I am not quite sure if universities are the best places for this kind of education. I do not find it very desirable if universities would become nothing more than gyms for elaborate leadership trainings." *Universities / Business Schools, Germany*
I - "Our society needs good leaders who can balance both sides (personality / leadership) versus knowledge. Without a combination of both, negotiations, compromise and agreement cannot occur. These skills are absolutely vital to large business deals, management on a large and small scale." *Companies / CEOs, Germany*	I - "Since it focus on individual personality, education has only little impact on it. Leadership education is a tool to be introduced to our students. If they use it or not depends more from persuasive examples than in class courses." *Universities / Business Schools, Brazil*

Table 22. Selected pro and contra comments of the experts for projection 1.

Conclusion

To summarize, in spite of clear differences in experts' opinions, the future trend that Master in Management programs will focus more on leadership and competencies rather than functional knowledge faces some challenges to become reality; nevertheless such a trend is desirable and will have a high impact on business leadership education in tertiary education for graduates in case of occurrence.

4.3.5.2.2   Projection 2 – Educational setting & development of competencies

Preliminary notes

Increasing the inclusion of practice and opportunity in order to apply the theoretical knowledge in a business setting is a matter of concern for most present Master's programs to foster competency development. Michael Arena, chief talent and development officer for General Motors Co. and member of AACSB board of directors, expects business graduates to master the "practice of theory in a less-than-ideal context" (as cited in Gellman, 2016). Differentiation is required between case studies – widely spread and traditionally used in management and leadership education, especially in MBA programs – and real-world challenges. Real-world challenges have to be embedded in the learning process in order to tie in with existing knowledge, experiences and competencies in order to enable students to systematically develop their competencies (Katz-Buonincontro & Ghosh, 2014).[67]

It is thought to be beneficial that Master in Management programs in tertiary education place equal emphasis on campus-related and company-related activities. Therefore, the second projection was formulated to discover whether such programs will take place both on campus and in companies in equal measure in the year 2030.

Experts' opinions

The estimated probability (EP) that, in 2030, Master in Management programs will take place both on campus and in companies in equal measure is 54.10 %, which signals a medium EP. Desirability (D) M = 3.87 and impact (I) M = 4.01 are quite high (Table 23). The interquartile range (IQR), which is the measurement of consensus for this RT Delphi survey, shows a strong dissent for EP. This indicates that the experts' opinions about whether this trend come into existence diverge to a high degree. For desirability and impact in case of occurrence, the IQR ranges show that consensus was achieved between the survey participants.

---

67   For details, please see Part 2, chapters 3.1.4.4, 3.2.5.4, 3.2.5.5.

No.	Projection for the year 2030
2	In 2030, Master in Management programs take place both on campus and in companies in equal measure.

EP statistics			D statistics		I statistics	
EP (mean)	IQR	Con	D (mean)	IQR	I (mean)	IQR
54.10 %	40	1.94 %	3.87	0	4.01	0

Legend: EP = Estimated probability of occurrence (0-100 %); IQR= Interquartile range; Con (SD) = Convergence of opinion (variation of standard variation: negative values equals convergence); D = Desirability of occurrence (1 = very low, 5 = very high); I = Impact in case of occurrence (1 = very low, 5 = very high).

Note degree of consensus / dissent: *Italic numbers* indicate that consensus among experts was achieved; i.e. for EP IQR ≤ 25 equals consensus, for D and I respectively IQR ≤ 1 equals consensus.

Table 23. Statistical data for projection 2 (n=105).

A qualitative examination of the recorded experts' comments revealed that 11 experts have revised their answers 18 times in total for the EP. 4 of 11 confirmed their first choice in completely different ranges of the 11-unit scale, regardless of the mean. 4 of 11 rated the EP higher than before and 3 of 11 ultimately rated EP lower than they did in their first choice and decreased the EP, regardless of the mean. Finally, only 7 final revisions imply that the experts continue to have their own expert opinion at the end, despite several revisions. This conclusion is also supported by the divergence of opinion, which is only 1.94 %.

Projection for the year 2030	2 (Educational setting & development of competencies)
Number of comments (total)	110
Number of comments (sub-questions 2.1, 2.2, 2.3)	47, 32, 31
Supportive comments ("pro")	61
Unsupportive comments ("contra")	20

Table 24. Details of comments for projection 2.

The qualitative content analysis revealed that the experts provided 110 written comments in total. There were 47 comments for EP, 32 comments for D and 31 comments for I (Table 24). There were mixed opinions of the diverse panel related to this issue. The analysis revealed 61 comments, which support the future trend that Master in Management programs will take place both on campus and in companies in equal measure, which shall be referred to as "pro" comments. A total of 20 comments were found to be unsupportive of this specific future trend, which shall be referred to as "contra" comments.

Pro comments	Contra comments
EP - "In 2030, there will presumably also be academically oriented continuing education programs which are narrowly associated with the apprenticeship and research at universities. However, the trend strongly goes in the direction of dual education which helps to overcome evident weaknesses of many existing programs at universities and colleges." *Universities / Business Schools, Liechtenstein*	EP - "The balance should depend on the business branch / area. Some might require more theoretical knowledge; some will require more practical experience. 50 / 50 should not be followed without serious branch nature scanning. It is acceptable in General Management programs, just like the medicine in general. Surgeon is more complex than family doctor practitioner." *Companies / CEOs, Croatia*
EP - "It is a good combination to give more practices and to create the innovative ideas." *Companies / CEOs, China*	EP - "I believe that on campus is more important, because not all Master's programs have experience with companies." *Universities / Business Schools, Brazil*
D - "Young leaders need guidance and chance to practice." *Companies / CEOs, China*	D - "I think crossing the lines from Education at the University level to the corporate level is good, but I do not think that Corporations want to take on the role of the University in most cases. We do see some of this already; I just don't believe it will be a huge trend." *Universities / Business Schools, USA*
D - "Value that the in-company exposure adds is immense." *Universities / Business Schools, India*	D - "The equal measure would be good (about 50 % in companies, 50 % in the Campus), but the danger is, that companies make their own specialists, which are not well prepared for other companies. Because of that it is important to ensure the quality of education in companies through binding rules." *Student, Germany*
I - "It could make it easier / less expensive and that could have a positive impact on businesses and the students enrolled from those businesses." *Politics / Associations, USA*	I - "In the future, the professionals will select the topics which are of interest and will mount they grid disciplines who want to know. And you do not need to go to the university to access those content." *Politics / Associations, Brazil*
I - "Higher number of people in the workforce, more cross-research projects. Better collaboration with better innovations." *Student, Germany*	

Table 25. Selected pro and contra comments of the experts for projection 2.

Some relevant comments were chosen to support the quantitative results of the second projection. The criteria used for choosing these comments were firstly the exactness displayed in the specific comment, secondly the category of experts and thirdly the nationality of the expert. For projection 2, the selective comments presented in Table 25 display the perspectives of all four groups of experts namely universities / business schools, companies / CEOs, students and politics / associations.

The selected experts' comments from different countries emphasize the collaboration between the universities and companies by providing guidance and opportunities for practices, which might lead to better innovations. This can have a positive impact on business leadership education. The content analysis showed that importance of training and practice was highlighted by 12 experts. One of the experts from Liechtenstein points out the trend strongly goes in the direction of dual education, which helps to overcome evident weaknesses of many existing programs at universities and colleges. On-campus and in-company was a good combination, which would generate innovative ideas, according to an expert from China. The analysis also highlighted importance and need for online learning, which was mentioned by 4 experts as an equally relevant option considering the future of Master in Management programs.

The differences in opinions displayed by the experts emerged clearly from the content analysis. Many experts highlight the possibility of 50-50 % role of universities and companies. According to a German student and a CEO from Croatia, the universities and companies should ensure the quality of the education through binding rules because each company might create their own specialists, which would not be suitable for other companies. An expert from Brazil believes that campus based education is more important. An American expert does not believe that this will be a huge trend because corporations would not take on the role of the universities. An expert from Croatia comments that the balance depends upon the business area or branch, as some courses place greater emphasis on theoretical knowledge whereas others require more experiential knowledge. Such a balance of even importance given to on-campus and in-company teaching will also affect business leadership education. The analysis further revealed the fact that more exposure to practice and real-world settings are needed for business leadership education, which a learner can get mostly in companies.

It is important to analyze quantitative and qualitative results together for a better understanding of the future implications of these programs taking place both on campus and in companies in equal measure. The quantitative results, namely a medium probability of occurrence and high desirability and impact in case of occurrence, are supported by the qualitative content analysis. Regardless of the fact that there were more supportive (61) than unsupportive (20) comments noted for this projection, the highest number of contra comments were shown for estimated probability supporting the dissent shown in quantitative results for EP and consensus shown for D and I.

Conclusion

To summarize, despite reasonable differences in experts' opinions, the future trend that Master in Management programs will take place both on campus and in companies in equal measure is uncertain and will face some challenges to come into existence in the year 2030. Nevertheless, such a trend is desirable and would have a high impact on business leadership education in tertiary education for graduates.

4.3.5.2.3   Projection 3 – E-learning

Preliminary notes

The "use of information and communications technology (ICT) to enhance and / or support learning" (OECD, 2005, p. 21) may have an effect on how business leadership education will function in tertiary education. E-learning comprises various types of media, technology applications, and processes facilitating different learning modes, such as learning inside or outside of the classroom, instructor-led synchronous or self-determined asynchronous learning, distance learning and flexible learning. Moreover, E-learning can be combined with face-to-face teaching and learning (blended learning) (Halarnkar & Kulkarni, 2013). Due to technological advances, digitization is taking place speedily. "Another force is the breathtaking pace at which educational technology is improving. There's been an explosion in the amount of high quality content that is readily accessible online." (Bailey et al., 2011, p. 8) The global mobile education market is expected to grow to 37.8 billion US dollars in 2020, up from 3.4 billion US dollars in 2011 (Statista, 2016). Driving force for the development of online education is the USA, where the numbers of students taking online courses has increased rapidly in recent years (Allen & Seaman 2013).

It is expected that the spending on digital education technologies in the USA will reach 26.8 billion US dollars in 2018 (Deloitte, 2015). Furthermore, new models for the supply of education will be developed by using technology not only to reach students which were previously marginalized (UNESCO, 2012b), but also to create new didactical concepts and to meet skills which are expected to be relevant in the 21st century (WEF, 2015; WEF, 2016). In a vision paper for open education 2030, it was stated that:

> "Naturally, our first assumption will be that the 2030 school education is (pre)designed. Experts agree that major changes are required in the way that learning is delivered, students are motivated, teachers are trained, and schools are managed. Education needs to open up to new contents, teaching practices and tools. A more individualized learning path and flexible core curriculum are among the key ingredients to this transformative process. Technology is seen as one of the main drivers to achieving major transformation both in and beyond the classroom." (Ullmo, 2013)

Universities have to attend to their duty of laying the foundations for innovations. They have to shape learning environments[68], which foster learning and creativity (NMC, 2015, p. 8). Therefore, the third projection was formulated in line with Becker and Gracht (2014) to know, whether advanced digitization (Web 2.x) will completely transform business leadership education in tertiary education in the year 2030.

Experts' opinions

The estimated probability (EP) that, in 2030, advanced digitization (Web 2.x) will completely transform business leadership education in tertiary education is 61 %. Desirability (D) M = 3.6 and impact (I) M = 3.84 are quite high (Table 26). The interquartile range (IQR), which is the measurement of consensus for this RT Delphi survey, confirms dissent regarding EP and impact in case of occurrence. This indicates that the panelists have different assessments of the future, even though the overall values for EP and I are reasonably high. In

---

68   See also Part 2, chapter 3.2.5.5.

contrast, for desirability, the IQR show that consensus was achieved between the experts.

No.	Projection for the year 2030
3	In 2030, advanced digitization (Web 2.x) has completely transformed business leadership education in tertiary education.

EP statistics			D statistics			I statistics	
EP (mean)	IQR	Con	D (mean)	IQR		I (mean)	IQR
61.00%	30	4.18%	3.6	*1*		3.84	2

Legend: EP = Estimated probability of occurrence (0-100%); IQR= Interquartile range; Con (SD) = Convergence of opinion (variation of standard variation: negative values equals convergence); D = Desirability of occurrence (1 = very low, 5 = very high); I = Impact in case of occurrence (1 = very low, 5 = very high).

Note degree of consensus / dissent: *Italic numbers* indicate that consensus among experts was achieved; i.e. for EP IQR ≤ 25 equals consensus, for D and I respectively IQR ≤ 1 equals consensus.

Table 26. Statistical data for projection 3 (n=105).

A qualitative examination of experts' comments discovered that 10 experts have revised their answers 17 times in total for the EP. 4 of 10 confirmed their first choice in completely different ranges of the 11-unit scale, regardless of the mean. 2 of 10 rated the EP higher than before and 4 out of 10 finally rated EP lower than they did in the first choice and decreased the EP regardless of the mean. The revisions suggest that the experts continue to have their opinion at the end in spite of several revisions. This conclusion is also supported by the divergence of opinion, which is 4.18%.

Projection for the year 2030	3 (E-learning)
Number of comments (total)	93
Number of comments (sub-questions 3.1, 3.2, 3.3)	39, 27, 27
Supportive comments ("pro")	38
Unsupportive comments ("contra")	37

Table 27. Details of comments for projection 3.

The qualitative content analysis revealed that the experts provided 93 written comments in total. There were 39 comments for EP, 27 comments for D and 27 comments for I (Table 27). The analysis showed mixed opinions of the experts of the diverse panel regarding projection 3. The analysis revealed that there were 38 comments, which support the third projection, which shall be referred to as "pro" comments. There were also differences found in the opinions of experts. A total number of 37 comments were found to be unsupportive of this specific future trend, which shall be referred to as "contra" comments.

For better perception of this technological trend, it was important to analyze quantitative and qualitative results together. The quantitative results revealed that such a trend would face some challenges to come into existence in the year 2030. On the other hand, such a trend would be highly desirable and would have a high impact on business leadership education as such an aspect of advanced digitization (Web 2.x) would provide advancement to the students and may completely transform business leadership education in tertiary education. The qualitative content analysis displayed support to this fact. Interestingly, there were 38 supportive and 37 unsupportive statements. The contra comments for desirability and impact were lesser compared to the comments noted for estimated probability, which is supporting the dissent shown in quantitative results for EP and consensus shown for D and I. Conclusively, there are mixed opinions expressed by the diverse expert panel regarding the probability of such a trend being realized in the year 2030; however, such a trend would be highly desirable and would have a high impact on business leadership education in tertiary education.

Some relevant comments were chosen to support the quantitative results. For projection 3, the selective comments are presented in Table 28 and display the perspectives of all four groups of experts, namely universities / business schools, companies / CEOs, students and politics / associations. It is to be noted that no supportive comments were mentioned by the fourth type of experts, namely politics / associations for this specific projection.

Strengths as well as weaknesses of the trend were seen frequently in the comments of the experts from different countries. An expert from Brazil sees this as an opportunity to save time by choosing the option of distance learning and internet based learning besides having a positive impact on business leadership education. Another expert from Switzerland showed a balanced approach towards this trend. According to him, it has already started changing the world by providing "flexi packages". It will gain importance and have a high impact on business leadership education. One of the experts from China points out that this trend will make teaching more interesting by providing

Pro comments	Contra comments
EP - "We are in the information age and people want to save time. An opportunity is to seek knowledge with courses over the Internet and distance learning." *Companies / CEOs, Brazil*	EP - "Despite all the technological developments, face to face interaction will retain its value and relevance." *Politics / Associations, Brazil*
EP - "Web 2.0 already transforms education since more courses on this Topic are offered as a "flexi"-package (online and on-Campus). Digital leadership and leading virtual Teams becomes more important. The Transformation trend will further gain in importance and will have a huge Impact. However, a 100 % occurrence is not possible because "in-class" practices will still have its Impact on leadership education." *Universities / Business Schools, Switzerland*	EP - "Like I said before, advanced digitization is NOT an effective way of passing on the skills and hands-on experience." *Universities / Business Schools, India*
D - "Will facilitate teaching methods and make them more interesting." *Universities / Business Schools, China*	D - "If I can afford the time and expense, I still prefer the conventional method to have the education, particularly the management and leadership issues which naturally request numerous discussions. Team work with the group showing on the screen would not create the same effectiveness and efficiency as face-to-face." *Companies / CEOs, China*
I -"To universities, this means a large financial and organizational relief. It seems like this could be the solution to manage the large number of students. Digitized education, however, should be well designed, in this lays the danger versus the benefits. Therefore, a combination between digitized and interpersonal education (blended learning) seems to be a good solution." *Student, Germany*	D -"Blended Learning will be the crème de la crème, as a mix of education formats. Full online learning develops. However, in order to train the increasingly important social-communicative competencies, it is required to practice offline and on-site by way of creative, sometimes theatrical manners. It will also be important to experience the teacher in persona. We still very much learn from idols." *Student, Germany*
I - "The impact will be very high because new skills need to be developed." *Universities / Business Schools, Brazil*	I - "I'd say no impact unless it is combined with superb instructional design principles, interactivity and applicability of the concepts in real life situations where there are consequences." *Universities / Business Schools, USA*

Table 28. Selected pro and contra comments of the experts for projection 3.

additional ways of teaching. A German student considers that it might imply financial advantages for the universities or educational institutions and could be a better solution for managing large numbers of students. Furthermore, according to the German student, blended learning is the best combination of advanced digitization and interpersonal communication is the suitable teaching manner. The expert from Brazil said that new skills should be developed by this trend. The analysis further highlighted the importance of and need for blended learning as a more balanced approach, considering the future of Master in Management programs.

Different solutions or alternatives for this trend also emerged from the differences of opinions expressed by the experts. An expert from Brazil believes that face-to-face interaction will maintain great value in spite of advancements. An Indian expert strongly considers this trend as not useful to gain practical knowledge and essential skills. A CEO from China stated that the conventional method of learning was more effective and efficient with regard to leadership and management that requires group discussions and face-to-face interactions; advanced digitization could not provide the same effectiveness. Another expert from Germany speaks in favor of blended learning. According to him, blended learning was required because human beings need idols to learn social communicative competencies, which are essential and can be practiced offline by knowing the personality of the teacher. An American expert says that an excellent educational basis and interactivity are required along with applicability in the real world, where real consequences occur.

Conclusion

To summarize, regardless of having some logical differences in experts' opinions, the future trend that advanced digitization (Web 2.x) will completely transform business leadership education in tertiary education is highly desirable and would have a high impact on business leadership education in tertiary education.

4.3.5.2.4 Projection 4 – Individualization

Preliminary notes

Custom-tailored programs allow learners to alter, plan, or build the curriculum according to individual needs based on competencies, personality, strengths and weaknesses. Custom-tailored programs have started gaining importance and popularity in today's world, not only because of technological opportunities. According to a vision paper for open education 2030, Devine (2013) stated that the "co-evolution of digital technologies, devices, infrastructure and resources that will occur in the coming decade suggests that a changed trajectory for formal education is inevitable." By 2030, he further stated, "Each student will have an individually negotiated curriculum." (Devine, 2013). However, the prime concern of Master's programs is the standardization procedure of such programs to ensure (high) quality and cost efficiency. Prima facie, these standardized programs appear effective and promising while, conversely, there are many controversial discussions regarding the individualization of programs. Klovert outlines the implications of individualized learning on education, which can also be transferred to tertiary education. Since there is no standardized definition for individualized learning, there are many different expectations and challenges to meet different demands. Higher expenditures for support and mentoring are assumed as well as a manifestation of inequalities. Last but not least access to and use of data should be regulated since they are required to determine and improve learners' learning rhythm and behavior (Klovert, 2015). Whether Master in Management programs for graduates will be highly individualized and custom-tailored in the future needs to be examined. Therefore, the fourth projection was formulated in line with Becker and Gracht (2014).

Experts' opinions

The estimated probability (EP) is 54.9 % that business leadership education in Master in Management programs for graduates will be highly individualized and custom-tailored in 2030. Desirability (D) M = 3.75 and impact (I) M = 3.97 are high respectively (Table 29). The interquartile range (IQR), which is the measurement of consensus for this RT Delphi survey, displayed a high degree of dissent regarding EP and D. Strong dissent with moderate values for EP and D entails that it is uncertain whether Master in Management programs for graduates would be highly individualized and custom-tailored in the future. Nevertheless, the IQR results for I show that consensus was achieved.

No.	Projection for the year 2030
4	In 2030, business leadership education in Master in Management programs for graduates is highly individualized and custom-tailored.

EP statistics			D statistics		I statistics	
EP (mean)	IQR	Con	D (mean)	IQR	I (mean)	IQR
54.9 %	40	1.75 %	3.75	2	3.97	*1*

Legend: EP = Estimated probability of occurrence (0-100 %); IQR= Interquartile range; Con (SD) = Convergence of opinion (variation of standard variation: negative values equals convergence); D = Desirability of occurrence (1 = very low, 5 = very high); I = Impact in case of occurrence (1 = very low, 5 = very high).

Note degree of consensus / dissent: *Italic numbers* indicate that consensus among experts was achieved; i.e. for EP IQR ≤ 25 equals consensus, for D and I respectively IQR ≤ 1 equals consensus.

Table 29. Statistical data for projection 4 (n=105).

A qualitative examination of the experts' comments revealed that 11 experts have revised their answers 19 times in total for the EP. 6 of 11 confirmed their first choice. 4 of 11 rated EP lower than they did in the first choice and decreased the EP regardless of the mean. 1 of 11 rated EP higher than before. The final assessments imply that the experts ultimately continue to have their own expert opinion in spite of several revisions. Furthermore, this conclusion is also supported by the divergence of opinion, which is only 1.75 %.

According to the content analysis, 93 written comments were noted from the experts for this projection. There were 42 comments for EP, 28 comments for D and 23 for I (Table 30). The analysis discovered that there were 49 comments, which support the future trend and shall be referred to as "pro" comments. 33 comments were found to be unsupportive of this specific future trend, which shall be referred to as "contra" comments.

Projection for the year 2030	4 (Individualization)
Number of comments (total)	93
Number of comments (sub-questions 4.1, 4.2, 4.3)	42, 28, 23
Supportive comments ("pro")	49
Unsupportive comments ("contra")	33

Table 30. Details of comments for projection 4.

Qualitative content analysis reveals some additional aspects of this particular projection. For projection 4, the selective comments presented in Table 31 display the perspectives of all four stakeholder groups of experts, namely universities / business schools, companies / CEOs, students, and politics / associations. A Chinese CEO opines that there are 50 % chances of this trend coming into reality because highly tailor-made programs will be too expensive for students. A Swiss professor mentioned that standardization of such an individualized and tailor-made program was mandatory. According to an American expert, the use of advanced resources will increase along with the productive learning by the students. A student from Germany believes that the learning process might become effective if individual needs are taken into account. An American professor thinks that this trend will open various options of Master's programs for the students. Though there are differences in the opinion regarding this particular trend, many experts believe that such programs may be advantageous for the underprivileged or migrants. Many experts also raised the issue of standardization of such programs and pointed out that some norms are mandatory to run these programs effectively.

Some challenging aspects of this trend also emerged from the unsupportive comments of the experts. A German student strongly believes that a leader should effectively work in multiple sectors of the businesses; custom-tailored programs may fall short in providing effective education to work in multiple sectors. An Indian expert is doubtful about the effectiveness and application of such programs and thinks that custom-made programs may limit the managers' mobility. According to a German student, fundamentals of leadership education will remain constant and everyone should adopt them equally; individualization will bring some specific skills related to a particular sector, which would not work at other places. A Swiss professor opines that custom-made programs were required at a higher level and not at graduation level. A German CEO expresses concern about the expenses required for the highly custom-tailored programs. The contra comments are also supporting the quantitative results for the dissent achieved for D. Many disadvantages were mentioned by the experts, which imply that the trend for Master in Management programs leans toward standardization to make the programs less expensive for students, contrary to individualization and custom-tailored programs.

Pro comments	Contra comments
EP - "Highly tailor-made education program would be perfect, if the solution could be found regarding the expense (I am not sure whether web 2.0 could help to eliminate the expense of individualized program) and the database including various industry segments covering all fields. Therefore I rate 50%." *Companies / CEOs, China*	EP - "I would not think that individualization is a proper way for good, efficient leadership education. Because a good business leader should not be an expert in only one part of the business, he should know general functions in business context over all branches and markets…" *Student, Germany*
EP - "Certain standardization is necessary." *Universities / Business Schools, Switzerland*	EP - "The basis of the customized programs is likely to be weak so far as the applicability and usefulness is concerned. Further, it may limit the possibility of managers moving from one sector to the other. In future, the manager mobility will of great value. And customized programs will not be able to meet this objective." *Universities / Business Schools, India*
EP - "This would improve student outcomes and may be enhanced by increased use of digital resources. It will be more satisfying to students than the old "one size fits all" approach." *Politics / Associations, USA*	EP - "Management programs itself provide management competences, which everybody should be able to learn in the same sense. The individualization comes from personality. This however is not part of competences. There might be some customization like specific management skills depending on functions (marketing, sales, finance, etc.)." *Student, Germany*
D - "Good education is always individualized and tailored on the needs of the learners. Through this the learn Processing becomes most effective." *Student, Germany*	D - "Technical People will specialize more, but managers need more general skills. Whatever kind of project you manage, the basic principles stay the same." *Companies / CEOs, Germany*
D - "The more individualized the learning experience, the better the outcomes will be for the learner." *Universities / Business Schools, USA*	D - "It is highly desirable on the Level of executive education. On the level of consecutive education it is not necessary." *Universities / Business Schools, Switzerland*
I - "Within reason, a targeted solution will greatly aid business. I can see, however, that this might lead to multiple "Master's" programs that an individual could take. Why stop at one if it can be greatly tailored?" *Universities / Business Schools, USA*	I - "Much more Support Needs to be provided; this will lead to higher cost." *Companies / CEOs, Germany*

Table 31. Selected pro and contra comments of the experts for projection 4.

It is essential to integrate quantitative and qualitative results for the enhanced understanding of the custom-tailored and individualized programs for graduates in business leadership education in tertiary education. The quantitative results showed that it is not very probable in the future. The results also showed that such a trend is rather undesirable; nevertheless, such a trend would have a moderate impact on how these programs will work and how business leadership education will undergo changes based on this projection in tertiary education. Regardless of the fact that there were more supportive (49) than unsupportive comments (33) noted for this projection, the contra comments for EP and D were maximum compared to contra comments for I, supporting the dissent shown in quantitative results for EP and D and consensus shown for I. It further implies that mixed opinions were expressed by the diverse expert panel with respect to the probability and desirability that Master in Management programs will be highly individualized and custom-made for graduates and would have a moderate impact on business leadership education in tertiary education for graduates in the year 2030.

Conclusion

To summarize, the possibility of highly individualized and custom-tailored programs for graduates is rather low and experts mentioned some mixed aspects associated with this trend. Quantitative and qualitative results together reveal that such a trend is seen as less desirable in the future and would have a moderate impact on business leadership education in tertiary education.

4.3.5.2.5 Projection 5 – Allocation to schools

Preliminary notes

At the beginning of this work, it was elaborated that leadership (and entrepreneurship) covers a broad spectrum and cannot be attributed solely to one academic discipline (Bijedić, 2013; Rosenstiel & Comelli, 2003). Subsequently, a holistic definition and model of business leadership was developed[69], comprising both the business perspective, i.e. goals and innovations as well as the perspective on the leader's individual personality, i.e. creative personality, business leadership competencies and networks. Moreover, the business leader is not conceived as being isolated, but rather acting in a complex sociocultural context with its multitude of influential factors. This holistic understanding laid the foundation for the conceptualization of business lead-

---

69 For details, please see Part 2, chapter 3, i.e. 3.1.4

ership education in tertiary education for graduates. Synthesizing the essential results of the proposed educational model reveals that business leadership education in tertiary education has to focus on student's familiarization with the scientific world on one hand, and the individual student's (creative) personality and its competency development on the other. Secondly, a curriculum with its elements – i.e. educational contents, educational methodologies, educational settings, and evaluation – has to ensure a consistent pedagogical infrastructure that nurtures the development of the individual student's business leader personality. Such an infrastructure is characterized by competency-based education. Literature supports that management and management education are more than just business and economy. One of the most famous representatives of an all-embracing management conception is Peter Drucker, who states:

> "[Management] deals with action and application; and it tests is results. This makes it a technology. But management also deals with people, their values, their growth and development – and this makes it a humanity. So does its concern with, and impact on, social structure and the community. Indeed, as everyone has learned who…has been working with managers of all kinds of institutions for long years, management is deeply involved in moral concerns – the nature of man, good and evil.
>
> Management is thus what tradition call a liberal art – 'liberal' because it deals with the fundamentals of knowledge, self-knowledge, wisdom, and leadership; 'art' because it is also concerned with practice and application. Managers draw on all the knowledges and insights of the humanities and the social sciences – on psychology and philosophy, on economics and history, on ethics – as well as on the physical sciences." (Drucker, 2010, p. 29-30).

Consequently, management and leadership education has to focus on more than mere business and economy due to the enormous impact of leaders / managers on nature, society, organizations and individuals. With regard to management education, Gagliardi (2006) states:

> "Conceiving management education solely as training in the management of an economy is to ignore the enormous power of managers in determining the individual and social quality of life in the community – small or large – entrusted to them, in making their organizations pleasant or oppressive places in which to

work, in fostering possible human happiness or at least reducing avoidable human suffering." (p. 6-7)

Furthermore, an example from the military context shall be mentioned. The German army (*Bundeswehr*) has established its own university – known as *Universität der Bundeswehr* – in the year 1973 in order to cope with increased requirements for military leaders. The *Universität der Bundeswehr* offers several study programs, wherein the field of educational sciences plays an important role for a (future) military leadership position. Education at the *Universität der Bundeswehr* can also be seen as a springboard to a career and / or leadership position in civil working environment (Bundeswehr, 2014; Universität der Bundeswehr, n.d.).

It was assumed that Business Schools rather focus on imparting functional management knowledge than consider the all-embracing topics needed for a holistic business leadership education. Hence, the fifth projection was formulated in a provoking manner to find out whether leadership and management programs will be a part of Schools for Social Sciences or Schools of Education in the future.

Experts' opinions

The estimated probability (EP) is 30.28 % that – in 2030, due to changed requirements for leaders, managers and talents – Master in Management programs are no longer part of Business Schools but rather a part of Schools of Education or Schools for Social Sciences, which is the lowest EP compared to the remaining 15 projections. Desirability (D) is $M = 2.70$, which is the lowest of all projections and impact (I) is M = 3.24, which is moderate (Table 32). The interquartile range (IQR), which is the measurement of consensus for this RT Delphi survey, confirms dissent regarding EP. This shows that the panelists have different assessments of the projection while the overall EP is low. Furthermore, for desirability and impact in case of occurrence, the IQR results show dissent.

No.	Projection for the year 2030
5	In 2030, Master in Management programs are no longer part of Business Schools but rather a part of Schools of Education or Schools for Social Sciences due to changed requirements for leaders, managers and talents,

EP statistics			D statistics		I statistics	
EP (mean)	IQR	Con	D (mean)	IQR	I (mean)	IQR
30.28 %	30	-0.96 %	2.7	2	3.24	2

Legend: EP = Estimated probability of occurrence (0-100 %); IQR= Interquartile range; Con (SD) = Convergence of opinion (variation of standard variation: negative values equals convergence); D = Desirability of occurrence (1 = very low, 5 = very high); I = Impact in case of occurrence (1 = very low, 5 = very high).

Note degree of consensus / dissent: *Italic numbers* indicate that consensus among experts was achieved; i.e. for EP IQR ≤ 25 equals consensus, for D and I respectively IQR ≤ 1 equals consensus.

Table 32. Statistical data for projection 5 (n=105).

A qualitative examination of the experts' comments revealed that 11 experts have revised their answers 13 times in total for the EP. 6 out of 11 confirmed their first choice. 4 out of 11 rated EP lower than they did in the first choice and decreased the EP regardless of the mean. 1 out of 11 rated EP higher than before. 5 final revisions imply that the experts continue to have their expert opinion at the end in spite of several revisions. Furthermore, this conclusion is also supported by the -.96 % convergence of opinion.

Projection for the year 2030	5 (Allocation to schools)
Number of comments (total)	84
Number of comments (sub-questions 5.1, 5.2, 5.3)	41, 21, 22
Supportive comments ("pro")	16
Unsupportive comments ("contra")	46

Table 33. Details of comments for projection 5.

As per the content analysis, 84 written comments were noted from the experts for this projection. There were 41 comments for EP, 21 comments for D and 22 comments for I (Table 33). The analysis revealed that there were only 16 comments, which support the future trend and are referred to as "pro" comments. 46 comments were found to be unsupportive of this specific future trend, which shall be referred to as "contra" comments. This projection did not receive much support from the experts meaning that Master in Management programs will not become a part of Schools of Education / Schools of Social Sciences but rather remain a part of Business Schools.

Pro comments	Contra comments
EP - "As there have been some educational changes putting together Philosophy, Sociology, History, Anthropology and Management will be necessary." *Universities / Business Schools, Brazil*	EP - "The best solution would be a strong cooperation between Business Schools and Schools of Education or Schools for Social Sciences." *Universities / Business Schools, Germany*
EP - "This might occur in education concepts / practice within low- and under developed societies / countries." *Companies / CEOs, Croatia*	EP - "That thesis is probably correct, but it won't happen. Since business schools will not be willing to give away management programs to social sciences. Also, the interconnectivity with other parts of Business studies will go missing. Furthermore, with the current set-up schools of education and social sciences are not able to teach management." *Politics / Associations, Germany*
D - "In my opinion this would be very desirable, because students of education schools would be perfect executives with optimal skills and competences for this occupation. Their strengths are, for example, explaining complicated issues in simple terms, understanding and learning quickly new subjects, social skills, handling with different people, empathy etc. Would a university mix pedagogical topics, connection to the professional practice (with companies) and leading and personality themes together, it would be the best education for executives and managers today and in the future. Nowadays students have to invest a lot of initiative and commitment to learn all these skills through independently commitment and activities." *Student, Germany*	EP - "Schools of education / social sciences will not be able to provide the necessary inputs that will suit the changed requirements.They are not geared to do that. It should not happen." *Universities / Business Schools, India*
D - "Business schools have usually a high competence in teaching management. This can take place in future digitized. The focus is development of leadership competences and personality - for these areas the competence lays in Schools of Education or Schools of Social Science." *Universities / Business Schools, Germany*	EP - "It's a mistake but will occur in some Universities. Business will still be "business". Leadership, in business, is not the same in education, sociology and politics." *Universities / Business Schools, Brazil*
I - "Even though I disagree with the concept, I can see advantages should this happen, and much learning could take place." *Universities / Business Schools, USA*	D - "I think this would be desirable, but I don't think it will happen because I don't think potential students in management are interested in gaining a degree at a School of Education but prefer Business Schools." *Companies / CEOs, Germany*

I - "A leader should have educational and social competences to lead humans the best way. Through this reason management education would greatly improve through this." *Student, Germany*	I - "If this was to occur, I would see a lessening of the organizational use for such a program." *Universities / Business Schools, USA*

Table 34. Selected pro and contra comments of the experts for projection 5.

For projection 5, the selective comments presented in Table 34 display the perspectives of all four groups of experts namely universities / business schools, companies / CEOs, students and politics / associations.

The content analysis displayed less support for this specific projection. The supportive comments uncover very few positive aspects of this projection. A Brazilian Professor commented that combining social sciences and management would be a necessity in the future due to the changes in education. A Croatian expert forecasts that such a trend might become a reality in under-developed countries. A German student views this trend as an advantage, as potential leaders would have the opportunity to learn social skills, interpersonal skills, empathy etc. and such individuals would be better managers according to him / her. Another German student agrees with this fact and suggests that management education in Schools for Social Sciences would be the best way to lead. According to a German CEO, Business Schools are specialized in imparting management knowledge whereas Schools for Social Sciences could be instrumental in developing leadership personalities, which focused on other competencies apart from pure technical management knowledge. An American expert foresees this change in trend to be quite beneficial, as it would promote better learning.

The comments analysis also revealed different aspects related to management programs becoming an integral part of Schools of Education and Schools for Social Sciences. Most experts believed that this trend would not be a reality in the year 2030; it is largely undesirable and would have a high negative impact on business leadership education. Most of the experts suggested that there should be an increased collaboration between Business Schools and Schools for Social Sciences. Furthermore, the experts clearly believed that these two types of schools are two different entities; each has its own strengths and weaknesses. Therefore, collaboration would be a more realistic option. A German Professor agreed with this fact and suggested that a strong co-operation would be beneficial. A German politician explained the different roles played by Business Schools and Schools for Social Sciences and disagreed with the fact that management programs should be adopted by Schools for Social Sciences / Schools of Education. An Indian expert shared the opinion of the German politician. The expert opined that Schools for Social Sciences were not equipped to handle management-related requirements. A Brazilian Professor distinguished between leadership in management and leadership in sociology, politics and education. A German CEO anticipated that students may not consider a degree awarded by schools of social sciences to be as valuable as that awarded by business schools. An American expert views this change in trend to be less applicable to organizations.

Conclusion

To summarize, it is less likely that Master in Management programs will no longer be part of Business Schools, but rather a part of Schools of Education or Schools for Social Sciences due to the changed requirements for leaders, managers and talents. It suggests that there are more negative than positive aspects associated with this trend. Both methods collectively showed that such a trend is not desirable at all and would have a high negative impact on business leadership education in tertiary education.

4.3.5.2.6 Conclusions for stakeholder dimension providers

As the findings of Part 2 demonstrate, it is urgently required to redesign business leadership education in tertiary education for graduates to equip tomorrow's business leaders with the competencies they need to cope with the challenges of the VUCA-world in the 21st century, to facilitate a pedagogical infrastructure that nurtures students' development of a (creative) personality. Consequently, providers (universities / business schools) of business leadership education in tertiary education have to scrutinize and rethink their educational goals, educational contents, educational methodologies, and educational settings. Therefore, projections 1-5 were developed and surveyed within this rubric. For all projections, different assessments and controversial discussions of the future were carried out by the diverse expert panel. Based on the analyses, the five projections can be clustered in two groups:

> The first group comprises projections 1-4 (personality & leadership competencies, educational setting & development of competencies, E-learning, individualization). The possibility that these trends emerge in the future is uncertain due to the EP values and the dissent shown by the IQR. Values for D and I are quite high, expressing the importance of the projections on the future of business leadership education in tertiary education.

> Projection 5 (allocation to schools) can be allotted to the second group. This projection seems to be improbable for future occurrence due to the low value for EP, being the lowest EP value of this RT Delphi survey. Values for D and I are also low. The possibility of this projection becoming a reality in the future is low due to the low overall values and the dissent shown by the IQR.

For all five projections, the quantitative results are supported by the qualitative content analysis, which provides reasons for experts' assessments and their thoughts on the potential trend. The detailed qualitative analysis of the experts' comments will play a crucial role for the subsequent scenario development. As the curriculum is conceived as an 'academic plan' experienced by its students, the next set of projections covers the stakeholder dimension participants / learners (students).

4.3.5.3 Stakeholder dimension participants / learners (students)

Participants of business leadership education in tertiary education are learners or students respectively, which can be considered as potential future business leaders. A participant or learner in the context of this work is: "A person who has changed behaviors through interaction with the environment or acquired new behaviors and thus enhances his own knowledge, skills and abilities. Furthermore, it is learning through engagement and motive" (Tenorth & Tippelt, 2012, p. 479). Learners in this context have to be active and intrinsically motivated to meet the challenges of their own development. "Development is not something you can do to or for someone. Development is something people do for themselves." (McCall in Mintzberg, 2005, p. 203) Therefore, the learner's portrait has to be complex.

In rabbinic Judaism with a learning tradition that is prevailing over several millenniums, learning (the Torah) was of first priority. To acquire Torah, a complex portrait of a perfect learner was designed in the Ethics of the Fathers (Pirkei Avot, Chapter VI, 6), comprising 48 qualities (Krochmalnik, 2009). Although of ancient and primarily religious origin, the challenging portrait of a perfect learner designed in Ethics of the Fathers can be adapted to modern secular learning ecology. The challenging portrait of a perfect learner designed in Ethics of the Fathers has been a topic as timeless as it is timely. Learners / students experience a curriculum. They are directly affected by the curriculum and are, thereby, one of the most important stakeholder groups for a future-oriented redefinition of business leadership education in tertiary education. To integrate the learner's dimension in business leadership education in tertiary education by the year 2030, projections 6-9 were developed.

4.3.5.3.1   Projection 6 – Requirements for leadership positions

Preliminary notes

Based on previous research, leaders will be faced with several challenges that are often specified as globalization, digitization and technological change, complexity, half-life period of knowledge, customer orientation, flat hierarchies, participation of employees, demographic change, value change etc. Those (future) challenges imply additional or changed requirements for leadership positions. Aspired leaders have to fulfill multifaceted, demanding and complex tasks (IBM, 2010; IBM, 2012a / b; Regnet, 2014; Weber, 2007).[70] Constant changes in the business environment may subsequently affect the future requirements for business leaders and business leadership education in tertiary education. Hence, the sixth projection was formulated in line with Becker and Gracht (2014) to find out whether the requirements for leaders, managers, and talents would change fundamentally by the year 2030 compared to today's requirements.

Experts' opinions

The estimated probability (EP) that the requirements for leaders, managers, and talents will change fundamentally in 2030 compared to 2015 is 59.1 %, de-

---

70   For details please see Part 2, chapter 3.2.2.2.

sirability (D) *M* = 3.51 and impact (I) *M* = 3.93 are relatively high (Table 35). The interquartile range (IQR), which is the measurement of consensus for this RT Delphi survey, shows a high degree of dissent. It implies that the requirements for leaders, managers and talents in the future may not change fundamentally when compared to 2015, because the experts have different judgments of the future. In contrast to EP, for desirability and impact in case of occurrence, the IQR results show that consensus was achieved between the experts.

No.	Projection for the year 2030
6	In 2030, requirements for leaders, managers, and talents have changed fundamentally compared to 2015.

EP statistics			D statistics		I statistics	
EP (mean)	IQR	Con	D (mean)	IQR	I (mean)	IQR
59.1 %	40	-1.57 %	3.51	1	3.93	1

Legend: EP = Estimated probability of occurrence (0-100 %); IQR= Interquartile range; Con (SD) = Convergence of opinion (variation of standard variation: negative values equals convergence); D = Desirability of occurrence (1 – very low, 5 = very high); I = Impact in case of occurrence (1 = very low, 5 = very high).

Note degree of consensus / dissent: *Italic numbers* indicate that consensus among experts was achieved; i.e. for EP IQR ≤ 25 equals consensus, for D and I respectively IQR ≤ 1 equals consensus.

Table 35. Statistical data for projection 6 (n=105).

A qualitative examination of the comments received from the experts revealed that 7 experts have revised their answers 11 times in total for the EP. 2 of 7 confirmed their first choice in completely different ranges of the 11-unit scale: 4 of 7 rated the EP higher than before and only 1 of 7 finally rated EP lower than before. There were 5 final revisions revealing that the opinions of those experts show tendency towards the mean. Furthermore, this conclusion is also supported by the convergence of opinion, which is -1.57 %.

Projection for the year 2030	6 (Requirements for leadership positions)
Number of comments (total)	77
Number of comments (sub-questions 6.1, 6.2, 6.3)	43, 16, 18
Supportive comments ("pro")	35
Unsupportive comments ("contra")	31

Table 36. Details of comments for projection 6.

The qualitative content analysis for projection 6 revealed that the experts provided 77 written comments in total. 43 comments were for EP, 16 for D and 17 comments for I (Table 36). The analysis also revealed that there were 35 comments supporting the future trend, which shall be referred to as "pro" comments. A total of 31 comments were found to be unsupportive of this specific future trend, which shall be referred to as "contra" comments.

Some relevant comments were chosen to explain the qualitative results of the sixth projection. For projection 6, the selective comments presented in Table 37 display the perspectives of four groups of experts namely universities / business schools, Companies / CEOs, students and politics / associations.

To know more about this future trend and the changing requirements of leaders, managers and talents, it is mandatory to analyze quantitative and qualitative results together. The quantitative results show that it is uncertain whether such a trend will be a reality in the year 2030. The experts suggested that such a change may occur, but only under certain circumstances, and that changes are bound to happen, yet there may not be fundamental changes in the requirements of leadership, managers and talents. Such a change is highly desirable even if it would not be a fundamental change in the future; it might have a high impact on business leadership education while setting the curriculum for the students of Master in Management programs in tertiary education. The qualitative content analysis supported this fact. Despite the fact that supportive statements were only slightly higher (35) than unsupportive comments (31), the contra comments for EP were higher compared to contra comments for D and I, thus, supporting the dissent shown in quantitative results for EP and consensus shown for D and I. It is to be noted that there were no contra comments for impact mentioned by the experts for this specific projection, affirming that experts foresee a high impact.

The comment by a German CEO highlights that different challenges will arise in the future, which will bring increasing complexity and continuous changes in the social, political and economic scenario. Some definite and deep changes will take place in the next decade, as predicted by a Brazilian expert. According to an American CEO, some requirements will definitely change due to a constant revolution in industry, energy, and digitization. Another German expert pointed out that a leader will have to take concrete decisions regarding the organization and make improvements at workplace based on the long-term vision with regard to these decisions. An American expert believes that the management programs need to update their learning tools, as competition will increase on a large scale in the future. Differences of opinions expressed by experts revealed that the requirements might not change fundamentally, but aspects such as collaboration, flexibility, certain skills like social and personal, virtual markets, digitization will carry greater importance than today.

Pro comments	Contra comments
EP - "In a constantly changing world (political, social and economic changes), where the half-life of knowledge is going to change rapidly, the challenges will change fundamentally and will be much more complex than today." *Companies / CEOs, Germany*	EP -"If you look back, how much the idea of leadership and entrepreneurship has changed over the last 15 years, one can only imagine, which challenges and topics (from ever increasing global interdependence to digital issues) will be part of the leadership canon 15 years from now. However, I don't believe that the core of leadership and management, i.e. to facilitate business success, will change." *Student, Germany*
EP - "In 2030, industry and energy and digitization revolutions will bring many requirements to leaders, management and talents, the fundament have changed." *Companies / CEOs, USA*	EP - "I don't believe so. Leader and Managers have needed the same skill since day one: ability to motivate and acquire good talent, ability to spot trends, and ability to make decisions under less than ideal situations. We just tend to emphasize different aspects as technology evolves and business cycle changes." *Companies / CEOs, USA*
EP - "We will certainly face deep changes in the next decades." *Universities / Business Schools, Brazil*	EP -"Human beings don't change fast. Situations might change. But the essence of leadership will remain." *Universities / Business Schools, Brazil*
D - "New requirements mean changes and changes can improve the policy of companies. I hope (in a positive thinking way) that through the changed requirements the company's focus on executives, who use their own mind, improve things in their company's and have a long-term view over decisions, which also consider social and environmental effects." *Student, Germany*	EP - "The expectations from leaders in terms of different management-based parameters will be hugely different in 2030. They will be expected to operate internationally across different cultures. So management by culture will play a huge role." *University / Business School, India*
I - "Programs might have to re-tool and it might even get more competitive than it is now." *Politics / Associations, USA*	D - "It will differ from Business to Business and Profession to Profession (for example Health care)." *Politics / Associations, Austria*

Table 37. Selected pro and contra comments of the experts for projection 6.

Some experts emphasize internationality linked with management programs. According to them, management programs will operate on a larger international level in the future compared to the year 2015. Policy makers should recognize emerging requirements of leadership and managers, such as the adjustment to generation Y, and that leaders / managers need to display more empathy as a part of their leadership styles.

The differences in opinions of the experts are worth taking into account. A German student believes that the core of business leadership and management will remain constant, which makes the business successful. He / she further compares this expected change with past and current situations, which showed that major changes did not take place in the past and that there only slight chances of this happening in the future. An American expert opines that leaders and managers required some basic skills to be successful and take decision regarding the organization, which will remain constant. However, they would need to modify their skills according to the emerging technological changes. An Indian expert expressed that management would operate more cross culturally in 2030. Leaders and managers across the globe would have to work with different cultures, which would change the parameters and expectations placed on leaders in the year 2030; culture-based management programs will play vital role. An Austrian politician believes that the change in requirements for leaders, managers and talents will not be equal for all the professions and businesses. Inferentially, the different opinions of experts show that there is a 50-50 chance for fundamental changes in requirements for leaders, managers, and talents. However, the qualitative analysis support the quantitative results of EP, D and I.

Conclusion

To summarize, qualitative and quantitative results reveal uncertainty and mixed opinions about the estimated probability that the requirements for leaders, managers, and talents will change fundamentally in 2030 compared to 2015 but such a trend is desirable. It would have a high impact on business leadership education in tertiary education.

4.3.5.3.2 Projection 7 – Entre- & intrapreneurship as a basis for innovations

Preliminary notes

The terms *entrepreneurship*, *intrapreneurship* and *innovations* were elaborated in detail in Part 2 of this work.[71] Generally, the term entrepreneurship refers to the creation of new companies and intrapreneurship refers to leaders within a company, which act like an entrepreneur but do not take the entrepreneurial risk and autonomy. Considering Schumpeter's oeuvre, the terms entrepreneurship and intrapreneurship are closely connected with the term *business leadership* due the immense importance of innovations as one of the main tasks required from business leaders. Based on Schumpeter, who described the entrepreneur (intrapreneur) as not merely an innovator but also as leader, the construct of *entrepreneurial leadership* emerged only recently. By combing, integrating, and exploring both entrepreneurship and leadership, the entrepreneurial leader is expected to cope with a rapidly changing business environment "to exploit opportunities to reap advantage for the organisation before and faster than others" (Karmarkar, Chabra & Deshpande, 2014, p. 160). Therefore, the seventh projection was formulated to find out if innovations, intrapreneurship and entrepreneurship would receive high importance in the future compared to other management- and leadership-related themes.

Experts' opinions

The estimated probability (EP) that, in 2030, intrapreneurship and entrepreneurship as well as innovations will be highly important parts of Master in Management programs compared to management related themes is 70.40 %; desirability (D) $M = 4.25$ and impact (I) $M = 4.32$ are quite high (Table 38). The interquartile range (IQR), which is the measurement of consensus for this RT Delphi survey, shows a strong dissent regarding EP. This shows that the panelists have different assessments of the projection even though the overall EP is high. For desirability and impact in case of occurrence, the IQR results show that consensus was achieved between the experts.

A qualitative examination of the recorded experts' comments revealed that only 6 experts have revised their answers a total of 12 times for the EP. 3 of 6

---

[71] For details, please see Part 2, chapters 3.1.1, 3.1.2.3, 3.1.4.2, 3.2.5.3.

confirmed their first choice in completely different ranges of the 11-unit scale, regardless of the mean. 3 of 6 rated the EP higher than before and none rated EP lower than they did in the first choice and decreased the EP regardless of the mean. Finally, only 3 final revisions imply that the experts retained their opinion at the end despite some revisions. Furthermore, this conclusion is also supported by the divergence of opinion, which is only - 0.43 %.

No.	Projection for the year 2030
7	In 2030, intrapreneurship and entrepreneurship as well as innovations are highly important parts of Master in Management programs compared to management related themes.

EP statistics			D statistics		I statistics	
EP (mean)	IQR	Con	D (mean)	IQR	I (mean)	IQR
70.40 %	30	-0.43 %	4.25	1	4.32	1

Legend: EP = Estimated probability of occurrence (0-100 %); IQR= Interquartile range; Con (SD) = Convergence of opinion (variation of standard variation: negative values equals convergence); D = Desirability of occurrence (1 = very low, 5 = very high); I = Impact in case of occurrence (1 = very low, 5 = very high).

Note degree of consensus / dissent: *Italic numbers* indicate that consensus among experts was achieved; i.e. for EP IQR ≤ 25 equals consensus, for D and I respectively IQR ≤ 1 equals consensus.

Table 38. Statistical data for projection 7 (n=105).

The qualitative content analysis revealed that the experts provided a total of 74 written comments. There were 36 comments for EP, and 19 comments each for D and I (Table 39). The analysis revealed 54 comments supporting the projection, which shall be referred to as "pro" comments. Only 5 comments were found to be unsupportive of this specific future trend, which are referred to as "contra" comments. The experts attached great importance to innovations, intrapreneurship and entrepreneurship and their role in management and leadership. On a qualitative level, there was enormous support for this projection.

Projection for the year 2030	7 (Entre- and intrapreneurship as a basis for innovations
Number of comments (total)	74
Number of comments (sub-questions 7.1, 7.2, 7.3)	36, 19, 19
Supportive comments ("pro")	54
Unsupportive comments ("contra")	5

Table 39. Details of comments for projection 7.

Some relevant comments were chosen to provide an overview of the results of the seventh projection. The selective comments presented in Table 40 display the perspectives of all four groups of experts, namely universities / business schools, companies / CEOs, students and politics / associations.

The selected experts' comments from different countries emphasize the different aspects related to innovation, intra- and entrepreneurship, asserting its importance in the future. According to an Indian expert, the current management programs are not focusing sufficiently on these important aspects; therefore, the importance will grow in the future.

Pro comments	Contra comments
EP - "Unfortunately, in the current programs, innovation management and entrepreneurship are not provided the required focus. In future both these elements will be extremely important, and will have to be made an integral part of management education." *Universities / Business Schools, India*	EP - "Intrapreneurship and entrepreneurship will only be important on bigger scales. Big companies are more likely to innovate and on some point there will be no space left for intrapreneurs and entrepreneurs." *Companies / CEOs, Germany*
EP - "This intuitively makes sense to me, especially taking advantage of the generational differences we will see." *Politics / Associations, USA*	EP - "Entrepreneurship on management level is not effective." *Companies / CEOs, Kazakhstan*
D - "Entrepreneurial thinking and action is necessary in some areas (e.g. research and development), but may not be transferred to all areas without speculation. Exploration and exploitation in relation to ambidexterity in an organization demonstrates the stressed environment." *Universities / Business Schools, Liechtenstein*	D - "It is good for starting level positions not for managers." *Companies / CEOs, Kazakhstan*
	D - "Some will remain in their tradition" *Politics / Associations, Austria*
I - "Development of entrepreneurs needs the development of personality." *Companies / CEOs, Germany*	
I - "A good leader has visions and these topics can promote such competences." *Student, Germany*	

Table 40. Selected pro and contra comments of the experts for projection 7.

An American politician opines that such a trend is nearing reality and sees the generational differences as an advantage. An expert from Liechtenstein specifies that the trend is desirable and suggests a cautious application of entrepreneurial thinking and action to the areas of management in an organization. A German CEO highlights the aspect of personality in the process of developing entrepreneurs and its impact on business leadership education. For successful leadership, vision was important, and innovation along with intra- and entrepreneurship would be significant to develop the necessary competencies, according to a German student. Indeed, the different aspects that emerged through content analysis may have an impact on business leadership education in the sense that many fundamental changes regarding how business leadership is taught to potential students are required.

A contra comment from a German CEO pointed out that only large-size enterprises will attach a great deal of importance to innovation and intra- and entrepreneurship. A CEO from Kazakhstan mentioned that entrepreneurship is not effective on a management level. Furthermore, such change in trend was more applicable for employees at a lower hierarchical level in organizations, but is not applicable for managers. An Austrian politician sees that such a trend may not be a reality for most of the organizations, as they would prefer to adhere to their traditions.

It is essential to integrate quantitative and qualitative results for a clearer understanding of the role of innovation intra- and entrepreneurship in business leadership education in tertiary education. Both methods showed consensus for D and I, implying that the increasing importance of innovation, intra- and entrepreneurship will be greater compared to other management themes; this high importance will have an impact on business leadership education. The quantitative results for EP indicate that such a trend is likely to occur in the year 2030, but the strong dissent shows that there are differences of opinions expressed by experts regarding the likelihood of intra-, entrepreneurship and innovations gaining importance compared to other management themes. The dissent can also be interpreted as experts foreseeing the trend, but they have mentioned several aspects related to innovation, intrapreneurship and entrepreneurship, which will serve as deciding factors of whether or not such a trend will be a reality. The qualitative content analysis for EP displayed converse results to quantitative results. It indicated clear support for the projection meaning that intrapreneurship, entrepreneurship and innovation will be highly important compared to other management themes. The support was further confirmed by the fact that there were only 3 "contra" comments for EP compared to 36 "pro" comments. The integration of quantitative and qualitative methods for this specific projection leads to conflicting results regarding the dissent shown for EP. This should not be considered a shortcoming of the present study rather as an insight into the studied issue. Such an insight would not have been realized if the results would have matched. Such a mismatch between qualitative and quantitative results leads to unexplored and novel perspectives of the studied topic (Greene, 2007; Lancy, 1993; Richardson, 2000; Teddlie & Tashakkori, 2009).

Another plausible explanation is the differences in data collection methods. When experts completed the RT Delphi survey, they based their responses on an 11-unit-scale from 0 % to 100 %. However, when they were asked to provide reasons and comments for their answers, they expressed themselves freely and clarified the given ratings; this may allude to other aspects of the projections compared to their quantitative ratings. Due to the fundamental differences in the methods, the findings do not complement, when trying to combine them – a phenomenon that is also explained and supported by (Slonim-Nevo & Nevo, 2009). Such a discrepancy implies mixed opinions expressed by the diverse expert panel. Nevertheless, considering the enormous support that was analyzed on a qualitative level for this projection, it can be assumed that the probability of such a trend to emerge by the year 2030 is very high.

Conclusion

To summarize, in spite of reasonable differences in experts' opinions expressed by the dissent in quantitative results, the future trend of intrapreneurship, entrepreneurship and innovation being highly important compared to other management themes will probably become reality. Additionally, the qualitative results showed massive support for the projection. Both methods collectively showed that such a trend is desirable and would have a high impact on business leadership education in tertiary education.

4.3.5.3.3 Projection 8 – International internships & development of competencies

Preliminary notes

Globalization and internationalization are common phenomena (Faix et al., 2006). Tertiary education in particular have always been influenced by international trends and operated – at least to a certain degree – in an international context. Nevertheless, global interconnectedness has gained in importance in 21st century (Altbach, Reisberg & Rumbley, 2009; Wannemacher & Geidel, 2016). Therefore, business leadership education in tertiary education has to explicitly facilitate international settings to foster the mobility of students (and scholars and teaching-staff) and contemporary cross-border education in a global world at a governmental, institutional and individual level e.g. by joint- or dual-degree programs, facilitating study abroad, field trips, internships etc. Providing international internships as real-world settings during the duration of Master's programs also fosters development of competencies.[72] More exposure and opportunity to gain practical experiences in an international business setting was a matter of concern for most Master's programs in recent years. The eighth projection was formulated to find out whether such programs would focus more on gaining leadership related experiences in an international work environment as compared to theoretical management knowledge in the year 2030.

Experts' opinions

The estimated probability (EP) that, in 2030, gaining leadership-related experiences in an international work environment will be more important compared to theoretical management knowledge is 73 %, desirability (D) $M = 4.16$ and impact (I) $M = 4.27$ are quite high (Table 41). The interquartile range (IQR), which is the measurement of consensus for this RT Delphi survey, confirms a strong dissent regarding EP. This indicates that the experts' opinions about whether this trend will come into existence diverge to a high degree. For desirability and impact in case of occurrence, the IQR results show that consensus was achieved between the survey participants.

---

72   See Part 2, chapters 3.2.5.3-3.2.5.5.

No.	Projection for the year 2030
8	In 2030, gaining leadership related experiences in an international work environment will be more important compared to theoretical management knowledge.

EP statistics			D statistics		I statistics	
EP (mean)	IQR	Con	D (mean)	IQR	I (mean)	IQR
73.00%	30	5.45%	4.16	*1*	4.27	*1*

Legend: EP = Estimated probability of occurrence (0-100%); IQR= Interquartile range; Con (SD) = Convergence of opinion (variation of standard variation: negative values equals convergence); D = Desirability of occurrence (1 = very low, 5 = very high); I = Impact in case of occurrence (1 = very low, 5 = very high).

Note degree of consensus / dissent: *Italic numbers* indicate that consensus among experts was achieved; i.e. for EP IQR ≤ 25 equals consensus, for D and I respectively IQR ≤ 1 equals consensus.

Table 41. Statistical data for projection 8 (n=105).

A qualitative examination of the experts' comments revealed that 6 experts have revised their answers 8 times for the EP. 2 out of 6 confirmed their first choice in completely different ranges of the 11-unit scale regardless of the mean. 1 out of 6 rated the EP higher than before and 3 out of 6 ultimately rated EP lower than they did in the first choice and decreased the EP regardless of the mean. Only 4 final revisions imply that the experts continue to have their own expert opinion at the end in spite of a few revisions. Furthermore, this conclusion is also supported by the divergence of opinion, which is 5.45%.

Projection for the year 2030	8 (International internships & development of competencies
Number of comments (total)	74
Number of comments (sub-questions 8.1, 8.2, 8.3)	40, 18, 16
Supportive comments ("pro")	38
Unsupportive comments ("contra")	24

Table 42. Details of comments for projection 8.

According to the content analysis, a total number of 74 written comments were received from panelists for this particular projection. There were 40 comments for EP, 18 comments for D and 16 comments for I (Table 42). The analysis revealed 38 comments, which support the future trend that Master in Management programs will place greater importance on gaining leadership-related experiences in an international work environment than theoretical management knowledge in the year 2030, which shall be referred to as "pro" comments. A total of 24 comments were found to be unsupportive of this specific future trend, which shall be referred to as "contra" comments.

For projection 8, the selective comments presented in Table 43 display the perspectives of all four groups of experts namely universities / business schools, companies / CEO, students and politics / associations.

The quantitative result shows that this trend is probable, but some concrete steps may be required and experts have different opinions about how these steps should be taken. However, desirability to make this trend reality is very high and its impact would be reasonably high on business leadership education, as such programs would focus more on experiential than theoretical knowledge, which is essential to develop leadership aspects to the students. The qualitative content analysis supports this fact. Although there were more supportive (38) than unsupportive statements (24) noted for this projection, the number of contra comments is worth mentioning. The number of contra comments for D and I were fewer compared to EP, supporting consensus shown in quantitative results for D and I and dissent shown for EP. It further implies that here are different opinions regarding EP, as quantitative results show dissent for EP. The results for desirability and impact lean towards high consensus and show a need for such trend to come into existence in the year 2030.

The emphasis of the selected expert comments was on the relevance of international exposure in the future (Table 43). This can have a positive impact on business leadership education. An Indian expert pointed out that the trend actually exists and is growing speedily which helps to overcome the most crucial part of business management of managing different people with different cultures, different government policies and talents across the world. The most challenging job for future leaders was to manage team members with different nationalities and cultures, according to a CEO from Germany. The experts from China and Germany express high desirability of such a trend. According to a German student, this represented an opportunity for students to develop their own vision, whereas an expert from China thinks of it as an addition and support to theoretical knowledge. A Brazilian expert believes that students should work internationally in different companies instead of working in the branches of the same organization. New opportunities are to be created for students globally and they should receive the opportunity to work internationally after the completion of formal education, as mentioned by an American politician. The above comments thus depict various aspects related to international exposure becoming increasingly important for Master in Management programs in the future.

Pro comments	Contra comments
EP - "This trend has already begun and will catch up rapidly as we progress. I have discussed this issue earlier. Managing people with different cultures, resources, governments, talents across the countries will be a very crucial aspect of successful business." *Universities / Business Schools, India*	EP - "To obtain the theoretical knowledge is the basic and to utilize the knowledge and to polish the leadership would be more important. Therefore, I agree that if the experiences obtain in an international work environment is important, but I do not believe that the theoretical knowledge is less important. They are equal." *Companies / CEO, China*
EP - "In my opinion there will be a dramatic change to an overall international management, one of the management key qualification will be the successful managing of members in teams with different cultures and nationality." *Companies / CEO, Germany*	EP - "In fact it's difficult to compare theory and practice in terms of importance; a successful program will integrate both intelligently: A mixture, such as 40 / 60, theory / practice will be fine. Or even better something like: 30 percent theory, 40 percent theory-based reflections of practice, 30 percent practice transfer. What is more important now? The right mixture is required." *Universities / Business Schools, Germany*
D - "Such experiences expand the own view, because of that they are desirable for the students." *Student, Germany*	D - "We need to balance these two educational pillars: experiences in an international work environment and theoretical management knowledge." *Universities / Business Schools, Brazil*
D - "It is always good to add more practice things into the theoretical education." *Companies / CEO, China*	D - "Not to forget that leadership also comprises thought leadership and here theoretical aspects are somehow an important foundation not to be missed." *Universities / Business Schools, Germany*
I - "We need international schools and students going abroad to study and to participate in internships in local companies, not only international branches from their national enterprises." *Universities / Business Schools, Brazil*	I - "Best Performer still will Need best theoretical models and implications" *Politics / Associations, Austria*
I - "It sounds as if more internship-type opportunities will need to be created in international settings. And the programs may have to do more in placements globally after graduation." *Politics / Associations, USA*	

Table 43. Selected pro and contra comments of the experts for projection 8.

The differences in opinions displayed by the experts show a balanced approach towards this trend. Many experts highlight the importance of theoretical knowledge with clear guidance and practical knowledge to expand theories into real situations. According to a CEO from China, it was necessary to place equal emphasis on theories as well as on practical knowledge, because theories are the basis and students need to utilize them in real situations. A German expert believes that the integration of theoretical knowledge and practical experience was important for any program to be successful and suggests that the curriculum must include 40 % theory and 60 % practical work. A Brazilian expert sees this division of theory-practice as educational pillars. A correct balance was required. According to a German expert, theories are a foundation for leadership education that contains certain leadership-related thought processes.

An expert from Austria comments that the knowledge of theoretical models and implications is necessary for a better performance. Considering the variety of comments mentioned by experts, who actually do not support the projection, it can be inferred that theory is equally important when compared to practical work. Thus, even if the probability that such a trend will be a reality in 2030 is high, universities may face challenges in attaching more importance to international work opportunities compared to theoretical knowledge.

Conclusion

To summarize, quantitative and qualitative results reveal that the probability of gaining leadership-related experiences in an international work environment will be more important compared to theoretical management knowledge to become reality is relative high, yet experts have different opinions on how this trend will come into existence. Nevertheless, both methods confirm that such a trend is highly desirable and would have a high impact on business leadership education.

4.3.5.3.4 Projection 9 – Transfer of knowledge by "real-world projects"

Preliminary notes

Real-world challenges are defined as complex, uncertain and open-ended projects that students have to accomplish autonomously. Such projects are unique and limited in time in order to solve corporate business challenges that may contribute to the organization's value and (sustainable) future. They are indicators for the (potential) business leaders' performance in uncertain and complex situations were self-organized action is indispensable. Real-world projects are – from a pedagogical point of view and based on Humboldt – an instrument, i.e. a means to an end for students to transform the world as much as possible according to their own perception. Thereby, students personal and competency development process is initiated, which is a crucial part of Faix's and Kisgen's educational cycle (see Figure 10). Moreover, real-world projects are an instrument to transfer knowledge to an organization.[73] More exposure for students and the opportunity to work in real-world business settings to gain practical experience is a top priority for most Master's programs. Real-world projects are a mandatory part of the curriculum in only a few Master's programs. Considering the required changes in business leadership education in tertiary education, it would be worth it to make real-world projects an integral part of Master's programs. Hence, the ninth projection was formulated to find out whether Master's programs would focus on real-world projects as a mandatory and integrated part in the year 2030.

Experts' opinions

The estimated probability (EP) that, in 2030, students are realizing "real-world projects" within companies by transferring knowledge as a mandatory and integrated part of their Master in Management programs is 68.10 %, desirability (D) $M = 4.39$ and impact (I) $M = 4.22$, which are quite high (Table 44). The interquartile range (IQR), which is the measurement of consensus for this RT Delphi survey, confirms a high degree of dissent regarding EP. This shows that the panelists have different assessments of the projection, even though the overall EP is relatively high. For desirability and impact in case of occurrence, the IQR results show that a consensus was achieved between the experts.

---

[73] For details, please see Part 2, chapters 3.1.4.5, 3.2.5.4 and 4.1.5.4

No.	Projection for the year 2030
9	In 2030, students are realizing "real-world projects" within companies by transferring knowledge as a mandatory and integrated part of their Master in Management programs.

EP statistics			D statistics		I statistics	
EP (mean)	IQR	Con	D (mean)	IQR	I (mean)	IQR
68.10 %	40	0.62 %	4.39	1	4.22	1

Legend: EP = Estimated probability of occurrence (0-100 %); IQR= Interquartile range; Con (SD) = Convergence of opinion (variation of standard variation: negative values equals convergence); D = Desirability of occurrence (1 = very low, 5 = very high); I = Impact in case of occurrence (1 = very low, 5 = very high).

Note degree of consensus / dissent: *Italic numbers* indicate that consensus among experts was achieved; i.e. for EP IQR ≤ 25 equals consensus, for D and I respectively IQR ≤ 1 equals consensus.

Table 44. Statistical data for projection 9 (n=105).

A qualitative examination of the experts' comments revealed that 11 experts have revised their answers 18 times for the EP. 6 out of 11 confirmed their first choice in completely different ranges of the 11-unit scale, regardless of the mean. 1 out of 5 rated the EP higher than before and 4 out of 5 ultimately rated EP lower than they did in the first choice and decreased the EP regardless of the mean. The final revisions imply that the experts continue to have their own expert opinion at the end. This conclusion is also supported by the divergence of opinion, which is only .62 %.

According to the content analysis, a total number of 65 written comments were received from the experts for this particular projection. There were 33 comments for EP, and 16 each for D and I. The analysis revealed that there were 55 comments, which support the future trend, which shall be referred to as "pro" comments. Only 4 comments were found to be unsupportive of this specific future trend, which shall be referred to as "contra" comments (Table 45). The experts showed great support for this projection.

Projection for the year 2030	9 (Transfer of knowledge by "real-world projects")
Number of comments (total)	65
Number of comments (sub-questions 9.1, 9.2, 9.3)	33, 16, 16
Supportive comments ("pro")	55
Unsupportive comments ("contra")	4

Table 45. Details of comments for projection 9.

Pro comments	Contra comments
EP - "The development of leadership competences needs real-world projects because competences and skills can be developed only in reality." *Companies / CEO, Germany*	EP - "It would be desirable, but conventional universities can and will probably not implement this. The problem could be the discrepancy between theory and practice, which is often difficult to combine. The reason for this is that conventional universities demanding scientific work, whereas companies demanding practice and implementation of the project work." *Student, Germany*
EP - "In case it is not so, the program will not be so attractive." *Politics / Associations, Brazil*	EP - "Good thinking but not easy to implement. it will be exciting if such "real-world project" could be part of the programs." *Companies / CEO, China*
D - "I think it will promote better learning and better outcomes for the students in the real-world." *Politics / Associations, USA*	EP - "Even when some universities implement that, I am not sure if all will do so." *Student, Germany*
D - "It would give students the necessary practical experience and insight into company and business. This is frequently absent today. However, if this is implemented, a support of the universities is necessary. This concerns on the one hand to give the Students the necessary knowledge and on the other hand organizational support (e.g. for the choice of a suitable company that wants not only cheap employees).That's the only way it can succeed." *Student, Germany*	D - "For programs it could be a core benefit but implementation is being questioned." *Universities / Business Schools, Germany*
D - "For the development of international leadership experiences projects are suitable especially because they generate an ideal practice field for Leadership." *Universities / Business Schools, Liechtenstein*	
I - "We'll need professors with active field experience, not only academic knowledge." *Universities / Business Schools, Brazil*	
I - "It sounds as if more internship-type opportunities will need to be created in international settings. And the programs may have to do more in placements globally after graduation." *Politics / Associations, USA*	

Table 46. Selected pro and contra comments of the experts for projection 9.

For projection 9, the selective comments presented in Table 46 display the perspectives of all four groups of experts, namely universities / business schools, companies / CEO, students and politics / associations. Please note that there were no "contra" comments for impact, meaning that the experts do not foresee a negative impact of real-world projects being mandatory or an integral part of Master in Management programs.

The comments analysis revealed different aspects related to real-world projects and their advantages. A German CEO clearly stated that leadership skills and competencies could develop well in such real-world projects. A German student sees real-world projects highly important for gaining practical knowledge and insights into the business world. A Brazilian politician sees these projects as very attractive for students. Another Brazilian expert, a university Professor, suggests a rising need for active and well-experienced Professors to cater to the needs of students working on real-world projects. An expert from Liechtenstein asserts that such projects served as a base for international leadership experiences.

The American experts believe that such projects will provide better learning opportunities to future leaders. Another American expert expresses concern that more opportunities for real-world projects should be created and subsequent placements should be global. Thus, even if there is a lot of support detected in expert comments, various aspects were mentioned by the panel. The comments clearly show that such a trend is certainly probable, highly desirable and can influence business leadership education in tertiary education.

Although there were only 4 "contra" comments, they elucidate important facets of real-world projections. A German student foresees this trend as desirable but expresses concern that conventional universities may not implement this, as they consider theory equally important as practice. It was also difficult to integrate theory and practice, which may be one of the reasons, why universities do not offer such projects on a mandatory basis. The issue of implementation seems to be a challenge, according to another German student, a German CEO and a Chinese CEO.

Furthermore, it is essential to integrate quantitative and qualitative results for enhanced understanding of the phenomena that real-world projects are well integrated in Master in Management programs and that they will be mandatory for students, considering the immense advantage they can offer to develop leadership competencies and skills. Both methods showed consensus for D and I, implying that the increasing importance of practical knowledge gained in the process of real-world projects, the increased understanding of the business world and enhanced skills to solve business-related problems through effective leadership. The integration of real-world projects into the management curriculum and making it mandatory for students will also have a positive impact on business leadership education, as there were no comments mentioned about its negative impact.

The quantitative results for EP indicate that such a trend is likely to occur in the year 2030, but the strong dissent shows that there are differences of opinions expressed by experts regarding the likelihood of real-world projects being an integral part of Master's programs. The dissent can also be interpreted as the experts foreseeing the trend, but expressing several aspects related to the real-world projects, which will serve as deciding factors as to whether or not such a trend will be a reality. The qualitative content analysis for EP displayed contrary results to quantitative results. There was clear support for the projection meaning that experts see the project opportunity as a major advantage for potential leaders. The support was further confirmed by only 4 "contra" comments for EP versus 55 "pro" comments. The integration of quantitative and qualitative methods for this specific projection leads to conflicting results regarding EP, a phenomenon that was also elaborated and discussed in the analysis of projection 7 (chapter 4.3.5.3.2) so that the previously discussed explanations shall be adapted analogously to this projection 9. Consequently, such a discrepancy implies mixed opinions expressed by the diverse expert panel. Nevertheless, considering the enormous support analyzed on a qualitative level for this projection, it may be assumed that the probability of such a trend becoming a reality by the year 2030 is very high.

Conclusion

To summarize, despite reasonable differences in the experts' opinions obvious by the dissent in quantitative results, the future trend of real-world projects becoming a mandatory and integral part of Master in Management programs will probably be realized. Moreover, the qualitative results showed massive support for the projection. Both methods collectively showed that such a trend is desirable and would have a great impact on business leadership education in tertiary education.

4.3.5.3.5 Conclusions for stakeholder dimension participants

Learners / students are one of the most important stakeholder groups for a future-oriented redefinition of business leadership education in tertiary education. Therefore, projections 6-9 were developed and surveyed within this rubric. For all projections, different assessments and controversial discussions of the future were carried out by the diverse expert panel. Based on the analyses, the four projections can be clustered in two groups:

> Projection 6 (requirements for leadership positions) can be allotted to the first group. It is uncertain whether this trend would be further accelerated in the future due to the moderate EP value – the lowest EP value of the four projections within this category – and the dissent shown by the IQR. The value for desirability is also moderate. In contrast, the value for impact in case of occurrence is high. The quantitative results are supported by the qualitative content analysis, which provides reasons for experts' assessments and their thoughts on the projection.

> The second group comprises projections 7-9 (entre- and intrapreneurship as a basis for innovations, international internships & development of competencies, transfer of knowledge by "real-world projects"). It is probable that these trends emerge in the future due to the high EP values. The interquartile range (IQR), which is the measurement of consensus for this RT Delphi survey, confirms a high degree of dissent for all three projections in terms of EP. However, the integration of quantitative and qualitative methods for projections 7 (entre- and intrapreneurship as a basis for innovations, international internships) and 9 (transfer of knowledge by "real-world projects") leads to conflicting results regarding the dissent shown for EP. On a qualitative level, there was enormous support for these two projections. Thus, it may be assumed that the probability of these two trends emerging by the year 2030 is very high. Moreover, the values for D and I are high and the highest of all 16 projections, expressing the importance of projections 7-9 on the future of business leadership education in tertiary education, which is supported by the qualitative content analysis on the comments provided by the experts.

As business leadership education in tertiary education aims to prepare business leaders for their future employers, the next set of projections was formulated.

4.3.5.4 Stakeholder dimension purchasers (employers / companies)

Purchasers of business leadership education consist of employers, i.e. business corporations, companies, enterprises, organizations etc. (employers / companies). The (future) challenges with which leaders are faced for participants or learners are described in chapter 4.3.5.3 and are not of minor relevance for purchasers and to be applied in the purchaser's dimension accordingly. As a consequence of change, purchasers (employers / companies) have to cope with enormous competition and cost pressure. Due to demographic change and shortage of talents, they have to recruit and develop the best talents for their relevant vacancies. Purchasers have to invest their expenses prudently and develop the right talents with profound international experience due to the specific organizations' needs. Investments in (training and) education also have to be worth it. Therefore, projections 10-13 were formulated.

4.3.5.4.1 Projection 10 – Return on education (ROE)

Preliminary notes

Education provides many benefits to students, such as social and cultural benefits, i.e. learning social skills, creating networks and developing of personality as well as specialized knowledge and technological skills. As education usually leads to higher incomes and greater productivity, it is a trend in the business community to verify the efficiency of education by return on education (ROE). The term ROE is based on the performance measure return on investment (ROI), which is a way of considering profits in relation to capital invested and can be referred to analyze and measure corporate success. According to Scholz (2009), a suitable way to identify the ROE could be to determine e.g. the period of time, which is used to amortize investments for education, which is frequently applied in practice (Boroujerdi & Wolf, 2015).

The ongoing trend to measure ROE in professional training analyzed for the year 2030 by Becker & Gracht (2014) is also visible in higher education (Oreopoulus & Petronijevic, 2013; The Economist, 2014). Furthermore, it was assumed that not only companies (i.e. departments of human resources development) ask universities / business schools to verify clearly the (monetary) benefits of management education due to the high cost awareness. In addition, students may ask for those (monetary) benefits as they are also interested in their income growth (Oreopoulus & Petronijevic, 2013; The Economist, 2014). Therefore, the tenth projection was adapted according to Becker & Gracht (2014) to establish whether companies and students will demand a measurable and comprehensible verification of the benefits of business leadership education in Master in Management programs from universities as "return on education" in the year 2030.

Experts' opinions

The estimated probability (EP) that, in 2030, companies and students will demand a measurable and comprehensible verification of the benefits of business leadership education of Master in Management programs from universities as "return on education" is 60.90 %; desirability (D) $M = 3.69$ and impact (I) $M = 3.83$ are relatively high (Table 47). The interquartile range (IQR), which is the measurement of consensus for this RT Delphi survey, confirms dissent regarding EP and I. This indicates that the panelists have different assessments of the future, even though the overall values for EP and I are reasonably high. In contrast, for desirability, the IQR show that consensus was achieved between the experts.

A qualitative examination of the comments discovered that 7 experts have revised their answers a total of 14 times for the EP. 3 out of 7 confirmed their first choice in completely different ranges of the 11-unit scale: 1 out of 7 rated the EP higher than before and 3 out of 7 ultimately rated EP lower than they did in the first choice and decreased the EP. There were only 4 final revisions revealing that the opinions of experts show no tendency towards the mean. Inferentially, the experts continue to have same opinion at the end. Furthermore, this conclusion is also supported by the 0.26 % divergence of opinion.

No.	Projection for the year 2030
10	In 2030, companies and students demand a measurable and comprehensible verification of the benefits of business leadership education of Master in Management programs from universities as "return on education" provided by these universities.

EP statistics			D statistics		I statistics	
EP (mean)	IQR	Con	D (mean)	IQR	I (mean)	IQR
60.90 %	30	0.26 %	3.69	*1*	3.83	2

Legend: EP = Estimated probability of occurrence (0-100 %); IQR= Interquartile range; Con (SD) = Convergence of opinion (variation of standard variation: negative values equals convergence); D = Desirability of occurrence (1 = very low, 5 = very high); I = Impact in case of occurrence (1 = very low, 5 = very high).

Note degree of consensus / dissent: *Italic numbers* indicate that consensus among experts was achieved; i.e. for EP IQR ≤ 25 equals consensus, for D and I respectively IQR ≤ 1 equals consensus.

Table 47. Statistical data for projection 10 (n=105).

Based on the qualitative content analysis, it can be inferred that the experts provided 64 written comments in total. There were 30 comments for EP and 17 comments each for D and I (Table 48). The analysis also revealed 40 comments which support the future trend that companies and students will demand a measurable and comprehensible verification of the benefits of business leadership education of Master in Management programs from universities as "return on education", which shall be referred to as "pro" comments. A total number of 13 comments were found to be unsupportive of this specific future trend, which shall be referred to as "contra" comments.

Projection for the year 2030	10 (Return on Education (ROE))
Number of comments (total)	64
Number of comments (sub-questions 10.1, 10.2, 10.3)	30, 17, 17
Supportive comments ("pro")	40
Unsupportive comments ("contra")	13

Table 48. Details of comments for projection 10.

Some relevant comments were chosen to support the quantitative results of the tenth projection. For projection 10, the selective comments presented in Table 49 display the perspectives of four groups of experts namely universities / business schools, companies / CEOs, students and politics / associations.

Pro comments	Contra comments
EP - "Very reasonable, especially for universities with a good rating." *Companies / CEO, Kazakhstan*	EP - "I do not think that companies measure the information / verification of the university. They will in general develop their own return on investment measures for education / employee development in general." *Student, Germany*
EP - "The benefit of education cannot be totally calculated. It depends too much on individual factors: which university, which Professor, what circumstances, the origin of the student, his social background, individual requirements etc. Furthermore, the benefit of an educated student is different for each company, so the value for each company is different. In that regard, the benefits of education cannot be defined uniformly. Nevertheless, there will be a growing demand for it, because we are in an economic world in which everything is to be measured, therefore, the need will certainly grow." *Student, Germany*	EP - "Some Business Schools will be still branded in their "old culture"." *Politics / Associations, Austria*
EP - "All want KPIs and ROI on educational Investment. Would be definitely helpful if a measurable Framework would be at hand." *Universities / Business Schools, Switzerland*	D - "Because the measurement is hardly possible." *Student, Germany*
D - "Return of Investment will be key." *Politics / Associations, Austria*	I - "The education would greatly adapt to business, which means that only the financial and economic outcome is important. Than the ideal of education and scientific education could be endangered." *Student, Germany*
I - "Students could get more motivated with new forms of evaluation." *University / Business School, Brazil*	I - "Impact not high, but the system will need to build in the necessary inputs." *University / Business School, India*

Table 49. Selected pro and contra comments of the experts for projection 10.

The selected expert comments indicate that Return on Education (ROE) is seen as a success factor for universities; institutions providing high ROE will be in high demand in the future. An expert from Kazakhstan pointed out that it is practical to provide ROE measurement and verification by the leading Universities. According to a German student, there is an increasing need of such trend but the measurement of educational benefits is difficult; individual differences as well as the need of the company were supposed to be considered while defining the benefits of education. The assessable structure for measuring ROE would be more helpful according to an expert from Switzerland. An Austrian politician believes that ROE will be the key of success for students and companies. A Brazilian expert pointed out that a new evaluation pattern would encourage the students to betterment. Two experts demanded that there should be a better way of measurement and verification of ROE. According to them, there should be a standardized method for measuring these expected benefits. Additionally, four experts mentioned that the competition among business schools would push this trend ahead.

While considering the supportive comments, it is also worth taking into account the differences in opinions displayed by the experts. A German student highlights that the companies make their own measurements to evaluate the progress of employees and verify received information from universities. An Austrian politician believes that some traditional business institutions would maintain the same customs. A German student opines that ROE is not easy to measure and thus less desirable in the future. Some essential changes needed to be made in the system according to an Indian expert who predicts a low impact of such trend on business leadership education in tertiary education. A converse comment made by the student from Germany demonstrates that great concentration on economic benefit may hamper core of education and it may transfer into business.

To understand the future implications for this projection, it is important to analyze quantitative and qualitative results together. The quantitative results show that it is uncertain that such a trend will come into existence in the year 2030. The qualitative content analysis supports this fact. Regardless of the fact that there were more supportive (40) than unsupportive comments (13) noted for this projection, the contra comments for EP were maximum compared to contra comments for D and I, supporting the dissent shown in quantitative results for EP and consensus shown for D and I. This indicates that the diverse expert panel had differences of opinions regarding the probability of such a trend becoming a reality in the year 2030; however, such a trend would be desirable and would have a great impact on business leadership education in tertiary education for graduates.

Conclusion

To summarize, quantitative and qualitative results reveal that there is a high estimated probability with clear differences of opinion in the group of experts. Thus, the trend that companies and students will demand a measurable and comprehensible verification of the benefits of business leadership education of Master in Management programs from universities as "return on education" is uncertain, although this trend is desirable and would have a great impact on business leadership education in tertiary education.

4.3.5.4.2 Projection 11 – Transformation of working environment & working conditions

Preliminary notes

Due to the main drivers, namely globalization, technological advancements and digitization along with the demographic change a transformation process of the working environment takes place. Buzzwords such as service economy, knowledge society, lifelong learning etc. were discussed in this context. Consequently, the structural changes (will) affect (future) working conditions (Priddat, 2013; Weber, 2007). It was assumed that project-based work and collaborations with freelancers will increase. Constant changes in the working environment and working conditions subsequently affect business leadership education in tertiary education. Hence, the eleventh projection was formulated to find out whether the working environment and the working conditions with respect to project-based work and collaboration with freelancers would be transformed by the year 2030 compared to today's conditions.

Experts' opinions

The estimated probability (EP) is 70.19 % that the labor market has transformed in 2030 and that project-based work and collaboration with freelancers has increased. Desirability (D) $M = 3.52$ and impact (I) $M = 3.94$ are fairly high (Table 50). The interquartile range (IQR), which is the measurement of consensus for this RT Delphi survey, confirms dissent regarding EP and I in case of occurrence. This indicates that the panelists have different assessments of the future, even though the overall values for EP and I are high. In contrast, for desirability, the IQR show that consensus was achieved between the experts.

No.	Projection for the year 2030
11	In 2030, the labor market has transformed. Therefore, project-based work and collaboration with freelancers has increased.

EP statistics			D statistics		I statistics	
EP (mean)	IQR	Con	D (mean)	IQR	I (mean)	IQR
70.19 %	30	0.09 %	3.52	*1*	3.94	1.75

Legend: EP = Estimated probability of occurrence (0–100 %); IQR= Interquartile range; Con (SD) = Convergence of opinion (variation of standard variation: negative values equals convergence); D = Desirability of occurrence (1 = very low, 5 = very high); I = Impact in case of occurrence (1 = very low, 5 = very high).

Note degree of consensus / dissent: *Italic numbers* indicate that consensus among experts was achieved; i.e. for EP IQR ≤ 25 equals consensus, for D and I respectively IQR ≤ 1 equals consensus.

Table 50. Statistical data for projection 11 (n=105).

A qualitative examination of the experts' comments revealed that 4 experts have revised their answers a total of 7 times for the EP. 3 out of 4 confirmed their first choice. 1 out of 4 rated EP lower than in the first choice and decreased the EP, regardless of the mean. The final assessments imply that the experts continue to have their expert opinion at the end in spite of very few revisions. Furthermore, this conclusion is also supported by the 0.09 % divergence of opinion.

Projection for the year 2030	11 (Transformation of working environment & working conditions)
Number of comments (total)	62
Number of comments (sub-questions 11.1, 11.2, 11.3)	28, 18, 16
Supportive comments ("pro")	39
Unsupportive comments ("contra")	17

Table 51. Details of comments for projection 11.

According to the content analysis, a total number of 62 written comments were received from the experts for this particular projection. There were 28 comments for EP, 18 comments for D and 16 comments for I. The analysis revealed that there were 39 comments, which support the future trend, which shall be referred to as "pro" comments. 17 comments were found to be unsupportive of this specific future trend, which shall be referred to as "contra" comments (Table 51).

The experts greatly supported this projection. For projection 11, the selective comments presented in Table 52 display the perspectives of all four groups of experts, namely universities / business schools, companies / CEOs, students and politics / associations.

Pro comments	Contra comments
EP - "The dynamics of the labor market will deep the current trends of project-based work." *Universities / Business Schools, Brazil*	EP - "Sad but true! And I am very pessimistic about that because I think this will mean the end of trade unions and the industrial democracy." *Universities / Business Schools, Germany*
EP - "Absolutely true for several branches which are also currently changing fast." *Student, Germany*	EP - "Depending on the industry and Level of experience needed. I do not see that this will significantly happen across all industries. The shift from production to Services will be much more significant." *Companies / CEOs, Germany*
EP - "The world will be filled with more entrepreneurs who will be making their own way." *Universities / Business Schools, USA*	EP - "This will happen to some extent but which labor market do you refer to? The developing countries will need to reach to the industrialized labor market first, in order to change towards collaboration. Locally I agree, but worldwide the percentage will be rather small." *Companies / CEOs, Germany*
D - "Present and future markets need this flexibility and agility to answer clients and markets. No other way to go!!!" *Universities / Business Schools, Brazil*	D - "Important knowledge which should be kept within the Company could be lost. Topics like patents need to be clarified." *Companies / CEOs, Germany*
D - "Such a trend will increase creativity." *Politics / Associations, Austria*	D - "One the one hand there are more flexible work conditions for employees, which is desirable, on the other hand it also can be dangerous, if companies avoid employees for which they have to pay insurance, etc. All in all I am not sure if that is desirable." *Student, Germany*
I - "Networking and knowing the experts will be a big part of having success." *Universities / Business Schools, USA*	I - "Freelancers do not make a big difference in management." *Companies / CEOs, Kazakhstan*
I - "Education must follow the same flexibility and modularity. Courses need to be actualized and tailored as well." *Universities / Business Schools, USA*	

Table 52. Selected pro and contra comments of the experts for projection 11.

The comments analysis revealed different aspects related to project-based work and collaborations with freelancers. 5 experts believed that encouraging project-based work and freelance collaboration could in turn affect the labor marker severely. Entrepreneurship will be instrumental in generating this trend, according to 5 experts. In general, experts opine that such a trend is desirable, but comes with risks such as social risk, namely a change in the employment trend, new technology, loss of tangible knowledge gained from workforce, less security, predictability and stability one gets from a job. Such a trend might have a great impact on business leadership education as it allows flexibility to cater to client and market needs, also flexibility of the labor market and in terms of geography, work / life balance, and could be an outgrowth of generational differences. A Brazilian Professor believes that the dynamics of the labor market will encourage more project-based work in companies. Another Brazilian Professor supports the projection by expressing the advantage of project-based work that it provides flexibility and agility to cater to market demands. A German student feels that this trend will be applicable to several branches in the market. An Austrian politician foresees that such a change in trend will increase creativity in organizational settings. The American Professors opine that networking, knowing the experts in the specific fields and entrepreneurship will lead to success in the future of management. They also believe that leadership education should be flexible and tailor-made to suit the changing trend of more freelance collaborations.

The experts mentioned several aspects that elucidate the negative impacts of project-based work and freelance collaborations. A German Professor opines that such a trend will bring trade unions and industrial democracy to an end. A German CEO believes that the important company related knowledge would be lost if there were more freelancers involved in the future trend and there will be patent-related issues which must be dealt with. Two German CEOs belonging to different branches mention that this trend may be a reality but may not be realized across all industries. A CEO from Kazakhstan commented that freelancers do not play an important role in management. Conclusively, the qualitative analysis revealed that, project-based work and more involvement of freelance collaborations in companies is probable due to the various advantages, it would be desirable and will also impact business leadership education in tertiary education.

To understand the future implications of project-based work and freelance collaborations for Master in Management programs, it is important to analyze quantitative and qualitative results together. The quantitative results show that it is probable that such a trend may occur in the year 2030, but there are different opinions about how it may come into reality. The results show that the desirability of such a trend coming into reality is high and that such a trend would have a high impact on how the curriculum for business leadership is designed, for example, and how business leadership as a topic will undergo changes in tertiary education. The qualitative content analysis displayed support to this fact. In spite of the fact that there were more supportive (39) than unsupportive comments (17) noted for this projection, the contra comments for EP were maximum compared to contra comments for D and I, supporting the dissent shown in quantitative results for EP and consensus shown for D and I. It means that the diverse expert panel had differences of opinions regarding the probability of such a trend to be a reality in the year 2030 but such a trend would be highly desirable and would have a great impact on business leadership education.

Conclusion

To summarize, in spite of reasonable differences in experts' opinions seen through the dissent in quantitative results, the future trend that project-based work and collaboration with freelancers will increase as a result of changed labor market will come into reality. Moreover, the qualitative results showed a huge support for the projection, which implies that there are many factors that must be considered in order to make this trend a reality. Both methods collectively showed that such a trend is desirable and would have a great impact on business leadership education in tertiary education.

4.3.5.4.3 Projection 12 – International and intercultural experiences

Preliminary notes

Based on previous research, it is stated that globalization and internationalization are common phenomena (Faix et al., 2006). Tertiary education in particular has always been influenced by international trends and – at least to a certain degree – operated in an international context. Nevertheless, global interconnectedness has gained importance in 21st century (Altbach, Reisberg & Rumbley, 2009; Wannemacher & Geidel, 2016).[74] Due to the increased and ever increasing mobility of students (and scholars and teaching-staff) in a global world, it was assumed that Master in Management programs, which are (completely) organized globally, would (even) foster students' transnational exposure, introduce students in the growing global competition and to increase students' variety of career opportunities. Organizing Master's programs (completely) on a global level would have an effect on business leadership education. Therefore, the twelfth projection was formulated to find out whether companies and students would demand Master in Management programs, which are (completely) organized globally by the year 2030.

Experts' opinions

The estimated probability (EP) that, in 2030, companies and students demand Master in Management programs which are organized globally is 70.20 %. Desirability (D) M = 4.06 and impact (I) M = 4.01 are quite high (Table 53). The interquartile range (IQR), which is the measurement of consensus for this RT Delphi survey, confirms a dissent regarding EP. This shows that the panelists have different assessments of the projection, even though the overall value for EP is high. For desirability and impact in case of occurrence, the IQR ranges show that consensus was achieved between the experts.

No.	Projection for the year 2030					
12	In 2030, companies and students demand Master in Management programs, which are organized globally.					

EP statistics			D statistics		I statistics	
EP (mean)	IQR	Con	D (mean)	IQR	I (mean)	IQR
70.20 %	30	-1.33 %	4.06	*1*	4.1	*1*

Legend: EP = Estimated probability of occurrence (0-100 %); IQR= Interquartile range; Con (SD) = Convergence of opinion (variation of standard variation: negative values equals convergence); D = Desirability of occurrence (1 = very low, 5 = very high); I = Impact in case of occurrence (1 = very low, 5 = very high).

Note degree of consensus / dissent: *Italic numbers* indicate that consensus among experts was achieved; i.e. for EP IQR ≤ 25 equals consensus, for D and I respectively IQR ≤ 1 equals consensus.

Table 53. Statistical data for projection 12 (n=105).

---

[74] See also projection 8 in chapter 4.3.5.3.3; furthermore, please see Part 2, chapters 3.2.5.3-3.2.5.5.

A qualitative examination of experts' comments discovered that 10 experts have revised their answers a total of 16 times for the EP. 7 out of 10 confirmed their first choice in completely different ranges of the 11-unit scale. 2 out of 10 rated the EP higher than before and 1 out of 10 ultimately rated EP lower than they did in the first choice. There were 3 final revisions, revealing that the opinions of experts show a tendency towards the mean. Furthermore, this conclusion is also supported by the convergence of opinion, which is only -1.33 %.

Projection for the year 2030	12 (International and intercultural experiences)
Number of comments (total)	67
Number of comments (12.1, 12.2,12.3)	33, 15, 19
Supportive comments ("pro")	44
Unsupportive comments ("contra")	19

Table 54. Details of comments for projection 12.

The experts have provided a total number of 67 comments. There were 33 comments for EP, 15 comments for D and 19 comments for I. The analysis revealed mixed opinions of the diverse panel regarding projection 12. The analysis revealed that there were 44 comments, which support the twelfth projection and shall be referred to as "pro" comments. There were also differences found in the opinions of experts. A total number of 19 comments were found to be unsupportive, which shall be referred to as called as "contra" comments (Table 54).

Some relevant comments were chosen to support the quantitative results. For projection 12, the selective comments are presented in Table 55 and display the perspectives of all four stakeholder groups of experts, namely universities / business schools, companies / CEOs, students, and politics / associations.

Some possibilities for this trend to become a reality as well as some potential threats came to the surface with the supportive and the unsupportive comments of the panelists. Most experts supported the demand for an international program. A German student believes that rising economical interdependencies required capable leaders to face the challenges in the changing global market. Many experts mentioned that leaders with global experience and intercultural skills would be in high demand as an effect of globalization. An Indian expert expresses certainty about this trend becoming a reality, but some requisite steps would have to be taken by management institutions at the right time. An American expert commented that global organization of management programs for students would unite various cultures and resources. A CEO from Kazakhstan points out that this trend would make the curriculum more appealing and exciting for students. According to a Brazilian expert, this trend is desirable to a great extent and students should learn to deal effectively with local and global pressures. Additionally, many experts mentioned the advantage that such international programs would increase employability as future leaders would gain international experience.

Differences of opinions are crucial for obtaining a better insight into this projection. An expert from Brazil believes that the fundamentals of leadership education will remain constant, therefore, global aspect should be given partial importance. A German CEO mentioned that working on an international level is an individual decision; not everyone would accept it and rather prefer to resign from the position. A contrary comment from a German student pointed out that different countries are having different patterns of studies and although globalization is taking place in education, the drastic change is impossible until the year 2030. According to an expert from Switzerland, some part of the entire curriculum should be organized internationally; even if Generation Y, which is supposed to be global, hesitantly goes abroad for a longer time. A German student argues that each country represents its uniqueness, which required local people or translators, and it was difficult for leaders to develop according to a particular country, which demands specific preparations. An American expert considers that the coordination and logistics would not be easy, which may increase the cost of programs and the benefits for students would be restricted.

The qualitative results are equally essential for better understanding of the specific trend. Therefore, it is necessary to analyze quantitative and qualitative results together. Although this trend is desirable by the students and companies and showing possible high impact on business leadership education in tertiary education, the quantitative results revealed that such a trend would face some challenges to become a reality in the year 2030. The quantitative results also disclose a trend of students and companies demanding global organization of Master in Management programs in the year 2030 are highly probable, but this probability comes with specific challenges in making programs work globally.

Pro comments	Contra comments
EP - "The interdependencies of the global economy increase continuously. Only globally educated leaders are able to get a grasp on these challenges." Student, Germany	EP - "I think the global vision is important, of course, but not entirely focused on that; remembering: the fundamentals do not change and will continue to be necessary to study them." Politics / Associations, Brazil
EP - "Yes, as I have said earlier, this is a very strong possibility, almost certain. And this should be looked at as an opportunity for a vital step forward. And Management Institutes need to plan for this right away. Else it will be too late." Universities / Business Schools, India	EP - "Some will-but not all. The willingness to act internationally is also a very personal decision. A lot of people rather stay "at home"." Companies / CEO, Germany
EP - "Students organized globally, will bind multi-culture and social sources integrated." Companies / CEO, USA	EP - "There will certainly be a slight tendency towards more globalization in education. However, today the studies in different countries are still hardly comparable (in spite of the Bologna process), so that a change in this direction will not be completely possible until the year 2030." Student, Germany
D - "That makes study more attractive and interesting." Companies / CEO, Kazakhstan	EP - "Would be nice if all students would like to have education globally. But even the Generation Y (digital natives) which is supposed to be a truly global Generation often has representatives in its cohort that don't match the "global" description. They prefer to stay in the home country and may be study only 1 Semester abroad in the best case. There will always be a part that will want to study locally." Universities / Business Schools, Switzerland
D - "The desirability is very high because business education's students have to face the tensions between the local and the global." Universities / Business Schools, Brazil	D - "I think for international business you always need local people and translators. It is not important that every leader is international educated in a strong way. Therefore the world is too complex to prepare for every country, if so. Works in another country always needs a special preparation." Student, Germany
I - "Gaining international experience will improve the employability of the students." Companies / CEO, Germany	I - "Coordination will be more difficult; logistics become more complex; programs may get more expensive which might limit the opportunities for some students to enter the programs." Politics / Associations, USA

Table 55. Selected pro and contra comments of the experts for projection 12.

The qualitative content analysis displayed support to this fact. 44 supportive and 19 unsupportive statements were received for this specific projection.

The contra comments for D and I were lesser compared to the comments noted for EP, which supports the dissent shown in quantitative results for EP and consensus shown for D and I.

Conclusion

To summarize, regardless of having some reasonable differences in experts' opinions, the future trend that companies and students will demand global organization of Master in Management programs in 2030 is probable, but various aspects are mentioned by experts, which should be taken into account. Moreover, this trend is highly desirable and would have a great impact on business leadership education in tertiary education.

4.3.5.4.4   Projection 13 – Corporate universities

Preliminary notes

Cooperation between enterprises and universities is a long discussed topic and of prime interest for business leadership education in tertiary education. The general aim of corporate universities is to match personnel and corporate development ideally, to enhance organization's learning aptitude and to integrate learning processes into corporate strategy (Gebauer, 2007; Hovestadt & Beckmann, 2010; Wimmer, Emmerich & Nicolai, 2002). Considering the competitiveness of enterprises in times of globalization, digitization and shortage of talents, it may be an option for enterprises to increase the already existing trend of corporate universities and own state-recognized corporate universities in order to succeed, to cater to management-related needs. Hence, the thirteenth projection was formulated.

Experts' opinions

The estimated probability (EP) is 46.80 % that, in 2030, enterprises have their own state-recognized degree-awarding corporate universities as an important success factor for competitiveness. Desirability (D) $M = 2.82$ and impact (I) $M = 3.43$ are quite low (Table 56). The interquartile range (IQR), which is the measurement of consensus for this RT Delphi survey, confirms a strong dissent regarding EP. This shows that the panelists have different assessments of the projection while the overall EP is quite low. The IQR value for D shows that there is a dissent. In contrast, the IQR value for I indicates that consensus was achieved.

No.	Projection for the year 2030
13	In 2030, enterprises have their own state-recognized degree-awarding corporate universities as an important success factor for competitiveness.

EP statistics			D statistics		I statistics	
EP (mean)	IQR	Con	D (mean)	IQR	I (mean)	IQR
46.80 %	40	-0.58 %	2.82	2	3.43	*1*

Legend: EP = Estimated probability of occurrence (0-100 %); IQR= Interquartile range; Con (SD) = Convergence of opinion (variation of standard variation: negative values equals convergence); D = Desirability of occurrence (1 = very low, 5 = very high); I = Impact in case of occurrence (1 = very low, 5 = very high).

Note degree of consensus / dissent: *Italic numbers* indicate that consensus among experts was achieved; i.e. for EP IQR ≤ 25 equals consensus, for D and I respectively IQR ≤ 1 equals consensus.

Table 56. Statistical data for projection 13 (n=105).

A qualitative examination of the experts' comments revealed that 8 experts have revised their answers a total of 9 times for the EP. 3 out of 8 confirmed their first choice. 4 out of 8 rated EP lower than they did in the first choice and decreased the EP regardless of the mean. 1 out of 8 rated EP higher than before. The final assessments imply that the experts continue to have their expert opinion at the end in spite of several revisions. Furthermore, this conclusion is also supported by the 0.58 % convergence of opinion.

Projection for the year 2030	13 (Corporate universities)
Number of comments (total)	72
Number of comments (sub-questions 13.1, 13.2, 13.3)	36, 20, 16
Supportive comments ("pro")	11
Unsupportive comments ("contra")	57

Table 57. Details of comments for projection 13.

As per the content analysis, 72 written comments were noted from the experts for this projection. There were 36 comments for EP, 20 comments for D and 16 comments for I. The analysis revealed that there were only 11 comments, which support the future trend and shall be referred to as "pro" comments. 57

comments were found to be unsupportive of this specific future trend, which shall be referred to as "contra" comments (Table 57).

This projection did not receive much support from the experts, meaning that enterprises owning state-recognized degree-awarding corporate universities may not be a reality in the future. For projection 13, the selective comments presented in Table 58 display the perspectives of all four stakeholder groups of experts, namely universities / business schools, companies / CEOs, students, and politics / associations.

The content analysis displayed less support for this specific projection. The supportive comments uncover very few positive aspects of this projection. A CEO from Kazakhstan comments that such a trend would become a reality only if the current education system is not flexible. A German CEO agrees with the probability of this trend and addresses the issue of quality control of education provided by such universities. The thesis written by students could be considered as a quality criterion. A German Professor is positive about companies having their own corporate universities and uses the USA as an example, where such a trend is already evident. A German student considers this trend to be desirable and believes that it would drive competitiveness among companies in the education market. Another German student considers this trend an opportunity for better education and lists a few advantages. An Austrian politician affirms that corporate universities have a bright future.

The comments analysis revealed different aspects related to enterprises owning degree-awarding corporate universities. Most experts believe that this trend will not be a reality in the year 2030; it is largely undesirable and may have a low impact on business leadership education. Four experts suggest that instead of enterprises owning degree-awarding corporate universities, there should be a cooperation between companies and universities, which would be a better option. Some experts believe that companies or enterprises would focus on internal training rather than awarding degrees. Another expert mentions that state recognition involves too many regulations, rendering such a trend challenging for enterprises. Six experts believe that programs conducted by corporate universities would be very expensive. Four experts believe that such a trend could be a reality only for big companies.

Pro comments	Contra comments
EP - "It could be possible if education system will be not flexible enough." *Companies / CEOs, Kazakhstan*	EP - "A corporate university will stay a corporate University with a strict focus on only one particular company. Enterprises will not enter educational market in this way: it costs too much and there is no retention guarantee for the great graduates." *Universities / Business Schools, Switzerland*
EP - "Very likely! This is just a form of 'quality control'. Today many companies use the 'Thesis' of students for recruiting. They offer a thesis and can check the quality without any risk." *Companies / CEOs, Germany*	EP - "Not sure if this will happen in next 15 years. First, companies have their own in-house programs. Second, the management institutes are anyways conducting Management Development Programs to suit companies' specific needs. However, the companies and the management institutes will need to work more closely and formulate programs to meet co's specific needs." *Universities / Business Schools, India*
EP - "See the trend in USA, where private persons or NBA teams open up own schools." *Universities / Business Schools, Germany*	EP - "In 2030 the most enterprises will have their own corporate universities - but not state recognized and degree-awarding only in cooperation with Business Schools." *Companies / CEOs, Germany*
D - "Very good for competitiveness and dynamic in the market. However they will lack research independence! *Student, Germany*	D - "More time (and unproductive time at that) will be spent on the regulatory side of state sponsorship. If started, this will die a quick death on the corporate side." *Universities / Business Schools, USA*
I - "More practical relevance, timeliness, better takeover opportunities for students etc. This means better education." *Student, Germany*	D - "The quality of the education is debatable if education is adapted to companies' needs." *Student, Germany*
I - "Corporate universities will dominate the market." *Politics / Associations, Austria*	I - "Companies will never cover all fields of specialization. They will offer some very specific (and good!) courses in some particular field of application but our students will need more comprehensive information." *Universities / Business Schools, Brazil*
	I - "It could negatively impact enrollment of students in the more traditional settings and maybe even stimulate closures." *Politics / Associations, Austria*

Table 58. Selected pro and contra comments of the experts for projection 13.

A Swiss Professor opines that a corporate university would focus only on one company and for enterprises to enter the educational market would be too expensive; in addition, he / she feared that there is no assurance that graduates could be retained. An Indian expert mentions the role of companies and management institutes, wherein companies conduct internal training and institutes conduct tailor-made training for companies, for cooperation to work well. A German CEO agrees to this fact and foresees the existence of corporate universities, but not as degree awarding state recognized universities. An American expert mentions the tedious regulatory part of sponsorship required by the state, which could be a challenge. According to five experts, the quality of education may decline and two experts state that research independence would be compromised. A sample comment from a German student expresses concern about the quality of education if the curriculum was designed to match the companies' requirements. A Professor from Brazil believes that companies could be capable of providing specific courses; however, they could not encompass all areas of specialization. Two experts comment that such a trend might limit student enrollment. An example from an Austrian politician implies a negative impact of such corporate universities on students' participation.

To understand future implications of this projection, it is important to integrate quantitative and qualitative results. The quantitative results showed that it is less probable that such a trend may occur in the year 2030. The results also showed that such a trend is not desirable; nevertheless, such a trend would have a moderate impact on how the curriculum for business leadership is designed, for example, and how business leadership as a topic will undergo changes based on this projection in tertiary education. The qualitative content analysis displayed support for this fact, as there were more unsupportive (57) compared to supportive (11) comments. It means that the diverse expert panel agreed regarding the low probability, and low desirability of this projection. The "pro" comments for I show a moderate impact on business leadership education, as a few positive aspects of corporate universities were mentioned. Conclusively, quantitative and qualitative methods complement each other for this specific projection.

Conclusion

To summarize, the likelihood of enterprises owning corporate universities, which are state recognized and award degrees is rather low, and experts suggest more negative aspects associated with this trend than positive aspects. Both methods collectively showed that such a trend is largely undesirable and would have a moderate impact on business leadership education in tertiary education.

4.3.5.4.5 Conclusions for stakeholder dimension purchasers

Business leadership education in tertiary education aims to nurture (potential) business leaders for the stakeholder group purchasers, which consist of employers, i.e. business corporations, companies, enterprises, organizations etc. (employers / companies). To integrate the purchaser's dimension in business leadership education in tertiary education by the year 2030, projections 10-13 were developed and surveyed within this rubric. Different assessments and controversial discussions of the future were carried out by the diverse expert panel for all projections. Based on the analyses, the four projections can be clustered in three groups:

> Projection 10 (return on education) can be allotted to the first group. It is uncertain whether this trend would emerge by the year 2030 due to the EP value and the dissent shown by the IQR. The value for desirability is also moderate. The value for impact is high, but the IQR value for I in case of occurrence confirms dissent. The qualitative content analysis, which provides reasons for experts' assessments and their thoughts on the projection, supports the quantitative results.

> The second group comprises projections 11 and 12 (transformation of working environment & working conditions, international & intercultural experiences). It is probable that these trends emerge in the future due to the high EP values. The interquartile range (IQR), which is the measurement of consensus for this RT Delphi survey, confirms a high degree of dissent for both projections regarding EP. However, the qualitative content analysis displayed support to this fact confirming that there are different opinions between the panelists. While the values for D and I in projection 11 are moderate to high, they are concordantly high for projection 12.

> Projection 13 (corporate universities) can be allotted to the third group. This projection seems to be improbable for future occurrence due to the low value for EP, which is the second lowest EP value of this RT Delphi survey. The results also showed that such a trend is not de-

sirable; nevertheless, such a trend would have a moderate impact on how the curriculum for business leadership is designed. The qualitative content analysis supported this fact.

The curriculum is conceived as an 'academic plan', which is embedded in a complex sociocultural context with its various influence factors. Along with the stakeholder groups, providers, participants and purchasers, the stakeholder group politics has a great impact on tertiary education and curriculum design. Therefore, the next set of projections was formulated.

4.3.5.5 Stakeholder dimension politics

"In all OECD countries (and in all countries where institutions are based), state / national governments play a significant role in the strategic direction and funding of higher education in general [...]. Even in countries where institutions have significant autonomy and governments are not expected to play a direct part in institutional management, governments play an important role in influencing the behavior of institutions by means of strategic funding / policy." (OECD, 2005, p. 18)

Consequently, politics and other associations are the fourth and last relevant stakeholder dimension in this RT Delphi, responsible for setting the framework for tertiary education particularly with regard to political, legal and also financial conditions. Therefore, projections 14-16 were developed and surveyed within this rubric.

4.3.5.5.1 Projection 14 – International student mobility & recognition of degrees

Preliminary notes

Increasing worldwide competition demands international experience for potential leaders. Management students need international (thus intercultural) experiences as early as possible to be well prepared for future performance in a global world. International (thus intercultural) experiences include knowledge of other countries, adaptability and flexibility, foreign language proficiency, communication skills and high self-esteem etc. International exposure is one of the options to develop leadership qualifications / skills systematically[75]. The current circumstances concerning student mobility very often create obstacles for students to gain international exposure and recognition of degrees following their study abroad. In times of globalization, it should be a matter of course to set globally comparable (quality) standards to make student mobility as easy as possible, e.g. based on the experiences and further development of Bologna Process / Bologna region. First efforts to develop "a global normative instrument on the recognition of qualifications in higher education" (UNESCO, 2015) were made by UNESCO in 1992. Afterwards, UNESCO and OECD jointly elaborated the "Guidelines for Quality Provision in Cross-border Higher Education", which were adopted in 2005 by the UNESCO General Conference. These guidelines aim to protect both students and other stakeholders from discredited providers and inferior quality and are still relevant to elaborate a global convention on the recognition of higher education qualifications. The project status was reported and presented in 2015, debates are still ongoing and are part of future work of international experts, committees and consultations both on theme-specific and regional level (UNESCO, 2015).[76] Therefore, the fourteenth projection was formulated to explore various aspects related to the promotion of student mobility through an international agreement for the recognition of degrees.

Experts' opinions

The estimated probability (EP) that, in 2030, an international agreement for recognition of degrees in tertiary education will be enacted to promote student mobility among different fields of study, institutions and nations in a global world is 60.40 %. Desirability (D) $M = 3.99$ and impact (I) $M = 4.02$ are quite high (Table 59). The interquartile range (IQR), which is the measurement of consensus for this RT Delphi survey, confirms dissent regarding EP. This shows that the panelists have different assessments about the development of such a trend. For desirability and impact in case of occurrence, the IQR results show that consensus was achieved between the experts.

A qualitative examination of the experts' comments revealed that 7 experts have revised their answers a total of 9 times for the EP. 3 out of 7 confirmed their first choice in completely different ranges of the 11-unit scale. 2 out of 7 rated the EP higher than before and 2 out of 7 ultimately rated EP lower than

---

[75] Please see also projection 8 (chapter 4.3.5.3.3) and 12 (chapter 4.3.5.4.3).
[76] For details please see Part 2, chapter 3.2.2.1.

they did in the first choice and decreased the EP. Only 4 final revisions showed tendency towards the mean. This conclusion is also supported by the convergence of opinion, which is only -0.15 %.

No.	Projection for the year 2030
14	In 2030, an international agreement for recognition of degrees in tertiary education is enacted to promote student mobility among different fields of study, institutions and nations in a global world.

EP statistics			D statistics		I statistics	
EP (mean)	IQR	Con	D (mean)	IQR	I (mean)	IQR
60.40 %	30	-0.15 %	3.99	*1*	4.02	*1*

Legend: EP = Estimated probability of occurrence (0-100 %); IQR= Interquartile range; Con (SD) = Convergence of opinion (variation of standard variation: negative values equals convergence); D = Desirability of occurrence (1 = very low, 5 = very high); I = Impact in case of occurrence (1 = very low, 5 = very high).
Note degree of consensus / dissent: *Italic numbers* indicate that consensus among experts was achieved; i.e. for EP IQR ≤ 25 equals consensus, for D and I respectively IQR ≤ 1 equals consensus.

Table 59. Statistical data for projection 14 (n=105).

According to the content analysis, a total of 68 written comments were received from the experts for this particular projection. There were 37 comments for EP, 16 for D and 15 for I. The analysis revealed that there were 48 comments, which support the future trend, which shall be referred to as "pro" comments. 17 comments were found to be unsupportive of this specific future trend, which shall be referred to as "contra" comments. Regardless of the fact that there were more supportive (48) than unsupportive comments (17) noted for this projection, the contra comments for EP were maximum compared to contra comments for I, supporting the dissent shown in quantitative results for EP and the consensus shown for I. Please note that there were no "contra" comments for desirability, meaning that the experts do not anticipate a negative desirability of such trend (Table 60).

Projection for the year 2030	14 (International student mobility & recognition of degrees)
Number of comments (total)	68
Number of comments (14.1, 14.2, 14.3)	37, 16, 15
Supportive comments ("pro")	48
Unsupportive comments ("contra")	17

Table 60. Details of comments for projection 14.

For projection 14, the selective comments presented in Table 61 display the perspectives of all four stakeholder groups of experts, namely universities / business schools, companies / CEO, students, and politics / associations.

The comments analysis revealed advantages as well as disadvantages of students' mobility among different fields globally. A German student stated that competitiveness amongst western countries would demand such type of agreements, which already exists at some places. A Chinese CEO strongly believes that governments of different countries would play a vital role in giving such type of cross-country recognition to the students; however, it was easier in European countries. A university professor from Germany mentioned that it would take some time to become a reality; although it was highly desirable, it would need a standardized agreement, which is in fact lacking at national levels. According to a CEO from Kazakhstan, the study costs may reduce and there would be more opportunities for students. A Brazilian expert believes in high desirability and impact of this trend on business curriculum globally. An Austrian expert states that globalization will drive this trend ahead.

On the other hand, different aspects of the same projection are revealed by the unsupportive statements of the experts. An American professor, along with five other experts from the panel, thinks that the year 2030 seems too early for this to occur globally. According to a CEO from Croatia, this change may be affected by the development in education and business system which is not same in each country. More barriers, namely policy-based, administrative and governmental were mentioned by the Austrian and Indian experts to restrict mobility. An Indian expert further added that this would be possible in European countries, but it seemed more difficult across other countries. A German CEO expresses that countries and institutions may be too bureaucratic to accept such an agreement, though there was a great need for such a change. According to an Austrian politician, the mobility may be hampered by the self-interest of universities in promoting own programs; thus greater collaboration was required.

To understand the future implications of this projection, it is important to place equal attention on both quantitative and qualitative results. Though this trend is desirable according to the students and companies and shows a promising high impact on business leadership education in tertiary education, the quantitative results revealed that such a trend would face some challenges to come into existence in the year 2030. The qualitative results also support this fact. Supportive comments of panelists revealed a few important aspects to promote student mobility through an international agreement for the recognition of degrees. Some barriers emerged through the unsupportive statements of the panelists regarding this particular trend. Inferentially, there are mixed opinions concerning the probability of such trend becoming reality, but the trend is highly desirable and will have a great impact on business leadership education in tertiary education.

Pro comments	Contra comments
EP - "In many cases, there are already agreements. With the demographic change, especially western countries will push to come to more extensive agreements in order to secure their competitiveness." *Student, Germany*	EP - "This would be great, but I am uncertain how quickly the Higher Education industry will undertake this. Fifteen years is not that long of a time frame for this to turn the industry around." *Universities / Business Schools, USA*
EP - "It is very much related to the willingness and negotiation between governments of different countries. It might be realistic to have such cross-country recognition in EU." *Companies / CEO, China*	EP - "This might depend on the country development level, both in terms of education system and business / economic development." *Companies / CEO, Croatia*
D - "Would be highly desirable once certain Standards are agreed upon. Today we are even not able to have a workable Agreement on a national Level therefore a Long way to go..." *Universities / Business Schools, Germany*	EP - "Obstacles of nation, authorities and pressure groups are always n against it." *Politics / Associations, Austria*
D - "Lower study cost and more opportunities for students." *Companies / CEO, Kazakhstan*	EP - "Not sure if it will happen on all these fronts by 2030. It is too early, according to me. There will be a few blocks (policy-based, administrative, governmental, etc. Lot of effort is required for this to happen. Perhaps it may happen across Europe but including developing countries in this will be difficult. " *Universities / Business Schools, India*
I - "The desirability is high and this trend would certainly impact the business curriculum around the world." *Universities / Business Schools, Brazil*	EP - "The need is much higher, but the countries and institutions are too bureaucratic to realize it." *Companies / CEO, Germany*
I - "Globalization is key success factor." *Politics / Associations, Austria*	I - "It would require a high degree of collaboration and work for the greater good, which conflicts with self-interest of existing programs. " *Politics / Associations, USA*

Table 61. Selected pro and contra comments of the experts for projection 14.

Conclusion

To summarize, in spite of the reasonable differences in experts' opinions obvious by the dissent in quantitative results regarding EP, the future trend that an international agreement for recognition of degrees in tertiary education is enacted to promote student mobility in different fields of study, institutions and nations in a global world may come into reality. Conclusively, this trend is forecasted if the standards for international agreement are clearly defined and implemented. Both methods collectively showed that such a trend is highly desirable and would have a great impact on business leadership education in tertiary education for graduates.

4.3.5.5.2 Projection 15 – Funding of tertiary education

Preliminary notes

Tertiary education is of great importance for the development of individuals, society, innovation and economic development. Due to its immense contributions to and benefit for society and economic development, tertiary education has been traditionally conceived as a public asset (Altbach, Reisberg & Rumbley, 2009). Nevertheless, on a transnational level, governmental tax revenues are neither willing nor able to cover rising costs of tertiary education (Salmi & Hauptman, 2006). Rising financial pressures hamper students' access to and success in tertiary education (Johnstone, 2016). Therefore, alternatives to public funding and innovative solutions are needed to finance tertiary education and cope with multitude of challenges. However, the funding resources of Master in Management programs differ from country to country. Various alternatives are already implemented and are a matter of course (Johnstone, 2016; Salmi & Hauptman, 2006; Ziegele, 2010).[77] Irrespective of the sources of funds, implications for respective stakeholders have to be thoroughly considered. Therefore, the fifteenth projection was formulated.

Experts' opinions

The estimated probability (EP) is 59 % that, in 2030, business leadership education in Master in Management programs for graduates is financed by com-

---

77 For details, please see Part 2, chapter 3.2.5.7.

panies, the private-sector or participants (students) themselves rather than public funded. Desirability (D) M = 3.25 and impact (I) M = 3.73 are moderately high (Table 62). The interquartile range (IQR), which is the measurement of consensus for this RT Delphi survey, confirmed a strong consensus for EP (Table 62). It is the only projection of this RT Delphi survey, for which consensus was achieved regarding EP. It signifies the experts' agreement to the fairly high probability that the funding for Master in Management programs focusing on business leadership education will not be public funded in the future, they would receive funding from companies, private sector or participants. The IQR results showed a strong dissent for D. It may be inferred that the experts have different assessments about whether such a trend is desirable for the potential leaders. Furthermore, a high consensus was reported for I, which means that the private funding from companies, other sectors and participants can have a high impact on business leadership education.

No.	Projection for the year 2030
15	In 2030, business leadership education in Master in Management programs for graduates is rather financed by companies, the private-sector or participants (students) themselves than public funded.

EP statistics			D statistics		I statistics	
EP (mean)	IQR	Con	D (mean)	IQR	I (mean)	IQR
59.00%	20	-3.00%	3.25	2	3.73	*1*

Legend: EP = Estimated probability of occurrence (0-100%); IQR= Interquartile range; Con (SD) = Convergence of opinion (variation of standard variation: negative values equals convergence); D = Desirability of occurrence (1 = very low, 5 = very high); I = Impact in case of occurrence (1 = very low, 5 = very high).

Note degree of consensus / dissent: *Italic numbers* indicate that consensus among experts was achieved; i.e. for EP IQR ≤ 25 equals consensus, for D and I respectively IQR ≤ 1 equals consensus.

Table 62. Statistical data for projection 15 (n=105).

A qualitative examination of the recorded experts' comments revealed that only 5 experts have revised their answers a total of 5 times for the EP. 1 out of 5 confirmed his / her first choice. 4 out of 5 experts changed their responses in completely different ranges of the 11-unit scale, regardless of the mean. 3 out of 5 rated the EP higher than before and 1 rated EP lower than they did in the first choice and decreased the EP with tendency to the mean. This conclusion is also supported by the convergence of opinion; which is only -3.00 %.

The qualitative content analysis revealed that the experts provided a total number of 64 written comments. There were 30 comments for EP, 18 for D and 16 for I. 23 comments, which support the projection, emerged from the analysis, which shall be referred to as "pro" comments. 35 comments were found to be unsupportive of this specific future trend, which shall be referred to as "contra" comments. Experts have mixed opinions about the funding Master in Management programs should receive (Table 63).

Projection for the year 2030	15 (Funding of tertiary education)
Number of comments (total)	64
Number of comments (15.1, 15.2, 15.3)	30, 18, 16
Supportive comments ("pro")	23
Unsupportive comments ("contra")	35

Table 63. Details of comments for projection 15.

On a qualitative level, the diverse experts' panel did not support this projection to a large extent. Some relevant comments were chosen to give an overview of the results of the fifteenth projection. The selective comments presented in Table 64 display the perspectives of all four stakeholder groups of experts, namely universities / business schools, companies / CEOs, students, and politics / associations.

Projection 15 received less support from the experts; nonetheless, the supportive comments present some relevant aspects. The selected experts' comments from different countries emphasize the different aspects related to private versus public funding. According to an American expert, if a person and / or a company considered the program beneficial, they would be willing to fund the education. A Brazilian expert discloses the reality in Brazil. The expert explains that a co-operation between students and companies was necessary and one had to invest a lot monetarily to achieve better results. An American expert points out the advantages of public and private funding. An expert from Liechtenstein opines that good education has its own cost and one had to bear this cost. An Austrian politician sees private investment as a success factor. A good relationship and vast networking with other institutions would be a requirement for business schools according to a Brazilian expert. As per an American Professor, market pressure will be high-impact factor for business leadership education, as the quality of education will improve. The overall comments show that there are fair chances that companies and private sector will surpass the public funding allotted for Master in Management programs and that public funding can have a high impact on business leadership education, implying that the quality of education may improve. There were hardly any comments that support the fact that students should fund their own education. Experts mostly considered the public and private sector funding including companies as a preferable funding option. The different positive aspects of this projection provide limited support to the consensus achieved for EP and I in quantitative examination, as there are fewer supportive than unsupportive statements.

There were many speculations about the funding options for Master in Management programs targeting graduate students. Two experts mention that such programs will be expensive for companies and that public funding may be a preference. Three experts mention that education is a public good, it should therefore be free of charge. According to an American expert, it is not easy to generalize this trend. Whether such a trend will be a reality depends upon individual nations and companies. An Indian expert highlights the role of world economy for making the international agreement possible. According to a Swiss expert, public funding will still dominate the market in the future, even if more private universities were to offer management programs. The expert forecasts cooperation between public and private sector. Public funding is desired as it will facilitate student mobility according to an American politician. A German student demands a combination of different financial resources and programs. The expert expressed concern that if only companies funded the programs, the education will be adapted only according to the companies' needs; which is not desirable as education is the right of everyone. Another German student anxiously commented that the quality of education will be compromised, meaning that if education became too expensive, the purpose of education would remain purely economic. As per an American politician, it would be extremely difficult to recruit such a diverse body of students. Thus, the opposing statements mainly support the strong dissent reported for D in the quantitative assessment of this projection. The experts have expressed many facets of funding for management programs, which show a tendency that this projection is not desirable.

Pro comments	Contra comments
EP - "I believe the organizations and individuals who see the benefit will fund the operation." *Universities / Business Schools, USA*	EP - "Depends upon the country, and to some extent the company I think." *Universities / Business Schools, USA*
EP - "This is the reality in Brazil already. The companies and students have to be involved intellectually and financially. Further, you can't ask for superior results in something for whichyou have compromised financially." *Universities / Business Schools, Brazil*	EP - "Likely to happen. But it depends on so many factors which are difficult to predict. One of factors is world economy. This is also linked to an earlier question linking companies running their own programs." *Universities / Business Schools, India*
EP - "Private funding will ensure that programs evolve to meet needs. Public funding tends to inhibit change and competition." *Companies / CEOs, USA*	EP - "Education will stay in public hand in the next decades. There will be more and more private universities that will offer such educational programs and as a consequence more cooperation between public and private educational institutions. And the quality will suffer if it happens because there will be no oversight." *Universities / Business Schools, Switzerland*
D - "The one, who has the benefit of further education, must meet the costs." *Universities / Business Schools, Liechtenstein*	D - "Public funding could improve access; otherwise, more diverse students may not be able to take part in these programs." *Politics / Associations, USA*
D - "Private Investment in individual programs will be key success factor." *Politics / Associations, Austria*	D - "A mixture of different systems and programs is desirable. A pure financing from companies would mean a total adaptation of education to this, which is not desirable. Education should be available to everyone (keyword: equal opportunities)." *Student, Germany*
I - "Business Schools need good relationship and big networking with other institutions and companies." *Universities / Business Schools, Brazil*	D - "Through this we could get a system like in the USA. Students have high depts. after university and education is orientated only in economic use. The ideal of education and science gets lost. This is not desirable." *Student, Germany*
I - "I think market pressure will help improve quality and relevance over time." *Universities / Business Schools, USA*	I - "It may be harder than ever to recruit a diverse student body." *Politics / Associations USA*

Table 64. Selected pro and contra comments of the experts for projection 15.

It is vital to integrate quantitative and qualitative results for enhanced understanding of the role of funding for management programs. In case of EP, the quantitative results show a strong consensus, whereas the qualitative results show some degree of support for this projection. It may be interpreted as being quite likely that this projection may become reality in the year 2030, but the experts have suggested various factors, which need to be taken into account with respect to funding by the private sector and companies. In case of I, both methods collectively suggest that private funding along with funding from companies instead of public funding for management education would impact business leadership education, though qualitative support is restricted for this projection.

Conclusion

Both methods assert the fact that even if there is a fair chance that this projection may become reality and impact business leadership education, such a trend that business leadership education in Master in Management programs for graduates is financed by companies, the private-sector or participants (students) themselves rather than public funded is not desirable due to several associated disadvantages.

4.3.5.5.3　Projection 16 – Duration of Master's programs

Preliminary notes

Management programs ideally concentrate on the overall development of the personality of potential leaders. To be observed in different markets, there are many differences in workload and duration of Master in Management programs – even within the Bologna region. The usual duration of Master in Management programs is two years, but there are also programs of just one year (e.g. Table 13). Based on the theory and the actual requirements for business leadership education[78] Master in Management programs not only have to impart knowledge and qualifications, but also need to set the framework that allows development of leadership personality and leadership competencies e.g. by applying the gained knowledge on the field through internships or real-world projects. Considering the (required) changes in business leadership

---

78　For details, please see Part 2, chapter 3.2.5.

education in the future, it should be discussed if the trend to reduce workload and time in Master in Management programs is reasonable so that most of the programs last only for 1 year. Therefore, the sixteenth projection was created to gain perspectives from the experts whether one year will be sufficient to complete Master in Management program for graduates in the year 2030.

Experts' opinions

The estimated probability (EP) is 48.20 % that, in 2030, most of the offered Master in Management programs for graduates will be completed in one year. Desirability (D) M = 2.73 is quite low and impact (I) M = 3.7 is moderate (Table 65). The interquartile range (IQR), which is the measurement of consensus for this RT Delphi survey, verified a strong dissent regarding EP. Low EP and strong dissent signify that, in the future, the probability is reasonably low that Master in Management programs for graduates will be completed within one year but experts have different opinions about the duration of Master in Management programs. The IQR result for D confirms dissent. Nevertheless, the IQR result for I showed that consensus was achieved.

No.	Projection for the year 2030
16	In 2030, most of the offered Master in Management programs for graduates can be completed in one year.

EP statistics			D statistics		I statistics	
EP (mean)	IQR	Con	D (mean)	IQR	I (mean)	IQR
48.20 %	40	-0.17 %	2.73	2	3.7	*1*

Legend: EP = Estimated probability of occurrence (0-100 %); IQR= Interquartile range; Con (SD) = Convergence of opinion (variation of standard variation: negative values equals convergence); D = Desirability of occurrence (1 = very low, 5 = very high); I = Impact in case of occurrence (1 = very low, 5 = very high).

Note degree of consensus / dissent: *Italic numbers* indicate that consensus among experts was achieved; i.e. for EP IQR ≤ 25 equals consensus, for D and I respectively IQR ≤ 1 equals consensus.

Table 65. Statistical data for projection 16 (n=105).

A qualitative examination of the experts' comments revealed that 7 experts have revised their answers a total of 10 times for the EP. 4 out of 7 confirmed their first choice. 2 out of 7 rated EP lower than they did in the first choice and decreased the EP regardless of the mean. 1 out of 7 rated EP higher than before. The final assessments imply that the experts continue to have their expert opinion at the end in spite of several revisions. Furthermore, this conclusion is also supported by the -0.17 % convergence of opinion.

According to the content analysis, 61 written comments were noted from the experts for this projection. There were 21 comments each for EP and D and 19 comments for I. The analysis revealed only 24 comments, which support the future trend and shall be referred to as "pro" comments. 37 comments were found to be unsupportive of this specific future trend, which shall be referred to as "contra" comments (Table 66).

Projection for the year 2030	16 (Duration of Master's programs)
Number of comments (total)	61
Number of comments (16.1, 16.2, 16.3)	21, 21, 19
Supportive comments ("pro")	24
Unsupportive comments ("contra")	37

Table 66. Details of comments for projection 16.

The experts do not support this particular projection, signifying that one year may not be sufficient for Master in Management program for graduates. For projection 16, the selective comments presented in Table 67 display the perspectives of all four stakeholder groups of experts, namely universities / business schools, companies / CEOs, students, and politics / associations.

Although the comments for EP show a low probability that Master programs should be completed in one year, a few experts have mentioned that this trend may be likely as the educational costs would increase in the future, so short courses will be preferred. A shorter duration could be acceptable if programs were well focused. Compared to unsupportive comments, fewer supportive opinions surfaced from the content analysis of the experts. A Brazilian expert commented that a short-term curriculum would gather more attention of students and companies. An American professor believes that a one-year program would concentrate more on specific aspects of the training and find a way to reach them practically. According to a German expert, long-term MBA programs are a fundamental need of the universities and they will remain; but the short-term programs are preferable. A CEO from Kazakhstan opines that this development seems to be in demand from companies and students. An expert from China commented about the impact this trend could have on business leadership education. According to a German professor, short-term programs would provide more flexibility to the learners. These programs would turn out to be a vital part of the permanent learning. A Chinese expert mentions that a one-year program might influence the knowledge transfer and the core topics of management. A German professor believes that different models will be required to realize this trend. Thus, the "pro" comments support the quantitative results for EP and D and demonstrate a tendency on a lower side that programs will be completed in one year and if this trend becomes reality, it will have a great impact on business leadership education.

Pro comments	Contra comments
EP - "Or in less time. More and more short-term programs will be more attractive." *Politics / Associations, Brazil*	EP - "There is a growing demand from the market (students and companies). But the development of leadership competencies and personality needs time. May be possible for programs for master's graduates." *Companies / CEOs, Germany*
EP - "I believe this will be true due to two factors; specificity of training and the need to get this done expediently." *Universities / Business Schools, USA*	EP - "Don't think so! Two year's courses are not working well and the market is not accepting these graduates. One year is impossible to cover all needed base." *Universities / Business Schools, Brazil*
EP - "Yes, time is money, and MBAs are expensive. Longer programs could become the domain of the virtual universities. Also, there will be more and more Special programs, which could lead to two MBAs so as to sharpen a Special Job aptitude Profile." *Companies / CEOs, Germany*	EP - "If modularly organized, it will need more time." *Politics / Associations, Austria*
D - "Companies and students want to start on as soon as possible" *Companies / CEOs, Kazakhstan*	D - "Such demand will exist to reduce the finance pressure on the student. Personally I do not prefer." *Companies / CEOs, China*
D - "Will make education more flexible and become an integral part of lifelong learning." *Universities / Business Schools, Germany*	D - "This will not improve the quality of education. You can see it even in vocational training, that shortening the time has immediate impact on education quality." *Companies / CEOs, Germany*
I - "It will influence the way to transfer the knowledge, and it may even influence the contents of the education program." *Companies / CEOs, China*	I - "Increased pressure and competition might mean less valuable programs in the long run; poorer student outcomes." *Politics / Associations, USA*
I - "Will Need different models." *Universities / Business Schools, Germany*	I - "Business education will be a mess in case of occurrence. Not even enough to form a specialist, neither a graduate." *Universities / Business Schools, Brazil*

Table 67. Selected pro and contra comments of the experts for projection 16.

An opposing comment by a German CEO reveals that, though there is a constant demand of such a development from students and companies, overall personality development and leadership competency development necessitate reasonable time. A Brazilian expert strongly believes that this trend is unfeasible and further added that some organizations or companies are not accepting students having degrees from one year courses. Well-focused programs require more time to complete, according to an Austrian politician. A Chinese CEO does not prefer such a development, but believes that short-term courses would decrease the costs of programs, which would be advantageous for the students. A German expert foresees that the quality of education would be jeopardized by reducing the time of the courses and therefore, they were not desirable. An American expert doubts the quality of management knowledge and skills gained by the students in short-term programs as this may imply compromising the value of such programs. As many experts explained, a Brazilian expert agrees that one year is insufficient time for business leadership education to create capable future leaders. The opposing statements greatly support the quantitative results for the dissent achieved for D. Various disadvantages were mentioned by experts, implying that management programs – especially Master's programs – should last more than one year so that enough time is spent on developing the whole personality of potential leaders. Some comments further uncover factors that may have a moderate yet negative impact on business leadership education.

To understand the future implications of this projection, it is important to concentrate on both quantitative and qualitative results. The quantitative results showed that this trend is less probable in the year 2030, even though there are mixed opinions about the duration of the Master's programs, and it is not desirable; nevertheless, such a trend would have a moderate impact on business leadership education in tertiary education. The qualitative content analysis indicates support to this fact, as there were more unsupportive (38) compared to supportive (25) comments. Mixed opinions were noted for EP regarding the duration of the Master's program. There were more contra statements (16) for D compared to pro statements (5). The comments for I also displayed moderate negative impact on business leadership education.

Conclusion

To summarize, it is less likely that the Master in Management programs for graduates can be completed in one year. The qualitative and quantitative analysis jointly demonstrated that such a trend is not desirable and would have a moderate negative impact on business leadership education in tertiary education.

4.3.5.5.4 Conclusions for stakeholder dimension politics

Along with the stakeholder groups, providers, participants, and purchasers, the stakeholder group politics has a great impact on tertiary education and curriculum design. Therefore, projections 14-16 were created and surveyed as the final set of projections of this RT Delphi survey. For all projections, different assessments and controversial discussions of the future were conducted by the diverse expert panel. Based on the analyses, the three projections can be clustered in two groups:

> The first group comprises projections 14 and 15 (international student mobility & recognition of degrees, funding of tertiary education). It is uncertain that these trends will emerge in the future due to moderate EP values. The interquartile range (IQR), which is the measurement of consensus for this RT Delphi survey, confirms dissent for projection 14 regarding EP. This indicates that the panelists have different assessments of the projection. The qualitative results also support this fact. Desirability and impact in case of occurrence were concordantly high. In contrast, consensus was confirmed for projection 15 regarding EP. It is the only projection of this RT Delphi survey, for which consensus was achieved regarding EP. However, in case of EP, the quantitative results show a strong consensus, whereas the qualitative results show some degree of support for this projection. It may be interpreted as being quite likely that this projection may become reality by the year 2030, but the experts have suggested various factors, which need to be taken into account with respect to funding by the private sector and companies. In case of I, both methods collectively suggest that private funding along with funding from companies instead of public funding for management education would impact business leadership education, though qualitative support is restricted for this projection.

> Projection 16 (duration of Master's programs) can be allotted to the second group. This projection seems to be improbable for future occurrence due to the low value for EP, which is the third lowest of this RT Delphi survey. The results also showed that such a trend is not desirable; nevertheless, it would have a moderate impact on how the curriculum for business leadership is designed. The qualitative content analysis displayed support for this fact.

According to the results of the Delphi survey, the scenario method was performed in five steps (see Figure 31) based on different methods of futures studies to ensure validity of results. Therefore, the results of the Delphi survey were prioritized by means of portfolio analysis, cross impact analysis and scenario axes analysis before scenario writing, discontinuity analysis and a final expert check. The scenario method is presented in the following chapter.

5. Scenario development

Following the overall research design and process (Part 1, Chapter 4), the aim of research and research questions, alternative scenarios and wildcards have to be created and developed based on results of the previous Delphi study. Bañuls and Turoff (2011) state that "scenarios have been widely used for exploring the detection of future events together, as well as an analysis of the path that leads to the desired future or prevents undesired futures" (p. 1580).

Scenarios in this thesis were defined in line with Markmann, Darkow and Gracht (2013, p. 1822) and Gracht and Darkow (2010, p. 47) as "internally consistent, plausible, and challenging narrative descriptions of possible situations in the future, based on a complex network of influencing factors". Remembering the aim of research, a scenario in the context of this research contains a rough proportion of technical and functional management versus personality and leadership aspects within education. The scenarios in this context will not include market-relevant trends such as branding etc. for providers of tertiary education (universities / business schools). Quality, accreditation and ranking issues will also not be discussed separately, due to the presumption that those aspects can be taken for granted for successful providers in the year 2030.

5.1 Prioritization

According to Fontela (1977), it can be stated: "The problem still remains that it is very often necessary to prepare "scenarios" in areas where quantification is difficult" (p. 87). Therefore, based on the results of the RT Delphi study analyzed above, the most relevant influencing factors for the future of business leadership education in tertiary education in Master in Management programs for graduates have to be prioritized. A methodological set of futures studies, consisting of portfolio analysis, cross impact analysis and scenario-axis technique, have been combined in order to reduce complexity and to enhance the final outcome. These methods will be presented consecutively in the following sections together with methodological background information in a first step, followed by description of implementation and results.

5.1.1 Portfolio analysis

Portfolio analysis by mapping quantitative Delphi data on scatterplots is one possible approach for scenario development (Markmann, Darkow & Gracht, 2013; Becker & Gracht, 2014). Based on this approach and the illustrations of Delphi results according to the before-mentioned researchers, the following Figure 33 and Figure 34 present the results of the RT Delphi survey and thereby the perspectives of a multi-stakeholder panel as analyzed and discussed in the previous chapter. 105 experts of international background participated in the RT Delphi survey and rated 16 projections for business leadership education in Master in Management programs for graduates in tertiary education in the year 2030 according to their estimated probability of occurrence, desirability and impact. Additionally, the respondents were requested to provide reasons and comments for their ratings wherever necessary. The collected data provides insights into stakeholders' (divergent) estimations for the future of business leadership education in tertiary education.

The strategic maps shown in Figure 33 and Figure 34 are based on the mean of the experts' opinions. The 16 surveyed projections according to the four stakeholder dimensions are represented by their numbers in the sequence in which they were surveyed, and may be retraced by headwords in the legend. According to experts' opinions, the 16 projections fall in the range of medium to high impact for the field of research; furthermore, almost all of projections seem to be desirable. Thus, the consistently overall high values can be evaluated as a quality criterion and an ex-post confirmation for the development and selection of the surveyed Delphi projections.

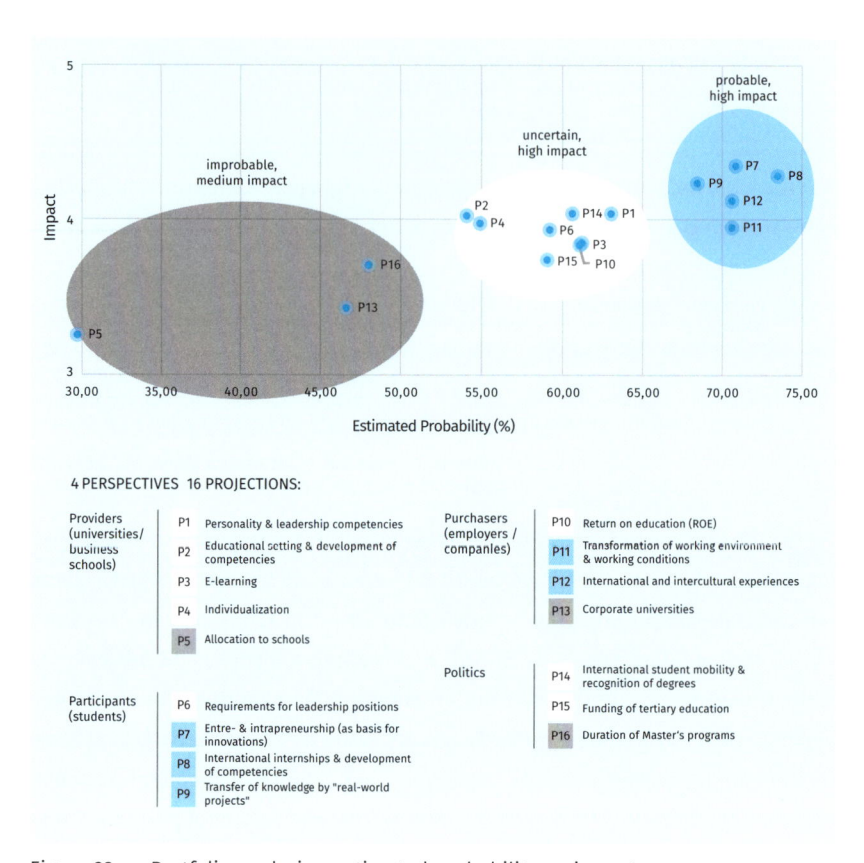

Figure 33.   Portfolio analysis – estimated probability vs. impact.

The quantitative results (mean values) were transferred into scatterplots according to the two dimensions estimated probability and impact (Figure 33) and estimated probability and desirability respectively (Figure 34). In the next step, the projections were grouped according to the three clusters "surprises", "eventualities" and "expectations", which is in line with Becker & Gracht (2014, p. 14). The clustering was carried out according to their apparent formation of groups in order to map the different characteristics. Markmann, Darkow and Gracht (2013) have mentioned two options for the clustering of projections that can be carried out subjectively or by cluster analysis. The subjective way of clustering was preferred to allow a natural formation of groups of projections. The process of clustering was necessary for further prioritization of the projections for the scenario development process.

As an overview, the three different clusters, namely surprises, eventualities and expectations, within the two different charts Figure 33 and Figure 34 respectively embrace the same projections. Altogether, three projections can be categorized as "surprises", which are marked gray. This means that projections 5, 13 and 16 show relatively low ratings for an estimated probability of occurrence and also have low impact and desirability ratings. It may be concluded that these three projections seem to be improbable for future occurrence and might be recognized as "eventual strategies" (Becker & Gracht 2014, p. 14) as a kind of back-up for decision making in case they will surprisingly occur.

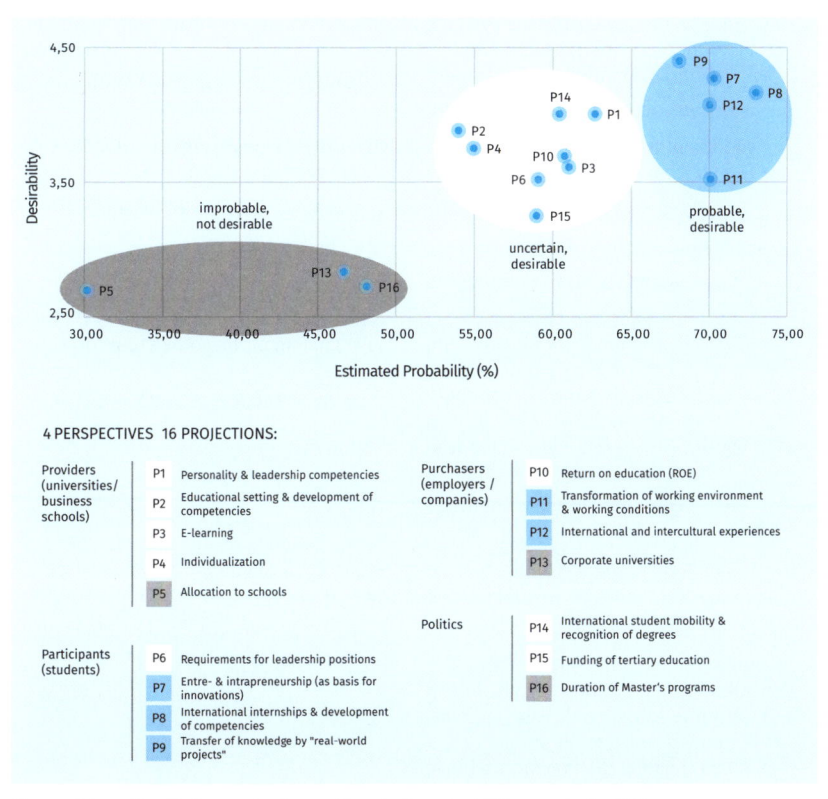

Figure 34. Portfolio analysis – estimated probability vs. desirability.

8 out of 16 projections can be categorized as "eventualities", which are marked white. Since the ratings for estimated probability show uncertainty for these eight projections 1-4, 6, 10, 14 and 15 which have high impact and are desirable according to the 105 experts, these projections can serve as a basis for future developments. This analysis is supported by Becker and Gracht (2014) who suggest that such eventualities play a vital role in monitoring the real developments based on tangible indicators.

The remaining five projections 7-9 and 11-12 can be categorized as "expectations" since they show high values for estimated probability of occurrence, which have high impact and are desirable according to the 105 experts' opinions. These five projections, which are marked blue, might be considered as crucial issues for the development of strategy and could be central elements in the description of alternative scenarios.

For the portfolio-based scenario development according to the dimensions estimated probability of occurrence and impact (Figure 33), it can be stated as a rule of thumb based on previous research:

> "Probable scenarios can be used to understand how a certain topic is expected to evolve, which decreases the inherent uncertainty. Instead, improbable scenarios should be considered in order to be aware of possible changes and wildcards which might seriously jeopardize business. Consequently, improbable scenarios assist in reducing an organization's vulnerability for worst case developments." (Markmann, Darkow & Gracht, 2013, p.1828 f.)

Using the portfolio analysis based on the dimensions, the estimated probability of occurrence and desirability has an advantage as it focuses on diverse perceptions and attitude of the involved experts (Markmann, Darkow & Gracht, 2013).

Although the portfolio analysis which was developed on basis of Delphi results shown above, seems to lay a plausible foundation for alternative scenarios, the shortcomings of the Delphi method must be considered while interpreting the findings. As the projections were presented in an isolated manner, the Delphi technique may not be able to fully consider the reactions between projected items, which is also reported as a weakness of the Delphi technique (Gordon & Hayward, 1968). To further explore the interdependencies and interactions between projections, a cross impact analysis was conducted and will be presented in the following section.

5.1.2 Cross impact analysis (CIA)

For an interdisciplinary and complex research topic as business leadership education in tertiary education, it might be assumed that developments are (highly) interrelated, interconnected and interdependent with other developments. Such interconnectedness between multiple incidents and developments is called "cross impact' (Gordon & Hayward, 1968). Interrelationships and interconnectedness of and between events or developments are analyzed by means of cross impact analysis. Bañuls and Turoff (2011) underline CIA to be used in analyzing "complex contexts with various interactions", as "an approximation to the real-world" and highlight CIA to be "one of the most commonly-used techniques for generating and analyzing scenarios" (p. 1580). The U.S. RAND Corporation developed cross impact analysis in the 1960s to balance the weakness of Delphi studies (Graf & Klein, 2003; Weimer-Jehle, 2006). Furthermore, numerous authors stated the flexibility of CIA in combination with the Delphi method (Campbell, 1971; Enzer, 1971; Bañuls & Salmeron, 2007) or other methods (Bañuls & Turoff, 2011).

One of the limitations of the cross impact analysis is "that it does not account for the effect of non-occurrence of events, a situation which leads to ambiguity in defining the initial likelihoods of occurrence" (Enzer, 1971, p. 53). In order to balance the methodological shortcomings and to decrease the inherent uncertainty, a combination with the Delphi method was preferred and conducted. Spickermann, Grienitz and Gracht (2014) conducted a cross impact analysis in order to prioritize strategic issues for development of projections for their Delphi survey, a cross-impact analysis in this research was applied in the post-Delphi process to assess and map the mutual effects and interactions of the 16 projections for a comprehensive development of scenarios. Therefore, the 16 projections were transferred into a cross-impact matrix. To support this analysis, the software CIM 8.1 was used, wherein 8 to 30 components can be processed.[79]

Four experts representing each of the stakeholder groups of business leadership education in tertiary education, which have also participated in the RT Delphi survey of this research, individually assessed the 16 projections based on their highest mutual effects. The final scores were defined by mutual agree-

---

[79] Possible alternative programs to map interdependencies between system components are SYSTEM-TOOLS www.frederic-vester.de, POWERSIM www.powersim.com etc. (Graf & Klein, 2003).

ment between the experts in an open discussion process. Scores of intensity of activity and interconnectedness were calculated and mapped in different modes. In a first step, the effect of projection 1 on each of the projections in horizontal direction was rated according to the following options:

0.0 = no effect / impact of projection x on projection y
0.3 = weak effect / impact of projection x on projection y
0.5 = medium effect / impact of projection x on projection y
0.7 = high effect / impact of projection x on projection y
1.0 = very high effect / impact of projection x on projection y

This procedure was conducted according to the concept of Graf and Klein (2003) and the software CIM 8.1 for each projection until the influence of each projection on each of the others was rated. The effect of a projection on itself is – logically – not to be rated. The results per line as TA (total active) show the sum of the rated active effect / impact of a projection on another projection; the results per column as TP (total passive) show the sum of the rated passive effect / impact how a projection is influenced by other projections. To calculate the intensity of activity (A), the total active has to be divided by the total passive (A = TA / TP) to express if a projection has an overall effect / impact on other projections (>1) or if it is totally influenced by other projections (<1). The intensity (I) of activity and interconnectedness (I = TA*TP) expresses the interrelation of a projection with other projections irrespective of the calculated active or passive effect / impact. If the product is $> ((n-1)^2 / 2)$, a projection has more than half of the possible interrelations, if the product is $< ((n-1)^2 / 2)$, a projection has less than half of the possible interrelations. The index of leverage (L) is the product of the normed intensity of activity and interconnectedness and is calculated by the following formula:

$$\left[\frac{(TA^2 - TP^2) * \sqrt{I}}{(TA^2 + TP^2) * (n - 1)} \right]$$

While the cross impact matrix (Figure 35) shows the ratings for all projections and the calculated results, Figure 36 highlights the intensity of influences (total active / total passive), Figure 37 the intensity of interconnectedness and Figure 38 the index of leverage. The 16 surveyed projections according to the four stakeholder dimensions are represented by their numbers in the sequence they were surveyed and may be retraced by headwords in the legends.

no.	name	1	2	3	4	5	6	7	8	9	10	11	12	13	14	15	16	TA	A (TA/TP)	I (TA*TP)	L	name	no.
1	Personality & lead...		1.0	1.0	1.0	1.0	1.0	1.0	1.0	1.0	1.0	0.7	1.0	0.5	0.5	0.5	1.0	13.2	2.9	59.4	0.27	Personality & lead...	1
2	Educational settin...	0.3		0.5	0.7	0.5	1.0	1.0	1.0	1.0	1.0	1.0	0.7	0.5	0.5	1.0	0.7	11.4	1.3	103.7	0.1	Educational settin...	2
3	E-learning	0.3	1.0		1.0	1.0	1.0	0.7	1.0	1.0	1.0	1.0	1.0	1.0	0.7	0.7	1.0	13.4	2.2	80.4	0.27	E-learning	3
4	Individualization	0.0	0.3	0.3		0.0	0.0	0.0	0.3	0.0	0.5	0.0	0.0	0.0	0.5	0.3	0.0	2.9	0.5	16.0	-0.1	Individualization	4
5	Allocation to scho...	0.5	0.0	0.3	0.0		0.5	0.5	0.0	0.0	0.0	0.0	0.0	0.0	0.0	0.0	0.0	1.8	0.4	7.6	-0.08	Allocation to scho...	5
6	Requirements for l...	1.0	1.0	0.5	0.0	1.0		1.0	1.0	1.0	1.0	0.7	0.5	1.0	0.3	0.3	1.0	11.3	1.3	94.9	0.12	Requirements for l...	6
7	Entre- & intraprene...	0.7	1.0	0.5	0.7	0.7	1.0		1.0	1.0	1.0	1.0	1.0	0.3	0.3	0.5	1.0	11.7	1.6	86.6	0.18	Entre- & intraprene...	7
8	International intern...	0.5	0.5	0.5	0.3	0.0	1.0	0.5		0.7	1.0	1.0	1.0	0.0	0.0	0.0	0.5	7.5	0.8	73.5	-0.1	International intern...	8
9	Transfer of knowle...	0.3	1.0	0.3	0.0	0.0	0.7	0.7	0.7		0.5	0.7	0.7	0.5	0.3	0.7	0.5	7.6	0.9	66.9	-0.05	Transfer of knowle...	9
10	Return on educatio...	0.3	1.0	0.5	0.0	0.0	0.7	0.7	1.0	1.0		0.7	0.7	0.0	0.0	0.7	0.3	7.6	0.8	70.7	-0.07	Return on educatio...	10
11	Transformation of l...	0.3	1.0	0.5	0.0	0.0	0.7	0.5	0.7	1.0	0.5		0.7	0.0	0.0	0.3	0.0	6.2	0.8	45.9	-0.05	Transformation of l...	11
12	International and i...	0.3	0.7	0.5	0.3	0.0	0.5	0.3	1.0	0.3	0.3	0.3		0.0	0.5	0.3	0.5	5.8	0.7	48.1	-0.11	International and i...	12
13	Corporate universit...	0.0	0.0	0.3	0.7	0.0	0.0	0.0	0.3	0.3	0.5	0.0	0.0		0.0	1.0	0.5	3.6	0.6	20.5	-0.09	Corporate universit...	13
14	International stude...	0.0	0.3	0.0	0.5	0.0	0.0	0.0	0.3	0.0	0.0	0.3	0.7	0.5		0.0	0.0	2.6	0.7	9.4	-0.04	International stude...	14
15	Funding of tertiary...	0.3	0.0	0.3	0.3	0.0	0.3	0.5	0.5	0.0	1.0	0.0	0.3	0.7	0.0		0.5	5.2	0.8	32.8	-0.05	Funding of tertiary...	15
16	Duration of Master'...	0.0	0.0	0.0	0.0	0.0	0.0	0.0	0.0	0.0	0.0	0.0	0.0	0.0	0.0	0.0		0.0	0.0	0.0	-0.0	Duration of Master'...	16
TP		4.5	9.1	6.0	5.5	4.2	8.4	7.4	9.8	8.8	9.3	7.4	8.3	5.7	3.6	6.3	7.5						

Legend: TA = total active; TP = total passive; A = TA / TP (intensity of influences: total active / total passive); I = TA * TP (intensity of activity and interconnectedness); L (index of leverage).

Figure 35.   Cross impact matrix.

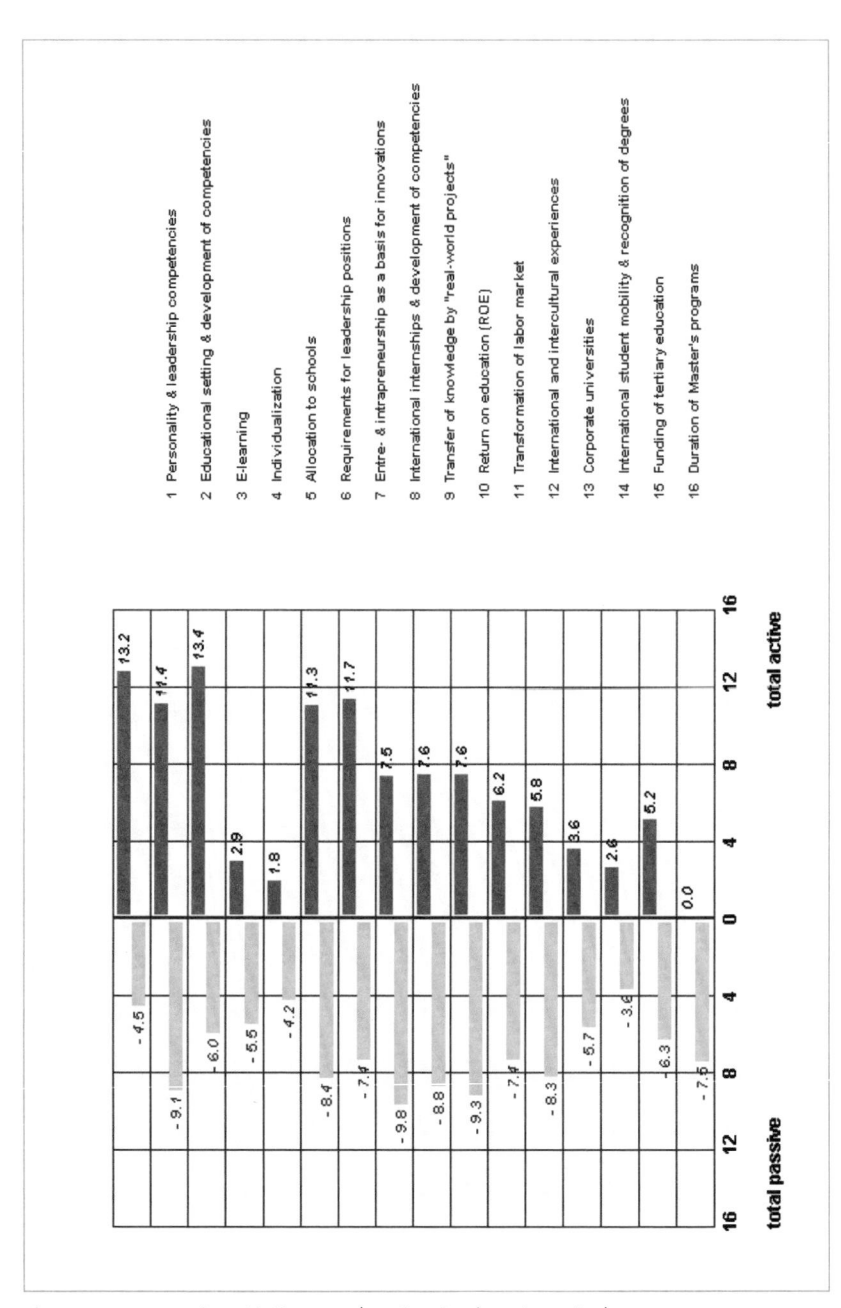

Figure 36.   Intensity of influences (total active / total passive).

Figure 37.   Intensity of activity and interconnectedness.

1 Personality & leadership competencies
2 Educational setting & development of competencies
3 E-learning
4 Individualization
5 Allocation to schools
6 Requirements for leadership positions
7 Entre- & intrapreneurship as a basis for innovations
8 International internships & development of competencies
9 Transfer of knowledge by "real-world projects"
10 Return on education (ROE)
11 Transformation of labor market
12 International and intercultural experiences
13 Corporate universities
14 International student mobility & recognition of degrees
15 Funding of tertiary education
16 Duration of Master's programs

Figure 38.   Index of leverage (degree of activity and interconnectedness).

An overall result of the cross impact analysis reflects a high degree of relationships and interactions between the 16 projections. Therefore, developments in the field of business leadership education in tertiary education for graduates cannot be viewed in an isolated way; they have rather to be perceived in a holistic manner. Furthermore, the results of cross impact analysis were consistent with the Delphi results. Thus, the results of the cross impact analysis further explain the dissent shown by IQR for 15 out of 16 projections probability ratings. One reason might be the high degree of uncertainty given by the high interconnectedness and multifaceted influences between developments. Therefore, experts might have discordant opinions of the future, although IQR results are showing high consensus for (high) desirability and impact assessments. By analyzing the high degree of interconnectedness as a result of the cross impact analysis, the holistic approach in analyzing the results of a heterogeneous Delphi panel by excluding further statistical analysis can be supported. The projections with the highest intensity of activity and interconnectedness were obviously projection 1 (personality & leadership competences) and projection 3 (E-learning), followed by projection 7 (entre- & intrapreneurship as basis for innovations), leading to a final prioritization in order to develop scenarios.

5.2   Scenario axes analysis

For the development of extreme scenarios, in line with previous research, the scenario axes technique (also called 2x2 matrix) was applied (Becker & Gracht, 2014; De Mooij & Tang, 2003; Markmann, Darkow & Gracht, 2013; Solnet et al., 2014; Heijden, 2005; WEF, 2009). According to Klooster and Asselt (2006), the scenario axes approach, which was first developed in strategic corporate management, is prevalent and recognized in futures studies in order to create scenarios in a coherent and systematic way. Furthermore, the authors highlight in their observations that futurists use the scenario axes technique in a flexible and less-standardized manner. The technique is seen to be a structuring device for contemplations and discussions about possible futures, but should not to be interpreted as a blueprint[80]. Since the scenario axes approach is considered to be a standard technique (Ramírez & Wilkinson, 2014; Kloost-

---

[80]   For different functions and/or interpretations of the scenario axes as backbone, building scaffold, foundation, "both-and grids" or "either/or-frames" see: Klooster & Asselt (2006); Ramírez & Wilkinson (2014).

er & Asselt, 2006) and its' application is presumed to be self-explanatory, it is scarcely described in futures studies, how the two axes have been chosen and been used. Although this approach is highlighted as structuring device for the unknown on one hand, criticism on the approach on the other has also to be noted. Some argue the scenario axes technique to be a subjective perspective on the future considering only two driving forces, which are rarely to be justified (Klooster & Asselt, 2006; De Mooij & Tang, 2003).

Applying the method, in line with numerous authors (Becker & Gracht, 2014; Markmann, Darkow & Gracht, 2013; Solnet et al., 2014; Heijden, 2005), the two most important driving forces or developments, which are both very uncertain and have a high impact have to be selected. Combining the two key uncertainties should ensure that they could potentially develop into different directions. The two identified, most important driving forces or developments are then to be plotted on two axes. Proceeding this way, four different scenario quadrants emerge, which are able to shed light on four potential different perspectives of the future wherein apparently unrelated or conflicting information can be made operationally useful (Klooster & Asselt, 2006). Although this frame is helpful to further foster the management of uncertainties on one hand, it has to be noted on the other that more than four scenarios have "proven to be counterproductive and organizationally impractical" (Heijden, 2005, p. 225). Ramírez & Wilkinson (2014) even recommend organizations do not create more scenarios than they can use.

In order to structure thinking and discussions about the future of business leadership education in tertiary education in Master in Management programs for graduates in the year 2030, the most important driving forces have been crystallized by a set of multiple methods of futures studies. After having conducted the RT Delphi study, portfolio analysis and CIA the two most important drivers that are very uncertain, have a high impact and were furthermore identified to be the most active and interconnected were:

> Projection 1: In 2030, Master in Management programs tend to focus on personality and leadership competencies rather than impart (functional) knowledge.

> Projection 3: In 2030, advanced digitization (Web 2.x) has completely transformed business leadership education in tertiary education.

The two selected most important driving forces for business leadership education in tertiary education in Master in Management programs for graduates in the year 2030 were plotted on two axes:

> X-axis: Knowledge, Qualification, Competencies & Leadership Personality with the two poles of "knowledge is power" and "conspicuous by action" and
> Y-axis: Digitization with the two poles of "face-to-face" and "online"

resulting in the following four different scenarios (Figure 39):

> Scenario 1:
> "2030: Management education 10.0"
> Scenario 2:
> "2030: Leadership trailblazer – grasping the 24 / 7 e-learning landscape & experiencing real-world settings"
> Scenario 3:
> "2030: Management education in the armchair"
> Scenario 4:
> "2030: Leadership explorer – coping with the blended learning environment online and off & exploring real-world settings"

Digital education landscape
online

Content conveyor
knowledge is power

Leadership evolYOUtion
conspicuous by action

Digitization

Scenario 1:
»Management education 10.0«

Scenario 2:
»Leadership trailblazer - grasping the 24/7 e-learning landscape & experiencing real-world settings«

Knowledge, qualifications, competencies & leadership personality

Scenario 3:
»Management education in the armchair«

Scenario 4:
»Leadership explorer - coping with the blended learning environment online and off & exploring real world settings«

on-campus
Face-to-face

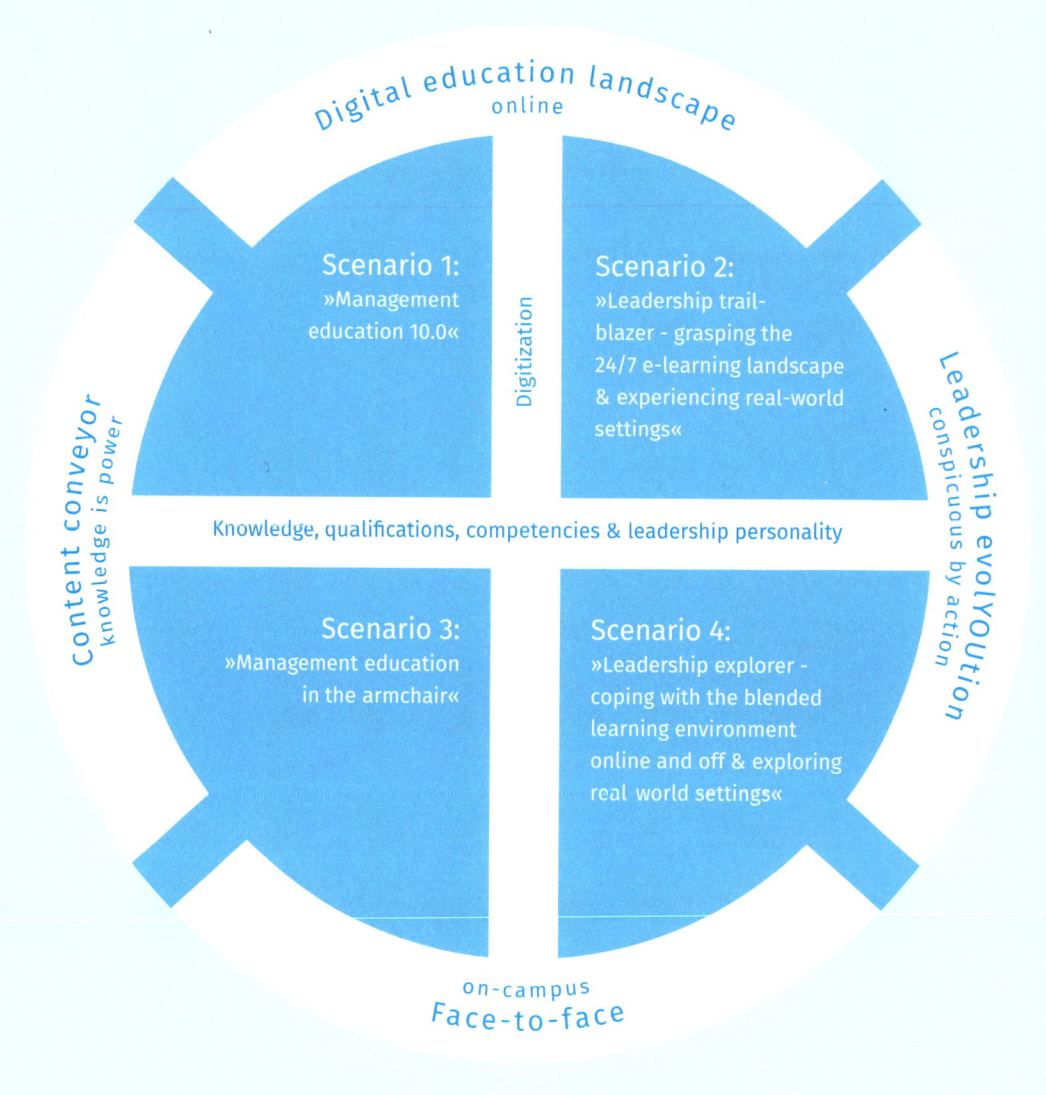

Figure 39. Business leadership education in tertiary education in Master's programs in the year 2030. Four scenarios in a nutshell.

5.3 Scenario stories

Using the comprehensive qualitative data provided by the Delphi expert panel along with additional secondary references, four narrative scenarios for business leadership education in tertiary education in Master's programs for graduates in the year 2030 were developed following different dimensions. The series of scenarios in this research were chosen to be vivid snapshots of possible futures in order to think outside of the box and challenge the audience. Fictitious prospects of business leadership education in tertiary education in Master's programs for graduates are presented to prepare the four stakeholder groups of business leadership education in tertiary education providers (universities / business schools), participants / learners (students), purchasers (employers / companies), and politics for decision-making and possible (extreme) situations in the future.

All four following scenarios are based on the premise of low to moderate global growth in an internationalized, highly digitized and innovative world (e.g. Gros & Alcidi, 2013; IDC, 2012; WEF, 2013). Due to the demographic development and an aging society, it is assumed that a shortage of talents is one of the major challenges for employers / companies and their competiveness (Manpower Group, 2014).

5.3.1 Scenario 1 – 2030: Management education 10.0

2030: Overview

Business leadership education in tertiary education in Master's programs for graduates follows the traditional curricula of management programs, which have proven their excellence for more than 50 years. The curricula are perfectly integrated in the digital learning landscape of 2030 based on highly developed technology and new teaching methods. The virtual classroom is the place to be. Classical management education e-loaded!

2030: Educational goal

Students will be familiarized with the practices of knowledge-building and scientific excercises to participate in scientific debates and / or grasp the utility of scientific knowledge. Furthermore, students will be qualified by classical management education for a management position in an accelerated technological and global working environment.

2030: Curriculum

Knowledge is power. Knowledge is available (for free) – without restraint. Nevertheless, universities and business schools have strengthened their authority over academic degrees also in the field of business leadership education and the relevant curricula. Since traditional management education programs, which have proven their excellence for more than 50 years, are highly glamorized in the business community, a "best of-version" is elaborated as an online edition tuned by newest teaching methods. Since the 100 % e-management classics fascinate students to be online 24 / 7, part of the curriculum is to verify sportive activities in order to balance virtual life and real life.

2030: Educational settings

Technological setting

Technological change is rapidly moving on. Not only constant learning, but also tech-enhanced learning is required. Due to technically matured online education, a highly digitized generation participates in a 100 % online Master's program. The program is very attractive as the study program is perfectly integrated in the digital learning landscape of 2030. New teaching methods and innovative feedback mechanisms motivate students to meet peers, tutors and teachers in virtual classrooms – to absorb more knowledge / content, participate in online simulations and case studies but finally also to pass written (multiple-choice) exams.

On-Campus versus real-world setting

E-Campus and its digital learning landscape is the favorite learning environment. As recent surveys have pointed out the need to better prepare graduates for today's labor market, a short period of in-company experience is a mandatory requirement to apply for final examinations. Students can choose to participate in an international consulting project or internship.

Transnational perspective

There is no way back for internationalization. As technology shrinks distances and removes communication barriers, students in the 100 % e-management program can be located anywhere in the world. International faculties and international student groups contribute to diverse discussions and a global mindset.

2030: Program profile – a rough rule of thumb

Degree:	Master's degree in Management
Knowledge & qualifications:	80-90 % of curriculum
Personality & competencies:	10-20 % of curriculum
Pedagogical approach:	focus on teaching, knowledge and qualifications
Duration:	1 year (full-time); 2 years (part-time)
Return on Education (ROE):	no relevance
Financials:	financed by participants (students), employers / companies or private-sector

2030: How to get there?

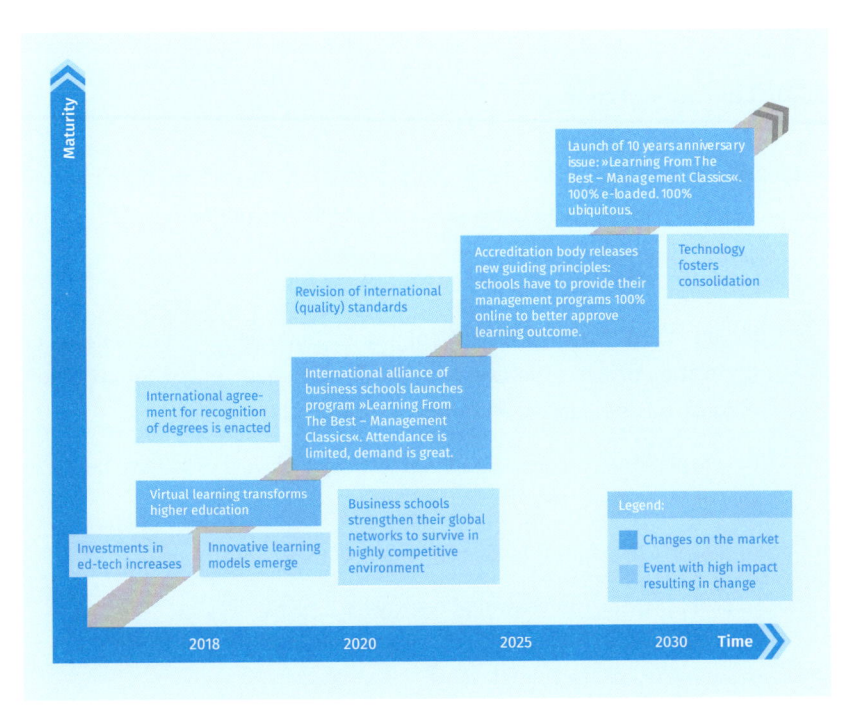

Figure 40.   Scenario 1 – Management education 10.0. Scenario pathway.

5.3.2 Scenario 2 – 2030: Leadership trailblazer – grasping the 24 / 7 e-learning landscape & experiencing real-world settings

2030: Overview

These are times of great transformation. Not only will highly developed technologies alter all aspects of our life, but also education supports the needful change. Learning, harnessing our minds and applying creative thoughts to new problems will allow leadership trailblazers to face, adapt and overcome any future transition (Sikka, 2016). Aspired leaders build the bridges between learning online and working offline, between theory and corporate practice, between action and reflection. A state-of-the-art curriculum in leadership fosters both knowledge & qualification and competencies & personality in order to lay the foundation for innovators in a transnational, highly technological, innovative and uncertain world beyond campus gates. Primarily, an optimal preparation for a successful (self-set) future in society and (business) world is possible due to integrated real-world projects within organizations, based on perfectly balanced functional and leadership knowledge. Leadership trailblazers march ahead!

2030: Educational goal

Students will be familiarized with the practices of knowledge-building and scientific excercises to participate in scientific debates and / or grasp the utility of scientific knowledge. Furthermore, students will be enabled

> to contribute to the generation of innovation quality by innovations or innovation projects for a sustainable development and benefits of individuals, businesses, economy and society,
> to set (personal, corporate and innovation) goals and to achieve the (self-set) goals and
> to develop (business) leadership competencies and
> to create strong international networks.

2030: Curriculum

The society needs leaders who can balance both sides (personality / leadership) versus knowledge. A combination of both is absolutely required to face not only worldwide challenges but also management on a large or small scale. Therefore, curricula of business leadership education in Master's programs for graduates focus on knowledge and qualification as well as on competencies and personality in equal parts. It has to be considered that knowledge and qualification are the basis for (leadership) competencies. In order to be well prepared for the real world after graduation, innovations, entre- and intrapreneurship will be a crucial part of the curriculum. Innovation is the most important success factor for sustainable wealth and growth. Innovations are realized by entre- and intrapreneurs.

Future leaders learn to be in touch with themselves; they learn about their respective strengths and weaknesses. They learn to understand themselves by learning how peers, lecturers and tutors see them. They learn in context, they are encouraged to be curious and to make knowledge adaptable in a collaborative and engaged setting. Authentic leadership evolYOUtion grown from within.

2030: Educational settings

Technological setting

Educational revolution also in higher education is successfully completed. These are times of new digital responsibility. Leading-edge education technology (ed-tech) is guaranteed to be learning-centered in order to take advantage of positive opportunities for a positive societal impact (Krueger, 2016). A highly digitized student generation is enrolled in highly developed interactive online education programs. The theoretical part of the Master's program is embedded in the innovative digital learning landscape of 2030, which is not only attractive but also motivating due to pedagogically well-designed interactive learning methods and novel feedback mechanisms. Students meet peers, tutors and teachers in virtual reality, allowing for intense discussions and exchange of learning experiences. Spaces for working as individuals, in pairs and groups are arranged. Study papers are uploaded to the digital examination office; oral exams take place in virtual exam halls. Aspired leaders will self-organize around their various electronic devices. Ed-tech is used to complement and enrich the real-world learning experience described in the following section.

On-Campus versus real-world setting

While the theoretical part of the program takes place on the virtual Campus and its interactive virtual learning landscape, students are integrated in an organization for the practical leadership experiences. The practical part of the Master's program is outsourced by universities to organizations, who offer real-world projects to enable students to gain real-world leadership experiences. Academic tutors within the organizations, assigned by universities / business schools, support students by building the bridges between theory and practice. We no longer talk about case studies and online simulations! Exploration, inquiry-based learning, project-based learning and work-integrated learning are the need of the hour. Welcome to real-world experiences!

Transnational perspective

In this world, transnational living, learning and working is state-of-the-art. Students participating in this leadership program can be located at any place in the world where an organization offers students the opportunity to realize and learn by real-world projects. Vice versa, organizations can get in touch with potential future leaders. International faculty, international student groups and a diverse working environment contribute to cosmopolitan discussions and a global mindset.

2030: Program profile – a rough rule of thumb

Degree:	Master's degree in Leadership
Knowledge & qualifications:	50 % of curriculum
Personality & competencies:	50 % of curriculum
Pedagogical approach:	focus on learning and competencies by exploration and inquiry in real-world setting
Duration	2 years (full-time)
Return on Education (ROE):	high relevance
Financials:	financed by employers / companies or private-sector; exceptionally by participants (students)

2030: How to get there?

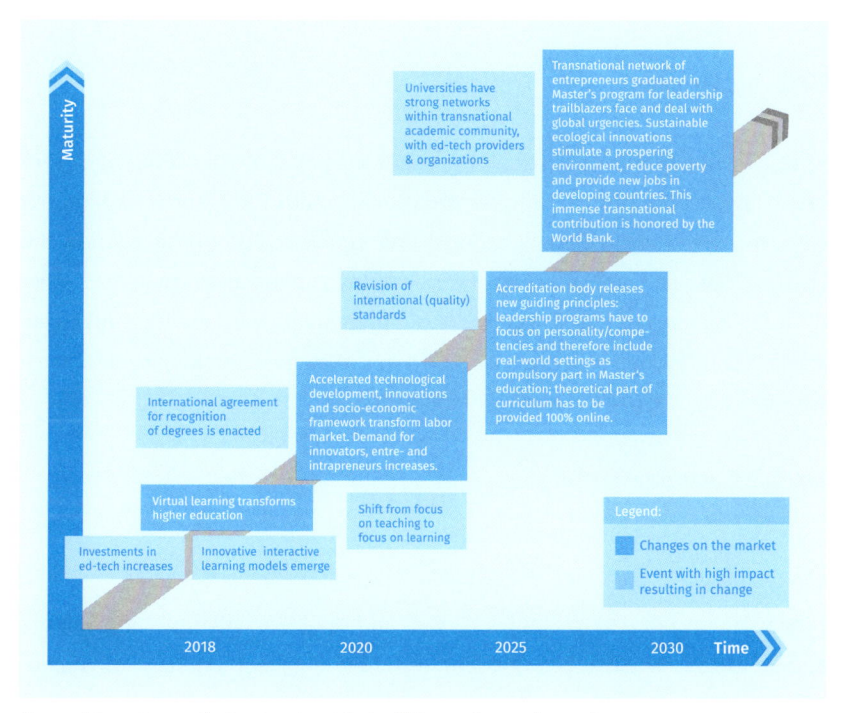

Figure 41. Scenario 2 – Leadership trailblazer. Scenario pathway.

5.3.3 Scenario 3 – 2030: Management education in the armchair

2030: Overview

Never change a running system! Functional knowledge, management tools and strategies are evergreens due to high acceptance by employers and future career entry for aspired managers. Why struggle? Let's keep the good old times. Management education can be acquired in a convenient way, sitting in the armchair.

2030: Educational goal

Students will be familiarized with the practices of knowledge-building and scientific excercises to participate in scientific debates and / or grasp the utility of scientific knowledge. Furthermore, students will be qualified by classical management education for a management position in a global working environment.

2030: Curriculum

As some companies focus on pure economic purposes, the academic and practice-relevant education comprises traditional courses in (functional) knowledge, tools and strategies. Functional and systematical approaches are the backbone of any prestigious Master's in Management program, where electives can be chosen due to the student's individual preference e.g. financial, marketing or human resources management. Functional management knowledge can truly assure the quality of education.

2030: Educational settings

Technological setting

Digitization is not a magic bullet. As web and Apps are only tools and helpers and cannot replace the way of communication and interaction between people, this Master's in Management program highlights face-to-face lectures in imparting functional and systematic approaches. A basic state-of-the-art digital learning infrastructure is accessible to deal with the administrative needs as e.g. study papers are uploaded to the digital examination office. Aspired leaders are disciplined in digital media use and well balance between virtual and physical realities.

On-Campus versus real-world setting

Although some smaller educational training parts always take place in companies, formal Master's degree programs take place on-campus in universities / business schools. The good old days are still alive in the traditional lecture halls! To enhance employability, brief internship (minimum of 4 weeks) as in-company experience is a mandatory requirement to apply for final examinations. Students have to apply for internships directly at organizations.

Transnational perspective

Due to a globalized world economy, where managers have to understand business from a world perspective, part of this Master's program is delivered by different universities worldwide, from which the students can choose. Global faculty and international student groups foster diverse discussions and a transnational mindset.

2030: Program profile – a rough rule of thumb

Degree:	Master's degree in Management
Knowledge & qualifications:	80-90 % of curriculum
Personality & competencies:	10-20 % of curriculum
Pedagogical approach:	focus on teaching, knowledge and qualifications
Duration:	1 year (full-time), 2 years (part-time)
Return on Education (ROE):	no relevance
Financials:	financed by participants (students), employers / companies or private-sector

2030: How to get there?

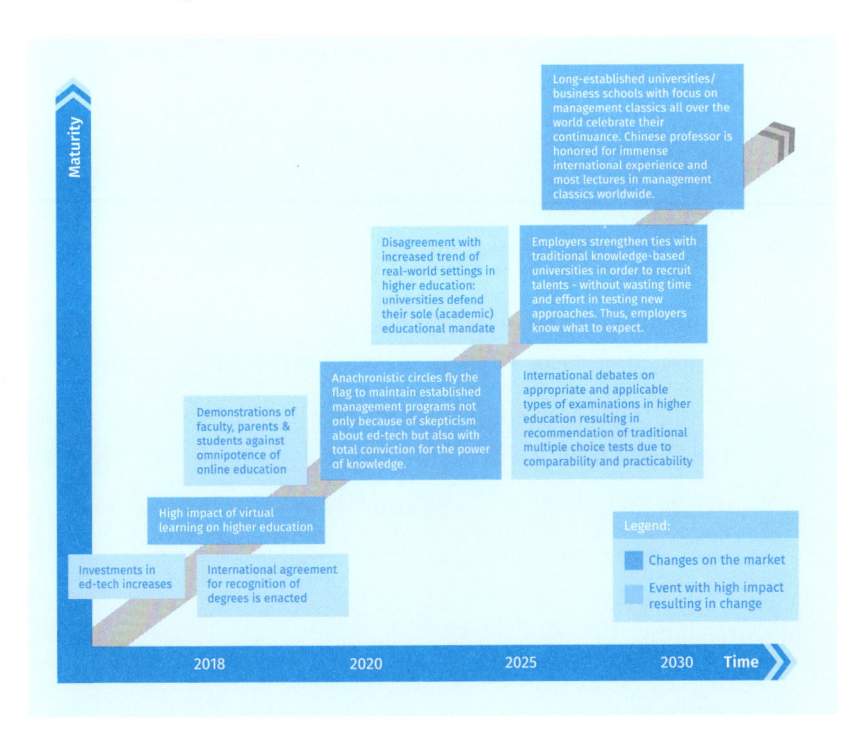

Figure 42. Scenario 3 – Management education in the armchair. Scenario pathway.

5.3.4 Scenario 4 – 2030: Leadership explorer – coping with the blended learning environment online and off & exploring real-world settings

2030: Overview

Traditional values are highly appreciated! Human interaction on a personal level is essential not only for educational excellence but also for a well-formed individual. Therefore, although functional knowledge is considered, Master's education focuses on personality and competencies in order to prepare aspired leaders in creating innovative future working landscapes and contribute to a prosperous and sustainable society in a highly innovative and transnational world. It is recognized that students need more than traditional academic learning to thrive in 21st century (WEF, 2016). Keystone of this philosophy is hands-on experience in a real-world working environment in addition to academic education on campus. This concept will shift the needle for organizations, address long-standing problems and improve the relevance of education.

2030: Educational goal

Students will be familiarized with the practices of knowledge-building and scientific excercises to participate in scientific debates and / or grasp the utility of scientific knowledge. Furthermore, students will be enabled

> to contribute to the generation of innovation quality by innovations or innovation projects for a sustainable development of a company,
> to set (personal, corporate and innovation) goals and to achieve the (self-imposed) goals,
> to develop personality and (business) leadership competencies and
> to create strong transnational networks.

2030: Curriculum

As most of the organizations have managerial problems at all levels, performance and creation of corporate culture based on common values have to be enhanced by leadership evolYOUtion from deep within. Although functional knowledge has to be considered, the difference of the programs need to be based on focusing in personality and leadership competencies. One of the biggest key points in the successful Master's program is innovation comprising the field of entre- and intrapreneurship. Theoretical education and practical exercises are equal parts of the curriculum. The new Master's in Leadership is highly appreciated on the mature Master's market.

2030: Educational settings

Technological setting

A basic state-of-the-art digital learning infrastructure is accessible to acquire basic knowledge and skills and to deal with the administrative needs as e.g. study papers are uploaded to the digital examination office. However, human interaction is the key to educational excellence. Socialization is the key to a well-formed individual. Aspired leaders are self-controlled in their media use and only use them in a beneficial way. Therefore, despite all fancy technological developments, face-to-face interaction has retained its value and relevance.

On-Campus versus real-world setting

Theoretical education and practical exercise are perfectly balanced also in terms of the learning environment. The theoretical part is held on-campus, where students meet experienced faculty with teachers and tutors with the highest academic background and practical experiences as well as peers. Learning and working effectively in (learning) groups in mixed (virtual and physical) realities have complementary roles. Development of personality and leadership competencies needs real-world projects because competencies and skills can only be developed in reality. Therefore, practical experience is gained in field-based practical projects in a real-world working environment. Both the theoretical and the practical part are perfectly connected. Theories have to be transferred and applied to entrepreneurial practice. Reflection and documentation is required for individuals, organizations as well as for universities / business schools. Exploration, inquiry-based, project-based and work-integrated learning are elaborated par excellence as a pivotal element of not only a creative but also an active learning process.

Transnational perspective

Leadership in a global world is a global task. As global markets are the only marketplace, aspired leaders have to be prepared for global roles. Therefore, theoretical education in this Master's program is delivered by numerous universities on different continents, for the students to choose. Ubiquity is in vogue. International faculty, international tutors and international peers foster a cosmopolitan mindset and form the basis for a strong international network.

2030: Program profile – a rough rule of thumb

Degree:	Master's degree in Leadership
Knowledge & qualifications:	50 % of curriculum
Personality & competencies:	50 % of curriculum
Pedagogical approach:	focus on learning and competencies by exploration and inquiry in real-world setting
Duration:	2 years (full-time)
Return on Education (ROE):	high relevance
Financials:	financed by employers / companies or private-sector; exceptionally by participants (students)

2030: How to get there?

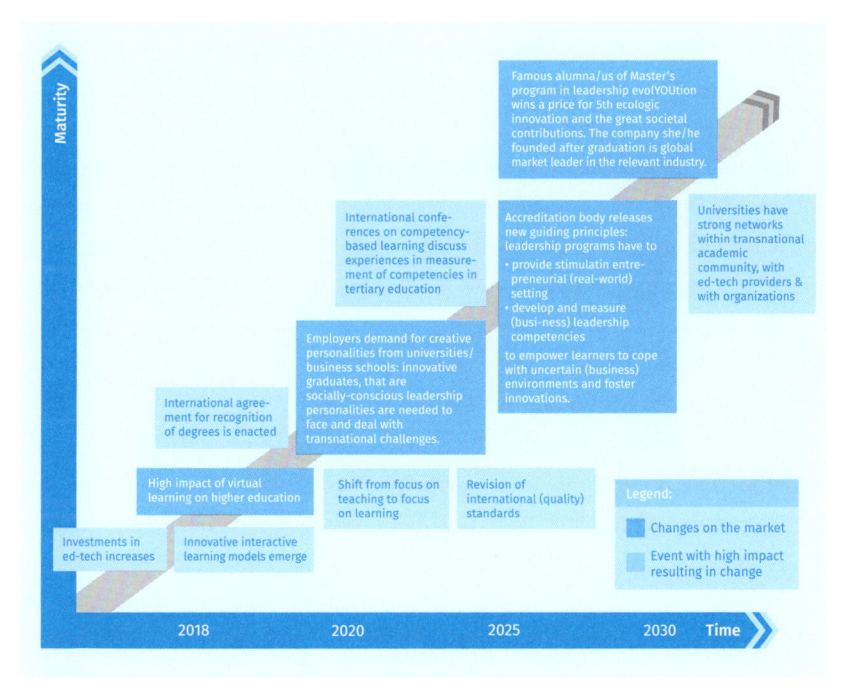

Figure 43. Scenario 4 – Leadership explorer. Scenario pathway.

5.4 Discontinuities and the surprising future

While scenario development in the past focused on probable, possible or desirable situations in the future, surprising future has gained in importance in recent scenario planning studies because of increased complexity, volatility and uncertainty in world economy (Gracht & Becker, 2014). Therefore, weak signals or wild cards have to be identified. Weak signals are defined as "past or current developments / issues with ambiguous interpretations of their origin, meaning and / or implications. They are unclear observables warning us about the probability of future events" (iKnow, 2016). Raising early awareness of such vague und incomplete insinuations, which might have positive (opportunities) or negative (threats) impact on future developments, is useful not only to reduce uncertainty, but also to benefit from these possibilities (Coffman, 1997; Markmann, Darkow & Gracht, 2013; Mendonça et al., 2004). Thus, qualitative data has to be thoroughly scrutinized. Furthermore, discontinuities or surprising futures describe structural interruptions, which are also named as wild cards or black swans. Although estimated probability of occurrence of disruptions might be very low to zero, their (positive or negative) impact in case of occurrence may be extremely high to devastating (Cornish, 2003; Grossmann, 2007; Mendonça et al., 2004; Notten, Sleegers & Asselt, 2005). In order to reveal wild cards, an inductive or deductive approach can be applied. In the inductive approach, common knowledge about certain possible events is accessed, while the deductive approach focus on creation of new and unexpected disruptive developments e.g. based on qualitative data analysis of Delphi studies (Markmann, Darkow & Gracht, 2013; Schuckmann et al., 2011).

Therefore, those discontinuities should be included in scenario development to underline both the necessity of breaking mental models and reduction of uncertainty and vulnerability. Taking potential changes with their positive or negative consequences in account at an early stage can help to develop relevant and adequate measures (Markmann, Darkow & Gracht, 2013).

Within this research, the vast qualitative data provided by the Delphi expert panel were analyzed carefully. Particular attention was paid to unique positive or negative arguments, which were easily accessible after the procedure of coding in pro and contra comments. This allows data to be analyzed for both weak signals and wild cards. Based on the discussion and the results of this RT Delphi study along with additional inquiries and browsing of different databases[81], two wild cards, two extreme situations with low-probability and serious impact in case of occurrence, for business leadership education in tertiary education in Master's programs for graduates were distilled. By creating the following wild cards, futures studies in this research were complemented in order to better support the different stakeholder groups in their robust strategies and action planning.

5.4.1 Wildcard 1 – Eradication of Master's degree programs

New technologies with leading-edge ed-tech and changes in the labor market along with changed requirements with which graduates are confronted are disrupting what, where and how students learn. Based on qualitative data

---

[81] Trendexplorer (TRENDONE), Shaping Tomorrow, iKnow WI-WE Bank, trendwatching.com and Google Trends.

provided by the expert panel the need for academic Master's degree programs is eradicated. A discontinuity that is not completely unthinkable, as a movement in USA called 'education hackers' is already known (Gerstlauer, 2014; Hansen, 2014; Stephens, 2013). Followers of this movement are not rushing to obtain a specific degree; rather, they inhale the learning process and learning outcomes. They configure their very individual curriculum from online course offerings e.g. massive open online courses (MOOCs) provided by top universities. As they have learned how to learn, they also apply advanced feedback mechanisms and lessons of neuroscience in order to improve their learning experiences. (Academic) education will remove from traditional institutions and their lecture halls. The new generation of learners will prefer continuous learning channels that are pervasive and of contextual relevance (IFTF, n.d.).

Such a transformation calls on all stakeholder groups of tertiary education, namely universities, students, employers (companies), and politics as well as the society, to challenge the assumptions and (re)think (about) the structures and principles of present tertiary education.

5.4.2   Wildcard 2 – Structural discontinuity

Based on the changed conditions and requirements in the labor market and the need for higher education in the working force, new education systems and programs are established. A complete transformation of higher education is of high relevance not only for individual countries, but for the whole world, since it is possible that basic compulsory education ends at the age of 18. Basic compulsory education comprises high school to be completed by the age of 15 followed by a first academic degree on Bachelor's level. An extreme situation is discussed by and available at the database iKnow, which is funded by the European Commission[82].

In case of the change and transformation of the entire education system including universities, such a structural discontinuity calls on all stakeholder groups of tertiary education, namely universities, students, employers (com-

---

82   In the iKnow Wild Cards & Weak Signals Bank (WI-WE Bank) 442 Wild Cards and 356 Weak Signals (total 798 as per 06.04.2016) are administered, complemented and rated by more than 5.400 active community members in 185 countries. The iKnow project "is aimed at interconnecting Knowledge on issues and developments potentially shaking or shaping the future of science, technology and innovation (STI) in Europe and the world." (Retrieved April 6, 2016, from http://wiwe.iknowfutures.eu/iknow-description/).

panies) and politics as well as parents and society to challenge the assumptions and (re)think about the structures and principles of present tertiary education.

5.5 Expert check

According to Heijden (2005), a final expert check of the scenario stories and wild cards was applied in order to agree with quality criteria. In order to conduct this "'validation' step" (Heijden, 2005, p. 264) the drafted scenarios and wild cards were distributed to a team comprising of four experts, representing each of the stakeholder groups of business leadership education in tertiary education. Thus, experts can prepare discussions and comments. In a subsequent workshop with the before mentioned expert team, scenarios and wildcards were presented and discussed according to logical aspects, specific content items and (in)consistency. The scenarios and wildcards were finalized based on minor changes and along with further desk research to substantiate plausibility and consistency – as presented above.

6. Transfer

The last step of the Delphi-based scenario development is transfer, which plays a central role in futures management in order to create a momentum of change. In contrast, Poteralska and Sacio-Szymańska (2014) state: "Foresight practitioners usually focus on developing methodologies and conducting foresight exercises and do not have an influence on the implementation of their results. Foresight sponsors (either public or private institutions) seldom contract further research aimed at the implementation of the achieved results" (p. 2). Thus, this research aims to picture a rough outlook to initiate, stimulate, and better prepare further transfer. Therefore, both checklist for stakeholders (Table 68) and a roadmap for the sponsor of this research (Figure 44) were elaborated in order to provide the context and navigation for decision makers to work with in practice.

The following checklist (Table 68) was compiled based on stakeholders' perspectives and motives. Following the main dimensions, which structure the scenario stories, relevant key questions were formulated for each stakeholder group. By answering the key questions, stakeholders build a bridge to their individual practice.

Stakeholder group	Motives	Key questions

Providers (universities / business schools)	Be competitive and successful in tertiary education	1. What is institution's goal in the year 2030?
		2. How will institution be positioned in 2030 (e.g. focus on leadership in quality or price)?
		3. Which concept of management or leadership does institution stand for?
		4. Which educational goals does institution pursue?
		5. Which learning environment and learning strategy does institution offer?
		  5.1 Which role does leading-edge ed-tech play for institution and learners? Is network and cooperation needed with ed-tech providers or other universities / (business) schools?
		  5.2 Which international academic network and cooperation is relevant for institution and learners?
		  5.3 Does institution require real-world experiences of learners? How can this be realized? Which cooperation does institution need to offer real-world experiences? Does institution have ties with organizations / companies? Are those ties to be strengthened? Or which new ways to combine theory and practice can be adopted?
		  5.4 Are other collaborations outside the campus needed to offer state of the art pedagogy and strengthen provider's (market) position?
		6. Is curriculum ready for 2030? Does curriculum reflect content and pedagogical concept for 2030?
		7. Does institution have adequate leadership and / or workforce?
		8. Does adequate faculty exist? Are practitioners and / or adjunct professors needed to complement faculty and / or academic research?
		9. When / how can institution's and educational goals be set and realized?
		10. When / How can measures to reach goals be defined?

		11. Who is responsible for topics above and implementation?
12. Is a controlling system for the process above implemented?
13. Is the budget calculated?
14. How is education funded?
…
Participants (students / learners)

Please note:

Key questions in this context are suitable for both applicants to better prepare decision for Master's program and students to challenge relevant Master's program, students are already enrolled | Search for a Master's program that best suits to self-set (individual / personal and professional) goals

Get management or leadership education that will equip for later (individual / personal and professional) life | 1. What are my (individual / personal and professional) goals?
2. Do I strive for a management or leadership position?
3. Is the Master's program I want to choose / have chosen suitable to reach my (individual / personal and professional) goals? Does Master's educational goal fit with my (individual / personal and professional) goals? Is Master's program suitable to prepare me for later (individual / personal and professional) life?
4. Does curriculum comprise both functional knowledge and personality / leadership aspects?
5. Are Master's programs learning environment and / or learning strategy state-of-the-art regarding technological setting and ed-tech, real-world experiences as well as transnational perspective?
6. Is adequate faculty available? Is academic faculty complemented by practitioners and / or adjunct professors?
7. Is marketing of the relevant Master's program plausible, coherent and reliable? Which ed-tech is used? How (strong) are the ties with companies / organizations? Are international aspects as part of program sufficient?
8. How is program success to be measured? Is ROE relevant?
9. How is education funded?
… |
| **Purchasers** (employers / companies / organizations) | Get well educated aspired leaders | 1. How to recruit the best talents and aspired leaders today and 2030? Can talented employees be encouraged and supported for a Master's program?
2. Which are higher education institutions company / organization can develop new or strengthen the ties with in order to recruit talented future leaders and / or support talented employees to study a Master's program? Which Master's program has an adequate and reasonable educational goal that fits to company's / organization's goals and culture? |

			3. Does Master's program enable students to cope with uncertain business reality in a transnational and highly technological world?
			4. Does curriculum comprise both functional management knowledge as well as leadership / personality aspects?
			5. Is adequate faculty available? Do practitioners and / or adjunct professors complement academic faculty?
			6. Is marketing of the relevant Master's program plausible, coherent and reliable?
			7. How is program success to be measured? Is ROE relevant?
			8. What are the Master's programs' costs?
			9. Does company / organization have opportunities for further (academic) research projects with higher education institution?
			...
Politics		Set the framework for tertiary education	1. How can an international agreement (comparable with worldwide extension of Bologna region) be fostered, accelerated and enacted in order to further improve student mobility and recognition of degrees among different fields of study, institutions and nations in a global world?
			2. How can framework for tertiary education be defined on a global level in order to enhance comparability among different institutions and nations? Can workload and program duration be defined and agreed transnationally in order to guarantee a reasonable, holistic and sustainable Master's education?
			3. How can budgets for education be reorganized e.g. according to the following principle: early childhood and basic compulsory education for free; the higher the education the more funded by private organizations or companies or learners themselves?
			4. How can framework be improved to foster leadership and entre- / intrapreneurship education in tertiary education in order to create sustainable growth and prosperity of nations?
			...

Table 68. Checklist: Are stakeholders prepared for Master's programs in 2030?

Furthermore, a roadmap for the sponsor of this research was elaborated (Figure 44), which can obviously be transferred to any institution of (higher) education. Consistently applying the tool of the holistic business development process according to Faix (Nagel et al., 2013) introduced in Part 1, the sponsor of this research has to conduct the following steps in phase of transfer:

Step 1: Deciding to apply the development process for the launch of a Master's program in (business) leadership education at the end of 2016 until the beginning of 2017 based on sponsor's mission, goals and culture.

Step 2: Analyzing the current stakeholders' situation and attitudes by conducting workshops in 2017 with selected representatives of the different stakeholder groups, learners / students, companies / organizations, faculty including adjunct professors and practitioners, network of cooperating universities and ed-tech suppliers. The framework has to be analyzed e.g. on the model STEEPL (Fleisher & Bensoussan, 2002), which is a recognized analytical technique in practical corporate management. According to the acronym STEEPL, the social, technological, economic, environmental, political and legal framework of (business) leadership education in tertiary education has to be analyzed in 2017.

Step 3: Defining and evaluating of current potentials and risks for Master's programs in (business) leadership education in tertiary education based on the results of previous steps in 2017.

Step 4: Defining the objectives for Master's program in (business) leadership education in tertiary education regarding positioning, educational goals, curriculum, learning environment, faculty and the relevant network comprising companies / organizations, cooperating universities and ed-tech suppliers in 2018.

Step 5: Defining the strategy as path to goals comprising a resource and project planning in 2018.

Step 6: Implementation of strategy beginning in 2018 / 19 in order to launch the redefined Master's program in 2019.

Step 7: Monitoring achievement of objectives along with a process of continuous improvement starting along with step of implementation.

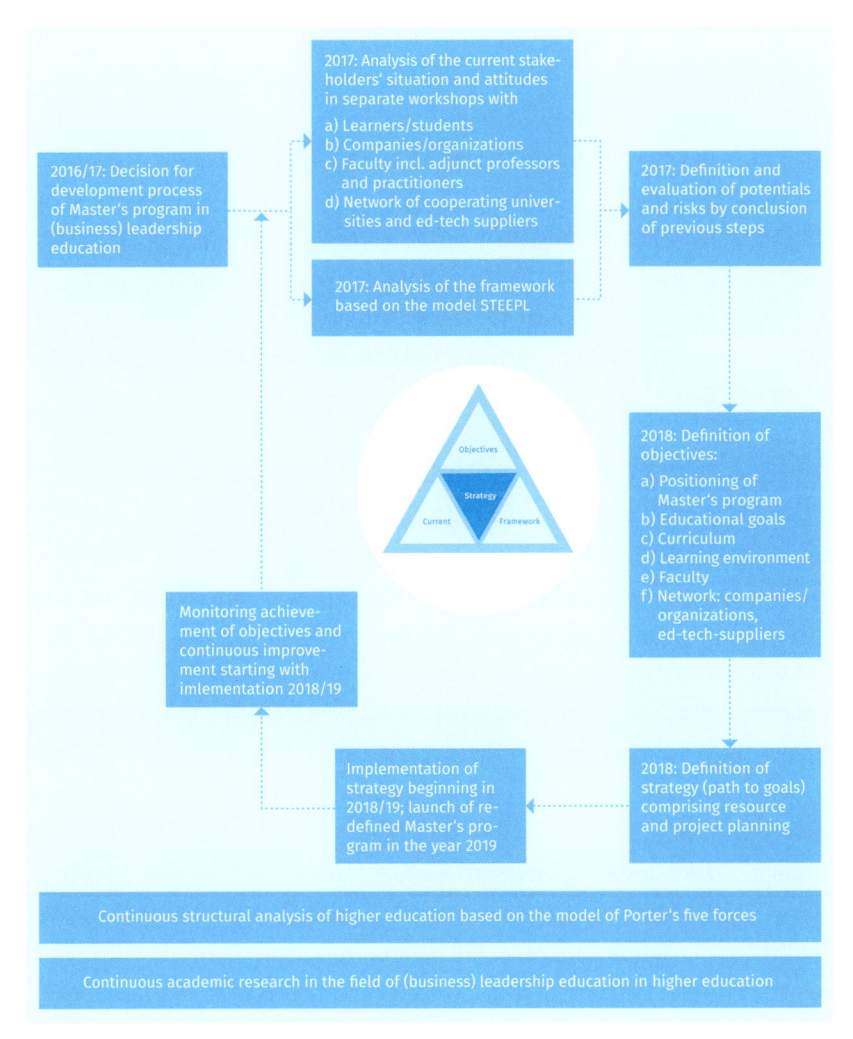

Figure 44.   Roadmap for sponsor of research.

Step 8:   Reentering the process.

The development process, which is originally structured in eight steps, is complemented in this roadmap by two additional steps, which have to be conducted systematically throughout the whole process. These two additional steps are:

Step 9:   A structural analysis of tertiary education based on the model of Porter's five forces has to be conducted. According to Porter (2004) "the state of competition in an industry depends on five basic competitive forces" (p. 3), which are the rivalry among existing industry competitors, potential new entrants, substitutes, bargaining power of suppliers and of buyers. In order to sustainably position sponsor's program on the market of tertiary education, the five competitive forces have to be monitored permanently.

Step 10: Based on the results of SIBE's current research project in leadership education in tertiary education, which comprises four individual sub-projects, further scientific research has to be conducted in order to systematically identify and close research gaps in this field of research.

To keep up with the times, SIBE, sponsor of this research, decided to be proactive and progressive in driving the future in business leadership education based on this research. Therefore, development process starts in 2016 / 2017 in order to launch the redefined Master's program in (business) leadership education with a pilot group in 2019, based on the results of a holistic analysis procedure. Depending on the results of analyzing the current situation and framework, aspirational goals will be set. Thus, SIBE's Master's program follows the principle of zeitgeist and market's maturity. Consequently, it has to be accepted that the Master's program has to be adapted in several rounds of development procedures. SIBE focus on developing creative personalities through project-based experiential learning pedagogy. Based on the assumption of SIBE's high competitiveness and long-term existence on the market of tertiary education along with the inherent principle of continuous development process, SIBE and SIBE's Master's program in (business) leadership education cannot reach a final stage. Thus, for SIBE the long-term horizon of 2030, which was set in Delphi-based scenario study, is only a rough time line in order to approach a long-term future horizon by a continuous development process starting in the present.

7. Limitations and future research

To obtain insights in the research topic of business leadership education in tertiary education, expert information and knowledge were aggregated and analyzed following a rigorous systematic research approach. The present RT Delphi study revealed the perception and views of the world of 105 international experts on business leadership education in tertiary education by the year 2030 from a multitude of stakeholder groups, such as providers (universities / business schools), participants / learners (students), purchasers (companies / employers), and politics. The multi-stakeholder panel embraces various perspectives, which are indicated by the high IQR values and thus the high dispersion. Numerous perspectives of the panelists on the surveyed projections were elaborated and discussed. Nevertheless, as with any research, some limitations of this RT Delphi study need to be mentioned. First, as a common phenomenon for any expert-based research methodology and due to a limited and not representative sample within this RT Delphi survey, the results may not be generalized for a bigger population. Second, only a limited number of projections were surveyed. Even though a vast amount of topics challenges business leadership education in tertiary education, the total number of projections was restricted in order to prevent response fatigue and to promote a substantial discussion between the experts. Third, the results of this RT Delphi survey were analyzed under holistic considerations (see chapter 4.3.5.1). Therefore, the four stakeholder groups were analyzed under equal conditions, irrespective of the gender. Moreover, it was decided to analyze a global panel as a total. On one hand, the sample size of some countries does not allow further statistical tests due to the limited number of cases. It was assumed that an analysis according to country groups would not provide further insights. On the other hand, business leadership education for graduates in Master in Management programs in tertiary education by the year 2030 was analyzed on a global perspective.

However, based on the analyses and results of this RT Delphi survey, the aim of research was the definition of objectives for the year 2030 and the creation of different future alternatives in order to be prepared for the future of business leadership education in tertiary education for graduates. Based on these elementary research results, future research could place greater emphasis on the details of curriculum implementation. Therefore, the professionalization of teaching staff for business leadership education in tertiary education for graduates is of high relevance along with development of suitable evaluation methods.

8. Conclusions Part 3

The principal purpose of this chapter was the definition of objectives for the year 2030 and the creation of different future alternatives to be prepared for the future of business leadership education in tertiary education for graduates. The scenarios of this research should support the main stakeholder groups of business leadership education in tertiary education in their decision-making process. The main stakeholder groups are providers (universities / business schools), participants (learners / students), purchasers (employers / companies), and politics. It was defined that a scenario in this context shall contain a rough proportion of technical and functional management versus personality and leadership aspects in education. The scenarios in this context do not illustrate market-relevant trends such as branding etc. for providers of tertiary education (universities / business schools). Quality, accreditation, and ranking issues are also not discussed separately, due to the presumption that those aspects can be taken for granted in successful providers by the year 2030.

In order to enhance the quality and validity of scenarios, Delphi-based scenario development was proposed. Two research questions provided the foundation for the design and implementation of this study. A suitable overall process to carry out the Delphi-based scenario study in this research was developed and applied. Therefore, the Delphi method was performed as basis for the subsequent scenario method, which was also the main structure of Part 3 of this work.

The Delphi process in this research was based on the classical procedure from the RAND Corporation, which is not only recognized and accepted, but also applied in various research articles. The Delphi process consisted of five steps. In a first step, projections were developed in workshop sessions with selected experts based on previous results of this research work. In a second step, appropriate experts were carefully selected in order to ensure validity and reliability. In a third step, the real-time Delphi survey was conducted to collect data following a pre-test. The quantitative and qualitative data were analyzed in step four in order to identify the contribution of the survey in the field of research and to create a basis for the scenario development process. Finally, the results were presented and discussed in general and separately for each projection according to the rubrics of the four stakeholder dimensions.

To summarize, a final set of 16 projections concerning four strategic perspectives of stakeholders on business leadership education in tertiary education was formulated and surveyed. 105 (13.78 %) experts from 13 countries and 16 industries participated in this RT Delphi survey. The multi-stakeholder panel embraces various perspectives, indicated by the high IQR values (average IQR of probability ratings was 30), and thus the high dispersion. The diverse panel provided a total number of 1,255 comments, which were a valuable contribution for the clarification of the given ratings. As this RT Delphi study involved quantitative and qualitative data collection, it was imperative to interpret these methods separately as well as together. Therefore, initially separate interpretations of each method were reported and an integrated overview of both methods was ultimately elaborately explained, as these methods together support the projection, provide less support to the projection or provide conflicting results, which uncovered various features of the projections that would have been lost, if only one method had been employed. Inferentially, employing two methods of analysis was a demanding task. However, this essentially served the prime purpose of the RT Delphi study, which was to build scenarios and wildcards for business leadership education in tertiary education for graduates based on these 16 projections.

On basis of the results of the Delphi survey, the scenario method was performed in five steps based on different methods of futures studies to ensure validity of results. Therefore, the results of the Delphi survey were prioritized by means of portfolio analysis, cross impact analysis and scenario axes analysis before scenario writing, discontinuity analysis and a final expert check.

The most important driving forces, crystallized by this set of multiple methods of futures studies in order to structure thinking and discussions about the future of business leadership education in tertiary education in Master in Management programs for graduates by the year 2030, derived from projection 1 (personality & leadership competencies) and projection 3 (E-Learning). They were plotted on two axes resulting in four different scenarios.

Using the comprehensive qualitative data provided by the Delphi expert panel along with additional secondary references, four narrative scenarios for business leadership education in tertiary education in Master's programs for graduates by the year 2030 were developed following different dimensions comprising potential systematic pedagogical approaches, through which the respective objectives can be achieved. The scenarios were presented to prepare the four stakeholder groups of business leadership education in tertiary education providers (universities / business schools), participants / learners (students), purchasers (employers / companies), and politics for decision-making and possible (extreme) situations in the future.

Based on the discussion and the results of this RT Delphi study along with additional inquiries, two wild cards, two extreme situations with low-probability and serious impact in case of occurrence, for business leadership education in tertiary education in Master's programs for graduates were distilled. Although their estimated probability of occurrence may be very low to zero, their (positive or negative) impact in case of occurrence may be extremely high to devastating. Therefore, those discontinuities were included in this research to underline both the necessity of breaking mental models and reduction of uncertainty and vulnerability.

The final transfer of scenarios prepares decision makers to apply theoretical results in their individual practice, based on a checklist for the different stakeholder groups and a roadmap for the sponsor of this research, which can obviously be transferred to any higher education institution.

Part 4: Conclusions

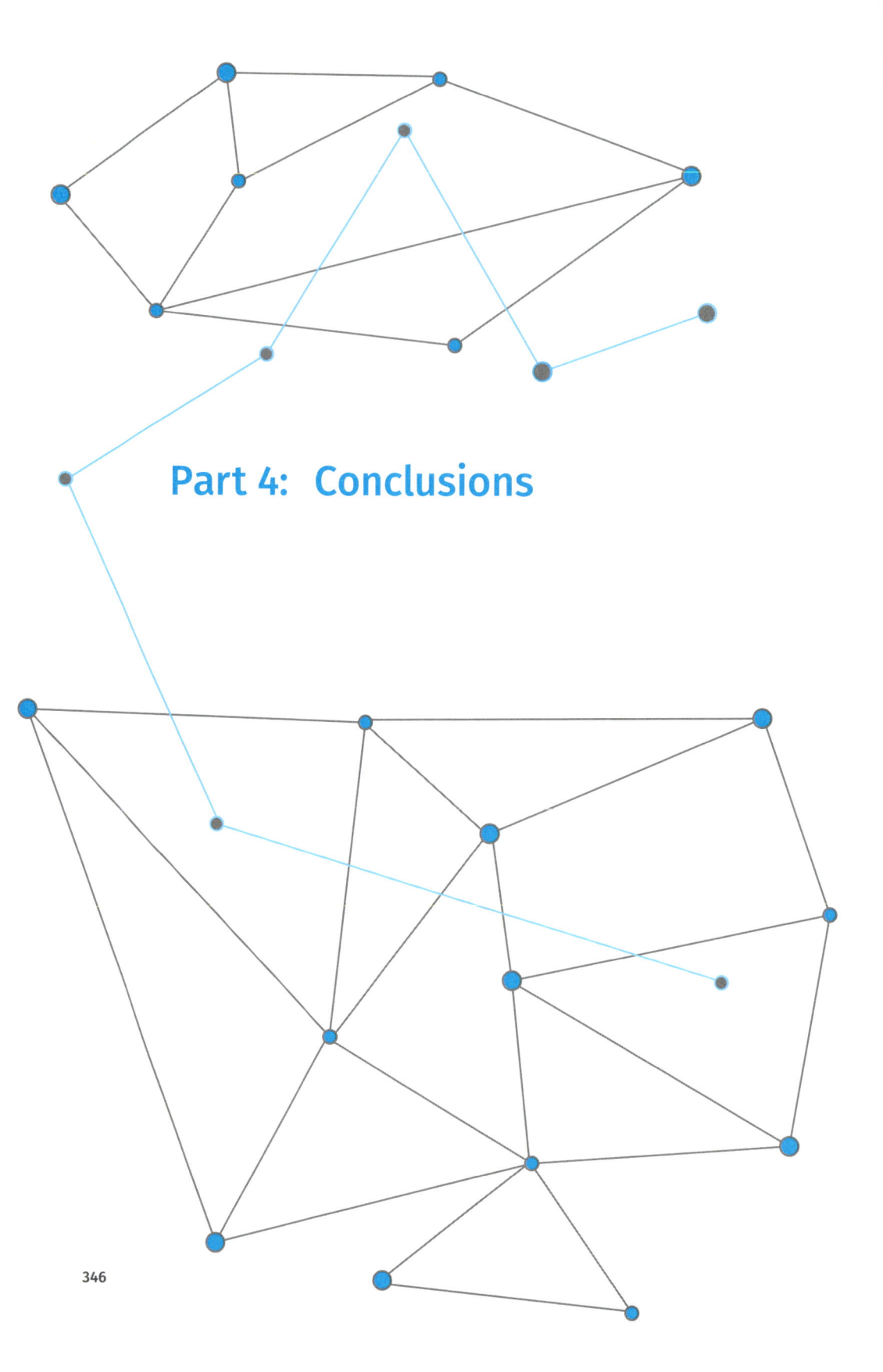

1. Conclusions and remarkable results

Based on the research background and with regard to the current development of the political, economic, social, and technological environment, business leadership education in tertiary education for graduates had to be scrutinized and redesigned in order to cope with the challenges of the 21st century. The overall aim of research was to contribute to the further improvement and continuously development of business leadership education in tertiary education to become state of the art, which was concretized on a two-fold level and structured in Parts 2 and 3 of this thesis. This thesis followed a rigorous research design and process.

In Part 2 of this research, it was aimed to introduce the principles of business leadership education in tertiary education for graduates based on thorough literature review. Therefore, it was indispensable to obtain an overview of the meaning of business leadership. Furthermore, the research aimed at uncovering how business leadership education in tertiary education is practiced in exemplary Master's programs for graduates. Two pivotal research questions guided the design and implementation of this chapter.

In order to answer the research questions, the most prevalent approaches to leadership were elucidated. As an immense number and variety of definitions and theoretical approaches to leadership exist, a choice was made. Thus, light was shed on the most prevalent approaches derive from the discipline of psychology. Despite their valuable contributions to leadership research, various strengths and (methodological) shortcomings were outlined. Moreover, it was pointed out that the (traditional) approaches reflect merely a fragmentary rather than a holistic perspective on leadership, failing to measure leaders' performance. Also the assessment center that belongs to the most popular diagnostic procedures was described. Considering ACs from a positive point of view, their main purpose may lie in a culture-oriented selection of (potential) business leaders, when assessors are (higher) leaders. Despite improvements, they are unable to predict leaders' future job performance, therefore rendering the reliance on just ACs to select future leaders seems to be insufficient and in many instances misleading.

Moreover, findings of different disciplines mainly from human ethology and organizational sciences, were compiled due to their high impact on leadership, and in order to obtain a comprehensive overview on the studied topic. Thus, as well as personal leadership behavior, also entrepreneurial leadership plays a vital role in business leadership.

A contemporary and holistic model of business leadership was developed based on previous findings and on exogenous influencing factors on (business) environment. This holistic model integrates both the business perspective as well as the perspective on the leader's individual personality. Moreover, the business leader is not considered as being isolated, but rather as acting in a complex sociocultural context with its multitude of influential factors.

This contemporary and holistic understanding of business leadership in a dynamic environment laid the foundation for a contemporary human-centered concept of business leadership education in tertiary education, deeply rooted in humanistic philosophy. Pivotal goal of this concept is the fostering of individuals throughout their entire life to develop their personalities, which is demonstrated by their actions and contributions to nature, other humans, society, organizations etc.

Against this background, the segment of tertiary education in general and the discipline of business leadership education in particular were examined; both have to cope with major trends and challenges on a global scale. Based on current debates, redesigning business leadership education in tertiary education from a pedagogical point of view was inevitable. To do so, the pedagogical infrastructure for business leadership education in tertiary education, the *curriculum*, was examined.

In order to answer the first research question of this work – how business leadership education in Master's programs for graduates in tertiary education shall be designed –, seven main principles were proposed for a curriculum of business leadership education in Master's programs in tertiary education. The seven principles are deeply rooted in theory and reflect the main questions that need to be answered with a didactic approach. The general principles of academic freedom, unity of research and teaching and each higher education institution's individual culture and (research) orientation were respected. Thus, the seven principles are conceived to serve as a kind of orientation and guidelines for curriculum design in business leadership education in tertiary education for graduates.

Synthesizing the essential results of curriculum design based on the seven proposed principles, two findings are established. Firstly, business leadership education in tertiary education has to focus on the student's familiarization with the scientific world on one hand, and the individual student's (creative) personality and its competency development on the other. Secondly, curriculum with its elements – i.e. educational contents, educational methodologies, educational settings, and evaluation – therefore has to facilitate a consistent pedagogical infrastructure that nurtures development of the individual student's business leader personality. Such an infrastructure is characterized by competency-based education. As competency-based education is conceived as an umbrella term, various implementations are possible. Each higher education institution has to find its own way best suited for its respective (research) orientation and (institutional) culture.

Based on previous findings, exemplary Master's programs in contemporary tertiary education were evaluated in order to answer the second research question of this work. A comprehensible systematic evaluation approach following strict rules was carried out to meet the demands of qualitative research. Considering the detailed analysis and its results, it was concluded that each program meets high quality demands demonstrated through at least one 'seal of approval' granted by AACSB. Moreover, each program has a distinct orientation, providing a highly attractive educational opportunity.

Nevertheless, crystallizing the essential results of the evaluation procedure yielded two findings. Firstly, exemplary Master's programs in the field of business leadership education for graduates focus on imparting functional management knowledge and development of management qualifications / skills in order to foster students' employability. Secondly, this educational approach is diametrically opposed to the earlier findings of this research. Hence, (creative) personality was revealed as the superior educational ideal, fostered through competency-based education.

In the subsequent Part 3 of this work, it was aimed to define objectives and create different future alternatives (scenarios) for the long-term future (2030) of business leadership education in tertiary education, which should comprise potentially systematic pedagogical approaches, through which the respective objectives can be achieved. Two pivotal research questions guided the design and implementation of this chapter.

In order to answer the research questions and, at the same time, enhance the quality and validity of different alternative futures, the Delphi-based scenario development was proposed. The scenarios of this research should support the main stakeholder groups of business leadership education in tertiary education in their decision-making process. The main stakeholder groups are providers (universities / business schools), participants (learners / students), purchasers (employers / companies), and politics. It was defined that a scenario in this context shall contain a rough proportion of technical and functional management versus personality and leadership aspects in education. The scenarios in this context do not illustrate market-relevant trends such as branding etc. for providers of tertiary education (universities / business schools). Quality, accreditation, and ranking issues are also not discussed separately, due to the presumption that those aspects can be taken for granted in successful providers by the year 2030.

A suitable, overall process to carry out the Delphi-based scenario study in this research was developed and applied, wherein the Delphi method was performed as basis for the subsequent scenario method. Thus, the Delphi process in this research was based on the classical procedure from the RAND Corporation, which is not only recognized and accepted, but also applied in various research articles.

To summarize, a final set of 16 projections concerning four strategic perspectives of stakeholders on business leadership education in tertiary education was formulated and surveyed. 105 experts (13.78 %) from 13 countries and 16 industries participated in this RT Delphi survey. The multi-stakeholder panel embraces various perspectives, indicated by the high IQR values (average IQR of probability ratings was 30), and thus the high dispersion. The diverse panel provided a total number of 1,255 comments, which were a valuable contribution for the clarification of the given ratings. As this RT Delphi study involved quantitative and qualitative data collection, it was imperative to interpret these methods separately as well as together. Therefore, initially separate interpretations of each method were reported and an integrated overview of both methods was ultimately elaborately explained, as these methods together support the projection, provide less support to the projection or provide conflicting results, which uncovered various features of the projections that would have been lost, if only one method had been employed. Inferentially, employing two methods of analysis was a demanding task. However, this essentially served the prime purpose of the RT Delphi study, which was to build scenarios and wildcards based on these 16 projections.

On basis of the results of the Delphi survey, the scenario method was performed according to strict rules. A set of multiple methods of futures studies was applied to ensure the validity of results. Therefore, the results of the Delphi survey were prioritized by means of portfolio analysis, cross impact analysis and scenario axes analysis before scenario writing, discontinuity analysis and a final expert check.

The most important driving forces, crystallized by this set of multiple methods of futures studies in order to structure thinking and discussions about the future of business leadership education in tertiary education in Master in Management programs for graduates by the year 2030, derived from projection 1 (personality & leadership competencies) and projection 3 (E-Learning). They were plotted on two axes:

> X-axis: Knowledge, Qualification, Competencies & Leadership Personality with the two poles of "knowledge is power" and "conspicuous by action" and
> Y-axis: Digitization with the two poles of "face-to-face" and "online"

resulting in the following four different scenarios:

> Scenario 1:
> "2030: Management education 10.0"
> Scenario 2:
> "2030: Leadership trailblazer – grasping the 24 / 7 e-learning landscape & experiencing real-world settings"
> Scenario 3:
> "2030: Management education in the armchair"
> Scenario 4:
> "2030: Leadership explorer – coping with the blended learning environment online and off & exploring real-world settings"

Using the comprehensive qualitative data provided by the Delphi expert panel along with additional secondary references, four narrative scenarios for business leadership education in tertiary education in Master's programs for graduates by the year 2030 were developed following different dimensions. The scenarios were presented to prepare the four stakeholder groups of business leadership education in tertiary education providers (universities / business schools), participants / learners (students), purchasers (employers / companies), and politics for decision-making and different future alternatives.

Based on the discussion and the results of this RT Delphi study along with additional inquiries, two wild cards, i.e. two extreme situations with low-probability and serious impact in case of occurrence, for business leadership education in tertiary education in Master's programs for graduates were synthesized. The first wild card deals with the eradication of Master's programs, while the second focuses on structural discontinuities on the (higher) education market.

The final transfer of scenarios prepares decision makers to apply theoretical results in their individual practice, based on a checklist for the different stakeholder groups and a roadmap for higher education institutions.

Thus, by following a rigorous research design and process and answering the four pivotal research questions, the aim of the research was achieved.

2. Contributions of research

Reflecting this thesis, eight pivotal contributions of this research shall be synthesized:

1. Holistic concept of business leadership:

    Based on previous findings of traditional and interdisciplinary considerations on leadership approaches, sound theory and influential external factors on (business) environment, a contemporary and holistic concept of business leadership was developed. This holistic concept comprises both the business perspective as well as the perspective on the leader's individual personality. Moreover, the business leader is not considered as being isolated, but rather as acting in a complex sociocultural context with its multitude of influential factors. Although the term *leadership* in this research is largely concerned with leadership in the business context, the holistic concept of business leadership can easily be adapted to other domains by considering the domain's specific mission and characteristics.

2. Educational cycle:

   A contemporary holistic human-centered concept of education was developed by Faix and Kisgen. It allows individuals to develop their personalities. This concept of education is deeply rooted in humanistic tradition, enriched by contemporary pedagogical perspectives. This approach of education is aimed at the personal potential of the individual, to convert it into actions and render it apparent in actions (see also Faix et al., 2017a).

3. Seven principles for curriculum design:

   Seven main principles were proposed for a curriculum of business leadership education in Master's programs in tertiary education. The seven principles – namely educational goals, personality as educational ideal, educational contents, educational methodologies, educational settings, evaluation, and financing – are deeply rooted in theory and reflect the main questions that need to be answered with a didactic approach. The general principles of academic freedom, unity of research and teaching and each higher education institution's individual culture and (research) orientation were respected. Thus, the seven principles are conceived to serve as a kind of orientation and guidelines for curriculum design. They can easily be adapted to other disciplines by considering the discipline's specific characteristics.

4. Systematic evaluation procedure for Master's programs from a pedagogical perspective:

   Based on sound theory, and particularly based on the seven principles for curriculum design and its respective sub-categories, a systematic evaluation procedure for exemplary Master's programs in contemporary business leadership education in tertiary education was developed. A comprehensible systematic evaluation approach following strict rules was carried out to meet the demands of qualitative research. This evaluation procedure can also be easily adapted to other disciplines by considering the discipline's specific characteristics.

5. Business leadership education in tertiary education means development of personality and the individual's leadership competencies:

   Considering the seven principles and the evaluation procedure, a gap between theoretical considerations on business leadership education in tertiary education and the practical implementation in exemplary contemporary Master's programs emerged. Sound theoretical considerations clearly yielded that business leadership education in tertiary education has to focus on the student's familiarization with the scientific world on one hand, and the individual (creative) personality and competency development of the student on the other. A curriculum with its different elements has to facilitate a consistent pedagogical infrastructure that nurtures development of the individual student's business leader personality. Such an infrastructure is characterized by competency-based education. Nevertheless, the evaluation procedure shows that exemplary Master's programs in the field of business leadership education for graduates focus on imparting functional management knowledge and development of management qualifications / skills in order to foster students' employability, but do not (adequately) promote competency development of future leaders. Furthermore, a graduate's future job performance as a leader cannot be predicted based on successful completion of contemporary business leadership education in tertiary education. This confirms the initially formulated (Part 1, 1) assumptions.

6. The Delphi-based scenario study to develop four scenarios and two wildcards for the long-term future (2030) of business leadership education in tertiary education:

   In order to enhance the quality and validity of different alternative futures (scenarios), the Delphi-based scenario development was conducted. Its objective was the development of the long-term future (2030) for business leadership education in tertiary education. Four different scenarios were developed based on the integrated analysis of quantitative and qualitative results of the cross-country real-time Delphi survey and a subsequent set of multiple methods of futures studies. The scenarios comprise potential systematic pedagogical approaches. Furthermore, two wildcards were developed to prepare for disruptive and unexpected developments. Considering different future alternatives was important as it was intended to support the main stakeholder groups in their decision-making process and prepare them to cope with different potential future settings.

7. Research gap is closed:

   Considering the field of research initially described (see Part 1, chapter 3), a profound theoretical and empirical analysis to conceptualize a holistic educational concept of business leadership education in tertiary education for graduates was not found. After completion and publication of this research project, the aim to close the research gap in the field of business leadership education in tertiary education is achieved.

8. Contributions to business leadership education in tertiary education:

   After completion and publication of this research project, the aim to contribute to the further improvement and continuous development of business leadership education in tertiary education for graduates to become state of the art is achieved.

3. Limitations and future research

This thesis followed a rigorous research design and process in order to answer the four pivotal research questions and achieve the research aim of this thesis regarding business leadership education in tertiary education for graduates. Nevertheless, as with any research, in spite of the notable findings and contributions, the discussions in this research have some limitations and generate questions for future research. Considering Parts 2 and 3 of this work, the main shortcomings and recommendations for future research shall be reflected and summarized.

Firstly, the holistic model and definition of business leadership, comprising both the business perspective as well as the perspective on the leader's individual personality, was developed based on previous findings of traditional and interdisciplinary considerations on leadership approaches, sound theory, and influential external factors on (business) environment. Along with the holistic model and definition of business leadership, concrete and specific KPIs were developed and proposed in order to evaluate the performance of (potential) business leaders. The verification of the previous assumption could be a project for future research.

Secondly, theoretical considerations on the conceptualization of business leadership education in tertiary education are based on a careful selection of the vast amount of existing literature. The state of the art of existing research literature on business leadership education and its associated topics was integrated as far as possible and necessary. It is important for future research to consider any newly released research literature in order to continuously develop business leadership education.

Thirdly, considering the evaluation procedure of exemplary Master's programs, deep insights into the curriculum design of exemplary Master's programs were provided and its nucleus uncovered. Nevertheless, as a common phenomenon for any exemplary research and due to a limited and not representative sample within this research, the results may not be generalized for all Master's programs in business leadership education. Moreover, information was – at least partly – difficult to obtain and was mainly based on official institutions' websites and / or program-specific documents available through official websites, which, in turn, are created for profiling and promotion. Although it may be assumed (hypothesized) that main findings of this research will not change – at least not significantly, future research could focus on a larger scale, using mixed-method approaches in order to obtain meaningful representative results.

Furthermore, to obtain insights in the research topic of business leadership education in tertiary education, expert information and knowledge were aggregated and analyzed following a rigorous systematic research approach. Nevertheless, as a common phenomenon for any expert-based research methodology and due to a limited and not representative sample within this RT Delphi survey, the results may not be generalized for a bigger population. Moreover, only a limited number of projections were surveyed. Even though a vast amount of topics challenges business leadership education in tertiary education, the total number of projections was restricted in order to prevent response fatigue and to promote a substantial discussion between the experts. Furthermore, this RT Delphi survey was analyzed under holistic considerations. Therefore, the four stakeholder groups were analyzed under equal conditions, irrespective of the gender. Moreover, it was decided to analyze a global panel as a total. On one hand, the sample size of some countries does not allow further statistical tests due to the limited number of cases. It was assumed that an analysis according to country groups would not provide further insights. On the other hand, business leadership education for graduates in Master in Management programs in tertiary education by the year 2030 was analyzed on a global perspective. Based on these elementary research results, future research could place greater emphasis on the details of curriculum implementation. Therefore, the professionalization of teaching staff for business leadership education in tertiary education for graduates is of high relevance along with development of suitable evaluation methods.

Finally, the Doctor of Business Administration (DBA) emerged as a new trend in business leadership education in tertiary education. The DBA program combines education and research and has to be, based on the findings of this research, a subject of future research.

4. Practical implications

The insights gained from this research on the future of business leadership education in tertiary education for graduates were manifold and of high relevance on a multidimensional level for the main stakeholder groups providers (universities / business schools), participants (students), purchasers (employers / companies), and politics. Thus, this research provides an in-depth understanding of the meaning of business leadership based on traditional and interdisciplinary approaches. A holistic concept of business leadership that can be adapted to the individual context is provided. Based on this broad understanding of business leadership, concrete and specific KPIs were developed in order to evaluate the performance of (potential) business leaders. Those KPIs are relevant for individuals and organizations in order to select and develop (potential) business leaders and / or to evaluate business leaders. By directing the company's working processes for the selection and development of (potential) business leaders to the holistic model of business leadership education and the KPIs developed above, one could hypothesize that the performance of (potential) leaders can be better predicted, rather than based on existing (selection) procedures. Evaluating KPIs developed within the model of business leadership for the selection and development of (potential) business leaders means to base ones decision on findings from previous works resulting from real-world settings vs. artificial situations created in ACs. In order to obtain meaningful results, it may be advisable to expose (potential) business leaders to real-world projects, which are unique and limited in time, in order to solve corporate business challenges that may contribute to the organization's value and (sustainable) future. Thus, real-world business projects are indicators for the (potential) business leaders' performance in uncertain and complex situations where self-organized action is indispensable. Thereby, goal identification, goal setting, and achievement procedure may be evaluated along with the project's contribution to the company's value and future as well as the business leader's competencies. However, previous assumptions have to be verified by future research.

Furthermore, Faix's and Kisgen's contemporary holistic human-centered concept of education aimed at the personal-potential of the individual, to convert it into actions and render it apparent in actions in order to allow individuals to develop their personalities can be transferred to any institution of (higher) education. Such a transfer to any institution of higher education is also possible for the seven principles for curriculum design of business leadership education in tertiary education for graduates and the subsequent evaluation procedure that were elaborated. In turn, this knowledge base provides the stakeholder groups, participants, and employers with the relevant information for their decision-making process. For the stakeholder group politics, the seven principles and the evaluation procedure may provide valuable information for setting the framework for tertiary education particularly with regard to political, legal, and financial conditions.

However, different alternative futures and wildcards for the long-term future (2030) of business leadership education in tertiary education for graduates were developed in order to support the main stakeholder groups in their decision-making process and to prepare them to cope with different potential future settings. Nevertheless, "[a] scenario is not an end in itself; it only becomes meaningful when its results and implications are embodied in real action." (Godet, 2000, p. 19 f.) To support and promote transfer to stakeholders' practice, a checklist was compiled based on stakeholders' perspectives and motives. Following the main dimensions, which guide the scenario stories, relevant key questions were formulated for each stakeholder group. By answering the key questions, stakeholders build a connection to their individual practice.

With respect to the sponsor of this research, the main implications shall be roughly outlined. Thus, the emerging results of this research were permanently summarized, presented, and discussed with the sponsor during the entire research process. Main findings of theoretical considerations and evaluation procedure in Part 2 of this work were already – as far as necessary – implemented and considered in the relaunch of the curriculum, i.e. supplementing educational goals and educational contents. The employment report as evaluation tool on a macro level was developed based on the recommendations of this research. Considering the findings of Part 3 of this work, a roadmap was elaborated and discussed, which can obviously be transferred to any institution of (higher) education. The roadmap presents a development process based on a holistic analysis procedure in order to launch the redefined Master's program in (business) leadership education. Therefore, it is required to analyze the current situation and framework, potentials and risks. Based on sponsor's individual situation influenced by multiple external factors, a decision about the future orientation and the objectives has to be made based on the different future scenarios and wildcards that are provided by this research. In order to implement the respective scenario successfully, it is proposed to involve all relevant internal and external stakeholders in the transformation process, e.g. by workshops, from the very beginning.

Finally, based on the work of Graf and Klein (2003), it has to be pointed out that considering potential alternatives impacts the corporate culture.

References

AACSB International (2010). *Business Schools on an Innovation Mission. Report of the AACSB International Task Force on Business Schools and Innovation.* Tampa: AASCB International.

Aalto University (n.d.). Master's Programme in Management and International Business Retrieved August 15, 2016, from http://www.aalto.fi/en/

Aalto University Design Factory (ADF, 2015). A year at Aalto Design Factory. Publication 2015. Retrieved August 19, 2016, from https://dl.dropboxusercontent.com/u/16170771/www.adf.fi/linked%20files/For%20Media/Publication%202015_web%20issuu.pdf

Albright, J. (2016). Transdisciplinarity in Curricular Theory and Practice. In D. Wyse, L. Hayward, & J. Pandya (Eds.), *The SAGE Handbook of Curriculum, Pedagogy and Assessment.* Volume 1 (pp. 525-543). Los Angeles: SAGE.

Alexander, R. J. (2000). *Culture and Pedagogy: International Comparisons in Primary education.* Oxford: Blackwell.

Allen, E., & Seaman, C. (2007). Likert Scales and Data Analyses. *Quality Progress*, 64-65. Retrieved January 16, 2016, from http://asq.org/quality-progress/2007/07/statistics/likert-scales-and-data-analyses.html

Allen, I. E., & Seaman, J. (2013). Changing Course: Ten Years of Tracking Online Education in the United States. San Francisco: *Babson Survey Research Group and Quahog Research Group,* LLC. Retrieved January 2, 2016, from http://www.onlinelearningsurvey.com/reports/changingcourse.pdf

Altbach, P. G. (2016). Patterns of Higher Education Development. In M. N. Bastedo, P. G. Altbach, & P. C. Gumport (Eds.), *American Higher Education in the Twenty-First Century. Social, Political, and Economic Challenges* (4th ed., pp. 191-211). Baltimore: Johns Hopkins University Press.

Altbach, P. G., Reisberg, L., & Rumbley, L. E. (2009). *Trends in Global Higher Education: Tracking and Academic Revolution. A Report Prepared for the UNESCO 2009 World Conference on Higher Education.* Paris: UNESCO.

Anger, C., Plünnecke, A., & Schmidt, J. (2010). *Bildungsrenditen in Deutschland – Einflussfaktoren, politische Optionen und volkswirtschaftliche Effekte.* Köln: Institut der Deutschen Wirtschaft Köln.

Armstrong, R. L. (1987). The midpoint on a five point Likert - type scale. *Perceptual and motor skills, 64* (2), 359-362.

Arnold, R. (2012). *Ich lerne, also bin ich. Eine systemisch-konstruktivistische Didaktik* (2. Aufl.). Heidelberg: Carl Auer.

Arnold, R., & Erpenbeck, J. (2014). *Wissen ist keine Kompetenz. Dialoge zur Kompetenzreifung.* Grundlagen der Berufs- und Erwachsenenbildung. Band 77. Baltmannsweiler: Schneider Verlag Hohengehren.

Arvey, R. D., Rotundo, M., Johnson, W., Zhang, Z., & McGue, M. (2006). The determinants of leadership role occupancy: Genetic and personality factors. *Leadership Quarterly, 17,* 1-20.

Arvey, R. D., Zhang, Z., Avolio, B. J., & Krueger, R. F. (2007). Developmental and genetic determinants of leadership role occupancy among females. *Journal of Applied Psychology,* 92(3), 693-706.

Ash, S. L., & Clayton, P. H. (2004). The Articulated Learning: An Approach to Guided Reflection and Assessment. *Innovative Higher Education, 29*(2), 137-154.

Ashkenas, R., & Hausman, R. (2016, April 12). Leadership Development Should Focus on Experiments. *Harvard Business Review.* Retrieved April 14, 2016, from https://hbr.org/2016/04/leadership-development-should-focus-on-experiments

Atwater, L., & Carmeli, A. (2009). Leader-member exchange, feelings of energy, and involvement in creative work. *Leadership Quarterly*, *20*, 264-275.

Autio, T. (2014). The Internationalization of Curriculum Research. In W. F. Pinar (Ed.), *International Handbook of Curriculum Research* (2nd ed.). New York: Routledge Taylor & Francis.

Bailey, A., Henry, T., McBride, L., & Puckett, J. (2011). Unleashing the Potential of Technology in Education. *Boston Consulting Group*, Boston.

Bañuls, V. A., & Turoff, M. (2011). Scenario Construction via Delphi and Cross-Impact Analysis. *Technological Forecasting and Social Change*, 78 (9), 1579–1602.

Bañuls, V. A. & Salmeron, J. L. (2007). A scenario-based assessment model – SBAM. *Technological Forecasting and Social Change,* 74 (6), 750-762.

Baregheh, A., Rowley, J., & Sambrook, S. (2009). Towards a multidisciplinary definition of innovation, *Management Decision, 47* (8), 1323-1339.

Barnett, R., & Coate, K. (2005). *Engaging the curriculum in higher education*. Berkshire: Society for Research in Higher Education & Open University Press.

Bartz, O. (2007). *Der Wissenschaftsrat. Entwicklungslinien der Wissenschaftspolitik in der Bundesrepublik Deutschland 1957-2007.* Stuttgart: Franz Steiner Verlag.

Basic Law for the Federal Republic of Germany in the revised version published in the Federal Law Gazette Part III, classification number 100-1, as last amended by the Act of 11 July 2012 (Federal Law Gazette I p. 1478). Retrieved July 30, 2016, from https://www.gesetze-im-internet.de/englisch_gg/englisch_gg.html#p0030

Bass, B. M. (1990). *Bass & Stogdill's Handbook of Leadership: Theory, Research, and Managerial Applications* (3rd ed.). New York: The Free Press.

Bass, B. M. (2007). Concepts of Leadership. In: R. P. Vecchio (Ed.), *Leadership. Understanding the Dynamics of Power and Influence in Organizations*, 2nd ed. (pp. 3-22). Notre Dame: University of Notre Dame Press.

Bauer, M. (2000). Classical content analysis: a review. In M. Bauer, & G. Gaskell (eds.), *Qualitative Researching with Text, Image and Sound - A Handbook* (pp. 131-150). London: Sage.

Bauer, W., & Karapidis, A. (2013). *Kompetenzmanagement in deutschen Unternehmen 2012/2013. Ergebnisse der empirischen Breitenstudie Fraunhofer IAO.* Stuttgart: Fraunhofer-Institut für Arbeitswissenschaft und Organisation.

Baum, S., Ma, J., & Payea, K. (2013). Education Pays 2013. Benefits of Higher Education for Individuals and Society. *Trends in Higher Education Series*. Retrieved August 6, 2016, from https://trends.collegeboard.org/sites/default/files/education-pays-2013-full-report.pdf

Beall, J. (2013). *Post-2015 agenda: why the UN must include higher education.* Retrieved August 2, 2016, from https://www.britishcouncil.org/voices-magazine/un-includes-higher-education-post-2015-development

Béchard, J. P., & Grégoire, D. (2005). Understanding Teaching Models in Entrepreneurship for Higher Education. In P. Kÿro, & C. Carrier (Eds.), *The Dynamics of Learning Entrepreneurship in a Cross-cultural University Context* (pp. 104-134). Tampere: Faculty of Education, University of Tampere.

Becker, M., & Gracht, H. v. d. (2014). *Lernen im Jahr 2030. Von Bildungsavataren, virtuellen Klassenräumen und Gehirn-Doping in der Führungs- und Fachkräfteentwicklung. Szenarien auf Basis einer Delphi-Experten-Befragung.* Berlin: Institute of Corporate Education e.V. (incore).

Becker, N., Höft, S., Holzenkamp, M., & Spinath, F. M. (2011). The Predictive Validity of Assessment Centers in German-Speaking Regions. A Meta-Analysis. *Journal of Personnel Psychology, 10*(2), 61-69.

Benner, D., & Stępkowski, D. (2011). Die Höhle als Metapher zur Beschreibung von Bildungsprozessen – eine Studie zur Transformation von Platons Höhlengleichnis in bildungstheoretisch relevanten Diskursen. In O. Zlatkin-Troitschanskaia (Hrsg.), *Stationen Empirischer Bildungsforschung. Traditionslinien und Perspektiven* (pp. 91-104). Wiesbaden: VS Verlag.

Bennis, W. G., & Nanus, B. (1985). *Leaders: The strategies for taking charge.* New York: Harper & Row.

Biggs, J., & Tang, C. (2007). *Teaching for Quality Learning at University* (3rd ed.). Berkshire: McGraw Hill, Society for Research into Higher Education & Open University Press.

Bijedić, T. (2013). Entwicklung unternehmerischer Persönlichkeit im Rahmen der Entrepreneurship Education. Didaktische Lehr-Lern-Konzeption und empirische Analyse für die Sekundarstufe II. *Flensburger Schriften zu Unternehmertum und Mittelstand. Band 4.* München und Mering: Rainer Hampp Verlag.

Björklund, T., Clavert, M., Kirjavainen, S., Laakso, M., & Luukkonen, S. (2011). *Aalto University Design Factory in the eyes of its community.* Retrieved August 22, 2016, from https://dl.dropboxusercontent.com/u/16170771/www.adf.fi/linked%20files/ADF_study_report_2011.pdf

Blumenthal, I., Djalali, A., Faix, W. G., Horne, A., Keck, G., Kisgen, S.,... Wittmann, P. (2012). *Werte. Bildung. Ethikkodex.* Stuttgart: Steinbeis-Edition. [Blumenthal et al., 2012a]

Blumenthal, I., Faix, W. G., Hochrein, V., Horne, A., Keck, G., Lenz, R., Mergenthaler, J. & Sax, S. (2012). Über einige Fronten des War for Talents. In W. G. Faix (Hrsg.), *Kompetenz. Festschrift Prof. Dr. John Erpenbeck zum 70. Geburtstag*. Band 4 (p. 491-539). Stuttgart: Steinbeis-Edition. [Blumenthal et al., 2012b]

BMBF (Hrsg.) (1998). *Delphi-Befragung 1996/1998. Potentiale und Dimensionen der Wissensgesellschaft – Auswirkungen auf Bildungsprozesse und Bildungsstrukturen. Integrierter Abschlußbericht*. München.

Boam, R., & Sparrow, P. (1992). *Designing and Achieving Competency*. London: McGraw-Hill.

Bologna Declaration (1999). Retrieved July 20, 2016, from http://www.magna-charta.org/resources/files/text-of-the-bologna-declaration

Boud, D., & Walker, D. (1991). Experience and Learning: Reflection at Work. EAE600 Adults Learning in the Workplace: Part A. Geelong: Deakin University.

Bourdieu, P. (1990). Principles for reflecting on the curriculum. *The Curriculum Journal*, *1*(3), 307-314.

Bourdieu, P., & Wacquant, L. (1999). On the Cunning of Imperialist Reason. *Theory, Culture & Society*, *16*(1), 41-58.

Bouroujerdi, R. D., & Wolf, C. (2015). *Emerging Theme Radar. What if I told you... Themes, Dreams and Flying Machines*. Retrieved December 21, 2015, from http://www.goldmansachs.com/our-thinking/pages/macroeconomic-insights-folder/what-if-i-told-you/report.pdf

Bowen, G. A. (2009). Document analysis as a qualitative research method. *Qualitative Research Journal*, *9(2)*, 27-40.

Bowden, J., & Masters, G. N. (1993). *Implications for higher education of a competency-based approach to education and training*. Canberra: AGPS.

Boyatzis, R. (1982). The *Competent Manager – A Model for Effective Performance.* New York: John Wiley & Sons.

Bradburn, N. M., Sudman, S., & Wansink, B. (2004). *Asking Questions. The Definitive Guide to Questionnaire Design – For Market Research, Political Polls, and Social and Health Questionnaires* (Revised edition). San Francisco: Jossey-Bass.

Braßler, M., & Dettmers, J. (2016). Interdisziplinäres Problembasiertes Lernen – Kompetenzen fördern, Zukunft gestalten. *Zeitschrift für Hochschulentwicklung, 11*(3), 17-37.

Braukmann, U., Bijedic, T., & Schneider, D. (2008). „Unternehmerische Persönlichkeit" – eine theoretische Rekonstruktion und nominaldefinitorische Konturierung. *Schumpeter Discussion Papers.* Wuppertal: Schumpeter School of Business and Economics, University of Wuppertal.

Brinker, T., & Temp, P. (Hrsg.) (2012). *Einführung in die Studiengangsentwicklung.* Bielefeld: Bertelsmann.

Brodbeck, F. C., Maier, G. W., & Frey, D. (2002). Führungstheorien. In D. Frey, & M. Irle (Hrsg.), *Theorien der Sozialpsychologie. Band II. Gruppen-, Interaktions- und Lerntheorien* (2. vollst. überarb. u. erw. Aufl., pp. 329-365). Bern: Verlag Hans Huber.

Brogden, H. E. (1949). When testing pays off. *Personnel Psychology, 2,* 171-183.

Brungardt, C. (1996). The Making of Leaders: A Review of the Research in Leadership Development and Education. *The Journal of Leadership Studies, 3*(3), 81-95.

Bundesministerium für Wirtschaft und Energie (BMWi, 2016). Nationales Reformprogramm 2016. Berlin: BMWi.

Bundeswehr (2014). *Studieren bei der Bundeswehr.* Retrieved July 11, 2015, from https://www.bundeswehr.de/portal/a/bwde/!ut/p/c4/04_8K8xLLM9MSSzPy8xBz9CP3I5EyrpHK9pPKUVL3sxKKizNSiVL3SvMyy1KLizJLE1JLUPP2CbEdFAHzXQ_o!/

Burke, L. M., & Butler, S. M. (2012). Accreditation: Removing the Barrier to Higher Education Reform. *The Heritage Foundation. Backgrounder*, No. 2728. Retrieved April 9, 2016, from http://thf_media.s3.amazonaws.com/2012/pdf/bg2728.pdf

Burns, J. M. (1978). *Leadership.* New York: Harper & Row.

Burns, A., & Burns, R. (2008). *Basic Marketing Research* (Second ed.). New Jersey: Pearson Education.

Businessweek (2008): *The Debate Room. The Financial Crises: Blame B-schools. Business schools are largely responsible for the U.S. financial crises. Pro or con?* November 2008. Retrieved January 3, 2016, from, http://www.businessweek.com/debateroom/archives/2008/11/us_financial_cr.html

Campbell, G. S. (1971). Relevance of Signal Monitoring to Delphi/Cross-impact Studies. *Futures*, December 1971, 401-404.

Canals, J. (2011a). In Search of a Greater Impact: New Corporate and Social Challenges for Business Schools. In J. Canals (Ed.), *The Future of Leadership Development. Corporate Needs and the Role of Business Schools* (pp. 3-30). New York: Palgrave Macmillan.

Canals, J. (Ed.) (2011b). *The Future of Leadership Development. Corporate Needs and the Role of Business Schools.* New York: Palgrave Macmillan.

Centre for Educational Research and Innovation (CERI, 2008). OECD / France International Conference. Higher Education to 2030: What Futures for Quality Access in the Era of Globalisation? Four Future Scenarios for Higher Education. Retrieved August 2, 2016, from http://www.oecd.org/edu/skills-beyond-school/42241931.pdf

Chen L.-L. (1997). Distance Delivery Systems in Terms of Pedagogical Considerations. A Reevaluation. *Educational Technology, 37*(4), 34-37.

Chermack, T. S., & Swanson, R. A. (2008). Scenario Planning: Human Resource Development's Strategic Learning Tool. *Advances in Developing Human Resources, 10* (2), 129-146.

Chien, I., Cook, S., & Harding, J. (1984). The field of American research. *The American Psychologist*, *3*, 43-50.

Chin, C., & Chia, L. (2004). Problem-based learning. Using students' questions to drive knowledge construction. *Science Education, 88*(5), 707-727.

Chung, K., & Ferris, M. (1971). An inquiry of the nominal process. *Academy of Management Journal, 14,* 520-524.

Cicero (55 B. C.). *De Oratore.* Retrieved June 15, 2014, from http://www.gottwein.de/Lat/CicDeOrat/de_orat01de.php

Cicero (2013). *De re publica / Vom Staat.* Stuttgart: Reclam.

Clayton, M. J. (1997). Delphi: A technique to harness expert opinion for critical decision-making tasks in education. *Educational Psychology, 17,* 373-386.

Coffman, B. S. (1997). *Weak Signal® Research.* Retrieved April 5, 2016, from http://www.mgtaylor.com/mgtaylor/jotm/winter97/wsrsampl.htm

Collinson, D., & Tourish, D. (2015). Teaching Leadership Critically: New Directions for Leadership Pedagogy. *Academy of Management Learning & Education*, *14*(4), 576-594.

Conger, J. (1992). *Learning to lead: The art of transforming managers into leaders.* SF: Jossey-Bass Publishers.

Constitution of the Free State of Bavaria (CFSB, 1998 / 2014). Constitution of the Free State of Bavaria in the version announced on 15 December 1998. Last update: 01 January 2014. Retrieved October 21, 2016, from https://www.bayern.landtag.de/fileadmin/Internet_Dokumente/ Sonstiges_P/BV_Verfassung_Englisch_formatiert_14-12-16_neu.pdf

Convention against Discrimination in Education (1960). Retrieved August 6, 2016, from http://portal.unesco.org/en/ev.php-URL_ ID=12949&URL_DO=DO_TOPIC&URL_SECTION=201.html

Cook, A., & Glass, C. (2014). Women and Top-Leadership positions: Towards an Institutional Analysis. *Gender, Work & Organization, 21*(1), 91-103.

Corbin, J. & Strauss, A. (2008). *Basics of qualitative research: Techniques and procedures for developing grounded theory* (3rd ed.). Thousand Oaks, CA: Sage.

Cornish, E. (2003). The WILD cards in our future. *The Futurist*, 37, 18-22.

Council of the European Union (2010). *Presidency conclusions on education targets in the Europe 2020 Strategy. 3013th education, youth and culture council meeting. Brussels, 11 May 2010.* Retrieved August 10, 2016, from http://www.dges.mctes.pt/NR/rdonlyres/0783B4AD-A6A8-4993-9B71-5A06AE49AADC/4359/Press_release_2020.pdf

Creuznacher, I. C. (2008). Persönlichkeitsentfaltung zu unternehmerischen Kompetenzen in Schule und Universität. Eine bildungsökonomische Antwort auf theoretische Zielvorstellungen von Schumpeter. *Publikationen des Marburger Förderzentrums für Existenzgründer aus der Universität, Band 13.* Marburg: Marburger Förderzentrum für Existenzgründer aus der Universität.

Cronbach, L. J. (1972). Evaluation zur Verbesserung von Curricula. In C. Wulf (Hrsg.), *Evaluation, Beschreibung und Bewertung von Unterricht, Curricula und Schulversuchen* (pp. 41-59). München: Piper.

Cronbach, L. J., & Meehl, P.E. (1955). Construct Validity in Psychological Tests. *Psychological Bulletin, 52*(4), 281-302.

Cube, F. v. (1986). *Fordern statt verwöhnen: Die Erkenntnisse der Verhaltensbiologie in der Erziehung.* München: Piper.

Cube, F. v. (2003). *Führen durch Fordern: Die BioLogik des Erfolgs.* München: Piper.

Cube, F. v. (1998). *Lust an Leistung: Die Naturgesetze der Führung.* München: Piper.

Czarniawska-Joerges, B., & Wolff, R. (1991). Leaders, Managers, Entrepreneurs On and Off the Organizational Stage. *Organization Studies, 12*(4), 529-546.

Dalai Lama, & Alt. F. (2016). An Appeal by the Dalai Lama to the World: Ethics Are More Important Than Religion. Wals: Benevento.

Dalkey, N. C. (1969). *The Delphi method: An experimental study of group opinion.* Santa Monica, CA: RAND Corporation.

Dansereau, F., Graen, G. B., & Haha, W. (1975). A vertical dyad linkage approach to leadership in formal organizations. *Organizational Behavior and Human Performance, 13*, 46-78.

Daudelin, M. W. (1996). Learning from Experience through Reflection. *Organizational Dynamics, 24*(3), 35-48.

Dawson, M. D., & Brucker, P. S. (2001). The Utility of the Delphi Method in MFT Research. *The American Journal of Family Therapy, 29*, 125-140.

De Leeuw, E. D. (2001). Reducing missing data in surveys: An overview of methods. Quality and Quantity, *35*, 147-160.

Deloitte (2015). Digital education 2.0. From contents to connections. Deloitte Review, 16. Retrieved from http://d27n205l7rookf.cloudfront.net/wp-content/uploads/2015/01/DR16_digital_education_2.0.pdf. [17.04.2016].

De Mooij, R. & Tang, P. (2003). Four futures of Europe. CPB. Retrieved January 23, 2016, from http://www.cpb.nl/en/publication/four-futures-europe

Development Dimensions International, & The Conference Board (DDI, 2015). *Ready-Now Leaders: 25 Findings to Meet Tomorrow's Business Challenges. Global Leadership Forecast 2014 / 2015* (revised ed.). s.l.: E. Sinar, R. S. Wellins, R. Ray, A. L. Abel, & S. Neal. Retrieved July 11, 2015, from http://www.ddiworld.com/DDI/media/trend-research/global-leadership-forecast-2014-2015_tr_ddi.pdf?ext=.pdf

De Vet, E., Brug, J., De Nooijer, A., Dijkstra, A., & De Vries, N.K. (2005). Determinants of forward stage transition: a Delphi study. *Health Education Research, 20,* 195-205.

Devine, J. (2013). *Personalized Learning Together. Open Schools 2030, Open Education 2030. Call for Vision Papers. School Education.* Retrieved January 1, 2016, from http://blogs.ec.europa.eu/openeducation2030/files/2013/05/Devine-OE-SE-2030-fin.pdf

De Vos, A., De Hauw, S., & Willemse, I. (2015). An integrative model for competency development in organizations: the Flemish case. *The International Journal of Human Resource Management, 26*(20), 2543-2568.

Dewey, J. (1938). *Experience and Education.* New York: Collier Books.

Dewey, J. (1910). *How We Think.* Boston, New York, Chicago: D. C. Heath & Co., Publishers.

Dewey, J. (1964a). Progressive organization of subject matter. In R. D. Archambault (Ed.), *John Dewey on education: Selected writings* (pp. 373-387). Chicago: University of Chicago Press.

Dewey, J. (1964b). Science as subject matter and as method. In R. D. Archambault (Ed.), *John Dewey on education: Selected writings* (pp. 182-195). Chicago: University of Chicago Press.

Diamond, R. M. (2008). *Designing and Assessing Courses and Curricula. A Practical Guide* (3rd ed.). San Francisco: Jossey-Bass.

Dillman, D.A. (2007). *Mail and Internet Surveys: the Tailored Design Method* (2nd ed.). New Jersey: John Wiley & Sons.

Ditton, H. (2010). Evaluation und Qualitätssicherung. In R. Tippelt, & B. Schmidt (Hrsg.), *Handbuch Bildungsforschung* (3. durchges. Aufl.) (pp. 607-623). Wiesbaden: VS Verlag für Sozialwissenschaften.

Ditton, H., & Reinders, H. (2011). Überblick Felder der Bildungsforschung. In H. Reinders, H. Ditton, C. Gräsel, & B. Gniewosz (Hrsg.), *Empirische Bildungsforschung. Gegenstandsbereiche* (pp. 69-74). Wiesbaden: VS Verlag für Sozialwissenschaften.

Djalali, A. (2017). *A didactic perspective on leadership education – focusing on the development of competencies within MBA programs.* Stuttgart: Steinbeis-Edition.

Docherty, P., & Marking, C. (1997). Understanding Changing Competence Demands. In P. Docherty, & B. Nyhan (Eds.), *Human Competence and Business Development. Emerging Patterns in European Companies* (pp. 19-42). London: Springer-Verlag.

Dörpinghaus, A., Poenitsch, A., & Wigger, L. (2012). *Einführung in die Theorie der Bildung* (4. Aufl.). Darmstadt: WBG.

Dörpinghaus, A., & Uphoff, I. K. (2011). *Grundbegriffe der Pädagogik.* Darmstadt: WBG.

Doughty, E. A. (2009). Investigating adaptive grieving styles: A Delphi study. *Death studies, 33,* 462-480.

Drucker, P. F. (1993). *Innovation and Entrepreneurship. Practice and Principles*. New York: Harper.

Drucker, P. F. (2010). *Was ist Management? Das Beste aus 50 Jahren* (6. Aufl.). Berlin: Econ.

Eagly, A.H., & Chin, J. L. (2010). Diversity and leadership in a changing world. *American Psychologist, 65*, 216-224.

Ecken, P., Gnatzy T., & Gracht, H. A. v. d. (2011). Desirability bias in foresight: Consequences for decision quality based on Delphi results. *Technological Forecasting & Social Change, 78,* 1654-1670.

École Supérieure de Commerce de Paris, Europe (ESCP). (n.d.). Master in ManagementGrand École. Retrieved June 1, 2014, from http://www.escpeurope.eu/escp-europe-programmes/master-in-management/overview-master-in-management-escp-europe-business-school/master-in-management-mim-escp-europe-business-school/overview-master-in-management-escp-europe-business-school/

École Supérieure des Sciences Économiques et Commerciales Business School (ESSEC). (n.d.). M.Sc. in Management Grand École. Retrieved June 4, 2014, from http://www.essec.edu/programs/master-of-science-in-management-grande-ecole.html

Edelson, D. C., Gordin, D. N., & Pea, R. D. (1999). Addressing the Challenges of Inquiry-Based Learning Through Technology and Curriculum Design. *The Journal of the Learning Sciences, 8*(3&4), 391-450.

Eibl-Eibesfeldt, I. (1984). *Die Biologie des menschlichen Verhaltens: Grundriß der Humanethologie*. München: Piper.

Eibl-Eibesfeldt, I. (1967). *Grundriß der vergleichenden Verhaltensforschung: Ethologie*. München: Piper.

Eisenbeis, U. (2008). *Ziele, Zielsysteme und Zielkonfigurationen von Medienunternehmen. Ein Beitrag zur Realtheorie der Medienunternehmen.* Strategie- und Informationsmanagement Band 22. München / Mering: Rainer Hampp Verlag.

„Eltern sollten eine Ausbildung in Menschenführung erhalten" (EAM, 2011). 2011, June 28). *Süddeutsche Zeitung*, p. 32.

Emlyon Business School. (n.d). Msc. In Management. Retrieved June 6, 2014, from http://graduate.em-lyon.com/en/MSc-in-Management

Enzer, S. (1971). Delphi and Cross-impact Techniques. An Effective Combination for Systematic Futures Analysis. *Futures*, March 1971, 48-61.

Erler, M. (2007). *Die Philosophie der Antike. Band 2 / 2. Platon.* Basel: Schwabe Verlag.

Erpenbeck, J. (2012a). Sind Kompetenzen Persönlichkeitseigenschaften? In W. G. Faix (Hrsg.), *Kompetenz. Festschrift Prof. Dr. John Erpenbeck zum 70. Geburtstag.* Band 4 (pp. 59-92). Stuttgart: Steinbeis-Edition.

Erpenbeck, J. (2012b). Was „sind" Kompetenzen? In W. G. Faix (Hrsg.), *Kompetenz. Festschrift Prof. Dr. John Erpenbeck zum 70. Geburtstag.* Band 4 (pp. 1-57). Stuttgart: Steinbeis-Edition.

Erpenbeck, J. (2009). Werte als Kompetenzkerne. 2. Ludwigsburger Symposium Bildungsmanagement. Wert und Werte im Management. Nachhaltigkeit - Ethik – Bildungscontrolling. Retrieved July 9, 2016, from http://dgbima.de/fileadmin/images/Symposium09/Erpenbeck.pdf

Erpenbeck, J., & Heyse, V. (2007). *Die Kompetenzbiografie. Wege der Kompetenzentwicklung* (2. Aufl.). Münster: Waxmann.

Erpenbeck, J., & Rosenstiel, L. v. (Hrsg.) (2007). *Handbuch Kompetenzmessung. Erkennen, verstehen und bewerten von Kompetenzen in der betrieblichen, pädagogischen und psychologischen Praxis* (2. überarb. u. erw. Aufl.). Stuttgart: Schäffer-Poeschel Verlag.

Erpenbeck, J., & Sauter, W. (2014): *Kompetenzentwicklung im Netz. New Blended Learning mit Web 2.0.* Berlin: epubli.

Esade Business School, Ramon Llull University. (n.d.). M.Sc. in International Management. Retrieved June 6, 2014, from http://www.esade.edu/management/eng/programmes/master-international-management

European Commission / EACEA / Eurydice (2015). The European Higher Education Area in 2015: Bologna Process Implementation Report. Luxembourg: Publications Office of the European Union. Retrieved December 28, 2015, from http://www.ehea.info/Uploads/SubmitedFiles/5_2015/132824.pdf

European Council (2000). *Presidency Conclusions. Lisbon European Council 23 and 24 March 2000.* Retrieved August 8, 2016, from http://www.consilium.europa.eu/en/uedocs/cms_data/docs/pressdata/en/ec/00100-r1.en0.htm

Eurostat (2016a). Educational attainment statistics. Retrieved August 4, 2016, from http://ec.europa.eu/eurostat/statistics-explained/index.php/Educational_attainment_statistics

Eurostat (2016b). *Statistics explained. Tertiary education statistics.* Retrieved August 4, 2016, from http://ec.europa.eu/eurostat/statistics-explained/index.php/Tertiary_education_statistics#Context

Eyler, J. (2001). Creating your reflection map. *New Directions for Higher Education, 114*, 35-43.

Eyler, J., Giles, D. E., & Schmiede, A. (1996). *A practitioner's guide to reflection in service-learning: Student voices and reflections.* A Technical Assistance Project funded by the Corporation for National Service. Nashville: Vanderbilt University.

Faix, W. G., Buchwald, C., & Wetzler, R. (1994). *Der Weg zum schlanken Unternehmen.* Landsberg / Lech: Verlag Moderne Industrie.

Faix, W. G., Djalali, A., Horne, A., Keck, G., Kisgen, S., Mezger, P., & Sailer, J. (2013). *Management von Wachstum und Globalisierung. Best Practice.* Band 5. Stuttgart: Steinbeis-Edition.

Faix, W. G., Kisgen, S., Lau, A., Schulten, A., & Zywietz, T. (2006). *Praxishandbuch Außenwirtschaft. Erfolgsfaktoren im Auslandsgeschäft.* Wiesbaden: Gabler.

Faix, W. G., Kisgen, S., Shah, S., & Faix, A.-V. (2017). Fostering creative personalities through real-world experiences. SIBE as a representative example. *The Journal of Competency-Based Education*, to be published. (Faix et al., 2017a)

Faix, W. G., & Laier, A. (1989 / 1991). *Soziale Kompetenz: Das Potenzial zum unternehmerischen und persönlichen Erfolg.* Wiesbaden: Gabler.

Faix, W. G., & Mergenthaler, J. (2015). *The creative power of education. On the formation of a creative personality as the fundamental condition for innovation and entrepreneurial success.* Translation of: Die schöpferische Kraft der Bildung, 2013 (2. Aufl.). Stuttgart: Steinbeis-Edition.

Faix, W. G., Mergenthaler, J., Ahlers, R.-J., & Auer, M. (2015). *Innovation-Quality. The Value of the New.* Translation of: InnovationsQualität. Über den Wert des Neuen, 2014. Stuttgart: Steinbeis-Edition.

Faix, W. G., Mergenthaler, J., Kisgen, S., Blumenthal, I., Djalali, A., Gracht, H. v. d., Horne, A., & Rygl, D. (2017). *Lehrphilosophie der SIBE.* Stuttgart: Steinbeis-Edition (to be published). (Faix et al., 2017b)

Faix, W. G., Rütter, T., & Wollstadt, E. (1995). *Führung und Persönlichkeit. Personale Entwicklung.* Landsberg / Lech: Verlag Moderne Industrie.

Faix, W. G., Schulten, A., & Auer, M. (2009). Das Projekt-Kompetenz-Studium der Steinbeis-Hochschule Berlin (SHB). In W. G. Faix, & M. Auer (Hrsg.), *Talent. Kompetenz. Management.* Band 1 (pp. 137-173). Stuttgart: Steinbeis-Edition.

Fiedler, F. E. (1964). A contingency model of leadership effectiveness. In L. Berkowitz (Ed.), *Advances in experimental social psychology* (Vol. 1, pp. 149-190). New York: Academic Press.

Fiedler, F. E. (1967). *A theory of leadership effectiveness.* New York: McGraw-Hill.

Fiedler, F. E., & Chemers, M. M. (1974). *Leadership and effective management.* Glenview, Ill.: Scott, Foresman & Co.

Financial Times Masters in management ranking (2013). Retrieved April 10, 2014, from http://rankings.ft.com/businessschoolrankings/masters-in-management-2013

Financial Times Masters in management ranking (2015). Retrieved August 28, 2016, from http://rankings.ft.com/businessschoolrankings/masters-in-management-2015

Fink, A., & Siebe, A. (2011). *Handbuch Zukunftsmanagement: Werkzeuge der strategischen Planung und Früherkennung* (2. Auflage). Frankfurt / New York: Campus.

Fischer, P., Frey, D., & Niedernhuber, J. (2013). Führung und Werte – Humanistische Führung in Theorie und Praxis. In K. Häring & S. Litzcke (Hrsg.), *Führungskompetenzen lernen. Eignung, Entwicklung, Aufstieg* (pp. 161-180). Stuttgart: Schäffer-Poeschel Verlag.

Fischer, F., Müller, H., & Tippelt, R. (2011). Multidisciplinary Cooperation in Education: the Munich Center of the Learning Sciences. *European Educational Research Journal, 10*(1), 153-159.

Flick, U. (2009). An introduction to qualitative analysis. London: Sage.

Flick, U., Kardorff, K. V., & Steinke, I. (2004). *A companion to qualitative research.* London: Sage.

Fleisher, C. S., & Bensoussan, B. E. (2002). *Strategic and Competitive Analysis. Methods and Techniques for Analyzing Business Competition.* Upper Saddle River, NJ: Prentice Hall.

Fletcher-Johnston, M., Marshall, S. K., & Straatman, L. (2011). Healthcare transitions for adolescents with chronic life-threatening conditions using a Delphi method to identify research priorities for clinicians and academics in Canada. *Child Care, Health and Development, 37,* 875-882.

Förster, B., & Gracht, H. v. d. (2014). Assessing Delphi panel composition for strategic foresight – A comparison of panels based on company-internal and external participants. *Technological Forecasting & Social Change, 84,* 215-229.

Fontela, E. (1977). Scenario generation by cross-impact analysis. *Futures,* February 1977, 87-89.

Francis, A. (1977). An experimental analysis of a Delphi technique: The effect of majority and high confidence-low confidence expert opinion on group consensus. *Dissertation Abstracts International, 38* (02), 566 (UMI No. 7717689).

Franklin, C., & Lytle, R. (2015). *Employer Perspectives on Competency-Based Education.* AEI Series on Competency-Based Higher Education. Retrieved May 11, 2016, from https://www.aei.org/publication/employer-perspectives-on-competency-based-education/

Fraser, S. P., & Bosanquet, A. M. (2006). The Curriculum? That's just a unit outline, isn't it? *Studies in Higher Education, 31*(3), 269-284.

Freeman, R. E. (1984 / 2010). *Strategic Management. A Stakeholder Approach.* New York: Cambridge University Press.

Frey, D., Nikitopoulos, A., Peus, C., Weisweiler, S., & Kastenmüller, A. (2010). Unternehmenserfolg durch ethikorientierte Unternehmens- und Mitarbeiterführung. In U. Meier, & B. Sill (Hrsg.), *Führung. Macht. Sinn. Ethos und Ethik für Entscheider in Wirtschaft, Gesellschaft und Kirche* (pp. 637-656). Regensburg: Pustet.

Frey, D., & Spielmann, U. (1997). Führung – Konzepte und Theorien. In D. Frey, & S. Greif (Hrsg.), *Sozialpsychologie. Ein Handbuch in Schlüsselbegriffen* (4. Aufl., pp. 164-173). Weinheim: Beltz Psychologie Verlags Union.

Friebel, H., Epskamp, H., Knobloch. B., Montag, S., & Toth, S. (2000). *Bildungsbeteiligung: Chancen und Risiken. Eine Längsschnittstudie über Bildungs- und Weiterbildungskarrieren in der „Moderne"*. Opladen: Leske + Budrich.

Friedman, H. S., & Schustack, M. W. (2012). *Personality: Classic Theories and Modern Research* (5th ed.). Boston: Pearson.

Furtner, M., & Baldegger, U. (2013). *Self-Leadership und Führung. Theorien, Modelle und praktische Umsetzung*. Wiesbaden: Springer Gabler.

Gagliardi, P. (2006). A role for humanities in the formation of managers. In: P. Gagliardi, & B. Czarniawska (Eds.), *Management Education and Humanities* (pp. 3-9). Cheltenham, UK / Northampton, USA: Edward Elgar.

Gagliardi, P., & Czarniawska, B. (Eds.) (2006). *Management Education and Humanities*. Cheltenham, UK / Northampton, USA: Edward Elgar.

Ganz, M., & Lin, E. S. (2012). Learning to Lead. A Pedagogy of Practice. In S. Snook, N. Nohria, & R. Khurana (Eds.), *The Handbook for Teaching Leadership. Knowing, Doing, and Being* (pp. 353-366). Los Angeles: SAGE.

Garfinkel, H. (1967). *Studies in Ethnomethodology*. Englewood Cliffs NJ: Prentice Hall.

Gauck, J. (2012). *Freiheit. Ein Plädoyer* (5. Aufl.). München: Kösel.

Gaugler, B. B., Rosenthal, D. B., Thornton III, G. C., & Bentson, C. (1987). Meta-Analysis of Assessment Center Validity. *Journal of Applied Psychology, 72*(3), 493-511.

Gausemeier, J., Fink, A., & Schlake, O. (1996). *Szenario-Management: Planen und Führen mit Szenarien* (2. Aufl.). München / Wien: Carl Hanser.

Gebauer, A. (2007). *Einführung von Corporate Universities, Rekonstruktion der Entwicklungsverläufe in Deutschland*, Heidelberg: Carl-Auer Verlag.

Geist, M. R. (2010). Using the Delphi method to engage stakeholders: A comparison of two studies. *Evaluation and Program Planning, 33, 147*-154.

Gellman, L. (2016, April 6). A New Push for Real-World Lessons at Business Schools. New guiding principles by nonprofit urge business programs to spend less time in research, pedagogy. *The Wall Street Journal.* Retrieved April 8, 2016, from http://www.wsj.com/articles/a-new-push-for-real-world-lessons-at-business-schools-1459972295

Gerholz, K.-H., & Sloane, P. (2013). Studiengangs- und Modulentwicklung – Aktuelle Herausforderungen und Potentiale zur forschungsorientierten Gestaltung. In K.-H. Gerholz, & P. Sloane (Hrsg.), *Studiengänge entwickeln – Module gestalten. Eine Standortbestimmung nach Bologna* (pp. 51-83). Paderborn: Eusl.

Gerstlauer, A.-K. (2014). Der Student ohne Uni. *Zeit Online*, 17.04.2014. Retrieved March 28, 2016, from http://www.zeit.de/studium/uni-leben/2014-04/selbststudium-education-hacking

Gervais, J. (2016). The operational definition of competency-based education. *Journal of Competency-Based Education*, May. Retrieved April 9, 2014, from http://onlinelibrary.wiley.com/doi/10.1002/cbe2.1011/full

Ghiselli, E. E. (1966). *The validity of occupational aptitude tests.* New York: Wiley.

Gibb, C. A. (1969). Leadership. In G. Lindzey & E. Aronson (Eds.), *The Handbook of Social Psychology* (Vol. 4, pp. 283-322). Reading, Mass: Addison-Wesley.

Giel, K., & Flitner, A. (2010). Einführung in die Schriften zur Theorie der Bildung. In A. Flitner, & K. Giel (Hrsg.), Wilhelm von Humboldt. Werke in fünf Bänden. Werke V. Autobiographische Dichtungen, Briefe. Kommentare und Anmerkungen zu Band I-V. Anhang (pp. 315-321). Darmstadt: WBG.

Gilbert, J. K., & Reiner, M. (2000). Thought experiments in science education: potential and current realization. *International Journal of Science Education, 22*(3), 265-283.

Gill, C. (2003). Plato's *Republic*: An Ideal Culture of Knowledge. In W. Detel, A. Becker, and P. Scholz (Hrsg.), *Ideal and Culture of Knowledge in Plato. Akten der 4. Tagung der Karl- und Gertrud-Abel-Stiftung vom 1.-3. September 2000 in Frankfurt* (pp. 37-55). Stuttgart: Franz Steiner Verlag.

Giuliani, R. W. (2002). *Leadership.* London: Sphere.

Gläser-Zikuda, M. (2011). Qualitative Auswertungsverfahren. In H. Reinders, H. Ditton, C. Gräsel, & B. Gniewosz (Hrsg.), *Empirische Bildungsforschung: Strukturen und Methoden* (pp. 109-119). Wiesbaden: VS Verlag für Sozialwissenschaften.

Glaser, B. G., & Strauss, A. L. (1967). *The discovery of grounded theory: strategies for* qualitative research. Chicago: Aldine.

Glass, A. (Ed.) (2014). *The State of Higher Education 2014. OECD Higher Education Programme (IMHE).* n. p.: OECD.

Gnatzy, T., Warth, J., Gracht, H. v. d., & Darkow, I. L. (2011). Validating an innovative real-time Delphi approach – A methodological comparison between real-time and conventional Delphi studies. *Technological Forecasting & Social Change, 78,* 1681-1694.

Godet, M. (1987). *Scenarios and Strategic Management.* London: Butterworth.

Godet, M. (2000). The art of scenarios and strategic planning: tools and pitfalls. *Technological Forecasting and Social Change, 65*, 3-22.

Godet, M. (2001). *Creating futures: Scenario Planning as a Strategic Management Tool*. London: Economica.

Goffman, E. (1983). The Interaction Order. *American Sociological Review, 48*, 1-17.

Gogolin, I., & Tippelt, R. (Hrsg). (2003). *Innovation durch Bildung. Beiträge zum 18. Kongress der Deutschen Gesellschaft für Erziehungswissenschaft*. Opladen: Leske + Budrich.

Gonzo, C. (1981 / 1982). A Critical Look at Competency-Based Education. *Contributions to Music Education, 9*, 77-84.

Google Trends (n.d.) Retrieved April 2, 2016, from https://www.google.de/trends/

Gordon, R. A. (1961). *Business Leadership in the Large Corporation*. Berkeley and Los Angeles / California: University of California Press.

Gordon, T., & Pease, A. (2006). RT Delphi: An efficient, "round-less" almost real time Delphi method. *Technological forecasting & social change, 73, 321*-333.

Gordon, T. J., & Hayward, H. (1968). Initial experiments with the cross impact matrix method of forecasting. *Futures*, December 1968, 100-116.

Gosling, J., & Mintzberg, H. (2006). Management Education as if Both Matter. *Management Learning, 37*(4), 419-428.

Gracht, H. A. v. d. (2012). Consensus measurement in Delphi studies. Review and implications for future quality assurance. *Technological Forecasting & Social Change, 79*, 1525-1536.

Gracht, H. A. v. d., & Darkow, I.-L. (2010). Scenarios for the logistics services industry: A Delphi-based analysis for 2025. *International Journal of Production Economics, 127*, 46-59.

Graen, G. B., & Uhl-Bien, M. (1995). Relationship-based approach to leadership: Development of leader-member exchange (LMX) theory of leadership over 25 years: Applying a multi-level, multi-domain perspective. *Leadership Quarterly, 6*(2), 219-247.

Graen, G. B., & Uhl-Bien, M. (1991). The transformation of professionals into self-managing and partially self-designing contributions: Toward a theory of leadership making. *Journal of Management Systems, 3*(3), 33-48.

Graf, H. G., & Klein, G. (2003). *In die Zukunft führen. Strategieentwicklung mit Szenarien.* Zürich / Chur: Rüegger.

Grebel, T. (2004). *Entrepreneurship: A New Perspective.* London: Routledge.

Greene, J. C. (2007). *Mixed Methods in Social Inquiry.* San Francisco, CA: Jossey-Bass.

Gregersen, J. (2011). *hochschule@zukunft 2030. Ergebnisse und Diskussionen des Hochschuldelphis.* Wiesbaden: VS Verlag für Sozialwissenschaften.

Grenoble École de Management. (n.d.). Master in International Management. Retrieved June 7, 2014, from http://www.grenoble-em.com/355-master-in-international-business-mib-2.aspx

Grimes, M. W. (2015). How Does Learning in Leadership Work? A Conceptual Change Perspective. *Journal of Leadership Education*, Special 2015, 26-45.

Grint, K. (1997). *Leadership: Classical, Contemporary, and Critical Approaches.* New York: Oxford University Press.

Grootings, P. (1994). Von Qualifikation zu Kompetenz: Wovon reden wir eigentlich? *Europäische Zeitschrift für Berufs*bildung (CEDEFOP), 1, 5-8.

Gros, D., & Alcidi, C. (Ed.) (2013). *The Global Economy in 2030: Trends and Strategies for Europe.* Retrieved from: http://europa.eu/espas/pdf/espas-report-economy.pdf. [17.04.2016].

Grossmann, I. (2007). Critical and strategic factors for scenario development and discontinuity tracing. *Futures, 39* (7), 878-894.

Gül, H., Gül, S. S., Kaya, E., & Alican, A. (2010). Main trends in the world of higher education, internationalization and institutional autonomy. *Procedia Social and Behavioral Sciences, 9,* 1878-1884.

Häder, M. (2009). *Delphi-Befragungen. Ein Arbeitsbuch* (2. Auflage). Wiesbaden: VS Verlag für Sozialwissenschaften.

Haerder, M. (2012, February 9). Auf den Spuren von Bologna. *Wirtschaftswoche.* Retrieved August 18, 2016, from http://www.wiwo.de/politik/deutschland/bildungspolitik-auf-den-spuren-von-bologna/6145066-all.html

Hager, P., Athanasou, J., & Gonczi, A. (1994). *Assessment – Technical Manual.* Canberra: AGPS.

Haken, H. (1990). *Synergetik. Eine Einführung. Nichtgleichgewichts-Phasenübergänge und Selbstorganisation in Physik, Chemie und Biologie* (3. Aufl.). Berlin / Heidelberg / New York: Springer.

Hamilton, D. (1996). *Learning About Education. An Unfinished Curriculum.* Bristol: Open University Press.

Handelshochschule Leipzig (Leipzig Graduate School of Management) (n.d.). M.Sc. in Management. Retrieved June 1, 2014, from http://www.hhl.de/en/programs/full-time-msc-program/

Hanges, P. J., Aiken, J. R., Park, J., & Su, J. (2016). Cross-cultural leadership: leading around the world. *Current Opinion in Psychology,* 8, 64-69.

Hansen, M. (2014). Vom Stipendiaten zum Campuscrasher. *Cicero*, 09.09.2014. Retrieved March 28, 2016, from http://www.cicero.de/berliner-republik/generation-y-das-dilemma-vom-erwachsen-werden/58145

Halarnkar, T., & Kulkarni, D. G. (2013). E-Learning: An Effective Way of Learning for Young Children. The Tenth International Conference on eLearning for Knowledge-Based Society, 12-13 December 2013, Thailand. Retrieved on June 20, 2015, from http://www.ijcim.th.org/SpecialEditions/v21nSP2/02_06_05F_Tasina.pdf

Harris, K. J., Wheeler, A. R., & Kacmar, K. M. (2009). Leader-member exchange and empowerment: Direct and interactive effects on job satisfaction, turnover intentions, and performance. *Leadership Quarterly, 20*(3), 371-382.

Harvard Business School. (n.d.). Master of Business Administration. Retrieved June 7, 2014 from http://www.hbs.edu/mba/Pages/default.aspx

Harvey, M. (2001). The Hidden Force: A Critique of Normative Approaches to Business Leadership. *SAM Advanced Management Journal, 66*(4), 36-48.

Hautes Études Commerciales (HEC) Paris. (n.d.). Master in Management. Retrieved June 7, 2014, from http://www.hec.edu/MSc/Programs/Master-in-Management-MiM-Grande-Ecole

Heid, H. (2012). Qualifikation. In H.-E. Tenorth, & R. Tippelt (Hrsg.), *BELTZ Lexikon Pädagogik (pp. 590-591)*. Weinheim und Basel: Beltz.

Heijden, K. v. d. (2005). *Scenarios. The Art of Strategic Conversation* (Second ed.). Chichester: John Wiley & Sons.

Hemphill, J. K., & Coons, A. E. (1957). Development of the leader behavior description questionnaire. In R. M. Stogdill, & A. E. Coons (Eds.), *Leader behavior: Its description and measurement* (pp. 6-38). Columbus: Bureau of Business Research, Ohio State University.

Herbold, A. (2013). Studenten wollen nicht abgerichtet werden. Ein Gespräch mit dem Philosophen Julian Nida-Rümelin über die Folgen der Bologna-Reform und sein humanistisches Bildungsideal. *Die Zeit*, *20*. Retrieved August 17, 2016, from http://www.zeit.de/2013/20/ruemelin-interview-bildungsideal

Hermelin, E., Lievens, F., & Robertson, I. T. (2007). The validity of assessment centres for the prediction of supervisory performance ratings: A meta-analysis. *International Journal of Selection and Assessment*, *15*, 405-411.

Hirsch, S., Burggraf, P., & Daheim, C. (2013). Scenario planning with integrated quantification – managing uncertainty in corporate strategy building. *Foresight*, 15 (5), 363-374.

Hochschulkompass. (2016). *Ein Angebot der Hochschulrektorenkonferenz. Studiengangssuche*. Retrieved from http://www.hochschulkompass.de/studium/suche.html [03.01.2016].

Hodgkinson, G., & Wright, G. (2002). Confronting strategic inertia in a top management team: Learning from failure. *Organization Studies*, *23*, 949-977.

Hoffmann, T. (1999). The meanings of competency. *Journal of European Industrial Training*, *23*(6), 275-286.

Horney, N., Pasmore, B., O'Shea, T. (2010). Leadership Agility. A Business Imperative for a VUCA World. *Human Resource Planning*, *33*(4), 32-38.

Horton, A. (1999). Forefront: a simple guide to successful foresight. *Foresight 1* (1), 5-9.

House, R. J., Hanges, P. J., Ruiz-Quintanilla, S. A., Dorfman, P. W., Javidan, M., Dickson, M., & Associates (1999). Cultural influences on leadership and organizations: Project GLOBE. In W. H. Mobley, M. J. Gessner, & V. Arnold (Eds.), *Advances in global leadership* (pp. 131-233). Stanford, CT: JAI Press.

Hovestadt, G., & Beckmann, T. (2010): *Corporate Universities. Ein Überblick.* Retrieved April 19, 2016, from http://www.boeckler.de/pdf/mbf_netzwerke_corporate_unis.pdf

Huang, H.-M. (2002). Toward constructivism for adult learners in online learning environments. *British Journal of Educational Technology, 33*(1), 27–37.

Huber, L. (1999). An- und Aussichten der Hochschuldidaktik. *Zeitschrift für Pädagogik, 1*, 25-44.

Humboldt, W. v. (1793 or 1794 / 2000). Theory of Bildung. Tanslated by G. Horton-Krüger. In I. Westbury, S. Hopmann, & K. Riquarts, *Teaching As A Reflective Practice. The German Didaktik Tradition* (pp. 57-62). New York and London: Routledge.

Humboldt, W. v. (1792 / 1854). *The Sphere and Duties of Government (The Limits of State Action).* Translated from the German by J. Coulthard. Retrieved July 22, 2016, from http://oll.libertyfund.org/titles/humboldt-the-sphere-and-duties-of-government-1792-1854

Hussler, C., Muller, P., & Rondé, P. (2011). Is diversity in Delphi panelist groups useful? Evidence from a French forecasting exercise on the future of nuclear energy. *Technological Forecasting & Social Change, 78*, 1642-1653.

Huynh, L. (2007). *A New Paradigm of Entrepreneurial Leadership: the mediating role of influence, vision and context. Honours Thesis.* Sydney: University of Sydney.

IBM (2010a). *Capitalizing on Complexity. Insights from the Global Chief Executive Officer Study.* Somers/NY: IBM Global Business Services.

IBM (2012a). *Connected generation. Perspectives from tomorrow's leaders in a digital world. Insights from the 2012 IBM Global Student Study.* Somers / NY: IBM Global Business Services.

IBM (2012b). *Leading Through Connections. Insights from the Global Chief Executive Officer Study.* Somers / NY: IBM Global Business Services.

IBM (2016). *Redefining competition. Insights from the Global C-suite Study – The CEO perspective.* Somers / NY: IBM Global Business Services.

IBM (2010b). *Working beyond Borders. Insights from the Global Chief Human Resource Officer Study.* Somers / NY: IBM Global Business Services.

IDC (2012). The Digital Universe in 2020: Big Data, Bigger Digital Shadows, and Biggest Growth in the Far East. Retrieved April 17, 2016, from http://www.emc.com/collateral/analyst-reports/idc-the-digital-universe-in-2020.pdf

iKnow project. European Commission (n.d). Retrieved March 28, 2016, from http://wiwe.iknowfutures.eu/bank/wild-card/view/basic-education-ends-in-the-age-of-18/

Imperial College London Business School. (n.d.). M.Sc. Management. Retrieved June 7, 2014, from http://wwwf.imperial.ac.uk/business-school/programmes/msc-management/

Instituto de Empresa Business School (IE Business School). (n.d.). Master in Management. Retrieved June 3, 2014, from http://www.ie.edu/business-school/degrees/master-management

Institute For The Future (IFTF) (n.d.): Future of learning. Retrieved March 28, 2016, from: http://www.iftf.org/iftf-you/programs-initiatives/future-of-learning/

James, A. (2009, April 7). Academies of the apocalypse? *The Guardian.* Retrieved January 3, 2016, from http://www.theguardian.com/education/2009/apr/07/mba-business-schools-credit-crunch

Jenert, T. (2016). Von der Curriculum- zur Studienprogrammentwicklung: Argumente für eine Perspektiverweiterung. In T. Brahm, T. Jenert, & D. Euler (Hrsg.), *Pädagogische Hochschulentwicklung. Von der Programmatik zur Implementierung* (pp. 119-132). Wiesbaden: Springer.

Johnstone, D. B. (2016). Financing American Higher Education: Reconciling Institutional Financial Viability and Student Affordability. In M. N. Bastedo, P. G. Altbach, & P. C. Gumport (Eds.), *American Higher Education in the Twenty-First Century. Social, Political, and Economic Challenges* (4th ed., pp. 310-341). Baltimore: Johns Hopkins University Press.

Joint Committee on Standards for Educational Evaluation (1999). *Handbuch der Evaluationsstandards.* Opladen: Leske + Budrich.

Jones, B. F., Rasmussen, C. M., & Moffitt, M. C. (1997). *Real-Life Problem Solving. A Collaborative Approach to Interdisciplinary Learning. A Collaborative Approach to Interdisciplinary Learning.* Psychology in the Classroom: A Series on Applied Educational Psychology. Washington, DC: American Psychological Association.

Jubb, R., & Robotham, D. (1997). Competences in management development: challenging the myths. *Journal of European Industrial Training, 21*(5), 171-175.

Jung, J.-H., & Pinar, W. F. (2016). Conceptions of Curriculum. In D. Wyse, L. Hayward, & J. Pandya (Eds.), *The SAGE Handbook of Curriculum, Pedagogy and Assessment.* Volume 1 (pp. 29-46). Los Angeles: SAGE.

Kahn, H., & Wiener, A. J. (1967). *The Year 2000: A Framework for Speculation on the Next Thirty-three Years.* New York: Macmillan.

Kant, I. (1784 / 2015). *Beantwortung der Frage: Was ist Aufklärung?* Bern: GURO.

Kant, I. (1803 / 1901). *Über Pädagogik* (3. Aufl.). Langensalza: Beyer & Söhne.

Karmarkar, Y., Chabra, M., & Deshpande, A. (2014). Entrepreneurial Leadership Style(s): A Taxonomic Review. *Annual Research Journal of Symbiosis Centre for Management Studies, 2*(1), 156-189.

Katz-Buonincontro, J., & Ghosh, R. (2014). Using Workplace experiences for learning about affect and creative problem solving: Piloting a four-stage model for management education. *International Journal of Management Education*, *12*, 127-141.

Keeney, S., Hasson, F., & McKenna, H. (2001). A critical review of the Delphi technique as a research methodology for nursing. *International Journal of Nursing Studies*, *38,* 195–200.

Keim, S. (to be published). *Kompetenzdefinition, -messung und -entwicklung in der Leadership Education am Beispiel der SIBE-Masterstudiengänge.* Stuttgart: Steinbeis-Edition.

Keim, S., Erpenbeck, J., & Faix, W. G. (2012). Der Poffenberger-KODE®X. In W. G. Faix (Hrsg.), *Kompetenz. Festschrift Prof. Dr. John Erpenbeck zum 70. Geburtstag.* Band 4 (p. 457-488). Stuttgart: Steinbeis-Edition.

Keim, S., & Wittmann, P. (2012). Zukunftsfähigkeit durch Kompetenzentwicklung. In W. G. Faix (Hrsg.), *Kompetenz. Festschrift Prof. Dr. John Erpenbeck zum 70. Geburtstag.* Band 4 (p. 425-455). Stuttgart: Steinbeis-Edition.

Kelchen, R. (2015). *The Landscape of Competency-Based Education: Enrollments, Demographics, and Affordability.* AEI Series on Competency-Based Higher Education. Retrieved May 11, 2016, from https://www.aei.org/wp-content/uploads/2015/04/Competency-based-education-landscape-Kelchen-2015.pdf

Kellerman, B. (2012a). Becoming Leadership Literate. A Core Curriculum. In S. Snook, N. Nohria, & R. Khurana (Eds.), *The Handbook for Teaching Leadership. Knowing, Doing, and Being* (pp. 35-45). Los Angeles: SAGE.

Kellerman, B. (2012b). *The End of Leadership.* New York: Harper Collins Publishers.

Kempfert, G., & Rolff, H. (2005): *Qualität und Evaluation.* Weinheim: Beltz.

Keough, S. M., & Shanahan, K. J. (2008). Scenario Planning: Toward a More Complete Model for Practice. *Advances in Developing Human Resources, 10* (2), 166-178.

Kerr, R., & Robinson, S. (2011). Leadership as an elite field: Scottish banking leaders and the crisis of 2007-2009. *Leadership, 7,* 151-173.

Kinkel, S., Armbruster, H., & Schirmeister, E. (2006). Szenario-Delphi oder Delphi-Szenario? Erfahrungen aus zwei Vorausschaustudien mit der Kombination dieser Methoden. In J. Gausemeier, J. (Ed.), *Vorausschau und Technologieplanung: 2. Symposium für Vorausschau und Technologieplanung Heinz Nixdorf Institut, 9. Und 10. November 2006, Schloss Neuhardenberg* (pp. 109-137). Paderborn: Heinz Nixdorf Institut.

Kisgen, S. (2010). Kompetenzmanagement mit dem Master of Science in International Management der SIBE. In W. G. Faix, & M. Auer (Hrsg.), *Talent. Kompetenz. Management. Global. Lokal,* Band 2 (pp. 163-260). Stuttgart: Steinbeis-Edition.

Kisgen, S. (2013). M.Sc. in International Management. In S. Kisgen, A. Dresen. & W. G. Faix (Hrsg.), *International Management* (pp. 1-76). Stuttgart: Steinbeis-Edition.

Klafki, W. (2012). Didaktik. In H.-E. Tenorth, & R. Tippelt (Hrsg.), *BELTZ Lexikon Pädagogik* (pp. 158-161). Weinheim und Basel: Beltz.

Klafki, W. (1995). On the problem of teaching and learning contents from the standpoint of critical-constructive Didaktik. In. S. Hopmann, & K. Riquarts (Eds.), *Curriculum and / or Didaktik* (IPN 147, pp. 187-200). Kiel: Institut für die Pädagogik der Naturwissenschaften.

Klafki, W. (2000). The Significance of Classical Theories of Bildung for a Contemporary Concept of Allgemeinbildung. In I. Westbury, S. Hopmann, & K. Riquarts, *Teaching As A Reflective Practice. The German Didaktik Tradition* (pp. 85-107). New York and London: Routledge.

Klein, G. (2001). Wissensmanagement und das Management von Nichtwissen – Entscheiden und Handeln mit unscharfem Wissen. In H. G. Graf (Hrsg.), *...und in Zukunft die Wissensgesellschaft? Der Umgang mit Wissen im Entscheidungsprozess* (pp. 73-80). Chur / Zürich: Verlag Rüegger.

Klink, M. R. v. d., & Boon, J. (2003). Competencies: The triumph of a fuzzy concept. *International Journal Human Resources Development and Management, 3*, 125-137.

Klooster, S. A. v.'t, & Asselt, M.B.A. v. (2006). Practising the scenario-axes technique. *Futures*, 38, 15-30.

Klovert, H. (2015, December 18). "Personalisiertes Lernen": So stellt sich Mark Zuckerberg Schule vor. *Spiegel online*. Retrieved from http://www.spiegel.de/schulspiegel/zuckerberg-will-personalisiertes-lernen-foerdern-was-bringt-das-a-1066491.html [21.12.2015].

Körner, T. (2015, August 31). Studenten und ihr "Bulimie-Lernen". *Deutschlandradio Kultur*. Retrieved August 18, 2016, from http://www.deutschlandradiokultur.de/ard-dokumentation-studenten-und-ihr-bulimie-lernen.2150.de.html?dram:article_id=329740

Kolb, D. A. (1984). *Experiential Learning. Experience as The Source of Learning and Development.* Upper Saddle River: Prentice Hall.

Korman, A. K. (1968). The prediction of managerial performance: A review. *Personnel Psychology*, 21(3), 259-322.

Korte, R. F., & Chermack, T. J. (2007). Changing organizational culture: Using scenario planning to change the collective mind of the organization. *Futures*, 39, 645-656.

Kossakowski, A. (1981). Disposition. In G. Clauß u.a. (Hrsg.), *Wörterbuch der Psychologie*. Leipzig: VEB Bibliographisches Institut.

Kotter, J. P. (1990). What Leaders Really Do. *Harvard Business Review*, May-June, 3-11.

Kreutz, P. (2008). *Romidee und Rechtsbild in der Spätantike: Untersuchungen zur Ideen- und Mentalitätsgeschichte*. Berlin: LIT.

Krochmalnik, D. (2009). Der "Lerner" und der Lehrer. Geschichte eines ungleichen Paares. In B. Schröder, H. H. Behr & D. Krochmalnik (Eds.), *Was ist ein guter Relegionslehrer? Antworten von Juden, Christen und Muslimen* (pp. 57-90). Berlin: Frank & Timme.

Krueger, U. (2016). *The promise and peril of digital cities*. Retrieved April 5, 2016, from https://www.weforum.org/agenda/2016/04/the-promise-and-peril-of-digital-cities

Künzli, R. (2000). German Didaktik: Models of Re-Presentation, of Intercourse, and of Experience. In I. Westbury, S. Hopmann, & K. Riquarts, *Teaching As A Reflective Practice. The German Didaktik Tradition* (pp. 41-54). New York and London: Routledge.

Küppers, B.-O. (2010). *Wissen statt Moral. Fünf Thesen zur Wissensgesellschaft*. Köln: Fackelträger.

Kultusministerkonferenz (Secretariat of the Standing Conference of the Ministers of Education and Cultural Affairs of the Länder in the Federal Republic of Germany) (KMK, 2015). *The Education System in the Federal Republic of Germany 2013 / 2014). A description of the responsibilities, structures and developments in education policy for the exchange of information in Europe*. Bonn: Secretariat of the Standing Conference of the Ministers of Education and Cultural Affairs of the Länder in the Federal Republic of Germany.

Lacey, A., & Murray, C. (2015). *Rethinking the Regulatory Environment of Competency-Based Education*. AEI Series on Competency-Based Higher Education. Retrieved May 11, 2016, from http://www.aei.org/wp-content/uploads/2015/05/Rethinking-the-CBE-regulatory-environment.pdf

Lancy, D. F. (1993). *Qualitative research in education: an introduction to the major traditions*. New York: Longman.

Lattuca, L. R., & Stark, J. S. (2009). *Shaping the College Curriculum. Academic Plans in Context* (2nd ed.). San Francisco: Jossey-Bass.

Le, C., Wolfe, R., & Steinberg, A. (2014). *The past and the promise: Today's competency education movement.* Students at the center: Competency Education Research Series. Boston, MA: Jobs for the Future.

Lewington, J. (2016, April 14). Business schools get a road map for change. *The Globe and Mail.* Retrieved April 16, 2016, from http://www.theglobeandmail.com/report-on-business/careers/business-education/business-schools-get-a-road-map-for-change/article29635951/

Lin, J. Y., & Pleskovic, B. (Eds.) (2008). *Annual World Bank Conference on Development Economics – Regional. Higher Education and Development.* Washington, D. C.: The World Bank.

Linstone, H.A., & Turoff, M. (2011). Delphi: a brief look backward and forward, *Technological Forecasting & Social Change, 78,* 1712-1719.

Linstone, H.A., & Turoff, M. (Eds.) (1975). *The Delphi Method: Techniques and Applications.* Reading / Mass.: Addison-Wesley.

Lizaso, F., & Reger, G. (2004). Paper 4: Scenario-based Roadmapping – A Conceptual View. *EU-US Seminar: New Technology Foresight, Forecasting & Assessment Methods.* Seville 13-14 May 2004, Retrieved January 21, 2016, from http://foresight.jrc.ec.europa.eu/fta/papers/Session%205%20Tales%20from%20the%20Frontier/Scenario-based%20Roadmapping.pdf

Locke, E. A., & Latham, G. P. (2013). Goal Setting Theory, 1990. In E. A. Locke, & G. P. Latham (Eds.), *New Developments in Goal Setting and Task Performance* (pp. 3-20). New York: Routledge.

Lohmann, I. (2003). *Neue Medien und der globale Bildungsmarkt. Vortragstyposkript, Bearbeitungsstand 5.5.2003.* Retrieved June 30, 2016, from http://www.epb.uni-hamburg.de/erzwiss/lohmann/Publik/hrvatska.pdf

Lorange, P. (2008). *Thought Leadership Meets Business. How Business Schools can become more successful.* Cambridge: Cambridge University Press.

Loveridge, D. (2002). *On Delphi questions. Ideas in progress.* Manchester: The University of Manchester.

Lüth, C. (2000). On Wilhelm von Humboldt's Theory of Bildung. In I. Westbury, S. Hopmann, & K. Riquarts, *Teaching As A Reflective Practice. The German Didaktik Tradition* (pp. 63-84). New York and London: Routledge.

Lysø, I. H., Mjøen, K., & Levin, M. (2011). Using collaborative action-learning projects to increase the impact of management development. *International Journal of Training and Development, 15*(3), 210-224.

Maastricht University (n.d.). Master of Science in International Business. Retrieved August 14, 2016, https://www.maastrichtuniversity.nl/education/master/master-international-business-track-entrepreneurship-and-small-and-medium-sized

Macharzina, K., & Wolf, J. (2005). *Unternehmensführung. Das internationale Managementwissen. Konzepte – Methoden – Praxis* (5. Aufl.). Wiesbaden: Gabler.

Machiavelli, N. (1515 / 2012). *The Prince.* Translated by W. K. Marriott. Retrieved June 26, 2016, from http://www.gutenberg.org/files/1232/1232-h/1232-h.htm#link2HCH0006

Manpower Group (2014). The Talent Shortage Continue. How the Ever Changing Role of HR Can Bridge the Gap. Retrieved April 5, 2016, from https://www.manpower.de/fileadmin/manpower.de/Download/2014_Talent_Shortage_WP_US2.pdf

Marginson, S., & Wende, M. v. d. (2007). Globalisation and Higher Education. *OECD Education Working Papers*, No. 8. OECD Publishing.

Markmann, C., Darkow, I.-L., & Gracht, H. v. d. (2013). A Delphi-based risk analysis – Identifying and assessing future challenges for supply chain security in a multi-stakeholder environment. *Technological Forecasting & Social Change, 80,* 1815-1833.

Marope, M., & Wells, P. (2013). University Rankings: The Many Sides of the Debate. In P. T. M. Marope, P. J. Wells, & E. Hazelkorn, E. (Eds.), *Rankings and Accountability in Higher Education. Uses and Misuses* (pp. 7-19). Paris: UNESCO Publishing.

Marquard, O., & Zimmerli, W. C. (1995). *Zukunft braucht Herkunft.* München: Siemens AG.

May, J. M. (2010). Cicero as Rhetorician. In W. Dominik, & J. Hall (Eds.), *A Companion to Roman Rhetoric* (pp. 250-263). Chichester: Wiley-Blackwell.

Mayring, P. (2004). Qualitative content analysis. In U. Flick, E. v. Kardorff & I. Steinke (Eds.), *A Companion to Qualitative Research* (pp. 266-269). London: Sage.

Mayring, P. (2000). Qualitative content analysis. *Forum Qualitative Sozialforschung / Forum Qualitative Social Research, 1(2).* Retrieved December 6, 2015, from http://nbn-resolving.de/urn:nbn:de:0114-fqs0002204

McClary, K. L., & Gaertner, M. N. (2015). *Measuring Mastery: Best Practices for Assessment in Competency-Based Education.* AEI Series on Competency-Based Higher Education. Retrieved May 11, 2016, from http://www.aei.org/wp-content/uploads/2015/04/Measuring-Mastery.pdf

McCraw, T. K. (2007). *Prophet of innovation. Schumpeter and Creative Destruction.* Cambridge: Belknap Press of Harvard University Press.

McCulloch, G. (2016). History of the Curriculum. In D. Wyse, L. Hayward, & J. Pandya (Eds.), *The SAGE Handbook of Curriculum, Pedagogy and Assessment.* Volume 1 (pp. 47-62). Los Angeles: SAGE.

McGrath, R. G., & MacMillan, I. C. (2000). *The Entrepreneurial Mindset: Strategies for Continuously Creating Opportunity in an Age of Uncertainty.* Boston, Mass.: Harvard Business School Press, 2000.

Mendonça, S., Pina a Cunha, M., Kaivo-Oja, J., & Ruff, F. (2004). Wild Cards, Weak Signals and Organizational Improvisation. *Futures, 36,* 201-218.

Menze, C. (1975). *Die Bildungsreform Wilhelm von Humboldts.* Hannover: Hermann Schroedel Verlag.

Merriam, S. B. (1988). *Case study research in education: A qualitative approach.* San Francisco: Jossey-Bass.

Mietzner, D., & Reger, G. (2004). Paper 3: Scenario Approaches – History, Differences, Advantages and Disadvantages. *EU-US Seminar: New Technology Foresight, Forecasting & Assessment Methods.* Seville 13-14 May 2004. Retrieved January 21, 2016, from http://foresight.jrc.ec.europa.eu/fta/papers/Session%201%20Methodological%20Selection/Scenario%20Approaches.pdf

Mintzberg, H. (2005). *Managers Not MBAs. A hard look at the soft practice of managing and management development.* San Francisco: Berrett-Koehler Publishers.

Mittelstraß, J. (1996). Vom Elend der Hochschuldidaktik. In G. Brinek, & A. Schirlbauer (Hrsg.), *Vom Sinn und Unsinn der Hochschuldidaktik* (pp. 56-76). Wien. WUV-Universitätsverlag.

Moules, J. (2015, June 21). Business schools adapt to changing times. *Financial Times.* Retrieved August 22, 2016, from http://www.ft.com/cms/s/2/b6b5e4a6-0945-11e5-b643-00144feabdc0.html#axzz4H-4MOTAYp

Mulgan, G., & Townsley, O. (2016). *The challenge-driven university: how real-life problems can fuel learning.* Part One. Retrieved August 22, 2016, from http://www.nesta.org.uk/sites/default/files/the_challenge-driven_university.pdf

Murphy, M. K., Black, N. A., Lamping, D. L., McKee, C. M., Sanderson, C. F., Askham, J., & Marteau, T. (1998). Consensus development methods and their use in clinical guideline development. *Health Technology Assessment, 2* (i-iv), 1-88.

Murphy, S. E., & Johnson, S. K. (2011). The benefits of a long-lens approach to leader development: Understanding the seeds of leadership. *The Leadership Quarterly, 22*(3), 459-470.

Myers, P. (2004). Max Weber: Education as Academic and Political Calling. *German Studies Review, 27*(2), 269-288.

Nabi, G., Liñán, F., Fayolle, A., Krueger, N., & Walmsley, A. (2016). The impact of entrepreneurship education in higher education: A systematic review and research agenda. *Academy of Management Learning & Education.* Published ahead of print, March 10, 2016. Retrieved April 9, 2016, from: http://amle.aom.org/content/early/2016/03/14/amle.2015.0026.full.pdf

Nagel, K., Faix, W.G., Djalali, A., Horne, A., Keck, G., Kisgen, S., & Sailer, J. (2013): *General Management Tools* (3. Aufl.). Stuttgart: Steinbeis-Edition.

Neiman, S. (2014). *Why Grow Up? Philososphy in Transit.* London: Penguin.

Nerdinger, F. W., Blickle, G., & Schaper, N. (2008). *Arbeits- und Organisationspsychologie.* Heidelberg: Springer.

Nida-Rümelin, J. (2014). *Der Akademisierungswahn. Zur Krise beruflicher und akademischer Bildung.* Hamburg: edition Körber-Stiftung.

Nida-Rümelin, J. (2011). Humanismus als Leitkultur. In W. G. Faix, & M. Auer (Hrsg.), *Kompetenz. Persönlichkeit. Bildung. Band 3* (pp. 117-137). Stuttgart: Steinbeis-Edition.

Nida-Rümelin, J. (2013). *Philosophie einer humanen Bildung.* Hamburg: edition Körber-Stiftung.

NMC (New Media Consortium) (2015). *Horizon Report 2015: Higher Education Edition (Hochschulausgabe).* Retrieved January 1, 2016, from http://www.mmkh.de/fileadmin/dokumente/Publikationen/2015-nmc-horizon-report-HE-DE.pdf

Northouse, P. G. (2013). *Leadership. Theory and Practice* (6th ed.). Los Angeles: SAGE.

Notten, P. W. F. v, Sleegers, A.M. & Asselt, M.B.A.v. (2005). The future shocks: on discontinuity and scenario development. *Technological Forecasting and Social Change*, 72 (2), 175-194.

Nowack, M., Endrikat, J., & Guenther, E. (2011). Review of Delphi-based scenario studies: Quality and design considerations. *Technological Forecasting & Social Change*, 78, 1603-1615.

Oreopoulus, P. & Petronijevic, U. (2013). Making College Worth It: A Review of Research on the Returns to Higher Education. NBER Working Paper (19053) also published in The Future of Children, (23) 1, 41-65. Retrieved April 17, 2016, from http://www.princeton.edu/futureofchildren/publications/docs/23_01_03.pdf

Ordorika, I., & Lloyd, M. (2014). International rankings and the contest for university hegemony. *Journal of Education Policy*, DOI: 10.1080/02680939.2014.979247.

Organisation for Economic Co-operation and Development (OECD) (OECD, 2015). *Bildung auf einen Blick 2015. OECD-Indikatoren.* Paris / Berlin: wbv.

Organisation for Economic Co-operation and Development (OECD) (OECD, 2005). *E-Learning in Tertiary Education. Where do we stand?* Paris: OECD.

Organisation for Economic Co-operation and Development (OECD). (n.d.). Glossary. Retrieved on August 2, 2016, from https://stats.oecd.org/glossary/index.htm

Organisation for Economic Co-operation and Development (OECD), & The International Bank for Reconstruction and Development / The World Bank (OECD, 2007). *Cross-border Tertiary Education. A Way Towards Capacity Development.* n.p.: OECD.

Oxford Dictionaries (n.d.). Ideal. Retrieved August 17, 2016, from http://www.oxforddictionaries.com/de/definition/englisch/ideal

Paetz, N.-V., Ceylan, F., Fiehn, J., Schworm, S., & Harteis, C. (2011). *Kompetenz in der Hochschuldidaktik. Ergebnisse einer Delphi-Studie über die Zukunft der Hochschule.* Wiesbaden: VS Verlag für Sozialwissenschaften.

Palin, A. (2013, June 23). Financial crisis forced business schools to change curriculum. *Financial Times.* Retrieved August 12, 2016, from http://www.ft.com/cms/s/2/80cba3fc-d9c3-11e2-98fa-00144feab7de.html#axzz4H4MOTAYp

Palmer, D. E. (2009). Business Leadership: Three Levels of Ethical Analysis. *Journal of Business Ethics, 88*(3), 525-536.

Parker, M. (2015). The quiet rebellion taking place in business schools. The stereotype of business schools teaching people how to be bastards and make money is no longer apt. *Acuity,* October, 42-43.

Parolin, P. (2016, April 10). *A letter to the Catholic University of the Sacred Heart.* Retrieved April 16, 2016 from http://aaog.blogspot.de/2016/04/a-letter-to-catholic-university-of.html

Parry, K. W. (1998). Grounded Theory and Social Process: A New Direction for Leadership Research. *Leadership Quarterly, 9*(1), 85-105.

Paulson, K. (2001). Using Competencies to Connect the Workplace and Postsecondary Education. In R. A. Voorhees (Ed.), *Measuring What Matters. Competency-Based Learning Models in Higher Education.* New Directions for Institutional Research. Number 110 (pp. 41-54). San Francisco: Jossey-Bass.

Peirce, C. S. (1878). Deduction, induction, and hypothesis. Popular Science Monthly, 13, 470-482. Retrieved January 23, 2016, from https://en.wikisource.org/wiki/Popular_Science_Monthly/Volume_13/August_1878/Illustrations_of_the_Logic_of_Science_VI

Pfäffli, B. K. (2015). *Lehren an Hochschulen. Eine Hochschuldidaktik für den Aufbau von Wissen und Kompetenzen* (2. Aufl.). Bern: Haupt.

Phadnis, S., Caplice, C., Sheffi, Y., Singh, M. (2015). Effect of Scenario Planning on Field Experts' Judgment of Long-range Investment Decisions. *Strategic Management Journal, 36* (9), S. 1401–1411.

Phelps, R., Chan, C., & Kapsalis, S.C. (2001). Does scenario planning affect performance? Two exploratory studies. *Journal of Business Research, 51* (3), 223-232.

Pittaway, L., & Cope, J. (2007). Simulating Entrepreneurial Learning. Integrating Experiential and Collaborative Approaches to Learning. *Management Learning, 38*(2), 211-233.

Plato (1969). *Republic. Plato in Twelve Volumes,* Vols. 5 & 6 translated by Paul Shorey. Cambridge, MA: Harvard University Press. Retrieved July 18, 2016, from http://www.perseus.tufts.edu/hopper/text?doc=Perseus:text:1999.01.0168

Podolny, J. M. (2009, March 30). Are Business Schools to Blame? Harvard Business Review. Retrieved August 12, 2016, from https://hbr.org/2009/03/are-business-schools-to-blame

Porter, L. R. (1997). *Creating the Virtual Classroom. Distance Learning with the Internet.* New York: John Wiley & Sons.

Porter, M. E. (2004). *Competitive Strategy. Techniques for Analyzing Industries and Competitors.* NY: Free Press.

Poteralska, B. & Sacio-Szymańska, A. (2014). Evaluation of technology foresight projects. *European Journal of Futures Research*, (26), 1-9. Retrieved March 30, 2016, from http://link.springer.com/article/10.1007%2Fs40309-013-0026-1

Powell, C. (2003). The Delphi technique: Myths and realities. *Journal of Advanced Nursing, 41*, 376-382.

Priddat, B.A. (2013). *Zukunft der Arbeit. Festvortrag anlässlich der Eröffnung des 78. Lehrgangs der Europäischen Akademie der Arbeit am 10. Oktober 2013*. Retrieved January 3, 2016, from http://www.europaeische-akademie-der-arbeit.de/fileadmin/user_upload/dokumente/Eroeffnungsrede_Priddat_Oktober_2013.pdf

Raithel, J., Dollinger, B., & Hörmann, G. (2009). *Einführung Pädagogik. Begriffe – Strömungen – Klassiker – Fachrichtungen* (3. Aufl.). Wiesbaden: VS Verlag für Sozialwissenschaften.

Ramírez, R. & Wilkinson, A. (2014). Re-thinking the 2X2 scenario method: grid or frames? *Technological Forecasting and Social Change, 86*, S. 254-264.

Raskin, M.S. (1994). The Delphi Study in Field Instruction Revisited: Expert Consensus on Issues and Research Priorities. *Journal of Social Work Education, 30*, 75-89.

Rasner, C., Füser, K., & Faix, W. G. (1999). *Das Existenzgründer-Buch. Von der Geschäftsidee zum sicheren Geschäftserfolg* (4. Aufl.). Landsberg / Lech: Verlag Moderne Industrie.

Rauch, W. (1979). The decision Delphi. *Technological Forecasting & Social Change, 15*, 159-169.

Rauhvargers, A. (2013). *Global University Rankings and Their Impact. Report II*. Brussels: European University Association.

Rayens, M. K., & Hahn, E. J. (2000). Building consensus using the policy Delphi method. *Policy, Politics & Nursing Practice, 1*, 308-315.

Rhode, D. L., & Packel, A. K. (2011). *Leadership: Law, Policy, and Management*. Frederick / MD: Wolters Kluwer Law & Business.

Richmond, R. C. (2009). The Future of the University Is Change. In G. Olson, & J. W. Presley (Eds.), *The Future of Higher Education. Perspectives from America's Academic Leaders*. Boulder: Paradigm Publishers.

Regnet, E. (2014). Der Weg in die Zukunft - Anforderungen an die Führungskraft. In L. v. Rosenstiel, E. Regnet, & M. Domsch (Eds.), *Führung von Mitarbeitern. Handbuch für erfolgreiches Personalmanagement* (7. überarbeitete Auflage) (pp. 29-45). Stuttgart: Schäffer-Poeschel.

Ricard, L., & Borch, K. (2011). From Future Scenarios to Roadmapping: A practical guide to explore innovation and strategy. *The 4th International Seville Conference on Future-Oriented Technology Analysis (FTA)*, May 12-13, 2011.

Richardson, L. (2000). Evaluating ethnography. *Qualitative Inquiry, 6*(2), 253-255.

Rikkonen, P., Kaivo-oja, J., & Aakkula, J. (2006). Delphi expert panels in the scenario-based strategic planning of agriculture. *Foresight, 8* (1), 66-81.

Rikkonen, P. (2005). *Utilisation of alternative scenario approaches in defining the policy agenda for future agriculture in Finland*. Doctoral Dissertation. Helsinki:

Rosenstiel, L. v., & Comelli, G. (2003). *Führung zwischen Stabilität und Wandel*. München: Verlag Franz Vahlen.

Rost, J. C. (1993). *Leadership for the Twenty-First Century*. Westport: Praeger.

Rotterdam School of Management Erasmus University. (n.d.). M.Sc International Management / CEMS. Retrieved June 1, 2014, from http://www.rsm.nl/master/msc-programmes/msc-international-management-cems/

Rousseau, J.-J. (1762 / 2010). *Émile oder über die Erziehung* (Translation of the French original *Émile ou De l'Éducation* by H. Denhardt). Köln: Anaconda.

Rütter, T. (2008). *Bildungsarbeit. Eine Betrachtung aus dem Anspruch personaler Existenz*. Berlin: Pro BUSINESS.

Ruey, S. (2010). A case study of constructivist instructional strategies for adult online learning. *British Journal of Educational Technology, 41*(5), 706-720.

Rutherford, P. (1995). Competency Based Assessment. Melbourne: Pitman.

Salancik, J. R., Wenger, W., & Helfer, E. (1971). The constructions of Delphi event statements. *Technological Forecasting & Social Change, 3,* 5-73.

Salden, P., Fischer, K., & Barnat, M. (2016). Didaktische Studiengangsentwicklung: Rahmenkonzepte und Praxisbeispiel. In T. Brahm, T. Jenert, & D. Euler (Hrsg.), *Pädagogische Hochschulentwicklung. Von der Programmatik zur Implementierung* (pp. 133-149). Wiesbaden: Springer.

Salmi, J., & Hauptman, A. M. (2006). Innovations in Tertiary Education Financing: A Comparative Evaluation of Allocation Mechanisms. *Education Working Paper Series Number 4.* Washington, D. C.: The World Bank.

Sarges, W. (2001). Die Assessment-Center Methode – Herkunft, Kritik und Weiterentwicklungen. In W. Sarges (Hrsg.), *Weiterentwicklungen der Assessment Center-Methode* (2. überab. u. erw. Aufl.; pp. VII-XXXII). Göttingen: Hogrefe.

Schäfer, A. (2008). *Die Kraft der schöpferischen Zerstörung. Joseph A. Schumpeter. Die Biographie.* Frankfurt / New York: Campus Verlag.

Schaper, N., Schlömer, T., & Paechter, M. (2012). Editorial: Kompetenzen, Kompetenzorientierung und Employability in der Hochschule. *Zeitschrift für Hochschulentwicklung, 7*(4), I-X.

Scheele, D. S. (1975). Reality construction as a product of Delphi interaction. In H. A. Linstone, & M. Turoff, (Eds.), *The Delphi method: Techniques and applications* (pp. 37-71). Reading / Mass.: Addison Wesley.

Scheibe, M., Skutsch, M., & Schofer, J. (1975). Experiments in Delphi methodology. In H. A. Linstone, & M. Turoff (Eds.), *The Delphi Method: Techniques and Applications* (pp. 257-281). Reading / Mass.: Addison-Wesley.

Schermutzki, M. (2012). Learning Outcomes – Lernergebnisse: Begriffe , Zusammenhänge, Umsetzung und Erfolgsermittlung. In J. Kohler, P. Pohlenz, & U. Schmidt (Hrsg.), *Handbuch Qualität in Studium und Lehre: Evaluation nutzen – Akkreditierung sichern – Profil schärfen!* (E 3.3). Retrieved August 17, 2016, from http://www.hqsl-bibliothek.de/index.php?option=com_docman&task=doc_details&gid=225

Schmidt, B., Hippel, A. v., & Tippelt, R. (2010). Higher Education Evaluation in Germany. *Research in Comparative and International Education, 5*(1), 98-111.

Schmidt, F. L. & Hunter, J. E. (1998). The validity and utility of selection methods in personnel psychology: Practical and theoretical implications of 85 years of research findings. *Psychological Bulletin, 124*(2), 262-274.

Schmidt, F. L., Hunter, I. E., McKenzie, R. C., & Muldrow, T. W. (1979). The impact of valid selection procedures on work-force productivity. *Journal of Applied Psychology, 64*, 609-626.

Schmidt-Huber, M., & Tippelt, R. (2014). *Auf der Suche nach den Wurzeln guter Führung. Born to be a leader?*, München: Roman Herzog Institut. Retrieved June 26, 2016, from: http://www.romanherzoginstitut.de/uploads/tx_mspublication/RHI-Information_Nr._15.pdf

Schmitter, E., & Schreiber, M. (2003). Wir brauchen viele Götter. Der Philosoph Odo Marquard über die Sehnsucht der Deutschen nach gründlicher Weltverbesserung, den Mut zur Bürgerlichkeit, die Wichtigkeit von Teddybären und sein neues Buch. *Der Spiegel*, 9, 152-154. Retrieved January 10, 2016, from http://magazin.spiegel.de/EpubDelivery/spiegel/pdf/26448590

Schneider, R. (2009). Kompetenzentwicklung durch Forschendes Lernen? *Journal Hochschuldidaktik, Forschendes Lernen: Perspektiven eines Konzepts*, 20(2), 33-37.

Schoelmerich, F., Nachtwei, J., & Schermuly C. C. (in press). Evaluating the quality of assessment centers used in employee selection – Development of a Benchmark for Assessment Center Diagnostics (BACDi). In: B. Krause, & P. Metzler (Eds.). *Empirische Evaluationsmethoden*. Berlin: ZeE Verlag.

Schoemaker, P. J. H. (1995). Scenario Planning: A Tool for Strategic Thinking. *Sloan Management Review*, 26, 25-40.

Scholz, C. (Ed.) (2009). *Vahlens Großes Personallexikon*. München: Franz Vahlen.

Schuckmann, S., Linz, M., Gracht, H. A. v. d. & Darkow, I.-L. (2011). Delphi based Disruptive and Surprising Transformation Scenarios on the Future of Aviation. In European Foresight Platform (EEEP) (Ed.), EFP Brief No. 192. Retrieved April 5, 2016, from http://www.foresight-platform.eu/wp-content/uploads/2011/08/EFP-Brief-No.-192_Future-of-Aviation.pdf

Schuler, H. (2007). Spielwiese für Laien? Weshalb das Assessment Center seinem Ruf nicht mehr gerecht wird. *Wirtschaftspsychologie aktuell*, 2, 27-30.

Schumpeter, J. A. (1939). *Business Cycles. A Theoretical, Historical, and Statistical Analysis of the Capitalist Process*. New York: McGraw Hill Book Company Inc.

Schumpeter, J. A. (1942 / 2003). *Capitalism, Socialism and Democracy.* London and New York: Routledge.

Schumpeter, J. A. (1947). The Creative Response in Economic History. *The Journal of Economic History, 7*(2), 149-159.

Schumpeter, J. A. (1911 / 2008). *The Theory of Economic Development. An Inquiry into Profits, Capital, Credit, Interest, and the Business Cycle.* Translated from the German by R. Opie. New Brunswick (USA) and London (UK): Transaction Publishers.

Schwartz, P. (1996). *The art of long view: Planning for the future in an uncertain world.* New York: Doubleday.

Schwartz, P., & Ogilvy, J. A. (1998). Plotting your scenarios. In L. Fahey, & R. M. Randall (Eds.), *Learning from the Future. Competitive Foresight Scenarios* (pp. 57-80). New York: John Wiley & Sons.

Sengstag, C. (2001). *Forschung und Lehre verknüpfen.* Retrieved August 1, 2016, from http://e-collection.library.ethz.ch/eserv/eth:25106/eth-25106-01.pdf

Shah, S. S. (2014). The Role of Work-Family Enrichment in Work-Life Balance & Career Success: A Comparison of German & Indian Managers. München. Retrieved February 16, 2016, from https://edoc.ub.uni-muenchen.de/16634/1/Shah_Shalaka.pdf

Shaping Tomorrow (n.d.). Retrieved April 2, 2016, from https://www.trendexplorer.com/de/

Sheridan, B. (2009). Are Business Schools to Blame for the Crises? Newsweek 8 / 1 / 09. Retrieved January 3, 2016, from http://europe.newsweek.com/are-business-schools-blame-crisis-81537?rm=eu

Shuell, T. J. (1986). Cognitive Conceptions of Learning. *Review of Educational Research*, 56(4), 411-436.

Sikka, V. (2016). What kind of education do we need in the future? Retrieved April 5, 2016, from https://www.weforum.org/agenda/2016/01/amplifying-our-human-potential-a-new-context-for-the-fourth-industrial-revolution

Sirelkhatim, F., & Gangi, Y. (2015). Entrepreneurship education: A systematic literature review of curricula contents and teaching methods. *Cogent Business and Management.* Retrieved April 9, 2016, from https://www.cogentoa.com/article/10.1080/23311975.2015.1052034.pdf

Skulmoski, G.J., Hartman, F. T., & Krahn, J. (2007). The Delphi Method for Graduate Research. *Journal of Information Technology Education,* 6, 1-21.

Skutsch, M., & Schofer, J. L. (1973). Goals-Delphis for urban planning: concepts in their design. *Socio-Economic Planning Sciences,* 7, 305-313.

Slonim-Nevo, V., & Nevo, I. (2009). Conflicting findings in mixed methods research: an illustration from an Israeli study on immigration. *Journal of Mixed Methods Research, 3* (2), 109-128.

Snook, S., Nohria, N. & Khurana, R. (Eds.) (2012). *The Handbook for Teaching Leadership. Knowing, Doing, and Being.* Los Angeles: SAGE.

Snow, D. L., & Tebes, J. K. (1992). Panel attrition and external validity in adolescent substance use research. *Journal of Consulting and Clinical Psychology, 60* (5), 804-807.

Solnet, D. J., Baum, T, Kralj, A., Robinson, R. N. S., Ritchie, B. W. & Olsen, M. (2015). The Asia-Pacific Tourism Workforce of the Future: Using Delphi Techniques to Identify Possible Scenarios. *Journal of Travel Research,* 53 (6), 693-704.

Spencer, L. M., & Spencer, S. M. (1993). *Competence at work: Models for superior performance.* New York, NY: Wiley.

Spickermann, A., Grienitz, V., & Gracht, H. A. v. d. (2014). Heading towards a multimodal city of the future? Multi-stakeholder scenarios for urban mobility. *Technological Forecasting & Social Change, 89,* 201-221

Spickermann, A., Zimmermann, M., & Gracht, H. A. v. d. (2014). Surface- and deep-level diversity in panel selection – Exploring diversity effects on response behaviour in foresight. *Technological Forecasting & Social Change, 85,* 105-120.

Spitzer, D. R. (1998). Rediscovering the Social Context of Distance Learning. *Educational Technology, 38*(2), 52-56.

Stake, R. E. (1995). *The art of case study research.* Thousand Oaks, CA: Sage.

Stanford Graduate School of Business. (n.d.). Master of Business Administration. Retrieved June 10, 2014, from http://www.gsb.stanford.edu/programs/mba

Statista (2016). Global mobile education market volume from 2011 to 2020 (in billion U.S. dollars). Retrieved April 17, 2016, from http://www.statista.com/statistics/273960/global-mobile-education-market-volume/

Steinert, M. (2009). A dissensus based online Delphi approach: An explorative research tool. *Technological Forecasting & Social Change, 76,* 291-300.

Stephens, D.J. (2013). *Hacking your education. Ditch the lectures, save tens of thousands, and learn more than your peers ever will.* New York: Penguin Group.

Sternberg, R., & Kolligian Jr. J. (1990). *Competence Considered.* New Haven / CT: Yale University Press.

Steyrer, J. (2009). Theorie der Führung. In H. Kasper, & W. Mayrhofer (Hrsg.), *Personalmanagement, Führung, Organisation* (4. Aufl., pp. 25-93). Wien: Linde.

Stogdill, R. M. (1948). Personal Factors Associated with Leadership: A Survey of the Literature. *Journal of Applied Psychology,* 25(1), 35-71.

Stone Fish, L., & Busby, D. M. (1996). The Delphi method. In D. M. Sprenkle & S. M. Moon (Eds.), *Research methods in family therapy* (pp. 469-482). New York: Guilford Press.

Strebler, M., Robinson, D., & Heron, P. (1997). *Getting the best out of your competencies.* Institute of Employment Studies. Report 334. Brighton: University of Sussex.

Sursock, A., & Smidt, H. (2010). *Trends 2010: A decade of change in European Higher Education.* Brussels / Belgium: European University Association.

Swedberg, R. (2002). The Economic Sociology of Capitalism. Weber and Schumpeter. *Journal of Classical Sociology, 2*(3), 227-255.

Szaif, J. (2003). Plato on the "Cultivation of the Soul through Philosophical Knowledge. In W. Detel, A. Becker, and P. Scholz (Hrsg.), *Ideal and Culture of Knowledge in Plato. Akten der 4. Tagung der Karl- und Gertrud-Abel-Stiftung vom 1.-3. September 2000 in Frankfurt* (pp. 25-35). Stuttgart: Franz Steiner Verlag.

Tapio, P. (2003). Disaggregative policy Delphi: using cluster analysis as a tool for systematic scenario formation. *Technological Forecasting and Social Change, 70,* 1557-1564.

Teddlie, C., & Tashakkori, A. (2009). *Foundations of Mixed Methods Research: Integrating Quantitative and Qualitative Approaches in the Social and Behavioral Sciences.* Thousand Oaks, CA: Sage.

Teichler, U. (2010). Hochschulen: Die Verknüpfung von Bildung und Forschung. In R. Tippelt, & B. Schmidt (Hrsg.), *Handbuch Bildungsforschung* (pp. 421-444) (3. durchges. Aufl.). Wiesbaden: VS Verlag für Sozialwissenschaften.

Tenorth, H.-E. (2012). Bildung. In H.-E. Tenorth, & R. Tippelt (Hrsg.), *BELTZ Lexikon Pädagogik* (pp. 92-95). Weinheim und Basel: Beltz.

Tenorth, H.-E. (2013). *Bildung – Zwischen Ideal und Wirklichkeit. Ein Essay.* Retrieved August 17, 2016, from http://www.bpb.de/gesellschaft/kultur/zukunft-bildung/146201/bildungsideale

Tenorth, H.-E., & Tippelt, R. (Hrsg.) (2012). *BELTZ Lexikon Pädagogik.* Weinheim und Basel: Beltz.

The Economist (2014, April 5). *Is college worth it?* Retrieved April 17, 2016, from http://www.economist.com/news/united-states/21600131-too-many-degrees-are-waste-money-return-higher-education-would-be-much-better

The Economist (2013, September 7). *The origins of the financial crisis. Crash course.* Retrieved January 3, 2016 from http://www.economist.com/news/schoolsbrief/21584534-effects-financial-crisis-are-still-being-felt-five-years-article

The Wharton School, University of Pennsylvania. (n.d.). Master of Business Administration. Retrieved June 12, 2014, from http://www.wharton.upenn.edu/mba/

Thom, N. (2015). Erfolgreiche Führungskräfte. Generelles und Spezifisches. *VM. Fachzeitschrift für Verbands- und Nonprofit-Management, 41* (3), 37-43.

Thomas, H. (2007). An analysis of the environment and competitive dynamics of management education. *Journal of Management Development, 26*(1), 9-21.

Thomas, H., Lee, M., Thomas, L., & Wilson, A. (2014). Securing the Future of Management Education. Competitive Destruction or Constructive Innovation? *Reflections on the Role, Impact and Future of Management Education: EFMD Perspectives. Volume 2.* Bingley: Emerald.

Thomas, H., Lorange, P., & Sheth, J. (2013). *The Business School in the Twenty-First Century. Emergent Challenges and New Business Models.* Cambridge: Cambridge University Press.

Tight, M. (2012). *Researching higher education* (2nd ed.). Maidenhead: Open University Press.

Tippelt, R. (2013). Bildung, Persönlichkeit und professionelle Führung. In W. G. Faix, J. Erpenbeck., M. Auer (Hrsg.), *Bildung. Kompetenzen. Werte* (pp. 245-263). Stuttgart: Steinbeis-Edition.

Tippelt, R. (1979). *Projektstudium. Exemplarisches und handlungsorientiertes Lernen an der Hochschule.* München: Kösel.

Tippelt, R., Mandl, H., & Straka, G. (2003). Entwicklung und Erfassung von Kompetenz in der Wissensgesellschaft – Bildungs- und wissenstheoretische Perspektiven. In I. Gogolin, & R. Tippelt (Hrsg), *Innovation durch Bildung. Beiträge zum 18. Kongress der Deutschen Gesellschaft für Erziehungswissenschaft* (pp. 349-369). Opladen: Leske + Budrich.

Tippelt, R., & Schmidt, B. (Hrsg.) (2010). *Handbuch Bildungsforschung* (3. durchges. Aufl.). Wiesbaden: VS Verlag für Sozialwissenschaften.

Totté, N., Huyghe, S., & Verhagen, A. (2013). *Building the curriculum in higher education: a conceptual framework.* Retrieved August 4, 2016, from http://www.enhancementthemes.ac.uk/pages/docdetail/docs/paper/building-the-curriculum-in-higher-education---a-conceptual-framework

Tourish, D., & Hargie, O. (2012). Metaphors of failure and the failures of metaphor: A critical study of metaphors used by bankers in explaining the banking crisis. *Organization studies*, 33, 1044-1069.

Tremblay, K., Lalancette, D., & Roseveare, D. (2012). *Assessment of Higher Education Learning Outcomes. AHELO. Feasibility Study Report. Volume 1. Design and Implementation.* n.p.: OECD.

Trendexplorer (n.d.). Retrieved April 2, 2016, from https://www.trendexplorer.com/de/

Trendwatching (n.d.). Retrieved April 2, 2016, from http://trendwatching.com

Turoff, M. (1970). The design of a policy Delphi. *Technological Forecasting & Social Change, 2,* 149-171.

Turoff, M., & Hiltz, S. R. (1996). Computer based Delphi processes. In M. Adler & E. Ziglio (Eds.), *Gazing into the oracle: The Delphi method and its application to social policy and public health.* London: Jessica Kingsley Publishers, 56-85.

Ullmo, P.-A. (2013). *Open Schools 2030, Open Education 2030. Call for Vision Papers. School Education.* Retrieved December 31, 2015, from http://blogs.ec.europa.eu/openeducation2030/files/2013/05/Ullmo-OE-SE-2030-fin.pdf

UNESCO (2015). *Draft Preliminary Report Concerning the Preparation of a Global Convention on the Recognition of Higher Education Qualifications.* Paris: UNESCO.

UNESCO (2012a). *International Standard Classification of Education ISCED 2011.* Montreal / Quebec: UNESCO Institute for Statistics.

UNESCO (2012b). *Turning on Mobile Learning. Global Themes. Working Paper Series on Mobile Learning.* Paris. Retrieved January 1, 2016, from http://www.unesco.org/new/en/unesco/themes/icts/m4ed/mobile-learning-resources/unescomobilelearningseries/

UNESCO (1998): *World Declaration on Higher Education for the Twenty-First Century: Vision and Action and Framework for Priority Action for Change and Development of Higher Education.* Retrieved August 2, 2016, from: http://www.unesco.org/education/educprog/wche/declaration_eng.htm

Universal Declaration of Human Rights (UDHR, 1948). Retrieved August 6, 2016, from http://www.un.org/en/universal-declaration-human-rights/

Universität der Bundeswehr (n.d.). *Department für Bildungswissenschaft.* Retrieved July 11, 2015, from https://www.unibw.de/hum/departments/dfb

University of St. Gallen (n.d.). Strategy and International Management (SIM). Retrieved June 1, 2014, from http://www.unisg.ch/en/studium/master/strategyandinternationalmanagement

University of Waterloo (n.d.). School of Finance and Accounting. Retrieved August 12, 2016, from https://uwaterloo.ca/school-of-accounting-and-finance/learning-model

U.S. News ranking Best Business Schools (2013). Retrieved April 10, 2014, from http://grad-schools.usnews.rankingsandreviews.com/best-graduate-schools/top-business-schools/mba-rankings?int=acf0d6

U.S. News ranking Best Business Schools (2016). Retrieved September 6, 2016, from http://grad-schools.usnews.rankingsandreviews.com/best-graduate-schools/top-business-schools/mba-rankings?int=acf0d6

Valero, A., & Reenen, J. v. (2016). The Economic Impact of Universities: Evidence from Across the Globe. *CEP Discussion Paper No. 1444*. London: Centre for Economic Performance / London School of Economics and Political Science.

Vecchio, R. P. (2003). Entrepreneurship and leadership: common trends and common threads. *Human Resource Management Review*, 13, 303-327.

Verbik, L., & Lasanowski, V. (2007). International Student Mobility: Patterns and Trends. *World Education News,* New York. Retrieved from http://www.wes.org/educators/pdf/StudentMobility.pdf [26.06.2015].

Viera, A. J., & Garrett, J. M. (2005). Understanding interobserver agreement: The kappa statistic. *Research Series (Family medicine), 35*(5), 60-64.

Visser, M. P., & Chermack, T. J. (2009). Perceptions of the relationship between scenario planning and firm performance: A qualitative study. *Futures, 41*(9), S. 581-592.

Vorhees, R. A. (2001). Competency-Based Learning Models: A Necessary Future. In R. A. Voorhees (Ed.), *Measuring What Matters. Competency-Based Learning Models in Higher Education.* New Directions for Institutional Research. Number 110 (pp. 5-13). San Francisco: Jossey-Bass.

Voros, J. (2003). A generic foresight process framework. *Foresight 5*(3), 10-21.

Wachs, M., & Schofer, J. L. (1969). Abstract Values and Concrete Highways. *Traffic Quarterly, 23*(1), 133-156.

Walterscheid, K. (1998). Entrepreneurship Education als universitäre Lehre. Retrieved June 15, 2014, from http://www.fernuni-hagen.de/GFS/pdf/entrepreneurship_lehre.pdf

Wannemacher, K., & Geidel, J. (2016). *Digitale Modelle internationaler Hochschulkooperation in der Lehre.* Berlin: Hochschulforum Digitalisierung.

Warth, J., Gracht, H. A. v. d., & Darkow, I.-L. (2013). A dissent-based approach for multi-stakeholder scenario-development – The future of electric drive vehicles. *Technological Forecasting & Social Change,* 80, 566-583.

Weber, B. (2007). Schöne neue Arbeitswelt? – die Zukunft der Arbeit. *Informationen zur politischen Bildung, 293.* Retrieved January 3, 2016, from http://www.bpb.de/izpb/8588/schoene-neue-arbeitswelt-die-zukunft-der-arbeit

Weber, M. (1904 / 1905 / 1930). *The Protestant Ethic and the Spirit of Capitalism.* Translated by T. Parsons. London: Routledge.

Weibel, A. (2015, October 23). Führung ist Vertrauen. *Wirtschaftswoche, 44,* 22.

Weimer-Jehle, W. (2006). Cross-impact balances: A system-theoretical approach to cross-impact analysis. *Technological Forecasting & Social Change,* 73, 334-361.

Weinert, F. E. (2001). Concept of Competence: A Conceptual Clarification. In D. S. Rychen, & L. H. Salganik (Eds.), *Defining and Selecting Key Competencies* (pp. 45-65). Seattle, WA: Hogrefe & Huber.

Weinert, F. E. (1999). *Definition and Selection of Competencies: Concepts of Competence.* Munich: Max Planck Institute for Psychological Research.

Welge, M. K., & Al-Laham, A. (2003). *Strategisches Management. Grundlagen – Prozess – Implementierung* (4. Aufl.). Wiesbaden: Gabler.

Werner, C. (2005). *Kompetenzentwicklung und Weiterbildung bei Mitarbeitern in der zweiten Berufslebenshälfte.* Dissertation, München: Ludwig-Maximilians-Universität. Retrieved January 11, 2016, from https://edoc.ub.uni-muenchen.de/3839/

Westbury, I. (2000). Teaching as a Reflective Practice: What might Didaktik teach Curriculum? In I. Westbury, S. Hopmann, & K. Riquarts, *Teaching As A Reflective Practice. The German Didaktik Tradition* (pp. 15-39). New York and London: Routledge.

Wester, K. L., & Borders, L. D. (2014). Research Competencies in Counseling: A Delphi Study. *Journal of Counseling & Development,* 92(4), 447-458.

Westera, W. (2001). Competencies in education: a confusion of tongues, *Journal of Curriculum Studies, 33,* 75-88.

Westera, W. (1999). Paradoxes in Open, Networked Learning Environments: Toward a Paradigm Shift. *Educational Technology, 39*(1), 17-23.

White, J. V., & Guthrie, K. I. (2016). Creating a Meaningful Learning Environment: Reflection in Leadership Education. *Journal of Leadership Education, 15*(1), 60-75.

WHU Otto Beisheim School of Management. (n.d.). Master in Management. Retrieved June 1, 2014 from http://www.whu.edu/en/programs/master-in-management-msc/

Wiersing, E. (2001). Humanistische Bildung und Platons „Politeia" heute. Anmerkungen zum Schreckensbild des Erziehungsstaates. In E. Wiersing (Hrsg.), *Humanismus und Menschenbildung. Zu Geschichte, Gegenwart und Zukunft der bildenden Begegnung der Europäer mit der Kultur der Griechen und Römer.* Detmolder Hochschulschriften. Band 4 (pp. 244-313). Essen: Verlag Die Blaue Eule.

Wildt, J. (2009). Forschendes Lernen: Lernen im „Format" der Forschung. *Journal Hochschuldidaktik, Forschendes Lernen: Perspektiven eines Konzepts, 20*(2), 4-7.

Wilhelm, W. J. (2001). Alchemy of the oracle: The Delphi technique. *The Delta Pi Epsilon Journal, 43* (1), 6-26.

Wimmer, R., Emmerich, A., & Nicolai, A. T. (2002). *Corporate Universities in Deutschland. Eine empirische Untersuchung zu ihrer Verbreitung und strategischen Bedeutung. Eine Studie im Auftrag des BMBF.* Retrieved December 16, 2015, from https://www.bmbf.de/pub/corporate_universities_in_deutschland.pdf

Wilson, B. G. (1998). What Is a Constructivist Learning Environment? In B. G. Wilson (Ed.), *Constructivist Learning Environments. Case Studies in Instructional Design* (pp. 3-8). Englewood Cliffs: Educational Technology Publications.

Wissenschaftsrat (2015). *Empfehlungen zum Verhältnis von Hochschulbildung und Arbeitsmarkt. Zweiter Teil der Empfehlungen zur Qualifizierung von Fachkräften vor dem Hintergrund des demographischen Wandels.* Bielefeld. Retrieved August 6, 2016, from http://www.wissenschaftsrat.de/download/archiv/4925-15.pdf

Wissenschaftsrat (2000). *Theses for the Future Development of the System of Higher Education and Research in Germany.* Cologne: Wissenschaftsrat, Secretariat.

World Economic Forum (WEF, 2016). *New Vision for Education: Fostering Social and Emotional Learning Through Technology.* Geneva: WEF. Retrieved April 5, 2016, from http://www3.weforum.org/docs/WEF_New_Vision_for_Education.pdf

World Economic Forum (WEF, 2015). *New Vision for Education: Unlocking the Potential of Technology.* Geneva: WEF. Retrieved April 5, 2016, from http://www3.weforum.org/docs/WEFUSA_NewVisionforEducation_Report2015.pdf

World Economic Forum (WEF, 2010). *Stimulating Economies through Fostering Talent Mobility* Geneva: WEF. Retrieved April 5, 2016, from http://www3.weforum.org/docs/WEF_PS_TalentMobility_report_2010.pdf

World Economic Forum (WEF, 2009). *The Future of the Global Financial System. A Near-Term Outlook and Long-Term Scenarios.* Geneva: WEF. Retrieved March 29, 2016, from http://www3.weforum.org/docs/WEF_Scenario_FutureGlobalFinancialSystem_Report_2010.pdf

World Economic Forum (WEF, 2013). The Global Information Technology Report 2013. Growth and Jobs in a Hyperconnected World. Geneva: WEF. Retrieved April 17, 2016, from http://www3.weforum.org/docs/WEF_GITR_Report_2013.pdf

World Future Society (WFS) (n.d.). Retrieved March 29, 2016 from http://www.wfs.org/

World Future Society (WFS) (2002). The Future: An Owner's Manual; a Brief Overview of the Study of the Future and the Services of the World Future Society. *The Futurist*, 36 (5), 31.

Wolter, A. (2011). Hochschulforschung. In H. Reinders, H. Ditton, C. Gräsel, & B. Gniewosz (Hrsg.), *Empirische Bildungsforschung. Gegenstandsbereiche* (pp. 125-135). Wiesbaden: VS Verlag für Sozialwissenschaften.

Yin, R. K. (1994). *Case study research: Design and methods* (2nd ed.). Thousand Oaks, CA: Sage.

Yukl, G. (2013). *Leadership in Organizations* (8th ed.). Harlow: Pearson.

Ziegele, F. (2010). Hochschulfinanzierung. In H. Barz (Hrsg.), *Handbuch Bildungsfinanzierung* (pp. 213-223). Wiesbaden: VS Verlag.

Ziglio, E. (1996). The Delphi method and its contribution to decision making. In Adler, M., & Ziglio, E., (Eds.), *Gazing into the oracle: The Delphi method and its application to social policy and public health* (pp. 3-36). *London:* Jessica Kingsley Publishers.

Zillner, S., & Krusche, B. (2012). *Systemisches Innovationsmanagement. Grundlagen – Strategien – Instrumente.* Stuttgart: Schäffer-Poeschel Verlag.

Zipfinger, S. (2007). *Computer Aided-Delphi – An Experimental Study of Comparing Round-based with Real-time Implementation of the Method.* Linz: Trauner.

Zorek, J. A., Sprague, J. E., & Popovich, N. G. (2010). Bulimic Learning. *American Journal of Pharmaceutical Education*, 74(8), Article 157.

Appendix

Template of data matrix for data collection.

No.	1	2	3.
study program	Master of Arts in Strategy and International Management	Master in Management	…
name of institution (university, business school,…)	University of St. Gallen	ESCP Europe	…
country of institution	Switzerland	France, UK, Germany, Spain, Italy	…
URL	https://www.unisg.ch/en/Studium/Master/StrategyAndInternationalManagement	http://www.escpeurope.eu/escp-europe-programmes/master-in-management/overview-master-in-management-escp-europe-business-school/master-in-management-mim-escp-europe-business-school/overview-master-in-management-escp-europe-business-school/	…
Framework			
degree			
private ownership (yes / no)			
state recognized (yes / no)			
public / state-owned / state-funded (yes / no)			
study fees (yes / no)			

study fees for locals (total in local currency)

study fees for locals (total / converted in Euro)

study fees for foreigners (total in local currency)

study fees for foreigners (total / converted in Euro)

exchange date

joint degree (yes / no)

if joint degree, name of partner university...

double degree option (yes / no)

if double degree, second degree awarded by...

standard period of study (in months)

fulltime

parttime option

online

credit points (ECTS or equivalent)

accreditation (yes / no)

FIBAA

AACSB

EQUIS

other (yes / no)

if other, name of institution

ranking yes / no

Financial Times (2013)

The Economist

other (yes / no)

if other, name of institution

admission requirements (besides copies of all degrees or diplomas, or certificate of attendance)

age

work experience (in years) / minimum

work experience (in time) / average

first academic degree (min. credit points)

consecutive (yes / no)

Bachelor's profile

GMAT (scores / min.)			
TOEFL (scores / min.)			
competency test			
interview			
language skills			
reference letters			
other (yes / no)			
if other, what?			
students			
number of students enrolled			
female students (%)			
international students (%)			
educational goal			
educational goal of study program (yes / no)?			
if yes, which goal?			
educational ideal			
educational ideal of study program (yes / no)?			
if yes, which ideal?			
educational contents			
curriculum splitted in core courses and elective courses / specialization (yes / no)			
courses mandatory or optional?			
Economics			
Accounting			
Finance			
Entrepreneur- / Intrapreneurship			
Marketing			
Management of goals			
Strategy			
Innovation			
Technology and Operations Management			
Supply Chain Management			
International Management			
Leadership knowledge and / or competency knowledge			
concrete name of the leadership course			

L & C definition				
L & C in theory				
L & C in practice				
Law				
HR				
Organizational Behavior				
other (yes / no)				
if other, what ?				
real-world setting / practice (in ECTS, US credits or time)				
Project (duration in ECTS, US credits or time)				
concrete name of the course				
if more than one project / duration in ECTS, US credits or time				
concrete name of the course				
other (duration in ECTS, US credits or time)				
other mandatory part of the curriculum				
concrete name 1				
definition of the course				
concrete name 2				
definition of the course				
concrete name 3				
definition of the course				
incl. course in the sense of leadership and competences				
Master thesis (in ECTS, US credits or time)				
leadership approach defined by institution				
program language / s				
English				
French				
Spanish				
German				
other				
methodologies				
teaching method defined yes / no?				
lectures				
working groups				

case studies

presentations

simulation games

project

definition of project

field trip

definition of field trips

internship

definition of internship

online learning

virtual classroom

mentoring program

other

if other, what?

definition of pedagogical approach

study abroad

description

number of countries

mandatory in ECTS, US credits or time

required exams?

written tests

transfer papers / Reflection learning papers / ...

seminar paper

examination paper (individually)

group examination paper

oral examination

presentations (group)

active participation

examination with link to practice / project...

others

if others, what?

Master thesis

link to practice / project / internship in Master thesis required?

final (oral) examination yes / no?

Alumni

Employment Report (yes / no)

Alumni career progress			
(weighted) salary (USD)			
(weighted) salary (USD) => converted in EUR (01.06.2014)			
current job title			
current sector			
Study and examinations regulations			
link to study and examinations regulations			
link to other relevant material			
Date of research			

Dr. Stefanie Kisgen

Stefanie Kisgen, born in 1979, studied Modern China Studies at the University of Cologne and Nanjing Normal University / China. After an additional qualification in business administration and management and an internship at the Bavarian Ministry of Economic Affairs, she completed her Master of Business Administration (MBA) at the School of International Business and Entrepreneurship GmbH (SIBE) of the Steinbeis University Berlin.

During this time, she developed the study program Master of Science in International Management at SIBE of the Steinbeis University Berlin.

Since 2008, she has been a Director of the Steinbeis Transfer Institute (STI) International Management at SIBE. In this capacity, she was responsible for the study programs Master of Science in International Management and Master of Science in Innovation and Technology Management as well as the Business Development of SIBE's Law School in cooperation with SIBE's international network. Since 2014, she has been COO at SIBE.

Since 2015, she is managing director and partner at the School of International Business and Entrepreneurship GmbH (SIBE) of the Steinbeis University Berlin, which currently includes approx. 700 students and 3,700 graduates in SIBE's Experience-Based Curriculum (EBC) in the fields of management and law.

Stefanie Kisgen also earned her doctoral degree at the Department of Educational Sciences at Ludwig-Maximilians-Universität (LMU) München (Munich, Germany). Her research was part of a joint research project of the Department of Educational Sciences at Ludwig-Maximilians-Universität (LMU) München and SIBE.

Her publications include various articles on Chinese and international law, foreign trade, international management as well as the management of competencies.